Assessment to Plan Instruction	Instructional Support for Struggling Readers
Assessment Purposes	**Determining Needs for Intervention**

Screening Assessment
- Identifying which students are on track to succeed, which students will need additional instructional support to succeed, and which students will need intensive instructional support to succeed

Progress-Monitoring Assessment
- Monitoring student progress on a weekly basis, bi-monthly, monthly, or three times each year, depending on level of instructional support needed

Diagnosis Assessment
- Identifying struggling readers' specific instructional strengths and needs

Outcome Assessment
- Determining student end-of-year achievement levels

Evaluating Data for Instructional Planning
- Data study meetings with grade-level team, reading coach, and other personnel
- Instructional foci
- Instructional groupings
- Pacing
- Preteaching and reteaching
- Number of minutes of daily instruction
- Appropriate interventions

Tier 1
- Core reading program, including differentiated small-group reading instruction for ALL students

Tier 2
- Additional in-class instructional support provided by the classroom teacher and other adult support personnel, sometimes using a supplemental instructional program
  - more minutes of small-group instruction with classroom teacher
  - an extra small group with Title 1 teacher, teacher aide
  - preteaching
  - reteaching

Tier 3
- Instruction, in addition to Tiers 1 and 2, from special education, ELL

Early Literacy Instruction

Teaching Readers and Writers in Today's Primary Classrooms

SECOND EDITION

John A. Smith
Utah State University

Sylvia Read
Utah State University

Allyn & Bacon
is an imprint of

Boston   New York   San Francisco
Mexico City   Montreal   Toronto   London   Madrid   Munich   Paris
Hong Kong   Singapore   Tokyo   Cape Town   Sydney

Vice President and Executive Publisher: Jeffery W. Johnston
Senior Editor: Linda Ashe Bishop
Senior Development Editor: Hope Madden
Senior Managing Editor: Pamela D. Bennett
Senior Project Manager: Mary Irvin
Editorial Assistant: Demetrius Hall
Design Coordinator: Diane C. Lorenzo
Cover Designer: Brian Huber
Cover Image: SuperStock
Operations Specialist: Laura Messerly
Director of Marketing: Quinn Perkson
Marketing Manager: Krista Clark
Marketing Coordinator: Brian Mounts

For related titles and support materials, visit our online catalog at www.pearsonhighered.com.

Between the time website information is gathered and then published, it is not unusual for some sites to have closed. Also, the transcription of URLs can result in typographical errors. The publisher would appreciate notification where these errors occur so that they may be corrected in subsequent editions.

Library of Congress Cataloging-in-Publication Data

Smith, John A.
  Early literacy instruction : teaching readers and writers in today's primary classrooms/ John A. Smith, Sylvia Read. — 2nd ed.
    p. cm.
  Includes bibliographical references and index.
  ISBN-13: 978-0-13-512903-6
  ISBN-10: 0-13-512903-6
 1. Language arts (Primary) 2. Reading (Primary) 3. English language—Composition and exercises—Study and teaching (Primary) I. Read, Sylvia II. Title.

  LB1528.S57 2009
  372.6—dc22

                                                                    2008005339

Printed in the United States of America

10 9 8 7 6 5 4 3 2 1   **BRR** 12 11 10 09 08

Allyn & Bacon
is an imprint of

About the Authors

Dr. John A. Smith is a professor in the Department of Elementary Education at Utah State University. He holds a bachelor's degree in elementary education from Brigham Young University, a master's degree in elementary curriculum from the University of Utah, and a doctorate in curriculum and instruction from the University of North Carolina at Chapel Hill.

Dr. Smith has 10 years of elementary classroom teaching experience in second and fifth grades and as a Chapter 1 reading teacher, and 20 years' experience teaching at the university level. Dr. Smith also taught at-risk students entering kindergarten and first grade for three summers at the Frank Porter Graham Child Development Center in Chapel Hill, North Carolina. He served 3 years as reading coordinator for the Chapel Hill City School District, during which time the district's Chapter 1 program was recognized by the U.S. Department of Education as an Exemplary Program. A highlight of Dr. Smith's teaching was taking a year off from university teaching to return to a first-grade classroom to implement the comprehensive literacy instruction framework described in this book.

Dr. Smith has worked extensively with teachers in elementary school classrooms as a Reading Excellence Act reading coach and currently as a consultant and Reading First technical assistant. Dr. Smith's publications and presentation topics include implementing balanced, comprehensive literacy instruction; implementing a variety of reading instruction strategies; and enhancing literacy instruction with children's songs. He is reviewer for *The Reading Teacher* and *Literacy Research and Instruction* journals, and currently serves as a member of the executive board of the College Reading Association.

Dr. Smith's teaching awards include USU College of Education Teacher of the Year, USU Department of Elementary Education Teacher of the Year, USU Extension Program Teaching Award, and the Mortar Board "Top Prof" award.

Dr. Smith and his wife, Joanne, are proud parents of five children and three grandchildren, so far.

Dr. Sylvia Read is an assistant professor in the Department of Elementary Education at Utah State University. She holds a bachelor's degree in English from the University of Illinois, a master's degree in education from the University of Illinois, and a doctorate in curriculum and instruction from Utah State University.

Dr. Read has 13 years of classroom teaching experience in first, second, sixth, and seventh grades and 6 years of experience teaching at the university level.

Dr. Read works extensively with teachers in elementary school classrooms as a writing instruction mentor, as a professional developer for school districts in the area of reading and writing, and as the leader of professional study groups locally. Dr. Read's publications and presentation topics include incorporating nonfiction in the reading and writing curriculum, implementing effective writing instruction strategies, and using children's literature effectively in language arts instruction. She is co-editor of *Literacy Research and Instruction*, a publication of the College Reading Association.

Preface

*E*arly Literacy Instruction: Teaching Readers and Writers in Today's Primary Classrooms* was written with teachers in mind. New and experienced teachers alike need a practical plan to help them coordinate the effective practices they've learned with the demands of today's primary classrooms—including federal legislation and adopted basal programs. Teachers need to be able to juggle these tools and demands, all the while focusing on the literacy needs and strengths of each individual student.

Because our second edition draws heavily on our experience as classroom teachers, we cover the practical aspects of K–3 literacy instruction. Through our current jobs as teacher educators, we share with you the reading research that should ground the organization and delivery of effective classroom reading and writing instruction. Our goal is to describe and model explicit instruction—so valuable to young learners and struggling learners—and provide you the supporting research and tools that will enable you to implement it in your primary classroom.

A COMPREHENSIVE READING AND WRITING INSTRUCTION FRAMEWORK

In this text we offer you a framework to help you plan and implement comprehensive reading and writing instruction. Within this flexible framework, we describe an explicit instruction model complete with lesson plans, strategies, and research-based practices for teaching reading and writing to young children.

The three-hour literacy instruction block upon which this book is based allows you to address five essential elements of reading as defined by the National Reading Panel: *phonemic awareness, phonics, fluency, vocabulary*, and *comprehension*. In addition, this block of time also provides for *oral language development* and *writing instruction*. It also specifically addresses assessment practices and options for meeting the needs of students who struggle with learning.

These topics are organized into blocks of time set aside for:

- Teacher read-alouds
- Word study and spelling instruction
- Differentiated small group reading instruction
- Independent work
- Writing

Explicit Instruction Model

This framework embraces a model of explicit instruction. Explicit instruction is a form of teaching that presents information to students efficiently and clearly. It's based on the principle of "a gradual release of responsibility" that begins with the teacher taking full responsibility for explaining and demonstrating, later sharing the responsibility with students as they work some examples together, and then finally releasing the responsibility to the students as they work through examples independently.

Implementing the Explicit Instruction Model

This new edition does more than just examine the framework and instructional model. We provide you the tools needed to implement this framework in your own classroom.

New!
- The Explicit Instruction Model Lesson Plan includes sections on explicit teacher explanation and demonstration, interactive guided practice, and monitored independent practice as well as assessment and accommodations for students who struggle.

Addressing Diverse Student Needs

Our framework and explicit instruction model gives you the flexibility to ensure all of your students are becoming literate. To draw your attention to the opportunities explicit instruction offers with diverse learners, we've pinpointed guidelines for students who struggle with literacy learning, as well as students for whom English is not the primary language.

- English Language Learner notes provide concrete suggestions for addressing the needs of students whose first language is not English.

New!
- A strengthened focus on struggling readers—in feature boxes within each chapter, as adaptation ideas within lesson plans, and in a complete chapter (Chapter 11, Interventions for Struggling Readers)—gives you the information you need to detect, assess, and address the needs of these students.

Modeling Effective K-3 Instruction

The chapters give you the research and background you need to make informed decisions about your teaching, but we also ensure that you can see how these teaching methods are put to use with real students in kindergarten through third grade.

- Vignettes open each chapter to help you envision the effective teaching of each chapter's topics.

New!
- MyEducationLab notes lead you to online video footage and articles that provide a clear vision of classroom implementation.
- Student work samples throughout chapters ground concepts and prepare readers for their own classroom.
- The last chapter in the book examines one teacher's classroom to see exactly how a comprehensive reading and writing instruction framework plays out in today's primary grades classrooms.

ORGANIZATION OF THE BOOK

Our new edition boasts two completely new chapters:

- Chapter 2: Organizing for Reading and Writing Instruction   *New!*
- Chapter 7: Independent Activities   *New!*

   Chapter 1, "What Is Reading?," still describes the components of the reading process—word identification and comprehension—but has been reorganized to make the relationships among these components more explicit. The word identification components have been expanded and reorganized to better reflect the sequence in which readers acquire and use them. The comprehension components section has been reorganized to better highlight precursors to comprehension and comprehension strategies.

   Chapter 2, "Organizing for Literacy Instruction," is an all-new chapter focusing on how to organize a classroom for reading and writing instruction. It describes an updated comprehensive reading and writing instruction framework and includes new sections on physical environment, instructional materials, explicit instruction, and building and using a classroom library. This chapter introduces the explicit instructional model, which we revisit in subsequent chapters with lesson plan features.

   Chapter 3, "Building Early Literacy Skills," retains its focus on oral language, alphabet knowledge, phonemic awareness, and print conventions, but weaves in an emphasis on making instruction in these areas more explicit. Building on the mode for explicit instruction described in Chapter 2, this chapter provides suggestions for teacher explanation and modeling, interactive guided practice activities, and independent practice activities.

   Chapter 4, "Reading Aloud to Children," retains its emphasis on using teacher read-aloud as an essential instructional tool, now focusing specifically on purposes for reading aloud: teaching children to respond to literature, teaching comprehension and vocabulary, developing comprehension strategies, and teaching about types of texts.

   Chapter 5, "Word Study," begins with an overview of research-based guidelines for teaching word identification and then describes common spelling patterns that all students will need to learn. A greatly-expanded section on building students' sight vocabularies as well as a new section on multisyllable word identification instruction round out the picture of word study instruction. A new section on explicit word identification instruction is accompanied by sample explicit instruction lesson plans.

   Chapter 6, "Differentiated Small-Group Reading Instruction," has been completely rewritten to examine differentiated instruction. More guidance is given on the use of screening, process-monitoring, and diagnostic assessment data when placing students into differentiated small groups. We take you step-by-step through differentiated small-group reading lesson activities, including several sample explicit instruction, small-group lesson plans. We've also added new sections emphasizing reading comprehension and fluency instruction within small-group lessons.

   Chapter 7, "Independent Activities," is an all-new chapter that describes how to organize independent reading, writing, and learning-centered activities to keep students productively engaged when they are working on their own, while the teacher meets with other students during small-group instruction time. Specific sections focus on preparing students to work independently and provide procedures for scheduling students to work on their own or in groups.

Chapter 8, "Effective Writing Instruction," explains both Writing Workshop and writing as a process, providing a balanced view of writing as both a skill and a meaning-making process. We emphasize the importance of having students write every day, teaching mini-lessons, conferring with students, and asking students to share their writing with the class. We've retained the strong focus on reading-writing connections, folding in information about explicit instruction, as well as specific guidance on selecting pre-writing strategies for different genres.

Chapter 9, "Reading and Writing Across the Curriculum," discusses the need for and the importance of reading and writing across the curriculum. It explains expository text structures and how to integrate instruction in expository text structures within Writing Workshop. The chapter explores ways to integrate reading and writing meaningfully in math, science, and social studies, including an explicit instruction lesson plan for teaching descriptive writing in the context of science.

Chapter 10, "Reading Assessment That Guides Instruction," has been completely reorganized to describe assessment instruments that are commonly used to measure student reading achievement in each of the essential areas of reading. Chapter 10 begins with expanded and updated sections on assessment purposes, validity, and reliability. Each subsequent section describes multiple assessment measures in each essential area.

Chapter 11, "Reading Interventions for Struggling Readers," begins with a focus on the pressing need for more attention to struggling readers and writers. New sections on the classroom teacher's responsibility to provide in-class interventions for struggling readers leads to the use of progress-monitoring and diagnostic assessment data to plan instruction. The chapter also presents new information on program interventions for students that need instructional support beyond what the classroom teacher can provide.

Chapter 12, "Putting It All Together," examines in detail one teacher's three-hour literacy block, which will enable you to envision how to allocate time and plan instruction.

SUPPLEMENTS

"Teacher educators who are developing pedagogies for the analysis of teaching and learning contend that analyzing teaching artifacts has three advantages: It enables new teachers time for reflection while still using the real materials of practice; it provides new teachers with experience thinking about and approaching the complexity of the classroom; and in some cases, it can help new teachers and teacher educators develop a shared understanding and common language about teaching. . . ."[1]

As Linda Darling-Hammond and her colleagues point out, grounding teacher education in real classrooms—among real teachers and students and among actual examples of students' and teachers' work—is an important, and perhaps even an essential, part of training teachers for the complexities of teaching today's students in today's classrooms. For a number of years, we at Pearson have heard the same message as we sat in your offices learning about the goals of your courses and the challenges you face in teaching the next generation of educators. Working with many of

[1]Darling-Hammond, I., & Bransford, J., Eds. (2005). *Preparing Teachers for a Changing World*. San Francisco: John Wiley & Sons.

our authors, we have created a website to provide the sample classrooms and student work that research on teacher education tells us is so important. Through authentic in-class video footage, interactive simulations, rich case studies, examples of authentic teacher and student work, and more, **MyEducationLab** offers you and your students a uniquely valuable teacher education tool.

MyEducationLab is easy to use! Wherever the MyEducationLab logo appears in the margins, you and your students can follow the simple link instructions to access the MyEducationLab resource that corresponds with the chapter content. These include:

Video: Authentic classroom videos show how real teachers handle actual classroom situations.

Case Studies: A diverse set of robust cases drawn from some of our best-selling books further expose students to the realities of teaching and offer valuable perspectives on common issues and challenges in education.

Simulations: Created by the IRIS Center at Vanderbilt University, these interactive simulations give hands-on practice at adapting instruction for a full spectrum of learners.

Student & Teacher Artifacts: Authentic student and teacher classroom artifacts are tied to course topics and offer practice in working with the actual types of materials encountered every day by teachers.

Readings: Specially selected, topically relevant articles from ASCD's renowned *Educational Leadership* journal expand and enrich students' perspectives on key issues and topics.

PEARSON myeducationlab

Vocabulary

Go to MyEducationLab, "Vocabulary," and watch the video *Introducing Words to Young Readers*.

As you view the video, notice how the teacher introduces two new words during the before-reading portion of a small-group lesson.

- What criteria might the teacher have used to select the two words she chose to teach?
- How did the teacher redirect a student's attention during the lesson?
- What other activities might the teacher use to introduce new words?

Other Resources

Lesson & Portfolio Builders: With this effective and easy-to-use tool, you can create, update, and share standards-based lesson plans and portfolios.

MyEducationLab is easy to assign, which is essential to providing the greatest benefit to your student. Visit www.myeducationlab.com for a demonstration of this exciting new online teaching resource.

Instructor Resource Center

The Instructor Resource Center at www.pearsonhighered.com has a variety of print and media resources available in downloadable, digital format—all in one location. As a registered faculty member, you can access and download passcode-protected resource files, course management content, and other premium online content directly to your computer.

Digital resources available for *Early Literacy Instruction: Teaching Readers and Writers in Today's Primary Classrooms*, Second Edition, include a test bank of multiple choice and essay tests.

To access these items online, go to www.pearsonhighered.com, click on the Instructor Support button, and then go to the Download Supplements section. Here you will be able to log in or complete a one-time registration for a user name and password. If you have any questions regarding this process or the materials available online, please contact your local Pearson sales representative.

 ## ACKNOWLEDGMENTS

We would like to thank the reviewers of our manuscript for their insights and comments: Carolyn Abel, Stephen F. Austin State University; Stacey A. Dudley, Bowling Green State University; Tobie R. Sanders, Capital University; Barbara A. Schaudt, California State University—Bakersfield; and Brenda H. Spencer, California State University—Fullerton.

Brief Contents

Contents

Special Features

Lesson Plans

For English Language Learners

What Is Reading?

by John A. Smith

1

The Importance of Knowing About Reading

"*Sound it out, José, /t/ /h/ /i/ /s/, you can do it, /t/ /h/ /i/ /s/," says student teacher Mr. Jones. "Say it the slow way." His student, José, methodically applies the blending process to the letter sounds. He points to the individual letters and pronounces their sounds, "/t/ /h/ /i/ /s/." Then he blends the letter sounds together and comes up with a word that sounds something like /t-hiss/. José is puzzled. Mr. Jones is puzzled too. The phonics isn't working.*

Serendipitously, the school reading coach, Mrs. Donaldson, just happens to be visiting the classroom, and because she knows reading, she instantly recognizes the problem that is perplexing both José and his student teacher. "May I give it a try?" she asks politely, recognizing that she'll be teaching both José and Mr. Jones.

"José, when you see a t *and an* h *together in a word, they most often make just one sound, the sound /th/ like in the word* that. *Sometimes they make the /th/ sound as in the word* think. T *and* h *together are called a consonant digraph," she adds for Mr. Jones's benefit, "like* ch, sh, *and* wh.*"Jose makes the /th/ sound and continues blending the* i *and* s *letter sounds so that he now comes up with the correct pronunciation /this/.*

Well-intentioned Mr. Jones, soon to finish his student teaching, was unable to help his student José because his own knowledge of the components and mechanics of reading was insufficient. Whether it's phonics spelling patterns, comprehension strategies, or ways to motivate reluctant readers, teachers must know how reading works in order to teach it effectively.

To be able to teach reading effectively, teachers must understand how reading works (Moats, 1998; Snow, Griffin, & Burns, 2005) and must be familiar with the components of reading and how they fit together. The more teachers understand the reading process, the better we will be able to recognize the reading skills and strategies our students possess and what they need to learn next. The more teachers understand the reading process, the better we will be able to recognize our students' various reading problems and give them the focused reading instruction

A comprehensive literacy instruction framework can meet learner's varying needs.

Steven Von Niederhausern

that they need. Specifically, this chapter provides information about the following topics:

 Reading is constructing meaning

 Components of reading

    Word identification

    Comprehension

 Attitude toward reading

READING IS CONSTRUCTING MEANING

There are many varying and often conflicting definitions of reading. Some people feel that reading means quickly and smoothly pronouncing words on a page. Others claim that reading is getting the meaning from a book, magazine, or other printed text. Still others argue that reading requires having an emotional or intellectual response to a text. A comprehensive view of reading includes elements of all these perspectives.

The 1985 landmark reading research summary published by the National Institute of Education titled *Becoming a Nation of Readers* (Anderson, Hiebert, Scott, & Wilkinson, 1985) contains a short sentence that provides a simple straightforward definition of reading. This definition, separated into four lines, highlights several important aspects of what it means to read.

> *Reading is a process in which information from the text and the reader's background knowledge act together to produce meaning. (p. 8)*

First, reading is a *complex process*. Reading is much like a symphony orchestra. String players, brass players, woodwind players, percussion players, and the conductor are all doing different things simultaneously to produce a magnificent single product: a symphony. While reading, the reader's eyes are tracking across the lines on each page, fixating on words and clusters of letters. The reader's brain automatically recognizes familiar words and spelling patterns. The recognition of familiar printed words triggers the reader's memory for both the spoken version of these words (print-to-sound) and their meaning versions (print-to-meaning). Adams (2001) describes how "recognition of a familiar word will automatically evoke its personal history of usage and interpretation in print and, through that, its previously experienced meanings in general" (p. 70). The reader's mind then carries out interactions and comparisons among the printed, spoken, and meaning aspects of words automatically, simultaneously, and "in mutual coordination" to confirm the identity and meanings of recognized words. When encountering unfamiliar words or spelling patterns, the reader often takes a second look, trying to recall other words with similar spelling patterns or similar words that might make sense. Like a symphony orchestra, all of these mental processes work together to produce a magnificent single product: meaning.

Second, information contained in the text is compared with and filtered by the reader's *background knowledge*. This results in adding to and in many cases changing the reader's knowledge in part or altogether. Each person has a unique collection of personal experiences. Each person has lived in different homes and communities, been to different schools, had different teachers, played with different friends, been to different places on vacation, seen different movies, pursued different hobbies, and read different books. Each reader's unique collection of background knowledge and experiences has the effect of emphasizing, disregarding, and connecting to different aspects of texts to create an individual interpretation. This is why 30 university students in a reading methods course could read a short story or poem and each write a one-page response that is different from all the others.

A *Family Circle* cartoon illustrated this principle of differing background knowledge very well. In the cartoon, Dad was reading aloud to four young children. He read the phrase "imagine that you're standing by the water's edge." For one of the children in the cartoon, this phrase recalled standing at the beach. Another child pictured standing at a mountain lake. A third child thought about standing by a river. The fourth child saw himself standing next to a stream behind the house. The phrase "standing by the water's edge" evoked four different images based on the children's varying experiences.

Third, the information in the text and the reader's background knowledge act together to *produce meaning*. Many people typically think of reading as getting information from the text. This implies that information involved in reading flows in one direction: from the book to the brain. However, the definition of reading described in this textbook suggests that the reader's background knowledge interacts with information from the text to produce a new and unique interpretation or meaning. The meaning of a text is actually created in a transaction somewhere between the text and the reader, influenced by the context or purpose of the reading situation. Rosenblatt (1994) states:

> Every reading act is an event, or a transaction involving a particular reader and a particular pattern of signs, a text, and occurring at a particular time in a particular context. Instead of two fixed entities acting on one another, the reader and the text are two aspects of a total dynamic situation. The "meaning" does not reside ready-made "in" the text or "in" the reader but happens or comes into being during the transaction between reader and text. (p. 1063)

Having a clear understanding of how reading works is important because that understanding will influence how you teach reading (Phelps, 2005; Snow et al., 2005). When you are aware of the critical role of your students' background knowledge in

Literacy learners
need instruction in all
aspects of reading
and writing.

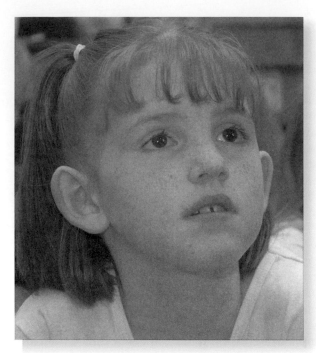

Steven Von Niederhausern

reading, you are more likely to spend instructional time activating and developing your students' background knowledge prior to reading and helping your students connect new information to what they already know. If you view reading primarily as blending letter sounds fluently, you may not guide your students to also use sentence structure and contextual information to help them process print. Conversely, if you are mostly concerned with making meaning and developing reader response, you may overlook the need to help your students process print fluently and automatically as a necessary contributor to reading comprehension.

Research has shown that effective reading teachers understand the need for helping readers attend to all aspects of the reading process (Pressley, Yokoi, Rankin, Wharton-McDonald, & Mistretta, 1997). Effective reading teachers simultaneously pay attention to the decoding skills and strategies of reading while also keeping in mind that reading is about meaning. Effective teachers use a comprehensive instructional framework to address these facets of reading.

 ## COMPONENTS OF READING

Classroom teachers, reading researchers, and others in the field of education generally agree that there are two major components of the reading process: *word identification* and *comprehension* (Hoover & Gough, 1990; National Reading Panel [NRP], 2000). These components are both necessary for reading to occur. In describing them, the NRP's (2000) report states:

> One process involves learning to convert the letters into recognizable words. The other involves comprehending the meaning of the print. When children attain reading skill, they learn to perform both of these processes so that their attention and thought are focused on the meaning of the text while word reading processes operate unobtrusively and out of awareness for the most part. (p. 2-106)

Although word identification is generally associated with the terms *phonics, word attack*, or *sounding out*, the term *word identification* refers to recognizing or decoding printed words. The term is more inclusive than *phonics* because it includes both words that are recognized and words that are decoded. *Comprehension* means making sense of what is read. Readers combine their background knowledge with information contained in the text to create meaning. For each of these two major components, there are several subcomponents. Your familiarity with these subcomponents or "parts" of reading will enable you to better understand what readers need to know and be able to do in reading, what they are doing well, and where they need additional support and guidance.

Another element of reading that needs to be acknowledged is attitude toward reading (Cunningham, 2005; Edmunds & Bauserman, 2006). The benefits of learning how to read are greatly diminished if students don't want to read. Students who do not enjoy reading will spend their time doing things other than reading and will miss the critical practice they need to improve as readers. Piano students who don't practice regularly will not improve their piano playing very quickly, if at all. Skiers who do not ski on a regular basis will not become better skiers as quickly as those who do. Readers who do not read often will have a harder time becoming better readers. If students are to read often and by choice, then it is imperative that teachers focus not only on the mechanics of reading, but also on building students' desire to read.

WORD IDENTIFICATION

Readers use several reading skills and sources of information to identify words: alphabet knowledge, phonemic awareness, phonics, structural analysis, sight vocabulary, context, and syntax (Bear, Invernizzi, Templeton, & Johnston, 2007; Cunningham, 2004). Good readers use all of these strategies flexibly, simultaneously, and automatically. Just as nutrition experts have long stressed the importance of a balanced diet, teachers should keep in mind the importance of providing students with a balanced and comprehensive approach to identifying printed words.

The following components of word identification are listed in a sequence that somewhat approximates the steps of learning to identify printed words.

Components of Word Identification

1. Alphabet knowledge — Students recognize alphabet letter names and sounds.
2. Phonemic awareness — Students understand that spoken words are composed of individual speech sounds.
3. Phonics — Students blend printed letter sounds to identify words.
4. Structural analysis — Students analyze and combine word parts to identify words.
5. Sight vocabulary — Students automatically recognize high-frequency and irregular words.
6. Context — Students use meaning to help confirm the identity of words.
7. Syntax — Students use sentence structure to help confirm the identity of words.

Alphabet Knowledge

Beginning readers often start by learning to recognize alphabet letter names and sounds (Bradley & Jones, 2007). They must also understand the alphabetic principle—that printed alphabet letters represent the sounds we make in spoken language. For example, the printed letter *t* represents the speech sound /t/ that we make at the beginning of the spoken word *top*. The printed letter *m* represents the speech sound /m/ that we hear at the end of the spoken word *Sam*. Chapter 3 describes ways to teach alphabet knowledge.

Phonemic Awareness

Beginning readers must also develop *phonemic awareness*, the understanding that spoken words are composed of individual speech sounds, and that individual speech sounds are manipulated and blended to form spoken words (McCormick, Throneburg, & Smitley, 2002). Unlike phonics where beginning readers recognize, blend, and segment printed letters, phonemic awareness involves only spoken words and sounds. Beginning readers must understand that the spoken word *dog* begins with the sound /d/ and that *dog* contains three speech sounds: /d/ /o/ /g/. They must be able to blend the three individual sounds /d/ /o/ /g/ together to pronounce the spoken word *dog*. Conversely they must be able to segment the spoken word *dog* into its three individual sounds: /d/ /o/ /g/. The understanding that individual speech sounds can be blended and segmented forms the foundation for learning phonics—the blending and segmenting of printed letter sounds.

Although reading research describes other phonemic awareness skills including rhyming, deleting, and manipulating speech sounds, the two skills of blending and segmenting are most directly related to reading and spelling printed words (NRP, 2000). Blending is the precursor to putting letter sounds together to pronounce (read) words. Segmenting is the skill needed for hearing and writing the individual sounds of words in spelling.

Phonics

Students are ready to use phonics to identify printed words when they know the sounds of the alphabet letters and understand the principle of blending sounds together to form words (Bear et al., 2007; Cunningham, 2004). The term *phonics* is used almost interchangeably with other terms including *sounding out*, *decoding*, *word attack*, and *word identification*. *Phonics* is based on the Latin root *phon*—meaning "sound"—as in the words tele*phon*e and *phon*ograph. Phonics simply means combining the sounds of the printed letters in a word to produce its pronunciation. For example, beginning readers will blend the sounds of the printed letters *s–a–t* to pronounce the word *sat* or the printed letters *th–i–s* to pronounce the word *this*. With phonetically regular words such as *cat*, *draft*, *steam*, *chip*, *floor*, and *twine* phonics works very nicely. With irregular words such as *does*, *is*, *love*, *said*, *some*, and *was*, using the sounds of the letters at least gives readers a place to begin trying to produce a pronunciation of the word.

There are several important reasons for beginning readers to learn to recognize spelling patterns as they read words. Our minds are wired to find visual and sequential patterns in our world. Recognizing and making patterns allows our minds to organize large amounts of data in useful categories so that we can more readily perceive, connect, store, retrieve, and process information. Many printed words are too long to be blended or "sounded out" letter-by-letter. For example, the word *championship* is too long to be sounded out. Instead, good readers will recognize spelling patterns within the word (*ch*, *amp*, *ion*, *sh*, *ip*) and simply blend the sounds of the patterns together. Recognizing and manipulating spelling patterns is the most efficient way to identify unfamiliar printed words.

Structural Analysis

As beginning readers use phonics to repeatedly blend simple words such as *bat*, *cat*, *fat*, and *hat*, they begin to notice the "at" spelling pattern and then use it to identify other *at*-family words more efficiently. Recognizing and using familiar parts of words is called structural analysis (Carlisle & Stone, 2005; Mountain, 2005).

FOR STRUGGLING READERS

Readers' Problems

An insufficient understanding of the alphabetic principle and an inability to easily blend letter sounds is at the heart of many struggling readers' problems. When some first-grade students begin to fall behind their classmates, one-on-one or small-group tutoring sessions with decodable texts provide the repetition and practice they need to catch up.

When good readers come across unfamiliar printed words they often recognize familiar spelling patterns and word parts and then combine these familiar word parts to identify the word. For example, a reader may not recognize the printed word *slight*, but may recognize the *ight* part of the word from other more familiar words such as *light*, *might*, and *right*. Structural analysis also involves recognizing and combining prefixes, root words, suffixes, and common letter combinations such as *ing*, *ble*, and *tion*. The following example of words from a medical journal should help you recognize just how important structural analysis is in word identification.

> neuropharmacology
> postganglionic
> phylogenetic
> renocorticotropic
> periacquaductal
> neospinalthalamic

Study these words for a moment and try to pronounce them out loud. As you do, chances are that you are using structural analysis to look for familiar parts of the words, such as *neuro*, *pharm*, and *ology* or *peri*, *acqua*, *duct*, and *al*. You still may not know what any of these words mean, but you should at least be able to pronounce them using structural analysis. Good readers use structural analysis continually, flexibly, and automatically.

Sight Vocabulary

As readers begin to recognize familiar word parts, they also begin to recognize many frequent words as whole units (Joseph, 2006). *Sight vocabulary* refers to words that readers can recognize instantly. There are two types of sight words.

One type of sight word is *high-frequency words*. High-frequency words appear so often in printed text that readers come to memorize or recognize them through sheer repetition. Words in a reader's sight vocabulary do not need to be sounded out or decoded. Many common words and spelling patterns that appear again and again in print (*the*, *and*, *for*, *some*) quickly become sight words through repetition. Other words easily become sight words because of their interest value to young readers (*love*, *dinosaur*, *mother*, *McDonald's*). Just as we come to instantly recognize people whom we see on a regular basis, readers can also come to instantly recognize many words that they see repeatedly. Following is a list of some high-frequency words:

a	funny	look	see
and	go	make	the
away	help	me	three
big	here	my	to
blue	I	not	two
can	in	one	up
come	is	play	we
down	it	red	where
find	jump	run	yellow
for	little	said	you

The second type of sight word is *irregular words*. Irregular words are words that do not follow the "phonics rules" and must simply be memorized because they cannot be sounded out or decoded.

The following list contains examples of irregular words. Try to apply phonics rules to the first word of each pair in the following columns of beginning reading words and see what you come up with. The second word in each pair represents how these words would be spelled if phonics rules really were applied consistently in our printed language. These are just a few of the many irregular words that simply must be memorized as sight words because the phonics rules don't apply to them.

a	u	does	duz	said	sed
above	ubuv	from	frum	says	sez
again	ugen	give	giv	school	skule
because	beekuz	love	luv	walk	wok
bought	bot	lose	luze	was	wuz
build	bild	of	uv	what	whut
come	cum	off	of		

Because quickly recognizing printed words and spelling patterns is a very efficient way to read and because many common words are irregular and can't be decoded using phonics rules, it is important that beginning readers quickly develop a strong sight vocabulary. A strong sight vocabulary will enable readers to recognize words quickly and effortlessly, which allows them to focus most of their attention on the meaning of the text. Sight vocabulary is also important because the words and spelling patterns that a reader can recognize instantly also become the building blocks for identifying more complex and multisyllabic words.

Context

Good readers identify printed words quickly and accurately by looking at and recognizing letters, word parts, and whole words. Good readers also use context, the *meaning of the sentence or passage*, not to identify words but rather to confirm or modify the pronunciations they have generated from looking at the letters.

How would you pronounce the following italicized word *read*? The vowel sound in *read* can be pronounced with the long *e* sound as in "I want to read this book" or the

Figure 1.1   A Fairy Tale

Ladle Rat Rotten Hut

Wants pawn term, dare worsted ladle gull hoe lift wetter murder inner ladle cordage honor itch offer lodge dock florist. Disk ladle gull orphan worry putty ladle rat cluck wetter ladle rat hut, and fur disk raisin, pimple colder Ladle Rat Rotten Hut.

Wan moaning, Ladle Rat Rotten Hut's murder colder in said, "Ladle Rat Rotten Hut, heresy ladle basking winsome burden barter and shirker cockles. Tick disk ladle basking tutor cordage offer groin-murder how lifts honor udder site offer florist. Shaker lake! Dun stopper laundry wrote! Dun stopper peck floors! Dun daily doily inner florist, and yonder nor sorghum stenches, dun stopper torque wet strainers!"

"Hoe-cake, murder," resplendent Ladle Rat Rotten Hut, and tickle ladle basking and stuttered oft.

Honor wrote tutor cordage offer groin-murder, Ladle Rat Rotten Hut mitten anomalous woof.

"Wail, wail, wail!" set disk wicket woof, "evanescent Ladle Rat Rotten Hut! Wares are putty ladle gull goring wizard ladle basking?"

"Armor goring tumor groin-murder's," reprisal ladle gull. "Grammar's seeking bet. Armor ticking arson burden barter and shirker cockles."

Source: Original version written in 1940 by H. L. Chace.

vowel sound can be pronounced as the short *e* sound, as in "I read this book yesterday." How you pronounce the word *read* depends on the context of the sentence.

The passage in Figure 1.1 provides a humorous example of how context helps readers identify words. The content of the passage is a very familiar fairy tale. The words have been changed so that a word-by-word oral reading will only give a vague approximation of the familiar spoken words, and will likely make no sense. As you read this passage notice how you must use the context of each paragraph and sentence to help identify the words. For those of you who need a head start, the first three printed words in the fairy tale translate to "Once upon a time."

As you can see, reading by phonics alone won't help with *Ladle Rat Rotten Hut*. You had to look at the letters in the words to generate a pronunciation. But because the pronunciations alone didn't make sense, you used contextual information to modify the pronunciations into words that did make sense. It was context that told you the printed word *ladle* was really the spoken meaningful word *little*. This principle holds true with all of our reading. We look at the letters to get a pronunciation, then use context to see if the pronunciation makes sense. If it makes sense we continue on. If not, we try another pronunciation. Good readers continually use phonics to derive word pronunciations and then context to confirm if their pronunciations are correct.

Syntax

Along with context, readers also use syntax to help confirm or modify the identity of printed words. Syntax is our knowledge of sentence structure. Our syntactic knowledge develops in early childhood along with our oral language. For example, our knowledge of English syntax tells us that the sentence "Sally lives in the house big down the street" is not right. Good readers use syntax as another check to see that they are identifying words correctly.

Figure 1.2 A Meaningless Passage

A Pidder Flaster Chiffel

Berm kerp a pidder flaster chiffel. Berm foober hep pidder flaster chiffel um vistar. At nogom Berm zonk hep pidder flaster chiffel. On Bister Berm foobers hep pidder flaster chiffel to meddar's seppum.

1. Who kerp a pidder flaster chiffel?
2. What did Berm do with hep pidder flaster chiffel?
3. Where did Berm zonk hep pidder flaster chiffel at nogom?
4. Where did Berm foober hep pidder flaster chiffel on Bister?

Read the passage in Figure 1.2 and try to answer the questions that follow. Phonics won't help because the pronunciations won't approximate real words. Context won't help because the passage has no meaning to rely on. Yet you will be able to "read" this passage and successfully answer the questions because of your familiarity with the syntax of the English language.

Fountas and Pinnell (2006) point out that good readers also use syntax to recognize the phrase units of printed text and to read in phrases, thus helping recognize the author's meaning. Students learn the rules of language structure from listening and speaking and then they apply those syntactic rules to printed language both to support word identification and to build comprehension.

FOR ENGLISH LANGUAGE LEARNERS

The Challenge of Syntax

Syntax is a particular challenge for ELL students. For example, the English oral language syntactic structure *big house* is reversed in the Spanish translation *casa grande*. In other words, the oral language patterns that native speakers rely on are of less or little help to ELL students.

The Need for Comprehensive Word Identification

Word identification strategies are not used individually, sequentially one-at-a-time, or in isolation from each other. Good readers use all of these strategies simultaneously, flexibly, and automatically (Cartwright, 2006). Take, for example, the following sentence: *Bob sleeps in his house.* Imagine a beginning reader reading this sentence and coming on the word *house*, which is not in his or her sight vocabulary. If we could peek inside that reader's mind, we might see a thought process like this:

> This is easy. I know the first words "Bob sleeps in his." Oh oh, I don't recognize this last word [sight vocabulary]. It's not an action word because of *in his.* . . . It must be someplace Bob sleeps [syntax and context]. It can't be his bed because it doesn't start with *b*. The first two letters are *ho* [phonics]. Maybe it's *home*, that makes sense [phonics and context]. Let's take another look at the word. Oops, it has an *s* toward the end and no *m* [phonics]. It can't be *home*. The middle has *ou* like *out* [structural analysis]. *H/ou/s . . . house.* And the *e* on the end is probably silent [phonics]. That must be it. It makes sense and all the letters fit [syntax, phonics, structural analysis, and context]. Bob sleeps in his house.

This example shows how good readers flexibly and simultaneously use letter–sound relationships, sight vocabulary, structural analysis, and syntactic and contextual information to identify words not in their sight vocabularies, much like fitting together the pieces of a jigsaw puzzle. A basketball team that relies on one star player to score most of its points will be seriously handicapped against a team that has even scoring from all of its players. Similarly, readers who rely on a single word identification strategy (i.e., phonics or context) every time they encounter an unfamiliar word will have a much harder time identifying words quickly, accurately, and automatically.

The Role of Oral Reading Fluency

Many beginning readers learning to recognize and process printed words and spelling patterns read slowly with many errors and little expression. Other beginning readers may develop the ability to recognize words fairly accurately, but still read very slowly and monotonously. Beginning readers can be accurate and still not be fluent. The goal of word identification instruction is to help all beginning readers develop oral reading fluency, defined by the National Reading Panel (2000) as reading quickly, accurately, and with expression (Pikulski & Chard, 2005; Rasinski, 2006). Although much of word identification instruction takes place at the word level (studying word families and word parts), fluency instruction takes place at the passage level as students practice reading large sections of text over and over until they can read aloud quickly, accurately, and with expression.

Being able to recognize and process printed words easily, quickly, and accurately is often referred to as *automaticity*. Automaticity has important implications for reading comprehension. Each of us has a limited amount of attention capacity that can be allocated among several items simultaneously. The more attention we shift to one item, the less there is to be allocated to other items. For example, most of us can drive a car with automaticity. We are so experienced with turning the wheel and pushing the pedals that we can drive a car almost effortlessly while focusing our attention on other things such as listening intently to the radio, thinking about upcoming events, or talking with our passengers.

Reading should operate the same way. Readers should be able to identify printed words effortlessly and automatically so that they can allocate greater portions of their attention to the more important component of reading: comprehension. Adams (1990) documents the important role of automaticity in reading. She writes:

> Laboratory research indicates that the most critical factor beneath fluent word reading is the ability to recognize letters, spelling patterns, and whole words effortlessly, automatically, and visually. The central goal of all reading instruction—comprehension—depends critically on this ability. (p. 54)

COMPREHENSION

The ultimate purpose of reading is to understand what authors have to say, to make meaning from texts, to comprehend (Block & Pressley, 2002; Liang & Dole, 2006). Alphabet knowledge, phonemic awareness, phonics, fluency, and vocabulary are only stepping stones that lead to comprehension. Without comprehension there would be no purpose for reading.

Like word identification, comprehension also has subcomponents, which are divided into three groups: precursors to comprehension, comprehension strategies, and levels of comprehension.

Precursors to Comprehension

Vocabulary and background knowledge	Students are familiar with word meanings and passage concepts.
Text structure	Students know how to use the organizational patterns of narrative, expository, and other texts.

Comprehension Strategies

Predicting	Students use background knowledge to predict passage content.
Clarifying	Students identify and then clarify words and passages that don't make sense.
Questioning	Students generate questions about passage content.
Summarizing	Students identify and organize important passage content
Visualizing	Students make mental images of passage content.

Levels of Comprehension

Literal comprehension	Students know the basic facts: who, what, when, where, how, why (there in black and white).
Inferential comprehension	Students use background knowledge to supplement information provided in the text (read between the lines).
Critical reading	Students evaluate the quality of the text.

Precursors to Comprehension

Vocabulary, background knowledge, and text structure are considered precursers to comprehension because they are the foundation on which comprehension is built. Teachers routinely incorporate instruction in these three comprehension subcomponents as the first step in teaching students to understand meaningful text.

Vocabulary

Vocabulary is considered by many reading experts to be the single largest contributor to reading comprehension (Blachowicz, Fisher, Ogle, & Watts-Taffe, 2006; Cunningham, 2006). Vocabulary is often discussed in two ways: sight vocabulary (printed words that students recognize easily and accurately) and meaning vocabulary (words for which students understand the meanings). Discussions of vocabulary linked to comprehension refer to meaning vocabulary.

Meaning vocabulary is necessary for comprehension to occur. Simply sounding out the phonetically regular word *cheetah* will not be of any use to a young reader who has never heard the word or seen a cheetah on television or at the zoo.

The following example illustrates the central role of meaning vocabulary in reading comprehension. These 10 words would be considered sight words for competent adult readers. Read them to yourself.

individual	variable
mean	blocks
error	square
effect	random
nuisance	differences

Now read the same words again, this time in a paragraph.

A randomized block design permits an experimenter to minimize the effects of individual differences by isolating that portion of the total effect due to blocks. As a result, the error term for testing the treatment mean square is free of the nuisance variable of individual differences.

Would you care to summarize the meaning of the paragraph? No? Why not? Even though most adult readers can read all of the individual words in that paragraph, most would have trouble comprehending the paragraph because they lack the necessary background knowledge of, in this case, inferential statistics. The point is that too many students come to our classrooms without the vocabulary knowledge needed to make sense of the materials they are expected to read. For such students, much of what they are given to read is as incomprehensible to them as statistics.

Teachers generally think of words as belonging to one of three tiers (Beck, McKeown, & Kucan, 2002). *Tier One* words are those very common words that most students will already be familiar with (*fast, pretty, house, happy, mother*) and do not need to be taught as vocabulary words. *Tier Two* words are words that many students will not yet know, yet are words that will be useful and important to learn (*impressive, furious, savor, invest*). Tier Two words are often encountered in general classroom reading and should be highlighted and used to build students' general vocabularies. *Tier Three* words are highly specific words, generally associated with a content area, that are taught in relation to content-area studies (*thorax, octave, emancipation*).

FOR ENGLISH LANGUAGE LEARNERS

The Challenge of Vocabulary

Vocabulary is also a major challenge for ELL students. An ELL student may be familiar with a background knowledge concept such as *horse*, but not know the specific English words associated with the concept of horse. Simply teaching ELL students the word identification skills needed to pronounce words such as *horse* will do little good unless we also give them ample instructional opportunities to develop the English vocabulary needed to understand what the pronounced words mean.

Background Knowledge

Where meaning vocabulary is associated with students' knowledge of specific word meanings, background knowledge has to do with students' knowledge of broader concepts. The following example shows a student's lack of background knowledge of geography concepts.

A Title 1 resource reading teacher was guiding a small group of struggling fifth-grade students through the novel *Island of the Blue Dolphins*. One of the struggling students, LaToya, lingered after class one day in the resource room. The teacher, seeing an opportunity for some extra teaching, brought LaToya to the classroom wall map to show her where the island is located. As the teacher pointed to the island, off the coast of Southern California, the following conversation ensued:

LaToya: Teacher, is this blue part the water?

Teacher: Yes, the blue part is the water and the colored parts are the different countries. Here's the United States; it's yellow. Here are Canada, Mexico, and South America. These dots in the ocean are islands, and these yellow dots are Hawaii, part of the United States.

LaToya: Could you drive to Hawaii?

Teacher: No, you'd have to take a boat or an airplane to get to Hawaii.

LaToya: Where's Hollywood and where's the Bahamas?

Teacher: (*Shows these locations on the map*)

LaToya: Is Norfolk in South America?

Teacher: No, Norfolk is over here in Virginia.

LaToya: Can you drive to Hollywood?

Teacher: Yes, you can drive to Hollywood from here and it would take about 4 days.

Based on this conversation, you can guess that LaToya did not have a lot of background knowledge, at least about geography. Her family was poorly educated and unable to provide a computer, music lessons, summer educational programs, vacations outside the county, books and magazine subscriptions, or other opportunities to learn about the world through travel and firsthand experiences, discussions, or wide reading.

Ironically, the teacher could hand LaToya a fifth-grade reading book, open it to any page, and say, "Read this to me." LaToya could read the words aloud almost effortlessly. She was bright and had learned the decoding aspects of reading very easily. But when the teacher would ask LaToya to explain what she had just "read," she would stare ahead with a blank expression on her face. She could seldom describe the ideas contained in the words she read. LaToya couldn't comprehend what she was reading because she generally lacked the necessary background knowledge.

Text Structure

Most texts that students will read are either narrative (stories) or expository (informational texts). Understanding how expository texts are structured differently from narrative texts will help students increase their comprehension (Dymock, 2005) by helping them better organize information from reading in their heads.

The text structure of narrative texts, or stories, is known as story grammar and generally contains the structural elements of *setting*, *characters*, *problem*, and *events*. For example:

> *One day in the deep dark woods (setting) Little Red Riding Hood's mother (character) asked her to take a basket of cookies to her grandmother (character, event). Her mother told her not to talk to anyone along the way. On the path Little Red Riding Hood met a wicked wolf (character, event) and stopped to chat with him (problem). The wolf hurried to Grandmother's house (setting), dressed up like Grandmother (event), and was about to gobbled up Little Red Riding Hood when a woodsman (character) saved them (event). The moral of this story is to always obey your mother.*

Conversely, the text structure of expository texts, informational texts, generally focuses on main ideas and details. For example:

> *Water on our planet goes continuously up into the air and back down to earth in a process known as the* water cycle (main idea). *Water comes down from the sky in the form of water and snow* (detail). *The water collects in streams and rivers and flows into lakes and oceans* (detail). *Then the water evaporates back up into the sky* (detail). *The water molecules in the sky collect together to form clouds* (detail). *When the clouds get full enough with water molecules, they fall back to earth as rain or snow* (detail).

Teaching students to recognize text structure gives them a way to anticipate, look for, and organize the information they will encounter. Many teachers like to begin each new reading lesson by inviting students to examine the text for a minute and then predict if it will be a story or an informational text. When the teacher and students have determined the text structure, the teacher will often draw a diagram or *graphic organizer* on the board corresponding to the text structure and use it as a vehicle for listing and organizing the information from the text (McMackin, & Witherell, 2005).

Comprehension Strategies

When teaching students to identify words, we refer to teaching word identification skills. The term *skills* denotes quick and accurate recognition of spelling patterns and word parts. Students should be able to apply skills automatically. Conversely, when teaching students to comprehend texts, we refer to teaching comprehension strategies. Strategies, unlike skills, are applied purposefully and selectively. Depending on the text, students will purposefully choose which comprehension strategies to apply. Reading comprehension strategies help readers become more mentally engaged with the content of texts by providing specific purposes for reading and specific ways of analyzing texts.

There are many lists of comprehension strategies (Bishop, Reyes, & Pflaum, 2006; Kragler, Walker, & Martin, 2005). The five comprehension strategies described in the following paragraphs (Oczkus, 2004) are found in most reading comprehension instruction programs. Reading comprehension strategies can be taught both individually (single-strategy instruction) and also in combination (multiple-strategy instruction) (NRP, 2000).

Predicting

Before reading, good readers will often consider the title and cover illustration, perhaps scan through the pages and subheads, and make a mental prediction of what information the passage will cover. Not random guessing, prediction involves incorporating the reader's background knowledge about the topic with the introductory information to make an informed prediction. For example, when looking at the cover of *Charlotte's Web*, a student may think to herself, "Hmmm, web; this book might be about a spider. It says Charlotte's web, so I think that this book might be about a spider named Charlotte."

During reading, readers pay attention to text content to learn the extent to which their predictions were accurate. During reading lessons, teachers may stop students occasionally to discuss their predictions of portions of the text read so far and to make predictions for upcoming portions of the text.

Clarifying

Also referred to as monitoring, clarifying involves readers purposefully looking for words and concepts whose meaning is unclear or unfamiliar. This is the aspect of reading where readers must continually monitor whether or not the text is making sense. For example, in reading a passage about rocks and minerals, students may need to stop and ask the teacher or a classmate to clarify terms such as *igneous* and *sedimentary*.

Occasionally during a reading lesson, teachers may ask if anyone has a word or passage that needs clarifying. This provides an opportunity for excellent instruction that is immediately relevant to students' instructional needs.

Questioning

Questioning may involve students answering teacher-generated questions about reading passage content, but more often it involves students generating their own questions to be answered by the teacher or discussed with classmates. For example, when reading *The Three Little Pigs*, students might ask why the Big Bad Wolf didn't eat the first little pig after blowing down the straw house, or why the wolf didn't simply break a window of the brick house to get in.

The National Reading Panel (NRP, 2000) found that having students generate their own questions was more powerful than simply having students answer teacher questions. During reading lessons, teachers may choose to stop students at selected points during reading and ask if anyone has questions about what they are reading.

Summarizing

Often considered the most difficult of the five comprehension strategies, summarizing involves readers distinguishing the most important information in a text from the least important information and then combining the most important information into a coherent summary of text content.

Students are taught ways to summarize narrative texts differently from information texts. For example, teachers often draw students' attention to the story grammar elements (setting, characters, events, theme) to help generate brief summaries of narrative texts. With information texts, teachers may use a simple T-chart to help students distinguish main ideas from details, then help the students combine the main ideas into a brief summary.

Visualizing

Visualizing simply involves asking students to make mental pictures of the story or information content as they read. With young readers this may involve telling students that they will be drawing a picture about the passage after they read, so they should be careful to remember the important parts. For example, a popular instructional activity is to have students fold a blank piece of paper into fourths and illustrate a story event or main idea in each of the four quadrants. Students also write a caption in each quadrant to describe the illustration. Showing and discussing these illustrations in small-group discussions brings students' attention to overlooked information that their classmates may have noticed.

Levels of Comprehension

Part of comprehending well has to do with understanding a text simultaneously on three levels. Readers must be able to know what is going on in a text, infer information from their background knowledge, and also evaluate the effectiveness and quality of a text. Educators generally refer to these three levels of comprehension as *literal*, *inferential*, and *critical*. These levels are generally found in the comprehension questions in basal reading program reading lessons, in informal reading inventories and other assessments, and in many curriculum guides.

Literal-Level Comprehension

Literal comprehension (also known as explicit comprehension) simply means understanding the literal meaning of the words on the page. We often say about literal comprehension, "It's right there, in black and white." In a story, this would mean understanding where and when the story takes place, who is in the story, and what is going on. At the literal level, the reader doesn't need to make any inferences about *why* characters are doing what they're doing. For example, read the following story:

> *Michael and Dianne were preparing to go for a bicycle ride on Sunday. The night before the bicycle ride, Michael broke Dianne's bicycle.*

Several literal questions could be asked about this little story. For example, "Who broke Dianne's bicycle?" or "Whose bicycle did Michael break?" or "When did Michael break Dianne's bicycle?" The point is, the reader doesn't need to know much about bicycles in order to answer these literal questions. As in the previous example of Berm and the pidder flaster chiffel, familiarity of English syntax will allow the reader to answer these questions simply by rearranging the order of the words in the sentences.

Inferential-Level Comprehension

Inferential comprehension (also known as implicit comprehension) is the next higher level of comprehension. The following analogy may help clarify the nature of inferential comprehension. A text is much like a fishing net. The structure of a fishing net allows a large catch of fish to be held together by a relatively small amount of string. The knots where the net's strings are tied together are much like the words in a text. A relatively small amount of words can evoke a large amount of meaning because readers use their background knowledge to fill in the gaps among the words. We often call this "reading between the lines."

Let's go back to the bicycle story. Inferential questions about that story might include, "Why did Michael break Dianne's bicycle?" or "How do you think Dianne felt when she learned that her bicycle was broken?" The answers to these two questions are not contained in the text. Perhaps Michael was unsuccessfully trying to tune up Dianne's bicycle before their ride. Perhaps breaking her bicycle was an accident. Maybe Dianne really wanted a new bicycle so she wasn't too upset about it. Readers are expected to use their background knowledge to make inferences by filling in the information gaps.

Critical Reading

At the critical comprehension level a reader goes beyond just understanding a text. The reader evaluates the quality and effectiveness of a text, just as critics evaluate the quality of a Hollywood movie or a Broadway play ("two thumbs up"). At this level, a reader should be able to answer questions such as

- How well did I like this Michael and Dianne story?
- Would I recommend this story to a friend? Why or why not?
- What was the author's purpose for writing the Michael and Dianne story?
- How well did the author achieve this purpose?

As we teach reading, it is important to teach students to comprehend at all three levels. A majority of the questions in a typical basal reading program teacher's manual tend to be at the literal level. Literal questions are important in reading instruction because they help students understand the basics. For example, when reading a story literal questions focus on who's in the story, where the story takes place, and what is going on in the story. But students also need plenty of opportunities to consider and respond to higher-level inferential and critical questions. Just as a comprehensive approach is most effective in word identification instruction, students also need a comprehensive approach to their comprehension instruction.

 ## ATTITUDE TOWARD READING

In addition to the two major components of the reading process—word identification and comprehension—there is a third critical component: attitude toward reading (Edmunds & Bauserman, 2006; Sipe & McGuire, 2006). The news media often run stories or documentaries about the personal and national costs of adult illiteracy in this country. Kozol (1985) provides horrifying accounts of large-scale industrial, agricultural, and military accidents and near accidents due to workers' inability to read operators' manuals or safety regulations. Most estimates place the adult illiteracy rate at about 20%, though some estimates go much higher depending on varying criteria for defining illiteracy.

There is another related problem in this country that receives very little media attention. This is *aliteracy*, the problem of people who can read but choose not to. It can be argued that our schools have focused almost exclusively on the mechanics of learning to read, and have often ignored teaching students to want to read. Trelease (2006) argues that in kindergartens nearly 100% of students enthusiastically want to learn to read, but by 12th grade only 24.4% of students read for pleasure.

The National Assessment of Educational Progress (NAEP, 2007), also known as the Nation's Report Card, paints an ongoing picture of two groups of students: those who choose to read and those who don't. Those students who read the most score the highest. Those who read the least score the lowest.

Educators must help students see that reading is a desirable pastime, a valuable means of relaxing and learning, a satisfying way of life. Calkins (2001) argues:

> Teaching reading, then, begins with helping children to want the life of a reader and to envision that life for themselves. It is important for the child just learning

to ride a bike to see others riding with vigor, joy, and power. "I want that for myself," the child says. In a reading workshop, children watch each other swapping books, gossiping about characters, reading favorite passages aloud to friends, or searching for information about a hobby, and they say, "I want that for myself." (p. 9)

To help students become genuine readers, teachers must provide opportunities for students to experience both the informational and recreational aspects of reading. Students should be able to cry when Little Ann and Dan die at the end of Wilson Rawl's *Where the Red Fern Grows* and laugh with the characters in *Tales of a Fourth Grade Nothing* by Judy Blume. It is this emotional response, more than classroom reading incentive charts and rewards, that will ultimately let students come to view reading as a valued means of recreation, relaxation, and learning.

 ## CONCLUDING THOUGHTS

When considering these many interrelated facets of the reading process and their implications for reading instruction, teachers must keep in mind the need for comprehensive reading instruction. Successful beginning readers are those who have a comprehensive approach to reading, those who can easily and effectively use alphabet knowledge, phonemic awareness, phonics, structural analysis, sight vocabulary, context, and syntax to identify words. Successful readers also know what words mean and can understand text at varying levels of comprehension. Comprehensive reading emphasizes the mechanics, meaning, and the pleasure of reading based on students' instructional needs.

This book recommends the development and implementation of a comprehensive and flexible *framework* for organizing reading instruction. Reading researchers (Bond & Dykstra, 1967, 1997; Pressley, 2002) and classroom teachers (Baumann, Hoffman, Moon, & Duffy-Lester, 1998) agree that there is no single best approach for teaching all students to read and write. Multiple research studies (Duffy, 1998; Pressley et al., 1997; Pressley, Rankin, & Yokoi, 1996) have shown that effective classroom teachers combine strong systematic phonics instruction and practice, reading and discussing engaging children's literature, and opportunities to write for personal and informational purposes.

Too often classroom teachers and administrators place heavy emphasis on "adopting a reading program," relying on instructional materials rather than highly knowledgeable and effective teachers. Rather than depending on commercially packaged one-size-fits-all reading programs, we must remember that knowledgeable, creative, dedicated teachers will have the greatest impact on students' reading success (Anderson et al., 1985). Teachers must be familiar with a wide variety of instructional materials and strategies and their purposes. Then, guided by carefully collected and analyzed ongoing assessment data, teachers must know how to organize instructional experiences for individual students and groups to teach the curriculum while adapting instruction to meet students' needs.

Teachers should ensure that they cover all important components of reading within a comprehensive instructional framework. The instructional specifics within the framework should vary from student to student and group to group, based on instructional needs. Every day teachers should do all of the following:

Organizing for Reading Instruction

Go to MyEducationLab, "Organizing for Reading Instruction," and read the article "Our Journey to Reading Success."

As you read this article notice how an effective reading instruction program can help students who struggle with literacy and includes attention to phonemic awareness, phonics, fluency, vocabulary, and comprehension using a combination of controlled readers and rich children's literature.

- How can teachers get the most instructional mileage from student workbooks?
- How can teachers use controlled-vocabulary reading materials effectively?
- What can teachers do to increase their students' reading fluency?

1. Read aloud and discuss captivating and informative books, poems, and other materials with their students.
2. Provide word study instruction to help students develop automaticity in recognizing printed words through using common spelling patterns and word parts.
3. Provide differentiated small-group reading lessons that focus on developing students' fluency and comprehension.
4. Provide time for students to read and write independently, in pairs, and at centers.
5. Help students write on a variety of topics for meaningful purposes.

By providing all students with these five instructional experiences each day, along with critical additional support for struggling readers, teachers can make huge strides in ensuring that all students learn to enjoy reading fluently and meaningfully.

SUGGESTED ACTIVITIES TO EXTEND YOUR LEARNING

1. Find a beginning reader (kindergarten or first grade) in your family or neighborhood. Invite him or her to read aloud a few beginner books with you. As the child reads, try to determine how well he or she uses the various word identification and comprehension strategies described in this chapter. Does the child rely primarily on phonics or context or both? Does the child make inferences about the content? What is the child's attitude toward reading?
2. Think back to how you learned to read. How much did your family read to you? Did your primary-grade teachers use materials that promoted primarily phonics or sight word recognition? Were you ever taught to comprehend what you read? Were you taught in small groups, whole-class settings, or both? Assemble a group of classmates and share your collective experiences about being taught to read.
3. Interview a local classroom teacher and discuss how he or she teaches the components of reading. Try to determine the level of balance between word identification and comprehension instruction. How comprehensive is the instruction of the various components? How does the teacher try to develop positive student attitudes toward reading?

REFERENCES

Adams, M. J. (1990). *Beginning to read: Thinking and learning about print.* Cambridge, MA: MIT Press.

Adams, M. J. (2001). Alphabetic anxiety and explicit, systematic phonics instruction: A cognitive science perspective. In S. B. Neuman & D. K. Dickinson (Eds.), *Handbook of early literacy research.* New York: Guilford Press.

Anderson, R. C., Hiebert, E. F., Scott, J. A., & Wilkinson, I. A. G. (1985). *Becoming a nation of readers: The report of the Commission on Reading.* Washington, DC: National Institute of Education.

Baumann, J. F., Hoffman, J. V., Moon, J., & Duffy-Lester, A. M. (1998). Where are teachers' voices in the phonics/whole language debate? Results from a survey of U.S. elementary classroom teachers. *The Reading Teacher, 51*(8), 636–650.

Bear, D. R., Invernizzi, M., Templeton, S. R., & Johnston, F. (2007). *Words their way: Word study for phonics, vocabulary, and spelling instruction* (4th ed.). Upper Saddle River, NJ: Merrill/Prentice Hall.

Beck, I. L., McKeown, M. G., & Kucan, L. (2002). *Bringing words to life: Robust vocabulary instruction.* New York: Guilford Press.

Bishop, P. A., Reyes, C., & Pflaum, S. W. (2006). Read smarter, not harder: Global reading comprehension strategies. *The Reading Teacher, 60*(1), 66–69.

Blachowicz, C. Z., Fisher, P. L., Ogle, D., & Watts-Taffe, S. (2006). Vocabulary: Questions from the classroom. *Reading Research Quarterly, 41*(4), 524–539.

Block, C. C., & Pressley, M. (2002). *Comprehension instruction: Research-based best practices.* New York: Guilford Press.

Bond, G. L., & Dykstra, R. (1997). The cooperative research program in first-grade reading instruction. *Reading Research Quarterly, 32*(4), 345–427.

Bradley, B. A., & Jones, J. (2007). Sharing alphabet books in early childhood classrooms. *The Reading Teacher, 60*(5), 452–463.

Calkins, L. M. (2001). *The art of teaching reading.* Portsmouth, NH: Heinemann.

Carlisle, J. F., & Stone, C. (2005). Exploring the role of morphemes in word reading. *Reading Research Quarterly, 40*(4), 428–449.

Cartwright, K. B. (2006). Fostering flexibility and comprehension in elementary students. *The Reading Teacher, 59*(7), 628–634.

Cunningham, P. M. (2005). "If they don't read much, how they ever gonna get good?" *The Reading Teacher, 59*(1), 88–90.

Cunningham, P. M. (2006). What if they can say the words but don't know what they mean? *The Reading Teacher, 59*(7), 708–711.

Cunningham, P. M. (2004). *Phonics they use: Words for reading and writing* (4th ed.). New York: Longman.

Duffy, G. G. (1998). Powerful models or powerful teachers? An argument for teacher as entrepreneur. In S. Stahl & D. Hayes (Eds.), *Instructional models in reading.* Mahwah, NJ: Erlbaum.

Dymock, S. (2005). Teaching expository text structure awareness. *The Reading Teacher, 59*(2), 177–181.

Edmunds, K. M., & Bauserman, K. L. (2006). What teachers can learn about reading motivation through conversations with children. *The Reading Teacher, 59*(5), 414–424.

Fountas, I. C., & Pinnell, G. S. (2006). *Teaching for comprehending and fluency: Thinking, talking, and writing about reading, K–8.* Portsmouth, NH: Heinemann.

Hoover, W., & Gough, P. (1990). The simple view of reading. *Reading and Writing, 2,* 127–160.

Joseph, L. M. (2006). Incremental rehearsal: A flashcard drill technique for increasing retention of reading words. *The Reading Teacher, 59*(8), 803–807.

Kozol, J. (1985). *Illiterate America.* Garden City, NY: Anchor Press/Doubleday.

Kragler, S., Walker, C. A., & Martin, L. E. (2005). Strategy instruction in primary content textbooks. *The Reading Teacher, 59*(3), 254–261.

Liang, L., & Dole, J. A. (2006). Help with teaching reading comprehension: Comprehension instructional frameworks. *The Reading Teacher, 59*(8), 742–753.

McCormick, C. E., Throneburg, R. N., & Smitley, J. M. (2002). *A sound start: Phonemic awareness lessons for reading success.* New York: Guilford Press.

McMackin, M. C., & Witherell, N. L. (2005). Different routes to the same destination: Drawing conclusions with tiered graphic organizers. *The Reading Teacher, 59*(3), 242–252.

Moats, L. (1998). *Teaching reading IS rocket science: What expert teachers of reading should know and be able to do.* Washington, DC: Learning First Alliance.

Mountain, L. (2005). ROOTing out meaning: More morphemic analysis for primary pupils. *The Reading Teacher, 58*(8), 742–749.

National Assessment of Educational Progress. (2007). *Reading report card.* U.S. Department of Education. Retrieved from http://nationsreportcard.gov/reading_2007

National Reading Panel. (2000). *Teaching children to read: An evidence-based assessment of the scientific research literature on reading and its implications for reading instruction. Report of the subgroups.* National Institute of Child Health and Human Development. Retrieved from http://www.nichd.nih.gov/publications/nrp/smallbook.cfm

Oczkus, L. D. (2004). *Super six comprehension strategies: 35 lessons and more for reading success.* Norwood, MA: Christopher-Gordon.

Phelps, G. (2005). *Content knowledge for teaching reading.* Unpublished doctoral dissertation, University of Michigan, Ann Arbor.

Pikulski, J. J., & Chard, D. J. (2005). Fluency: Bridge between decoding and reading comprehension. *The Reading Teacher, 58*(6), 510–519.

Pressley, M. (2002). *Reading instruction that works: The case for balanced teaching* (2nd ed.). New York: Guilford Press.

Pressley, M., Rankin, J., & Yokoi, L. (1996). A survey of instructional practices of primary teachers nominated as effective in promoting literacy. *Elementary School Journal, 96,* 363–384.

Pressley, M., Yokoi, L., Rankin, J., Wharton-McDonald, R., & Mistretta, J. (1997). A survey of instructional practices of Grade 5 teachers nominated as effective in promoting literacy. *Scientific Studies of Reading, 1*(2), 145–160.

Rasinski, T. (2006). Reading fluency instruction: Moving beyond accuracy, automaticity, and prosody. *The Reading Teacher, 59*(7), 704–706.

Rosenblatt, L. M. (1994). The transactional theory of reading and writing. In R. B. Ruddell, M. R. Ruddell, & H. Singer (Eds.), *Theoretical models and processes of reading* (4th ed.). Newark, DE: International Reading Association.

Sipe, L. R., & McGuire, C. E. (2006). Young children's resistance to stories. *The Reading Teacher, 60*(1), 6–13.

Snow, C. E., Griffin, P., & Burns, M. S. (Eds.). (2005). *Knowledge to support the teaching of reading: Preparing teachers for a changing world.* San Francisco: Jossey-Bass.

Trelease, J. (2006). *The read-aloud handbook* (6th ed). New York: Penguin.

Organizing for Literacy Instruction

2

by John A. Smith

Where to Start?

Two weeks before the beginning of her first year of teaching, Ella walked into her school district's new teacher workshop for a half-day presentation on reading instruction. As a new second-grade teacher Ella was very excited and appreciative.

The new teacher workshop presenter gave Ella a large blue three-ring binder with the school district's logo on the front along with the words GORP: Goal-Oriented Reading Program. The district had invested a lot of money developing its own reading program that looked to Ella like a large collection of tests and worksheets.

Ella was instructed to give all of her students Reading Skill Pretest 1. Students who passed this test with 80% mastery (4 of 5 correct) could be given Reading Skill Pretest 2. Students who didn't pass the test would then be given instruction and worksheets 1 to 5 and then Reading Skill Posttest 1. Students who didn't pass this posttest would be given more instruction and worksheets 6 to 10. Ella was also given a list of the 180 GORP reading skills and a punch card on which she was to keep track of each student's progress.

When Ella got back to her school, she went to see the teacher in the classroom next door (her team leader). Ella showed her the big blue GORP binder and asked, "How do we teach reading here?" The team leader took Ella to the supply room and showed her a shelf full of second-grade basal reading program materials and said, "Here are the reading books." She also said, "Make sure to read them a story each day." Actually, Ella's team leader was very helpful and spent a lot of time answering her many questions about how to start and maintain a reading program. Ella's principal came by and gave her some forms so she could send her struggling readers down the hall to the Resource room.

But the fact remained that Ella's students would arrive in 7 days and she really didn't know how to teach reading. Although she was becoming familiar with some of the pieces of a reading program, what Ella lacked was the big picture—a conceptual framework for reading instruction within which she could fit the individual pieces into a coherent whole.

This chapter provides a comprehensive literacy instruction framework, a big picture of reading and writing instruction components that teachers should include each day in their classrooms. The literacy instruction framework described here is depicted on the inside front cover of this book and should help pull the many reading and writing instruction pieces together into a coherent and effective instructional whole. The chapter begins with a rationale for using an instruction framework rather than relying on a single commercial reading program, and then outlines a comprehensive literacy instruction framework. Subsequent sections of the chapter describe additional aspects of effective literacy instruction. Specifically, this chapter covers the following topics:

- Why a literacy instruction framework rather than a reading program
- A comprehensive literacy instruction framework
- The classroom physical environment
- Instructional materials
- Explicit instruction
- The classroom library
- Matching books to students

WHY A LITERACY INSTRUCTION FRAMEWORK RATHER THAN A READING PROGRAM

READING PROGRAMS AND FRAMEWORKS

The vast majority of elementary classrooms in U.S. public schools rely on a basal reading program as the foundation for day-to-day reading and writing instruction. A basal reading program is a commercially published program designed to provide most of the instructional activities and materials that a teacher will need to teach reading. A basal reading program generally consists of a teacher's manual, student reading materials, and accompanying instructional materials.

On the other hand, a literacy instruction framework is a set of broad and comprehensive reading and writing instruction components that need to be taught each day. Just as nutrition experts recommend the food pyramid as a general framework for determining a healthy daily diet, literacy instruction experts generally agree on a daily instructional diet of teacher read-aloud and instruction in phonemic awareness and phonics, fluency, vocabulary, comprehension, and writing. Literacy instruction framework components are taught daily and may incorporate instructional materials from a variety of specific programs. Many teachers use a basal reading program as the basis for their reading instruction, but add to the basal program with components from additional or supplemental reading programs such as an additional phonics or fluency program.

Several literacy instruction frameworks have become popular in recent years. Perhaps the first well-known example of a literacy instruction framework is Cunningham's popular Four Blocks framework (Cunningham & Allington, 2003). The Four Blocks framework is divided fairly evenly among four major emphases in reading instruction: (1) guided reading, (2) self-selected reading, (3) writing, and (4) working with words. Fountas and Pinnell (1996) suggest a three-part literacy instruction framework consisting of word study, reading workshop, and writing workshop. The National

Reading Panel (NRP, 2000) presents its own framework based on five "essential elements" of reading: (1) phonemic awareness, (2) phonics, (3) fluency, (4) vocabulary, and (5) comprehension.

No Single Approach Is Best

Reading researchers and classroom teachers generally agree that there is no single best approach or program for teaching all students to read and write successfully (Pressley, 2002). Biancarosa and Snow (2004) in a recent research summary wrote, "No single intervention or program will ever meet the needs of all struggling readers and writers" (p. 11). In the largest reading research study ever conducted in this country, Bond and Dykstra (1967, 1997) compared reading test scores of students in over 700 first-grade classrooms across the country to see what kind of reading instruction was best. Among their many conclusions (1997), they found that "combinations of programs, such as a basal program with supplementary phonics materials, often are superior to single approaches" and "no one approach is so distinctly better in all situations and respects that it should be considered the one best method and the one to be used exclusively" (pp. 44 and 416, respectively). Reliance on any single approach or program cannot meet all of the students' diverse instructional needs. Wise teachers know from experience that *the best instructional method is a combination of methods*.

A comprehensive literacy instruction framework, rather than a single program, gives teachers the flexibility to focus on individual students' instructional needs. Every student and every class of students presents unique instructional strengths and challenges. A comprehensive and flexible literacy instruction framework allows teachers to make instructional adjustments in the amount of time allotted and the specific activities and materials used with each component, and yet still include all aspects of the framework. Like a roadmap, a flexible framework provides an overall route to follow but also allows for necessary instructional detours.

Duffy (1998) writes:

> In practice, however, there are no panaceas. The best teachers never follow a single program, theory, model, or philosophy, nor do they play a single role or employ one set of materials to the exclusion of others. Instead the best teachers draw thoughtfully from various sources, play many roles, and use many techniques and materials. (p. 360)

 ### A LITERACY INSTRUCTION FRAMEWORK

The chart on the inside front cover of this book provides an overview of a literacy instruction block. This 3-hour block of time comprises a typical morning in a primary-grade classroom and provides for instruction in each of the five essential elements of reading identified by the NRP (2000): phonemic awareness, phonics, fluency, vocabulary, and comprehension. In addition, this block of time also provides for oral language development and writing instruction. Although reading and writing are the focus of the literacy instruction block, there are opportunities to also integrate instruction in the content areas such as science and social studies.

A comprehensive literacy instruction framework consists of the following five parts: (1) teacher read-aloud, (2) word study, (3) differentiated small-group reading instruction, (4) independent reading practice, and (5) writing instruction. The teacher read-aloud and word study components are provided in a whole-class setting. Differentiated small-group reading instruction and independent reading practice are provided during group time. Writing instruction includes a combination of whole-class writing instruction, teacher conferencing during independent writing practice, and whole-class student sharing of drafts in progress. A typical 3-hour literacy block might look something like the following:

9:00–9:30 a.m.	Whole-class teacher read-aloud and discussion from a picture book. Also, some background knowledge building for the basal reading program selection.
9:30–10:00 a.m.	Whole-class word study lesson.
10:00–11:00 a.m.	Four small-group differentiated reading lessons while classmates practice reading independently, in pairs, and complete some center activities.
11:00–11:15 a.m.	Recess.
11:15–12:00 noon	Writing workshop.

WHOLE-CLASS TEACHER READ-ALOUD

Many teachers begin the instructional day with a whole-class teacher read-aloud (Doyle & Bramwell, 2006; Lane & Wright, 2007). Teacher read-aloud, and accompanying instructional activities, which may last 30 minutes, promotes a strong sense of classroom community and provides students with much of the vocabulary and background knowledge needed for reading comprehension. Teacher read-aloud should expose students to a wide variety of literature including picture books, chapter books, information books, newspapers, magazines, and poetry. This whole-class instructional time is also great for building students' oral language skills through singing songs, rehearsing and performing readers' theater, and enjoying chants and other language-play activities.

Whole-class teacher read-aloud is also a great time to introduce reading selections from the basal reading program. A good introduction to a reading selection can activate and build background knowledge, preteach selected vocabulary words, introduce a graphic organizer to guide comprehension, or teach comprehension strategies such as predicting, clarifying, generating and discussing questions, summarizing, and making visual images. Teachers may choose to first read the basal reading program selection aloud to the class so that all students can understand the reading selection.

An important aspect of teacher read-aloud is the accompanying discussions that maximize student enjoyment and learning. Teachers ask open-ended questions about the read-aloud that lead students to discover important insights about setting, characters, events, and themes in narrative reading selections and main ideas and details in information selections. Students share their personal responses, connections, questions, and favorite parts as they enjoy and learn from literature.

Teacher read-aloud provides students with an enjoyable positive experience with books and is one of the most powerful ways of building students' motivation to read (Trelease, 2006). Teachers should read aloud every day to give students daily opportunities to discover books and genres that they love.

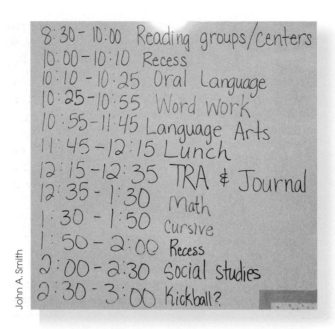

8:30 – 10:00 Reading groups/centers
10:00 – 10:10 Recess
10:10 – 10:25 Oral Language
10:25 – 10:55 Word Work
10:55 – 11:45 Language Arts
11:45 – 12:15 Lunch
12:15 – 12:35 TRA & Journal
12:35 – 1:30 Math
1:30 – 1:50 Cursive
1:50 – 2:00 Recess
2:00 – 2:30 Social Studies
2:30 – 3:00 Kickball?

John A. Smith

A daily schedule helps students know the routines.

WHOLE-CLASS WORD STUDY INSTRUCTION

Whole-class word study instruction often follows teacher read-aloud time. Word study instruction includes the study of phonemic awareness and phonics (Bear, Invernizzi, Templeton, & Johnston, 2007; Cunningham, 2004). It also includes the study of high-frequency words (*a*, *the*, *and*, *for*) that appear over and over in print and also irregular words (*was*, *some*, *does*, *said*) that can't be sounded out, words that students must simply learn to recognize by sight (Joseph, 2006).

Word study in kindergarten and first grade emphasizes learning the names and sounds of the alphabet letters and blending the alphabet letter sounds to pronounce spoken words. Word study in these grades also focuses on blending the sounds of printed letters to identify words and recognizing common spelling patterns and sight words that make up much of our printed language. Chapter 5 presents common spelling patterns that enable beginning readers to read approximately 2,000 words. Word study in Grades 2 and 3 moves on to focus on studying multisyllable words through identifying prefixes, suffixes, word roots, and base words, and then blending these word parts together.

Good word study lessons are explicit and systematic (Duffy, 2003). Explicit instruction is precise, direct, and clear to students. Systematic word study instruction follows a carefully designed sequence where each new word study concept builds on previously learned concepts. Explicit instruction also employs clear instructional language that carefully guides student listening, learning, and responding.

Explicit word study lessons begin with teacher explanation and modeling. For example, the teacher provides printed examples of words containing a common spelling pattern, explains how the pattern works, and models blending the letters and pattern to identify the word. Then the teacher provides interactive guided practice opportunities for students to practice applying the concept with teacher guidance and feedback. Finally, the teacher provides opportunities for monitored

Acknowledging and Elaborating ELL Student Participation

ELL students may be hesitant to participate in classroom discussions because they are in the silent time of receiving rather than producing language, they are less confident with academic language, or because they are unsure of the appropriateness of questioning an authority figure, the teacher. Mohr and Mohr (2007) point out that when ELL students do respond, "their responses may fall into one or more of the following six categories: an appropriate or correct response; a partially correct response; an incorrect or inappropriate response; a response in their native language, rather than in English; another question; or no response" (p. 444). When ELL students do participate in classroom discussions, teachers should acknowledge and value their efforts to respond and also support these efforts by inviting and helping them elaborate on their responses. Mohr and Mohr provide guidelines for supporting ELL students in classroom discussions and suggest that teachers should:

- Expect all students to participate.
- Demonstrate to students with verbal and nonverbal gestures that their responses are welcomed and valued.
- Allow sufficient wait time for students to respond and repeat questions and prompts as needed.
- Accept phrases and partial answers so that students can show their knowledge without needing to use complete sentences. Focus on the content of students' responses rather than on grammatical structure.
- Model standard pronunciation and grammar rather than oversimplifying or talking down to ELL students.
- Make time for casual, less-threatening one-on-one conversations with ELL students.
- Videotape some class discussion in order to self-evaluate the effectiveness of interactions with ELL students.
- Learn some key phrases in ELL students' native languages to develop connections and share in the language-learning process.

independent practice where students apply the word study concepts independently in follow-up activities or in reading connected texts. Throughout word study lessons teachers assess students' progress by noticing and recording how well students learn and apply word study skills and concepts.

DIFFERENTIATED SMALL-GROUP READING INSTRUCTION

After the whole-class teacher read-aloud and word study lessons, many classrooms change to a 60-minute block of time that involves teachers meeting with small groups of students on a rotating basis for reading instruction while other students practice reading independently and in pairs and also engage in a variety of learning center activities.

Differentiated small-group reading instruction occurs when teachers meet with instructional groups of three to six students who share common instructional needs and provides each group with differing instruction and materials based in those needs (Tyner, 2004; Walpole & McKenna, 2007). Differentiated small-group lessons, designed to focus primarily on building reading fluency, often last about 15 to 20 minutes, and are comprised of four or five quick components. Differentiated small-group lessons often begin with quick instruction and review in high-frequency words and irregular words. Next, the teacher may provide a phonics lesson that focuses on spelling patterns that a particular group of students needs to learn. This may be followed by the teacher having the students read a decodable text to provide immediate practice with the spelling pattern just taught. Then the teacher introduces a leveled text or basal reading program selection and quickly highlights unfamiliar printed words and provides necessary background knowledge as appropriate. Students sometimes read the text aloud in unison, softly to themselves (whisper reading), or silently to themselves. The teacher listens to each student's reading and guides him or her through the text by providing on-the-spot instruction with difficult words.

Following the students' reading the teacher may lead students in follow-up activities such as discussions of the reading content, related writing experiences, and other projects designed to extend student learning. Small-group reading lessons often conclude with an assignment for students to reread the texts individually or in pairs to build fluency.

Differentiated small-group reading instruction is the foremost time when students at varying reading ability levels receive instruction that is closely tailored to their instructional needs. Because students' reading abilities differ within one classroom, instruction for struggling reader groups may focus on learning and reviewing letter sounds, whereas on-grade-level groups may be learning to recognize various vowel-sound spelling patterns. Above-level readers may be studying multisyllable words.

During this differentiated instruction time it is important that struggling readers receive instruction that is more intense in order for them to catch up to their classmates (Torgesen, 2004). Teachers can increase instructional intensity by providing more minutes of instruction each day to students in lower-achieving reading groups. Teachers in many classrooms also increase instructional intensity by using additional adults such as teacher's aides, Title 1 teachers, special education teachers, and ELL teachers to provide additional doses of adult-directed small-group reading instruction.

INDEPENDENT READING PRACTICE

Independent reading practice takes place during the time that teachers are providing small-group reading instruction. Those students who are not meeting with the teacher in small-group instruction engage in a variety of instruction activities that should flow directly from the lessons provided in the small groups. These activities may include reading independently or with a partner, rereading song lyric or poem charts for fluency, or completing writing activities such as personal journals, reading journals, content-area writing, or personal writing.

During independent practice time students may also work at a variety of learning centers. Some centers are designated classroom areas such as a table or corner with instructional materials. Other centers may simply be a set of materials and tasks that students complete at their desks or other classroom area. Common center activities include listening to recorded books on tape or CD, doing follow-up reading activities on computers, doing integrated reading and writing content-area activities, working with word parts in a pocket chart or on an overhead transparency, and practicing a readers' theater.

Some teachers have their students move from activity to activity as groups in 15-minute time intervals. Other teachers allow students to self-select activities.

FOR STRUGGLING READERS

Comprehensive Reading Instruction Is the Best Approach

A comprehensive approach to reading instruction is especially important for struggling readers because multiple sources of reading problems exist for these readers. Joseph Torgesen (2004), director of the Florida Center for Reading Research and a national authority on interventions for struggling readers, points out that some students begin school with strong oral language skills, but with problems in reading words accurately and fluently. Other students, particularly those from disadvantaged backgrounds, begin school with problems in both oral language ability and in the ability to read words. For struggling readers, Torgesen recommends a strong focus on the five instructional components of phonemic awareness, phonics, fluency, vocabulary, and comprehension and concludes:

> It is now generally understood, however, that skills and knowledge in these five areas each contribute to becoming a good reader during elementary school. Thus, it should not be surprising that prevention and intervention research since the 1980s has demonstrated that at-risk and struggling readers show greater reading growth with interventions that focus directly on strengthening these components than with methods that do not address them in a comprehensive manner. (p. 357)

Teachers should ensure that independent practice activities provide opportunities for genuine reading and writing practice. Ideally independent practice activities flow directly from the differentiated instruction provided in small groups. Independent practice time should not be wasted on worksheets or other less productive time-fillers. Teachers should also require student accountability so students know they are expected to accomplish something during independent reading practice time.

WRITING INSTRUCTION

After teacher read-aloud, word study instruction, and differentiated small-group and independent practice time, students are ready for recess. Following this much-needed break is a good time for 45 to 60 minutes of writing instruction (Calkins & Mermelstein, 2003). Writing instruction not only teaches students to express themselves fluently and meaningfully, but also deepens students' understanding of every aspect of the reading process.

Teachers generally begin writing instruction with whole-class mini-lessons: 10- to 15-minute lessons where the teacher explains and demonstrates writing concepts and skills that students will apply in their own writing. Next, students return to their seats to begin or continue working on writing pieces, often on self-selected topics. As students write, teachers go from student to student, conferencing individually with students, providing instruction on both the content and mechanics of the student writing. At the end of writing time each day, a few students are invited to sit in the "authors' chair" and share excerpts from their writing with classmates and receive feedback and ideas. Finally, some pieces are revised and edited for publication. These polished writing pieces are displayed for classmates and eventually taken home for family recognition and praise.

Much of writing instruction involves students writing personal narratives—self-chosen stories about grandparents, pets, family vacations, friends, birthday parties, and school experiences. Such stories are important to students and are highly motivating. It is important that students are also taught to write other genres such as informational texts, letters, journals, and poetry.

 ## PHYSICAL ENVIRONMENT

The effectiveness of classroom reading and writing instruction will be diminished if the physical environment of the classroom is barren, disorganized, or cluttered. The classroom physical environment can be organized in ways that will facilitate and support reading and writing instruction. The sections of this chapter are intended to provide an overview of what a literacy-rich classroom should look like, what it should contain, and how it should function (Wolfersberger, Reutzel, Sudweeks, & Fawson, 2004).

INSTRUCTIONAL AREAS

The spatial arrangement of the classroom should contain designated space for three forms of instruction: whole-class, small-group, and individual. For whole-class instruction, a rug, large enough to hold all students in the class, should be situated in front of the large classroom whiteboard. An overhead projector and a chart-stand with chart paper should be nearby for whole-class instruction. A comfortable chair also belongs in the whole-class instruction area for teacher read-aloud and student sharing in the authors' chair and readers' chair.

For small-group instruction, a kidney-shaped table large enough to seat six to seven students is ideal. This table should be placed in a corner of the room so that small-group instruction can take place relatively undisturbed. Position the table so that the teacher can view the remainder of the classroom and keep an eye on the students who are working independently. A second table is also desirable for additional small-group instruction provided by a Title 1 teacher or teacher's aide. A chart-stand, easel with whiteboard, individual student whiteboards with markers and erasers, and similar instructional materials should be placed near each small-group instruction table.

For individual student work, desks may be arrayed individually in rows or in a horseshoe configuration surrounding the whole-class rug with the open end of the horseshoe facing the instructional whiteboard (see Figure 2.1). Alternatively, many teachers group student desks in sets of four to six to facilitate group discussions and cooperative learning.

An effective classroom environment also includes centers for individual or small-group follow-up practice activities after students meet with the teacher for

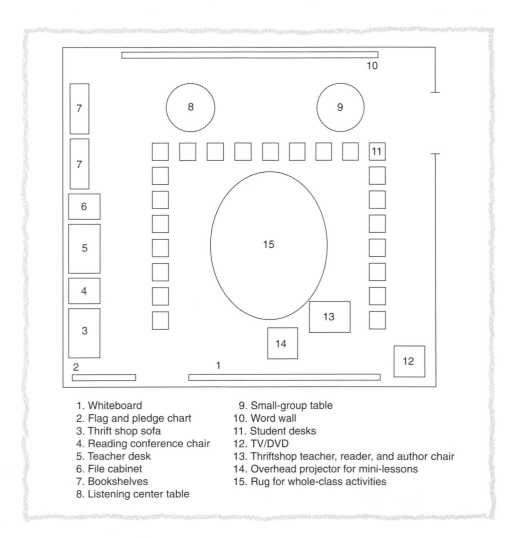

Figure 2.1
Classroom Diagram

1. Whiteboard
2. Flag and pledge chart
3. Thrift shop sofa
4. Reading conference chair
5. Teacher desk
6. File cabinet
7. Bookshelves
8. Listening center table
9. Small-group table
10. Word wall
11. Student desks
12. TV/DVD
13. Thriftshop teacher, reader, and author chair
14. Overhead projector for mini-lessons
15. Rug for whole-class activities

A classroom word wall.

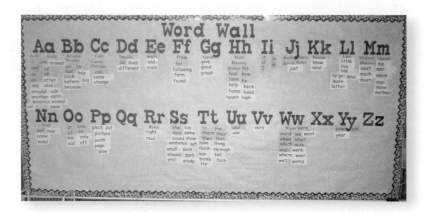

John A. Smith

small-group instruction. Centers may be as simple as a small desk with instructional materials. Such centers can be labeled with their purpose, procedures, and accountability. Some teachers store materials for various center activities in portable containers for students to retrieve and use during independent work time.

In addition to instructional areas, many classrooms have a "reading area" with comfortable seating and plenty of books. One enterprising teacher turned a corner of his classroom into a reading area that simulated a comfortable family living room. This included a bookshelf, coffee table with an assortment of magazines, lamp, a wall hanging, and two old recliner chairs from a local thrift shop.

CLASSROOM WALLS

Classroom walls should do much more than hold up the ceiling. Classroom walls should display procedural aides such as class schedules; school lunch menus; lists rules; charts containing steps for instructional strategies taught; project guidelines; sign-up sheets; and daily, weekly, or monthly assignments. Classroom walls should also function as instructional aides by displaying alphabet letters, word walls of high-frequency words or selected words from content-area studies, charts of common spelling patterns, teacher-made instructional posters, interactive bulletin boards, and pocket charts. Some wall space should always be allocated to displaying student-centered items such as student-written products and artwork, murals, and photo displays with captions.

PEARSON
myeducationlab

Vocabulary

Go to MyEducationLab, "Vocabulary," to watch the video *Creating Word Walls.*

Notice how the teacher uses the word wall to teach a variety of concepts.

STORAGE

Classrooms often overflow with teacher and student instructional materials and supplies, not to mention coats, backpacks, and lunchboxes. One important aspect of setting up a classroom is to identify places and methods for storing all the materials. Many teachers use large plastic crates with a labeled hanging file folder for each student to store student work samples, tests, and other instructional artifacts. Classroom libraries should be organized, with books stored in smaller labeled plastic baskets according to genre, content area, and level of difficulty. Other instructional materials should be stored in clearly labeled drawers, cupboards, trays, storage bins, closets, and bookshelves. In addition to teaching students to read, write, calculate, and understand science and social studies, teachers need to make sure that students learn to follow classroom procedures including where to access instructional materials and how to put them back when finished.

 ## INSTRUCTIONAL MATERIALS

Classroom teachers have many instructional materials available to help support their instruction, including basal reading programs, supplemental reading programs, and reading and writing assessment materials. It is important that teachers understand the scope and purposes of reading instruction materials in order to use them properly and effectively and to help students reach high levels of reading achievement.

BASAL READING PROGRAMS

Teacher's Manuals

Basal reading programs are the foundation of most reading instruction in U.S. elementary schools. Produced by large commercial publishing companies such as Harcourt, Houghton Mifflin, Open Court, and Scott Foresman, basal reading programs are designed to provide most of the necessary materials for classroom reading instruction at each grade level.

The centerpiece of all basal reading programs is the teacher's manual. The teacher's manual contains extensive lesson plans for teaching numerous reading selections included in the program. Although lesson plans vary from one publishing company to another, they are generally organized into three parts: (1) before-reading activities to prepare students to read the selection successfully, (2) during-reading activities for the teacher to guide the students through the selection, and (3) after-reading activities to review selection content and extend student learning. Common before-reading activities include building student interest for the selection, activating and building background knowledge, teaching selected vocabulary, teaching decoding skills, and setting a purpose for reading. During-reading activities generally focus on comprehension questions and discussion points to guide ongoing discussion of the selection. After-reading activities include summarizing important selection content, providing follow-up decoding and writing activities, and integrating selection content with other curriculum areas.

Many basal reading programs also provide detailed suggestions for day-to-day planning. For example, many basal reading program teacher's manuals provide a chart at the beginning of each reading selection with a 5-day plan for teaching all the essential areas of reading and writing. Such plans are designed to ensure that each of the instructional areas in the left column is taught each day.

Another helpful feature of teacher's manual lessons is suggestions for differentiated small-group instruction activities. Within a single lesson, the manual provides separate instructional options for small-group lessons for students reading above grade level, at grade level, and below grade level. Teacher's manuals also provide additional instructional suggestions for students who are learning to speak English.

Student Reading Materials

Along with the teacher's manual, basal reading programs also provide a variety of student reading materials. Three common types of student reading materials are the basal program anthology, leveled readers, and decodable reading books. The anthology is the main student reading book, often hardback, that contains a mixture of stories, informational selections, and poetry. The selections in an anthology are often grouped thematically in units of four or five selections. Teachers often use the anthology during whole-class instruction to focus on vocabulary and comprehension instruction.

Leveled readers are smaller paperback books that usually contain only one story or informational selection per book. Whereas the anthology contains selections at grade level, the leveled readers come in sets of six to eight and span a variety of grade levels. Leveled readers are designed for use in small-group differentiated reading instruction. Small-group reading instruction with leveled readers focuses on comprehension of the selection content and also reading and rereading the selection to build reading fluency.

Decodable reading books are also smaller paperbacks that come in sets of six to eight. The selections are composed of sentences with a high percentage of decodable words (e.g., The green boat floats on the smooth lake; Ben and Sam ride in the boat). The sole purpose of decodable books is to give students practice with applying decoding skills.

Other Basal Reading Program Materials

In addition to the teacher's manual and student reading materials, basal reading programs also provide other materials designed to support reading instruction. Many basal programs provide placement tests. Placement tests are given at the beginning of each school year to provide teachers an indication of each student's reading level. Basal programs may also provide unit tests, which are designed to be given at the conclusion of each four- or five-selection unit in the anthology. Unit tests provide teachers with ongoing data on how well students are succeeding in the program.

Other basal reading program instructional materials include audiotapes, instructional charts, and word cards. The audiotapes of the anthology selections allow students who may not be able to read the selection on their own to access the selections by following along in the printed texts while listening to the tapes. Instructional charts allow teachers to guide students through a text, usually a poem or short selection, while pointing to the words in the large chart format. Basal programs also make available sets of word cards that allow teachers to teach and review selected vocabulary words with students.

SUPPLEMENTAL PROGRAMS

Even though basal reading programs are designed to be complete reading programs, no basal reading program is perfect. Many teachers also use a supplemental reading program to strengthen an area of reading where the basal reading program may be lacking. For example, the *Read Well* program published by Sopris West is a supplemental program designed to help struggling readers become successful in the basal reading program. *Read Well* focuses on 30-minute small-group lessons that are mastery based and guided by assessment. *Read Naturally*, published by Read Naturally, Inc., is a supplemental reading program that focuses specifically on increasing students' oral reading fluency. *Read Naturally* begins with students studying a short reading passage then reading the passage with a fluent model, then measuring fluency progress through a series of 1-minute timings. *Building Language for Literacy*, published by Scholastic, is a supplemental reading program designed specifically to provide foundational language skills for very young learners. The program focuses on students using language through singing songs and interacting with poems. Instruction also focuses on basic literacy skills such as developing letter knowledge and phonemic awareness. *Soar to Success*, published by Houghton Mifflin, is a supplemental reading program that focuses on improving reading comprehension for students in Grades 3 to 8. *Soar to Success* focuses on teaching students to learn and apply reading comprehension strategies through teacher modeling and student application of predicting, clarifying, questioning, and summarizing.

Supplemental reading programs can be very valuable resources when students may need additional instruction above and beyond what is provided by the basal reading program. The Florida Center for Reading Research website provides a thorough review of many supplemental reading programs at http://www.fcrr.org/FCRRReports/LReports.aspx.

ASSESSMENT MATERIALS

Assessment is an important aspect of effective reading instruction, and classrooms need to be equipped with assessment materials so that teachers may use four types of reading assessments: screening assessments, progress-monitoring assessments, diagnostic assessments, and outcome assessments. Screening assessments allow teachers to establish a baseline of where each student's reading level is at the beginning of the year. Teachers may have students read alphabet letter lists, word lists, and short passages to gather initial screening data. Progress-monitoring data may be gathered in the form of unit tests, ongoing checklists, teacher–student reading conference records, and graphs of weekly or monthly 1-minute samples of students' reading ability. Students who fail to make progress in reading will benefit from diagnostic testing as teachers dig deep to identify students' specific reading strengths and weaknesses. Diagnostic testing materials generally include word lists containing specific spelling patterns and graded reading passages that teachers can use to pinpoint and analyze students' reading errors. Outcome measures are often end-of-year state-mandated standardized tests that allow teachers, administrators, and parents to learn how well each student is reading at the end of each school year.

It is important to note that gathering assessment data alone will not improve student reading achievement. Teachers, and grade-level teams of teachers, must review and use assessment data to plan instruction. Assessment data can suggest to teachers which instructional materials to use, how many minutes of daily instruction are needed, and how to group students with similar instructional needs for instruction. School-based reading coaches can be very helpful in helping teachers and grade-level teacher teams gather, analyze, and use assessment data in instructional planning.

EXPLICIT INSTRUCTION

A vast body of instructional research (Blair, Rupley, & Nichols, 2007; Carnine, Silbert, Kame'enui, & Tarver, 2003; NRP, 2000) has shown the importance of ensuring that instruction is well-designed, systematic, and explicit. Explicit instruction is a form of teaching that presents information to students efficiently and clearly. Duffy (2003) points out that explanations contain "how-to" information, presented in forthright and unambiguous ways early in lessons and, sometimes, repeatedly across several lessons. Explanations attempt to describe the mental activity required to make sense of text. (p. 9)

A teacher who begins a lesson with a phrase such as "Who can tell us about . . . ?" is not teaching explicitly.

Explicit instruction can be thought of on two levels: (1) the overall flow and structure of a lesson from start to finish and (2) the explicit instructional language that a teacher uses during each lesson. Effective teachers develop an explicit teaching mindset so that they begin to think about planning instruction in terms of clearly explaining and demonstrating, working with students together, and having students work independently.

LESSON FLOW AND STRUCTURE

Explicit instruction is based on the principle of "gradual release of responsibility" (Pearson & Gallagher, 1983), which begins with the teacher taking full responsibility for explaining and demonstrating, sharing the responsibility with students as they work some examples together, then releasing the responsibility to the students as they work through examples independently. This is the same process that parents use to teach their children to ride a bicycle, providing full support at first, then gradually releasing that support until the child can ride the bicycle independently. Figure 2.2 shows this process of teachers gradually releasing responsibility to students during the course of a lesson.

The gradual release of responsibility principle includes several sequential steps when applied to formal instruction: (1) an introduction that connects today's instruction to previous instruction and sets a purpose for the lesson, (2) explicit teacher explanation and demonstration where the teacher clearly explains the new concept and demonstrates with examples, (3) interactive guided practice where the teacher and students work through some examples of the concept together with teacher guidance, (4) monitored independent practice with students working through some examples on their own with teacher feedback, and (5) assessment where the teacher gathers informal data on how well the students have learned the concept in order to plan subsequent lessons.

The explicit instruction model lesson plan shown is an example of an explicit lesson. This model will be used throughout the textbook as an example of how to apply explicit teaching across the components of reading and writing instruction.

Figure 2.2
Gradual Release of Responsibility

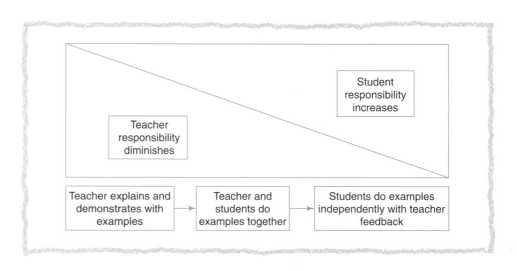

Explicit Instruction Model Lesson Plan

Concept or Objective: Blending short *a* CVC words: small-group lesson   **Date:** _____

Lesson Steps	Activities	Materials
Introduction • Connect today's lesson to previous lessons • Give a purpose for today's lesson	"Students, you remember that we have been studying the sounds of the alphabet letters. Today we will learn how to blend the letter sounds together to read words. Learning to blend letter sounds together is the first big step in learning to read most of the words you'll see."	
Explicit teacher explanation and demonstration	1. Write the word *mat* on the teacher's whiteboard. 2. Point to each letter and make its sound. 3. Blend the three sounds together slowly, then pronounce the word. Sweep your hand below the letters as you blend the sounds slowly, then tap below the word as you pronounce it. 4. Repeat this blending process with several other short *a* CVC words until you feel that the students are ready to move on.	Teacher's whiteboard Markers Eraser
Interactive guided practice	1. Write the word *sad* on the teacher's whiteboard and have the students write the word *sad* on their student whiteboards. 2. Using the teacher's whiteboard as an example, lead the students in blending and pronouncing the word *sad* in unison on their whiteboards. 3. Repeat the blending process with the students on several more short *a* CVC words. Provide guidance as needed.	Teacher's whiteboard Student whiteboards Markers Eraser
Monitored independent practice	1. Write the word *fat* on the teacher's whiteboard. Have the students copy the word onto their whiteboards. 2. Say to the students, "When I say *think*, you look at the letters on your whiteboard and figure out the word in your head. When I say *word*, you tell me the word." 3. Repeat this process with more short *a* CVC words until you feel that the students are beginning to understand the blending process well. 4. Have the students read a short *a* decodable text for additional practice.	Teacher's whiteboard Student whiteboards Markers Eraser
Assessment	1. Write 5–6 short *a* CVC words on index cards. 2. Use the *think* and *word* procedure to see how well each student can read the words. 3. Make notes of each student's ability to do this.	3 × 5 index cards with short *a* CVC words Notepad for recording students' success at reading the cards
Accommodations for students	Use drawings, photographs, and explanations to ensure that ELL students understand the meanings of the short *a* words that we're blending.	Drawings and photos of applicable short *a* CVC words

EXPLICIT INSTRUCTIONAL LANGUAGE

The second aspect of explicit instruction is the clear direct instructional language that teachers use during reading and writing lessons. Explicit instructional language provides a consistent set of teacher cues that tell students when to listen and when and how to respond.

Explicit Instructional Language for Word Identification Lessons

Word Identification Concept	Explicit Instructional Language
Letter-name recognition	"My turn. This is the letter _____." (*teacher points*) "Your turn. What letter?" (*teacher taps*) (*Review previously taught letter names.*)
Letter-sound recognition	"My turn. The sound this letter makes is _____." "Your turn. What sound?" (*Review previously taught letter sounds.*)
Combining letter names and sounds	"My turn. The name of this letter is _____. The sound of this letter is _____." "Your turn. What name? What sound?" (*Review previously taught letter names and sounds.*)
Blending: sound-by-sound	"My turn. I'll read this word the slow way, then I'll read it the fast way." (*Teacher models blending letter-by-letter.*) "Your turn. Read this word the slow way." (*Students pronounce the letter sounds as you sweep your hand below each letter.*) "Now you read this word the fast way." (*Students pronounce the word as you tap below it.*)
Blending: onset-rime	"My turn. I'll say the first sound(s) and the end part of the word." (*Teacher models.*) "Your turn. Say the first sound(s) and the end part of the word." (*Students pronounce the first sounds and the end part of the word as you sweep your hand below the word parts.*) "Now read the word the fast way." (*Students pronounce the word as you tap below it.*)
Word reading	"My turn. When I slide my hand under a word, figure out the word in your head. When I tap below a word, you say the word." "Your turn." (*Students think as you slide your hand below the word, then pronounce the word as you tap below it.*)

Source: Adapted from the Western Regional Reading First Technical Assistance Center.

For example, the heart of an explicit instruction lesson is the sequence of teacher explanation and demonstration, guided practice, and independent practice. Teachers can guide students through these lesson steps with the simple instructional phrases "My turn," Our turn," and "Your turn." "My turn" tells students that it is the teacher's turn to talk and that they should sit quietly and listen attentively. "Our turn" tells students that they will now perform a task together in unison with teacher guidance and support. "Your turn" tells students that it is their turn to show the teachers how well they can perform the task on their own. Such simple instructional language makes lessons flow quickly and effectively.

Reading instruction experts have also developed explicit instructional language that can guide students through the procedures for learning and blending letter sounds and word parts. The chart on page 38 is adapted from explicit instructional language developed by the Western Regional Reading First Technical Assistance Center (WRRFTAC).

BUILDING AND USING A CLASSROOM LIBRARY

Classroom libraries are an essential part of an effective classroom. Students need access to a large number of books. Recent research shows that access to books significantly increases students' literacy development (Neuman, 1999). The books should be attractive, high-quality, and arranged at the sightline of students. Research recommends five books per child minimum in your classroom library. Teachers also need to have a classroom library so that students can take books home for independent reading. Parent and family involvement in literacy development is also correlated with higher language development and reading achievement (Snow, Burns, & Griffin, 1998).

Building a classroom library takes time, but school book clubs like Scholastic and Trumpet Club are invaluable. Small grants of $100 to $250 can go a long way toward building a good book collection. Other sources for books are thrift stores and garage sales; however, don't expect children to get very excited about extremely old or worn-out books.

Sylvia Read

This is only part of one teacher's extensive classroom library.

The other way to build a classroom library, though it is temporary, is to use your school library and/or your public library. School libraries often have no limit to the number of books that teachers can check out. Public libraries often allow teachers to check out up to 30 titles at a time.

By combining books from all of these sources, you eventually should have a collection sufficient to read aloud to your students and for them to choose from for independent reading, with one caveat: Having a large collection of books does not guarantee that you have books at appropriate levels of difficulty for your students. A good classroom library should include books that are leveled, or can be leveled, according to difficulty. Although you can build your own classroom library of leveled books, it's more efficient to work with the other teachers in your school to build a schoolwide leveled book library with multiple copies of books to use for guided reading lessons.

The bulk of the leveled books you use for instruction will be included in your school's reading program. Some schools use federal and state monies to purchase books which they then level, organize, and store in a common area of the school.

ORGANIZING BY LEVEL

You can organize a portion of your classroom library by level and use that portion of your collection to guide students to books on their independent and instructional levels. Teachers sometimes use the student-friendly term "just right" to describe books that are at students' instructional levels. The Goldilocks analogy explains this well: She wanted a bed that was not too soft and not too hard, but just right. Similarly, we want our students to read books that are not too hard and not too easy, but just right.

When children are reading independently, they need to have access to books at their independent level, which is 95% to 100% accuracy. While reading books at their independent level, they have a chance to consolidate their reading skills, especially comprehension, because they aren't using all of their attention to decode. Reading

A well-organized classroom library.

John A. Smith

books that are somewhat easy also allows children to build fluency, which enhances comprehension as well.

There are many leveling systems and criteria available. We caution against leveling every book in your room (some libraries do this using Accelerated Reader levels or Lexile levels). Some books, particularly picture books, can and should be enjoyed by all children regardless of their reading ability through emergent reading of the pictures, retelling the story based on having heard it, or rereading a familiar old favorite. Children, like adults, enjoy reading books that do not challenge them (like the books adults buy in the airport to read on the plane or at the beach!).

Table 2.1 shows a list of books that represent each guided reading level. You can use these books as benchmark books for assessing children's reading levels or as comparison books when leveling other books. By examining features such as words per

Table 2.1　Benchmark Books for Guided Reading Levels

Level		Title	Author
A	K	*Do You Want to Be My Friend?*	Eric Carle
B	K	*Lunch at the Zoo*	Wendy Blaxland
C	K/1	*Rainbow of My Own*	Don Freeman
D	K/1	*Bears on Wheels*	Stan and Jan Berenstain
E	1	*All by Myself*	Mercer Mayer
E	1	*The Foot Book*	Dr. Seuss
E	1	*Go Dog, Go*	Philip D. Eastman
F	1	*Cookie's Week*	Cindy Ward
F	1	*A Bug, a Bear, and a Boy*	David McPhail
F	1	*Who Will Be My Friends?*	Syd Hoff
G	1	*Just for You*	Mercer Mayer
G	1	*Mine's the Best*	Crosby Bonsall
G	1	*Sheep in a Jeep*	Nancy Shaw
G	1	*Spot's First Walk*	Eric Hill
H	1	*Sammy the Seal*	Syd Hoff
H	1	*Just Me and My Dad*	Mercer Mayer
H	1	*We Are Best Friends*	Aliki
I	1	*Dragon Gets By*	Dav Pilkey
I	1	*Father Bear Comes Home*	Else Holmes Minarik
I	1	*Hattie and the Fox*	Mem Fox
I	1	*Henny Penny*	Paul Galdone
J	1/2	*Cat in the Hat*	Dr. Suess
J	1/2	*Danny and the Dinosaur*	Syd Hoff
J	1/2	*Henry and Mudge* books	Cynthia Rylant
J	1/2	*Mr. Putter and Tabby* books	Cynthia Rylant
K	2	*Arthur's Loose Tooth*	Lillian Hoban

Table 2.1   Continued

Level		Title	Author
K	2	*Dinosaur Time*	Peggy Parish
K	2	*Harold and the Purple Crayon*	Crockett Johnson
K	2	*Nate the Great* books	Marjorie Weinman Sharmat
L	2	*Amelia Bedelia* books	Peggy Parish
L	2	*Cam Jansen* books	David Adler
L	2	*George and Martha* books	James Marshall
L	2	*Horrible Harry* books	Suzy Kline
M	2/3	*Arthur* chapter books	Marc Brown
M	2/3	*Freckle Juice*	Judy Blume
M	2/3	*Junie B. Jones* books	Barbara Park
M	2/3	*The Littles*	John Peterson
N	3	*The Adam Joshua Capers* books	Janice Lee Smith
N	3	*Amber Brown* books	Paula Danziger
N	3	*The Leftovers* books	Tristan Howard
N	3	*Rumpelstiltskin*	Paul O. Zelinksky
O	3	*Baby Sitter's Club* books	Ann M. Martin
O	3	*Baby-Sitter's Little Sister*	Ann M. Martin
O	3	*The Boxcar Children* books	Gertrude Chandler Warner
O	3	*Can't You Make Them Behave?*	Jean Fritz
P	4	*Encyclopedia Brown* books	Donald and Rose Sobol
P	4	*Magic School Bus* books	Joanna Cole
P	4	*Time Warp Trio* books	Jon Scieszka
P	4	*Stone Fox*	John Reynold Gardiner
Q	4	*Wayside School Is Falling Down*	Louis Sachar
R	4	*Babe the Gallant Pig*	Dick King-Smith

page, page layout, familiarity of vocabulary, and correlation between words and illustrations, you can determine whether a book should be considered easy or difficult for your students. For more information on leveling books, refer to Fountas and Pinnell (1996 and 1999).

Books should also be organized in ways that help children learn more about reading and content areas.

ORGANIZING BY GENRE

When you display other books in your classroom library in baskets according to their genre, you give students a chance to build their understanding of various genres. Books grouped by genre are usually books that you have either read aloud or done a

Sylvia Read

Sylvia Read

Leveled books in baskets.

book talk about. In addition, you may have taught the students the features of the genre in a mini-lesson.

Books can also be grouped according to topic, which may change throughout the year. Depending on the content unit being taught, the basket containing books about rocks may be replaced with a basket of books about weather. Other genres, such as poetry, biography, or fairy tales, may stay out all year. In addition to organizing books by genre, arranging books in baskets labeled by author, such as Eric Carle or Mem Fox, allows children to choose to read books by a familiar author and explore the topics that author writes about and the author's writing style.

MATCHING BOOKS TO STUDENTS

Because students need to choose books for independent reading, teachers need to teach them how to choose books with which they will feel successful and that they will enjoy. In fact, if students are not taught how to choose books many of them will feel overwhelmed by the number and variety of books that are available to them. They need to learn how to find books that match their reading ability and how to find books that match their personal interests.

MATCHING BOOKS TO STUDENTS' ABILITY

In addition to teachers assessing students' reading ability using formal and informal measures, students need to know how to judge a book's difficulty. The "five-finger test" is easy to teach. If students run into five words on a page that they can't figure out, the book is not just right. If they encounter only two or three difficult words, the book is probably just right. Teachers assess students' reading levels in various ways and assessment is ongoing throughout the school year.

MATCHING BOOKS TO STUDENTS' INTERESTS

You can certainly pinpoint the level at which children read in terms of accuracy and provide a book that is at an appropriate difficulty level, but that means little if the child isn't engaged. Reading aloud and doing book talks helps students decide what books interest them. Some students will have serious problems becoming engaged in their reading if the books aren't interesting to them. This is when you must really listen to them. Not just during reading time, but all day—before school, in the hall, on the way to recess, in the lunch line. Sometimes you'll even need to eavesdrop as they talk with a friend to figure out what interests them. Interest inventories (Atwell, 1998; Ruddell, 1999) are available that can help you figure out what most children like, but some children won't respond to them and you must take covert action!

I had a student one year whose passion was snakes. It wasn't hard to figure out; Damien talked a lot about wanting a pet snake. He latched onto the snake books I had in my nonfiction book rack. I found more in the library. He exhausted my supply of snake books and those I had checked out from the library. After reading them multiple times, he began to be less interested in them and correspondingly less interested in reading. This is where I had to start doing detective work. I watched Damien chase butterflies at recess and provided jars for the crickets he caught and wanted to take home. So I made sure my insect books were out and found more in the library. He became interested in reading again. This cycle happened a few more times that year, but by paying attention and making sure I had books that interested him, he stayed engaged. If I asked him directly what kind of books he wanted to read, he couldn't answer. I had to be attentive to his interests. Damien grew as a reader because I made the effort to keep finding books that would keep him engaged.

Pay attention to students' levels of enthusiasm toward the books in the classroom library. We want students to be able to read as well as *willing* to read.

CONCLUDING THOUGHTS

Many primary-grade classrooms flow through the 3-hour literacy instruction block like a well-rehearsed symphony orchestra flows through a concerto. Some classrooms don't. Much of the difference depends on the teacher's level of organization. Effective classroom teachers know what instructional concepts need to be taught and what sequence of instruction will best allow for cumulative review and learning. Effective classroom teachers are familiar with the variety of available instructional materials and coordinate a seamless blend of basal and supplemental reading program instruction, often involving resource personnel to help support struggling readers. Effective classroom teachers teach explicitly and minimize student guessing. Students in effective classrooms know and follow classroom routines consistently so that little if any instructional time is wasted. Effective classroom teachers consistently gather and analyze assessment data and use this information for instructional planning. Effective classrooms are productive and joyous places to be.

SUGGESTED ACTIVITIES TO EXTEND YOUR LEARNING

1. Contact a local classroom teacher and discuss his or her daily literacy instruction schedule. How many minutes of instruction does the teacher devote to teacher read-aloud, word study, differentiated small-group reading instruction, independent reading practice, and writing instruction? Are all of the important components being taught well? Are some components minimized or left out altogether?
2. Contact a local classroom teacher and ask to examine his or her teacher's manual. Choose a reading selection from the middle of the manual and list the

suggested before-reading, during-reading, and after-reading activities. Discuss with the teacher how well you like the suggested activities. How well would you be able to teach the lesson yourself? Examine the manual's introductory information and appendix materials. How helpful are they?

3. Ask the classroom teacher if he or she uses a supplemental instructional program. If so, what program is it and what is its purpose? Who chose this supplemental program? How effective is the program?

4. Observe a reading lesson in a local elementary school classroom to determine the level of explicitness. Compare the observed lesson with the sample explicit instruction model lesson plan provided in this chapter. Does the teacher provide an introduction to the lesson along with explicit teacher explanation and modeling, guided practice, independent practice, and an assessment component? Did the teacher make accommodations for students with specific instructional needs? What recommendations would you suggest to the teacher?

5. Observe a classroom's physical environment in terms of the number of books available, how books are displayed, and students' level of interaction with books. Also note other print in the room. Are there charts, sets of instructions, sign-in sheets, displays of student writing? Are other literacy materials (charts, big books, paper, writing and drawing implements) organized and accessible to students? Are there areas designated for small-group instruction, whole-group instruction, and individual work? Record your observations and critically evaluate the literacy environment in terms of the information provided in this chapter.

 *REFERENCES*

Atwell, N. (1998). *In the middle: New understandings about writing, reading, and learning*. Portsmouth, NH: Heinemann.

Bear, D. R., Invernizzi, M., Templeton, S. R., & Johnston, F. (2007). *Words their way: Word study for phonics, vocabulary, and spelling instruction* (4th ed.). Upper Saddle River, NJ: Merrill/Prentice Hall.

Biancarosa, C., & Snow, C. E. (2004). Reading next: A vision for action and research in middle and high school literacy: A report to the Carnegie Corporation of New York (2nd ed.). Washington, DC: Alliance for Excellent Education.

Blair, T. R., Rupley, W. H., & Nichols, W. (2007). The effective teacher of reading: Considering the "what" and "how" of instruction. *The Reading Teacher, 60*(5), 432–438.

Bond, G. L., & Dykstra, R. (1997). The cooperative research program in first-grade reading instruction. *Reading Research Quarterly, 32*(4), 345–427.

Calkins, L. M. (2001). *The art of teaching reading*. New York: Longman.

Calkins, L. M., & Mermelstein, L. (2003). *Units of study for primary writing: A yearlong curriculum*. Portsmouth, NH: Heinemann.

Carnine, D. W., Silbert, J., Kame'enui, E. J., & Tarver, S. (2003). *Direct instruction reading*. Upper Saddle River, NJ: Merrill/Prentice Hall.

Cunningham, P. M. (2004). *Phonics they use*. Boston: Pearson/Allyn & Bacon.

Cunningham, P. M., & Allington, R. L. (2003). *Classrooms that work: They can all read and write* (3rd Ed.). New York: Longman.

Cunningham, P. M., Hall, D. P., & Defee, M. (1998). Non-ability grouped multilevel instruction: Eight years later. *The Reading Teacher, 51*(8), 652–664.

Doyle, B., & Bramwell, W. (2006). Promoting emergent literacy and social–emotional learning through dialogic reading. *The Reading Teacher, 59*(6), 554–564.

Duffy, G. G. (1998). Powerful models or powerful teachers? An argument for teacher as entrepreneur. In S. Stahl & D. Hayes (Eds.), *Instructional models in reading.* Mahwah, NJ.: Erlbaum.

Duffy, G. G. (2003). *Explaining reading: A resource for teaching concepts, skills, and strategies.* New York: Guilford Press.

Fountas, I., & Pinnell, G. S. (1996). *Guided reading: Good first teaching for all children.* Portsmouth, NH: Heinemann.

Fountas, I., & Pinnell, G. S. (1999). Matching books to readers: Using leveled books in guided reading, K–3. Portsmouth, NH: Heinemann.

Joseph, L. M. (2006). Incremental rehearsal: A flashcard drill technique for increasing retention of reading words. *The Reading Teacher, 59*(8), 803–807.

Lane, H. B., & Wright, T. L. (2007). Maximizing the effectiveness of reading aloud. *The Reading Teacher, 60*(7), 668–675.

Mohr, K. J., & Mohr, E. S. (2007). Extending English language learners' classroom interactions using the response protocol. *The Reading Teacher, 60*(5), 440–450.

National Reading Panel. (2000). *Teaching children to read: An evidence-based assessment of the scientific research literature on reading and its implications for reading instruction. Report of the subgroups.* National Institute of Child Health and Human Development. Retrieved from http://www.nichd.nih.gov/publications/nrp/smallbook.cfm

Neuman, S. B. (1999). Books make a difference: A study of access to literacy. *Reading Research Quarterly, 34*(3), 286–311.

Pearson, P. D., & Gallagher, M. C. (1983). The instruction of reading comprehension. *Contemporary Educational Psychology, 8*(3), 317–344.

Pressley, M. (2002). *Reading instruction that works: The case for balanced teaching* (2nd ed.). New York: Guilford Press.

Pressley, M., Rankin, J., & Yokoi, L. (1996). A survey of instructional practices of primary teachers nominated as effective in promoting literacy. *Elementary School Journal, 96,* 363–384.

Ruddell, R. B. (1999). *Teaching children to read and write: Becoming an influential teacher,* (2nd ed.). Boston: Allyn & Bacon.

Snow, C. E., Burns, M. S., & Griffin, P. (1998). *Preventing reading difficulties in young children.* Washington, DC: National Academy Press.

Torgesen, J. K. (2004). Lessons learned from research on intervention for students who have difficulty learning to read. In P. McCardle & V. Chhabra (Eds.), *The voice of evidence in reading research.* Baltimore: Brookes.

Trelease, J. (2006). *The read-aloud handbook* (6th ed). New York: Penguin.

Tyner, B. (2004). *Small-group reading instruction: A differentiated teaching model for beginning and struggling readers.* Newark, DE: International Reading Association.

Walpole, S., & McKenna, M. C. (2007). *Differentiated reading instruction: Strategies for the primary grades.* New York: Guilford Press.

Wolfersberger, M. E., Reutzel, D. R., Sudweeks, R., & Fawson, P. C. (2004). Developing and validating the classroom literacy environmental profile (CLEP): A tool for examining the "print richness" of early childhood and elementary classrooms. *Journal of Literacy Research, 36*(2), 211–272.

Building Early Literacy Skills

3

by John A. Smith

Moving On Without Sally

One Wednesday morning I went to visit a first-grade classroom in the school district where I worked as reading coordinator. I recognized Sally, a girl that I had taught in a summer reading program for at-risk students. I knelt down beside her desk to say a cheerful hello and noticed that she had tears in her eyes. I asked her what was wrong and she pointed to a pile of 11 worksheets on her desk. The plaintive look in her eyes told me that she didn't understand what to do on the worksheets. Her teacher was in a corner of the classroom with a reading group.

Unfortunately, Sally frequently didn't understand what to do or what was happening during her reading instruction. The problem was that Sally's home environment provided her very little literacy preparation or support. She seldom observed family members reading and writing. There were virtually no reading or writing materials available to her at home. Nobody read to her. Vacations, dance and music lessons, and other enriching experiences were beyond her family's means.

Sally's lack of literacy preparation put her at a great disadvantage during reading instruction. She didn't know what many of the stories were about. Many of the words she heard and saw were unfamiliar to her. She didn't understand what to do with the letter sounds that her teacher pronounced. Sally saw many other classmates responding confidently to the teacher, and wondered why she couldn't do what they did.

Just as a house without a solid cement foundation will most likely encounter serious structural problems, beginning reading students who don't have a solid foundation of early literacy skills are at substantial risk for experiencing reading problems (Dickinson & Neuman, 2006; Strickland & Shanahan, 2004). A solid literacy foundation comprises early literacy skills in four areas: (1) *oral language*, building background knowledge and vocabulary; (2) *alphabet knowledge*, learning letter names and sounds; (3) *phonemic awareness*, understanding how speech sounds form spoken words; and (4) *print awareness*, learning the conventions of print.

It is important to realize that these four early literacy skill areas should not be considered sequential. They can be developed very effectively together and can complement and reinforce each other. This chapter is organized around these four early literacy skill areas:

- Oral language: building a necessary foundation
- Alphabet knowledge: learning letter names and sounds
- Phonemic awareness: recognizing and using speech sounds
- Print awareness: understanding how print works

ORAL LANGUAGE: BUILDING A NECESSARY FOUNDATION

The foundation of learning to read successfully actually begins in infancy as parents speak to and with their children. Students' ability to use oral language is a precursor to their ability to use written language. Students who have never heard or don't know the meanings of written words they are being asked to decode are at a severe disadvantage.

Varying home environments provide some students with tremendous oral language advantages and others with very little language preparation. Adams (1990) points out that many mainstream children experience "thousands of hours of pre-reading activities" at home during their preschool years, while their less fortunate classmates may receive as few as 200 hours of such support. Hart and Risley (1995) found that 3-year-old children from professional homes had vocabularies four times

One literacy learner helps another learn foundations concepts.

Brenda Richards

larger than children from welfare homes, and that children from professional homes would experience over 30 million more words in conversations at home by age 5 than children from low-income homes.

The varying levels of oral language activities found in students' homes are also found in their classrooms. Many classrooms provide rich oral language opportunities for students including verbal models and instructions, extended adult–child dialogues, questions and answers, poetry, singing and chanting, and especially many hours spent enjoying and discussing picture books, fairy tales, and Mother Goose. Unfortunately, other less-effective classrooms provide "teacher-dominated language environments" that do little to stimulate students' oral language growth (Christie, Enz, & Vukelich, 1997, p. 89).

The following sections of this chapter provide suggestions for creating language-rich classrooms that will help build the necessary oral language foundations that students need in order to read and understand written language successfully.

> ### FOR ENGLISH LANGUAGE LEARNERS
>
> **English Learners Need an Oral Language Foundation**
>
> ELL students need increased amounts of oral language development activities. Time spent teaching word identification skills will be of little value unless ELL students develop a solid foundation in oral English.

ORAL LANGUAGE MODELING

Children develop oral language, in large part, through their verbal interactions with adults and peers. Classroom teachers who actively and consistently promote oral language use can have a tremendous impact on their students' oral language development, particularly for those students from disadvantaged homes and homes where little or no English is spoken. Many students with limited levels of oral language will benefit from direct instruction and teacher modeling of oral language.

Several effective methods for teaching oral language directly to limited-language students have been described by Pullen and Justice (2003). *Self-talk*, like think-aloud, is when a teacher describes his or her activities for students ("I am putting my chair under my desk"). *Parallel-talk* is when a teacher describes a student's actions ("You are sitting by me"). *Repetitions* involve teachers repeating verbatim what students say, often with praise and encouragement. For example:

Student: Pencil.
Teacher: That's right, pencil.

Expansions involve elaborating on students' spoken words with questions and additional elaborations to provide a model of oral language that is slightly above the student's level. For example:

Student: Pencil.
Teacher: Whose pencil?.
Student: My pencil.
Teacher: That's right. This is your pencil.

SHARING TIME

Show-and-tell has long been a fixture in many primary-grade classrooms. Students bring toys, books, dolls, and pets and tell about everything from the family's trip to Disneyland to Dad's trip to jail for hunting ducks out of season.

Traditional show-and-tell has not always been as effective a strategy for developing oral language as it could have been because one student would make a brief presentation while the others were expected to sit quietly and listen. Discussion was not encouraged. When done properly, sharing time can provide opportunities to develop students' oral language skills through rich classroom discussions of students' shared objects or events.

Sharing time should be structured to maximize learning and minimize confusion. Teachers can post a sharing time weekly schedule on which each student is assigned a day of the week as his or her sharing day throughout the entire school year. Parents should be advised to not send toys for sharing time, but instead be encouraged to send items or stories of educational value with their children.

The most important aspect of sharing time is the opportunity for classroom discussions associated with the items and stories brought to class. Teachers can stimulate oral language development during sharing time discussions with questions for the sharer such as:

- Where did you get this?
- How does it work?
- What do you do with it?
- What happened next?
- What did you say (to the people involved)?
- How did you feel about that experience?

Classmates should be encouraged to ask similar questions. When classmates know they will be invited to ask questions they are more likely to become active listeners. Seating students close on the carpet or rug during sharing time brings them closer together, enhancing opportunities to see an item or hear about an event.

Parents may also be encouraged to participate during sharing time. They can bring pets or items too bulky or fragile for their children to carry to school, and parent classroom visits can provide an excellent opportunity for classmates to ask questions and engage in sharing time discussions.

LITERACY-ENRICHED PLAY

Literacy educators recognize the vital role of play in developing young children's oral language skills. Time spent playing in literacy-enriched play centers such as a homemaking center, grocery store, or business office is not just for fun. The verbal interactions among students as they engage in make-believe provides important opportunities to develop language by using language. Literacy props such as pens and pencils, notepads, stationery and envelopes, file folders, telephones, menus, books and magazines, and wall signs increase opportunities for students to generate and share language (Justice & Pullen, 2003).

Literacy-enriched play helps support children's ongoing cognitive development. Through play, children learn to understand and respond to the content of oral language, integrate new information into their conceptual understandings, clarify misunderstandings, ask questions, create meaning, and solve problems.

Cooper and Dever (2001) describe a Card Shop learning center in which students created and exchanged greeting cards. Teacher Jaclyn Cooper showed her first-grade students a number of sample greeting cards and told them that they were going to create a classroom card shop. Together Cooper and her students looked through the contents of a prop box that she had assembled and the students took the responsibility for making signs and additional props that they felt necessary for their classroom card shop. Cooper showed examples of birthday cards, friendship cards, holiday cards, wedding cards, and thank-you cards. She helped the students develop a pricing structure for their cards. The students took on roles of cashier, clerk, customers, and observers. The level of student engagement, learning, and motivation was understandably very high as students integrated math, literacy, and art curriculum concepts during their activities in the card shop.

FOR ENGLISH LANGUAGE LEARNERS

Social Interaction

Role-playing games are effective for promoting language acquisition. In role-playing games students need to interact (and sometimes read) in order to participate. Interactions naturally have comprehensible input, especially when native speakers of English are also participating (Pica, Young, & Doughty, 1987).

NURSERY RHYMES

Nursery rhymes provide wonderful opportunities to build students' vocabulary and oral language skills, along with phonological awareness. The vocabulary and content of nursery rhymes is delightful. The sing-song rhythm and rhyme help students recite familiar nursery rhymes along with the teacher. Research studies (Bryant, Bradley, Maclean, & Crossland, 1989; Maclean, 1987) have found correlations between children's early knowledge of nursery rhymes and their reading achievement scores in later years.

Students in beginning reading and writing programs should be taught to recite, dramatize, and do many other follow-up activities with nursery rhymes. Some teachers write nursery rhymes on chart paper to help students learn to read and recite the nursery rhymes through shared reading activities. Other teachers display nursery rhymes on overheads and give students individual copies of nursery rhymes to illustrate and practice reading.

Students' oral language grows as they chant and recite nursery rhymes along with the teacher. Students can recite nursery rhymes aloud in unison or in parts. They can use stuffed animals as props for dramatizing nursery rhymes. Cunningham (2004) suggests dividing the class into two groups and having Group 1 say the first two lines of a nursery rhyme, but allowing Group 2 to say the rhyming word at the end of the second line. For example:

Group 1: Hickory dickory dock. The mouse ran up the . . .
Group 2: clock.

POETRY

Like nursery rhymes, poetry also has the power to delight beginning readers and help them develop insights about the nature of oral and written language. Teachers should read poetry aloud regularly and involve students in follow-up activities that provide opportunities for them to recite poetry, learn to love poetry, and learn the meanings of poems' rich vocabulary words and concepts.

There are many ways to use poetry in elementary school classrooms to build students' oral language. Poetry can be a regular part of daily teacher read-alouds. Poetry provides a way to make effective use of those occasional spare moments waiting in the lunch line. Students can illustrate and compile favorite poems in personal poetry anthologies.

There are many opportunities for using poetry to stimulate students' love for words, language, and literature (Parr & Campbell, 2006; Sekeres & Gregg, 2007). Students may keep favorite poems in their writer's notebooks and use the poems as a seedbed for writing ideas (Harwayne, 1992). Gill (2007) reads her own poetry aloud to her students as a model for helping them capture images of their own worlds and describe these images in their own poetic language.

First-grade teacher Vicki Olson has her students read and memorize favorite poems that they add to their personal poetry collection and take home at the end of the year. It is not uncommon for Olson's entire class to march unannounced into a neighboring classroom at any time of the school day, recite a newly learned poem in unison, and then smugly turn around and march back out.

There are many wonderful children's poetry anthologies available, in addition to the well-known poetry books by Shel Silverstein and Jack Prelustky. John Ciardi's delightful book *You Read to Me, I'll Read to You* has poems printed in two colors for partner reading with a classmate. *Sing a Song of Popcorn* (de Regniers, Moore, White, & Carr, et al, 1988) contains poems illustrated by Caldecott Award–winning artists. Online booksellers have extensive lists of children's poetry anthologies listed in order of popularity.

SINGING

One of the most enjoyable activities of the school day may also be one of the most effective for developing students' oral language. Singing provides a vehicle for students to produce large amounts of oral language meaningfully and enjoyably. Fifteen to 20 minutes of singing to begin each day also develops a wonderful sense of classroom community and warmth (Smith, 2000).

Many teachers write and display song lyrics in large print on chart paper and designate one of the students as the "song chooser" and another student as the "song pointer" for the day. The song chooser selects a song for the day (the teacher also selects a song or two) and the song pointer uses a yardstick or other pointing device to point to the words on the chart as the class sings. Some teachers play piano or guitar to accompany the singing; others use a CD player.

Singing with song charts provides a wonderful opportunity to discuss the song's background knowledge, vocabulary, and spelling patterns. For example, when singing John Denver's song "Grandma's Featherbed," begin by activating students' background knowledge with a class discussion of visits to their grandparents. It is also important to discuss the meaning of unfamiliar words and expressions such as *bolt of*

Singing can help children develop phonemic awareness.

Steven Von Niederhausern

cloth, tick, ballad, cobwebs filled my head, and of course *featherbed.* Song charts also provide an opportunity to develop students' familiarity with spelling patterns (*featherbed* and *homemade* are compound words, or that *wake, made, whole,* and *wide* follow the CV_e pattern).

There are many sources of wonderful children's songs. Teachers can find songs in their own music collections at home, in children's sections at libraries and music stores, from friends, and from the students themselves. Popular children's song singers like Bob Chapin, Hap Palmer, Jean Feldman, Raffi (see their websites) and artists from *Sesame Street* are a great source of delightful children's songs. Public and university libraries often have anthologies of American folk songs that sometimes include lyrics, chords, melody lines, and background notes (Lomax, 1960).

ALPHABET KNOWLEDGE: LEARNING LETTER NAMES AND SOUNDS

Just as oral language is the foundation for understanding written language, alphabet knowledge is one of the foundations for decoding written language. Researchers have found "the best predictor of beginning reading achievement to be a child's knowledge of letter names" (Adams, 1990, p. 61). A child who can already name the letters will have an easier time learning about letter sounds and spelling patterns than a child who is still learning the letters. Children who are confident with letters will be in a better position to focus on words and recognize that words are composed of patterns of letters. And, the sounds of many letters closely resemble their names, providing an easy transition from names to sounds.

Understanding the connection between printed letters and their sounds, called the alphabetic principle, is a critical first step toward the ability to decode words. Teachers can employ numerous methods and activities to teach alphabet letter names and sounds directly.

DIRECT TEACHING OF LETTER NAMES AND SOUNDS

Direct teaching of letter names involves a simple three-step procedure: (1) the teacher points to the letter and pronounces its name for the students, (2) the teacher asks the students for the name, and (3) the students pronounce the letter's name. For example:

Teacher (*points to letter* a): The name of this letter is *a*.

Teacher: What name?

Students: *a* (*as teacher taps on the letter*).

If students cannot correctly pronounce the letter name, then go back and repeat the three steps. When students can correctly identify the name of the letter *a*, follow the same procedure to introduce the letter *b*, then go back and review the letter *a*. If the students can't remember the name of letter *a*, reteach the letter *a* using the three-step procedure again. As more letter names are learned, review the previously learned letter names in random order. If students have forgotten a letter name, reteach the name using the three steps. Cumulatively go through the letter names teaching, reviewing when necessary, and adding more letters.

The same three-step procedure is also used to teach the sounds of letters.

Teacher (*points to letter* a): The sound of this letter is /a/.

Teacher: What sound?

Students: /a/ (as teacher taps on the letter).

Many kindergarten teachers follow the time-honored tradition of teaching an alphabet letter each week. This "letter-a-week" curriculum does not provide for the cumulative review that is so critically important. Recently, some kindergarten teachers have found great success teaching a letter a day. This accelerated pacing through the alphabet provides generous practice and review as teacher and students cycle through the alphabet six times in a 180-day school year. Letter-a-day is also much more effective in classrooms where students move in and out on a regular basis.

FOLLOW-UP ACTIVITIES FOR TEACHING LETTER NAMES AND SOUNDS

Alphabet knowledge instruction should begin each day with direct teaching and review of letter names and sounds, followed by activities that provide opportunities for students to further learn and practice the names and sounds.

A B C S o n g

a b c d

e f g

h i j k

l m n o p

q r s

t u v

w x

y z

Now I know my ABCs

Next time won't you

sing with me?

Figure 3.1 Alphabet Song Chart

Alphabet Song

Perhaps the most common activity for teaching the names of the alphabet letters is singing the alphabet song—also know as the "ABC Song"—to the tune of "Twinkle Twinkle Little Star." Many students entering kindergarten already know this song, but some don't. Kindergarten and first-grade teachers should sing this song frequently at the beginning of the school year, and regularly thereafter.

When all students can sing the song proficiently, display a chart like that shown in Figure 3.1. Point to the printed letters as the students sing, much like choral reading with a big book.

Sing through the alphabet song several times. Then focus on singing and pointing to the letters in just the first line. Ask students to come to the chart and point to the letters that you name ("Who can come to the chart and point to the letter *b*?" "Who can come to the chart and point to the letter *a*?"). Cumulatively add lines until students can successfully identify all letter names. A follow-up activity is to distribute alphabet letter cards for the letters being learned and ask, "Who has the letter _____? Would you bring it to the chart and hold it next to the printed letter _____?"

Alphabet Flashcards

Alphabet flashcards are a common follow-up activity for teaching alphabet letter names and sounds. Teachers should begin with the flashcards for the first five alphabet letters and review them with students during small-group differentiated instruction. When all students in the group can recognize all five letters instantly, add another letter and review all six letters. When the students can automatically identify all six letters, add one more letter and review until all students can recognize seven letters.

Review the previously learned letters and cumulatively add letters each day. The number of letters to add each day depends on how quickly the group members make progress in recognizing them instantly.

FOR STRUGGLING READERS

Recognizing Alphabet Letters

For students who lag behind in recognizing alphabet letters, do the flashcard activity individually, using only the letters from the student's own name. Help the student locate the same letters displayed in classroom print.

Students' Names

Cunningham (2004) has shown that student names can provide an effective vehicle to help teach the alphabet letter names and sounds. Begin by writing a student's name (for example, *Abbey*) on an index card and display it on a classroom bulletin board. Point out that the word *Abbey* has five letters. Chant the letters with the students and point out any other characteristics: for example, *Abbey* has two *b*s and begins with the first letter of the alphabet.

Print the word *Abbey* on a second index card and cut this second card into individual letters. Mix up the order of the letters and have students reassemble the letters

Figure 3.2   Some Favorite Alphabet Books

A Is for Asia by Cynthia Chin-Lee. New York: Orchard, 1997.

A Mountain Alphabet by Margriet Ruurs and Andrew Kiss. New York: Tundra Books, 1996.

Alpha Bugs: A Pop-Up Alphabet Book by David A. Carter. New York: Little Simon, 1994.

Alphabet Adventure by Audrey Wood. New York: Blue Sky Press, 2001.

The Alphabet Tree by Leo Lionni. New York: Knopf, 1990.

Alphabet Under Construction by Denise Fleming. New York: Henry Holt, 2002.

Anno's Alphabet by Mitsumas Anno. New York: Crowell 1975.

Antelope, Bison, Cougar: A National Wildlife Alphabet Book by Steven Medley. Boston: Houghton Mifflin, 2002.

Antler, Bear, Canoe: A Northwoods Alphabet Year by Betsy Bowen. New York: Little, Brown, 1991.

Chicka Chicka Boom Boom by Bill Martin and John Archambault. New York: Simon and Schuster, 1989.

The Construction Alphabet Book by Jerry Pallota and Rob Bolster. Watertown, MA: Charlesbridge, 2006.

Cowboy Alphabet by James Rice. Gretna, LA: Pelican 1990.

Dr. Seuss's ABC by Dr. Seuss. New York: Random House, 1991.

Eating the Alphabet: Fruits and Vegetables from A-Z by Lois Short. San Diego: Harcount Brace, 1989.

Eh? to Zed: A Canadian Abecedarium by Kevin Major and Alan Daniel. Red Deer, Alberta: Red Deer College Press, 2003.

The Farm Alphabet Book by Jane Miller. New York: Scholastic, 1987.

The Graphic Alphabet by David Pelletier. New York: Orchard, 1996.

Kipper's A to Z by Mick Inkpen. San Diego: Harcourt Brace, 2000.

Maisy's ABC by Lucy Cousins. Cambridge, MA: Candlewick Press, 1995.

Merriam-Webster's Alphabet Book by Ruth Heller. Springfield, MA: Merriam-Webster, 2005.

My Pop-Up Surprise ABC by Robert Crowther. New York: Orchard Books, 1997.

Navajo ABC: A Dine Alphabet Book by Luci Tapahonso and Eleanor Schick. New York: Aladdin, 1999.

Parading with Piglets by Biruta Akerbergs-Hansen. Washington, DC: National Geographic Society, 1996.

Prairie Primer A to Z by Caroline Stutson. New York: Puffin, 1999.

Q Is for Duck by Mary Elting and Michael Folsom. New York: Clarion, 1985.

Robert Crowther's Most Amazing Hide-And-Seek Alphabet Book by Robert Crowther. Cambridge, MA: Candlewick Press, 1999.

The Turn-Around, Upside-Down Alphabet Book by Lisa Campbell. New York: Simon and Schuster, 2004.

The Z Was Zapped by Chris Van Allsburg. Boston: Houghton Mifflin, 1987.

in the proper order. Finally, have each student write the word *Abbey* on one side of a piece of paper and then draw a picture of Abbey on the other side.

The next day, add another student's name to the board and repeat the process. Compare the two names. Which name has more letters? How many more letters does the longer name have? Do the two names have any letters in common? Repeat this procedure each day by adding another name to the bulletin board and going through the examining and comparing process.

Alphabet Books

Alphabet book read-alouds are a popular and effective follow-up to direct alphabet teaching. Research (Bradley & Jones, 2007) suggests that in addition to reading alphabet books aloud, teachers should provide explicit talk about the features of the letters and connect the alphabet book letters to other meaningful contexts. Bradley and Jones (p. 461) also provide an example of a class-made alphabet book where the teacher displayed photographs with alliterative captions below each photograph ("Helga and Hillary hike happily").

There is an increasing number of captivating alphabet books available to teachers and students. Refer to Figure 3.2 for a list of favorites.

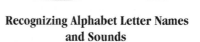

FOR STRUGGLING READERS

Recognizing Alphabet Letter Names and Sounds

Struggling readers may need more direct instruction in alphabet letter names and sounds than will their higher-functioning classmates.

DON'T WAIT

Some students will have a difficult time learning the names and sounds of letters. Memorizing letter names and sounds is rote learning, much like learning people's names or phone numbers. The important principle is that it is not necessary to postpone formal decoding instruction until a student has learned all of the letter names and sounds perfectly. Decoding instruction includes constant use of the letter names and sounds, and many students will learn these more easily from hearing and seeing them used in the context of decoding lessons. Students who cannot seem to catch on to mastering alphabet letter names and sounds through the activities already described may have learned them inductively while participating with their classmates in simple word family decoding activities. Other students have learned the alphabet letter names and sounds most readily by using their personal alphabet charts and books to figure out the sounds they want to use in their writing.

 ## PHONEMIC AWARENESS: RECOGNIZING AND USING SPEECH SOUNDS

WHAT IS PHONEMIC AWARENESS?

Phonemic awareness is the understanding that oral speech is composed of individual speech sounds called *phonemes*. For example, the spoken word *tan* has three phonemes: /t/ /a/ /n/. The spoken word *stop* has four phonemes: /s/ /t/ /o/ /p/. Phonemes don't necessarily correspond exactly with alphabet letters. Although the word *choose* has six letters, it still has only three phonemes: /ch/ /oo/ /z/.

Phonemic awareness also includes the understanding that phonemes can be blended together in varying combinations to form words (Dickinson & Neuman, 2006). For example, the three phonemes from *tan* can also be blended together to form the spoken words *Nat* and *ant*. The four phonemes from the spoken word *stop* can also forms the words *spot* and *pots*.

Phonemic awareness comes under the umbrella term *phonological awareness*, which is the larger understanding that streams of speech can be segmented into individual words. For example, the three-word spoken question "Did you eat?" may sound to a listener like a one-syllable speech stream, "Jeet?" Phonological awareness also includes the understanding that individual spoken words can be broken down into individual syllables (*wonderful*: *won–der–ful*).

WHY IS PHONEMIC AWARENESS IMPORTANT?

Beginning readers' understanding of how phonemes are blended together to form spoken words is the foundation for their later understanding of how printed letter sounds can be blended together in reading printed words. Where oral language provides the foundation for reading comprehension, phonemic awareness in connection with alphabet knowledge forms the foundation for decoding printed words. Adams (1990), in her extensive review of beginning reading research, concluded that "knowledge of letters and phonemic awareness were found to bear strong and direct relationship to success and ease of reading acquisition" (p. 82).

Research also suggests that the lack of phonemic awareness may impede an individual's ability to benefit from phonics instruction (Juel, Griffith, & Gough, 1986) and is a "primary source of difficulty for children with reading disabilities" (Pullen & Justice, 2003, p. 88).

GUIDELINES FOR TEACHING PHONEMIC AWARENESS

Phonemic awareness is best nurtured through direct teaching supported by follow-up activities that encourage students' exploring and playing with the sounds of spoken language. Activities such as stumbling over tongue twisters, chanting jump-rope rhymes, playing with pig latin, singing children's songs, and reciting poems and nursery rhymes all help students become aware of the sounds of spoken language and the interrelationships among the sounds. A sufficient amount of phonemic awareness can be taught in a few months, and an overabundance of phonemic awareness instruction does not add to students' reading achievement (Reading & Van Deuren, 2007).

Members of the National Reading Panel (NRP, 2000) formulated the following guidelines after reviewing 52 phonemic awareness research studies.

- **Keep it simple and explicit.** The NRP (2000) recommends focusing on just one or two phonemic awareness skills.
- **Teach students to segment and blend phonemes.** The NRP found that segmenting and blending were most directly involved in reading and spelling. Segmenting is a precursor to spelling. Blending is a precursor to reading.
- **Keep it short.** The panel also found that phonemic awareness instruction does not need to be lengthy to be effective. Assessment of students' instructional needs is the best indicator of how much phonemic awareness training is necessary.

📖 **Teach phonemic awareness to students in small groups.** The NRP found that teaching phonemic awareness in small groups was more effective than teaching to individual students or the whole class together.

📖 **Include printed letters.** The NRP concluded that phonemic awareness instruction is more effective when printed letters are added. Adding printed letters to phonemic awareness instruction provides a natural transition to phonics instruction.

TEACHING PHONEMIC AWARENESS

Before beginning phonemic awareness instruction, many teachers give their students screening assessments such as the DIBELS Initial Sound Fluency and Phoneme Segmentation Fluency subtests to determine which of their students have already mastered phonemic awareness concepts and which students will need varying levels of instruction. Chapter 10 contains descriptions of several phonemic awareness screening and progress-monitoring assessments. This chapter section on teaching phonemic awareness begins with rhyming activities as a means to draw students' attention to the sounds of spoken words. Then activities for teaching students to segment and blend speech sounds are described. Finally, this section presents activities for adding printed letters to phonemic awareness and also teaching phonemic awareness through writing.

Rhyming

The most basic of rhyming activities is to ask students for rhyming words. The following example describes a simple playful rhyming activity.

Teacher modeling: I like to think of rhyming words, words that end with the same sound. Listen to me rhyme some words: *tan: fan, man, Dan, ran; tall: fall, small, hall, wall.*

Teacher: Now, who can say a word that rhymes with *cat*?

Students: *bat, mat, fat, hat, sat*

Teacher: Who can say a word that rhymes with *bed*?

Students: *said, fed, head, red, Ted*

Teacher: Who can say a word that rhymes with *go*?

Students: *snow, slow, no, toe, show*

Teachers can also use a "rhyming phrases" variation (Adams, Foorman, Lundberg, & Beeler, 1998) of this activity. Pronounce a phrase and invite students to complete it with a rhyming word.

Teacher modeling: I also like to think of rhyming sentences. Listen to me make some rhyming sentences: *I saw a **dog** sit on a **log**. I know a **boy** who has a new **toy**.* Now you help me make some rhyming sentences.

Teacher: I know a **cat** who's wearing a _____.

Students: hat

Teacher: I see a **goat** that is sailing a _____.

Students: boat

Teacher: Airplanes **fly** up in the _____.

Students: sky

Songs and poems can be used for a variety of rhyming activities. For example, sing or recite two rhyming lines from a song or poem and ask the students to listen for and identify the rhyming words.

Teacher modeling: I like to think of rhyming words in nursery rhymes and poems and songs. Listen to me find some rhyming words in a nursery rhyme: *Jack and Jill went up the hill*. *Jill* and *hill* rhyme because they end with the same sound. Now you help me find some rhyming words in nursery rhymes and poems.

Teacher: Humpty Dumpty sat on a **wall**, Humpty Dumpty had a great **fall**. Which two words rhyme?

Students: wall, fall

Segmenting Speech Sounds

The ability to segment speech sounds is critically important for beginning readers because it gets to the heart of listening for individual speech sounds in spoken words. Segmenting is necessary for spelling, as students listen for the individual sounds in words in order to be able to write them.

Teacher modeling: I like to say and count the sounds I hear in words. Listen to me say and count some sounds in words, and watch how I use my fingers to help me count: (*Cat*: /c/ /a/ /t/. There are three sounds in the word *cat*. *Me*: /m/ /e/. There are two sounds in the word *me*. Now you help me say and count some sounds in words. Remember to use your fingers to help you count.

Teacher: Let's say and count the sounds in the word *bed*: /b/ /e/ /d/. How many sounds are in the word *bed*?

Students: three

Teacher: Let's say and count the sounds in the word *flat*: /f/ /l/ /a/ /t/. How many sounds are in the word *flat*?

Students: four

Remember to keep phonemic awareness activities simple and playful. Many teachers have found that using a hand puppet to say and count the sounds makes phonemic awareness activities especially motivating (e.g., "This is Sylvester. Sylvester likes to say and count sounds . . .").

Blending Speech Sounds

Teaching students to blend speech sounds is an important precursor to their blending the sounds represented by letters in print. Pronounce the individual sounds of a simple consonant–vowel–consonant (CVC) word and let the students blend and pronounce the word back to you. For example:

Teacher modeling: I like to make secret words from word sounds. Listen to me make some secret words from word sounds: /h/ /a/ /t/—*hat; /t/ /o/ /p/— top*;

/s/ /a/ /m/—*Sam*. Now, I'll say some word sounds and you put the sounds together in your mind and see if you can tell me what the secret word is.

Teacher: /m/ /a/ /d/
Students: *mad*
Teacher: /b/ /i/ /g/
Students: *big*

Repeat the process with other CVC words. When the students become proficient with CVC words, challenge them with four-letter words beginning or ending with consonant blends (*play, grin, stop, past, hold, jump*).

Adding Printed Letters

When students demonstrate that they are catching on to the concept of blending speech sounds, repeat the activity, this time including the printed letters along with the sounds. Select three students to stand up in front and hold up letter cards that spell the word *big*. Have the three students stand a foot or so apart from each other. Ask the non-card-holding students to pronounce each individual sound with you as you point to the letter cards.

Then ask the three students holding the letter cards to move together side-by-side so the word *big* is shown intact, and model the blending process.

Teacher modeling: Watch me point to the three letters and say their sounds one at a time, "the slow way:" Then I'll say the word "the fast way": /b/ /i/ /g/—*big*. Now you say the word the slow way as I point to the letters, then say the word the fast way.

Students: /b/ /i/ /g/—*big*

Repeat this blending process with other CVC words.

The following phonemic awareness activity adds printed letters to both segmenting and blending. The teacher begins by pronouncing a CVC word and asks the students to say it the slow way (segmenting), then the fast way (blending). Then the teacher writes the word on the board and asks students to *read* the the slow way, then the fast way.

Teacher: Listen to me say a word the fast way: *hot*.
Now let's say the word together the slow way, then the fast way:
Students: /h/ /o/ /t/—*hot*
Teacher: Watch me *write* the word. Now, let's *read* the word the slow way, then the fast way (teacher points to each letter, then the whole word).
Students: /h/ /o/ /t/—*hot*

The strength of this activity is that it makes very clear to students the direct link between phonemic awareness and reading. The lesson plan at the end of this section provides another activity for adding printed letters to phonemic awareness instruction. The following lesson plan and the spelling and reading chart shown in Figure 3.3 provide an additional example of a lesson for adding printed letters to a phonemic awareness lesson.

Phonemic Awareness Explicit Instruction Lesson Plan

Concept or Objective: Developing phonemic awareness with letters: small-group lesson

Date: _____

Lesson Steps	Activities	Materials
Introduction • Connect today's lesson to previous lessons • Give a purpose for today's lesson	"Students, you remember that we have been segmenting and blending the sounds of spoken words. Today I'll teach you how segmenting and blending sounds in words that we say helps us segment and blend the sounds in words that we see in books."	
Explicit teacher explanation and demonstration	1. Draw a 4×4 matrix on the teacher's whiteboard (see Figure 3.3). 2. Tell the students that you will show them how matching letters and sounds helps us read words. 3. Pronounce the CVC word: *run*. Count the phonemes on your fingers. Demonstrate putting a little dot in each of the first three boxes in the first row because you counted three phonemes. 4. Say to the students, "The first sound I hear in the word *run* is /r/. The letter *r* makes the sound /r/, so I'm going to write an *r* in the first box." 5. Repeat this process with the sounds /u/ and /n/. 6. Say, "Now watch how I can read this word the slow way, then the fast way." Demonstrate blending and reading the word *run*. 7. Repeat this modeling process with three or four more phoneme words.	Teacher's whiteboard Markers Eraser
Interactive guided practice	1. Distribute copies of the spelling and reading chart in Figure 3.3 to the students. 2. Pronounce a CVC word and guide students through the segmenting (saying and counting) process, making dots, writing the letters in their boxes, and reading the word the slow and fast ways. Write the letters in boxes on the teacher's whiteboard as a model. 3. Repeat #2 with another three or four phoneme words from the second row of the chart in Figure 3.3.	Student copies of Figure 3.3 Teacher's whiteboard Markers Eraser
Monitored independent practice	1. Pronounce a CVC word and tell the students to say and count the sounds of the word in their head, make the dots in the boxes in row three of their paper, then write the letters. Have each student read the word to you the slow and fast ways. 2. Repeat #1.	Student copies of Figure 3.3 Teacher's whiteboard Markers Eraser
Assessment	Listen in as students go through the segmenting, blending, and reading processes in rows three and four of their paper. Ask each student to do the process aloud for you in a whisper voice. Note how well each student can do this.	Notepad for recording students' success at segmenting, blending, and reading
Accommodations for students	Reteach as needed. Provide more explanation/demonstration and/or guided practice as needed.	Additional student copies of Figure 3.3 Teacher's whiteboard Markers Eraser

Figure 3.3   Spelling and Reading Chart

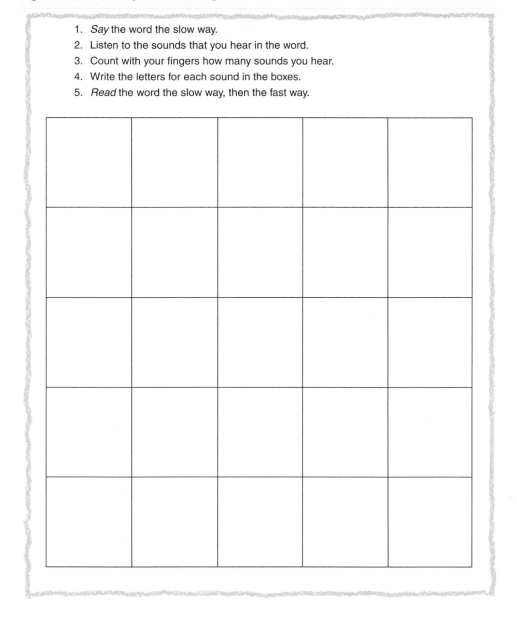

1. *Say* the word the slow way.
2. Listen to the sounds that you hear in the word.
3. Count with your fingers how many sounds you hear.
4. Write the letters for each sound in the boxes.
5. *Read* the word the slow way, then the fast way.

Writing

As students write (using invented spellings) they necessarily go through the process of listening for, segmenting, and organizing the sounds in the words they want to write on paper. A daily writing journal serves this purpose well. Model this process at the beginning of the year by drawing a picture of something interesting or meaningful. When the drawing is complete, label it with a short caption underneath. As you write the caption, model stretching out the sounds in the words and writing what you hear. Students can "help" you with this. This kind of think-aloud allows students to see the process in action.

Then invite the students to draw a picture in their journals of something important, and write a caption underneath. When students ask for help with spelling the
captions early in the year teachers may want to write the captions for the students
and discuss the words and letters. Later in the year teachers may nudge students to
write the captions themselves, instructing them to, "Write down the letters that you
hear in the words."

Even in second grade, some students need to strengthen their phonemic awareness through writing. Teachers can kneel beside a student who has asked for help to
spell a word, and pronounce the word very slowly, stretching out the sounds so the
student can hear and write them.

Students' written journals make a nice chronological record of their development over time. These journals are especially helpful in discussions with parents at
conference time. Writing experiences, coupled with other phonological awareness
activities, allow students to develop these understandings from two perspectives:
interpreting print and producing print.

PRINT AWARENESS: UNDERSTANDING HOW PRINT WORKS

All professions have their own ways of describing what they do. Physicians, attorneys,
economists, and other professionals often use vocabulary that seems incomprehensible. Similarly, the terminology of reading and writing may seem baffling to many
beginning readers and writers, particularly those with meager literacy preparation.
For example, many beginning readers know perfectly well that a letter comes in the
mailbox, a sentence is what you do in jail, a title is for champion athletes, and that a
capital is where the president lives. Imagine the consternation of beginning readers
asked to "point to the diphthong in the third capitalized word of the second sentence
in the first paragraph."

For beginning reading and writing instruction to be fully effective, beginners need
to be familiar with the conventions and terminology of reading and writing. Students
usually learn these concepts best in the context of reading and writing lessons.

Some common *print conventions* that beginning readers and writers must
learn are:

- Reading and writing proceed from left-to-right and from top-to-bottom.
- Words are made up of letters.
- Sentences are made up of words.
- There are spaces between words.
- Sentences begin with capital letters and end with periods, question marks, or
  exclamation points.

Some common reading and writing *terminology* includes:

letter	word	sentence	period	capital
uppercase	lowercase	consonant	vowel	long/short
blend	edit	publish		

Print awareness is often taught through print-referencing behaviors as teachers
read picture books aloud and also through literacy-enriched play (Pullen & Justice,

2003). Print-referencing behaviors include teachers pointing to and explaining print features and pointing to the words while reading aloud. Students can also increase their awareness of print during literacy-enriched play as described in the oral language section of this chapter. It is important for teachers to bring students' attention, during literacy-enriched play, to the existence and functions of print on literacy artifacts such as notepads, menus, labels, and shopping lists. Students also learn much about print as they observe their teachers writing words and sentences on classroom writing surfaces.

THE LANGUAGE-EXPERIENCE APPROACH (LEA)

An effective method for teaching students about print conventions and jargon is the language-experience approach (LEA) (Nelson & Linek, 1999; Stauffer, 1970). LEA allows students to focus their full attention on print conventions because they are learning to read words that are very familiar to them, words they have generated themselves. LEA consists of the following basic steps:

1. Students dictate to the teacher an account of an event or topic that is important to them.
2. As the students watch, the teacher writes their dictated sentences on a piece of chart paper and points out features of the letters and words.
3. The teacher teaches the students to read the LEA chart by reading it aloud *to them*, reading it *with them* aloud in unison, and then having *the students read it* aloud on their own.
4. After reading the LEA chart, the teacher directs the students in follow-up activities that focus their attention on print conventions along with beginning decoding concepts.

The following vignette illustrates an LEA lesson. Notice the high level of student motivation as they learn about print conventions while generating and reading meaningful text.

Six kindergarten and first-grade students, who were enrolled in a special summer program for rural, low-income, at-risk students, chattered excitedly after their morning field trip to a nearby sheep ranch. Their teacher, Robyn, guided them in a discussion about the trip, then suggested (as if this were a spontaneous idea), "Hey, let's write a story about our trip to the sheep ranch." The students thought this was a great idea.

Robyn then asked, "How should we begin?" The students eagerly contributed sentences about their field trip as Robyn wrote them on a piece of chart paper.

The Sheep Ranch

We went to the sheep ranch. (Donyell)

The sheep like to "Baaaa." (Shanika)

The sheep like to eat. (Michael)

A literacy learner matches a sentence strip to a language experience chart.

Steven Von Niederhausern

The sheep like to run. (Devon)

The sheep like to play. (Jesse)

The sheep like to sleep. (Vince)

The students watched and listened as Robyn pointed out features of the letters, words, and sentences as she wrote. "Let's count the words on this first line," Robyn says as she ensures that her students are watching as they count words together. Next Robyn moves on to helping her students count letters within words. As she continues writing the students' dictated sentences, Robyn brings her students' attention to capital letters and periods.

After each of her students has contributed a sentence, Robyn reads the LEA chart back to them, then several times with them aloud in unison. Next Robyn has the students read the sheep ranch story back to her as she points to the words.

Robyn spent the remainder of the week rereading the LEA chart with her students, counting words and sentences, matching sentence strips and word cards to the original chart, studying spelling patterns in the words, and playing a variety of games with the words from the chart. Each of her students also illustrated a personal edition of the sheep ranch story. On Friday, all of Robyn's students were thrilled to take home a book about the class trip to the sheep ranch that they could read successfully to their families.

Generating an LEA Chart

For beginning readers, LEA stories can be only one to two sentences long. Teachers may also want to use a "patterned LEA" format in which the students' dictated sentences repeat a pattern such as:

> *I like to eat pizza.*
> *I like to eat apples.*
> *I like to eat spaghetti.*
> *I like to eat peanut butter.*
> *I like to eat grapes.*

Most LEA charts are between five and eight sentences long. Charts that get much longer may overload students' ability to learn to read the chart quickly. Teachers should read aloud each sentence as it is being written, pointing to the words, left-to-right, then inviting the students to read along.

After the LEA chart is finished, teachers should read the completed chart aloud to the students, then with the students in unison. As the teacher points to the words and continues to provide support, the students read the chart aloud on their own.

FOR ENGLISH LANGUAGE LEARNERS

Formal and Informal Language Development

An effective teacher of English language learners will give students plenty of opportunities to develop their language skill through informal means such as peer discussion, instructional conversations, and small-group cooperative learning activities. But because academic language takes longer to develop and has specialized syntax and vocabulary, formal instruction in the English language is also necessary (Dutro & Moran, 2003).

Students collaborate to reconstruct a sentence from a language experience chart.

Steven Von Niederhausern

The following LEA story examples show the variety of styles and topics that LEA stories can take.

Our Walk (Tiffany)

On our walk, we saw dandelions.
We saw tulips.
We saw a robin and his home.
We saw violets.
We saw ants.
We saw blossoms.
We saw a prickly bush that scratches.
We saw rocks.
We saw a spider.

Soccer (Michael)

Today I played a game of soccer. It was so much fun. And they were very good. But, I must admit that we won instead of them. During the last part of the game, I was goalie, that was my favorite part. This time we wore blue uniforms. Sometimes we wear yellow. Soccer is my favorite game.

The Garden (Marci)

Planting a garden is hard work.
We tilled the dirt.
We put manure on it.
We made signs.
We planted the seeds.
We gave the seeds water.
It was hard work, but it was fun.

The Butterfly (Justin)

A butterfly was born in time for summer. It was red and green and purple—really pretty. The butterfly wanted to have babies so it laid eggs. It is sad but the butterfly died on the front of someone's car.

LEA Follow-Up Activities

The second part of an LEA lesson is using the LEA chart to focus on print conventions and selected reading skills. Sentence strip matching is a popular LEA follow-up activity. The teacher copies each LEA chart sentence onto a sentence strip. He or she introduces the sentence strips to the students by showing one of the strips, reading it aloud, then showing the students how it corresponds to one of the sentences on the LEA chart. The students take turns matching the sentence strips to the sentences on the chart paper. Afterward, pairs of students can reconstruct the entire chart with the sentence strips.

A next step is to use individual word cards from the LEA chart. Teachers can give students a word card and ask them to match the card to the corresponding word on the LEA chart.

Another activity is to distribute the word cards from an LEA sentence to a group of students. The students stand in mixed-up order in front of their classmates, displaying the word cards. Then the students must rearrange themselves in the proper sequence to reconstruct the sentence. Cunningham (2004) calls this activity "Being the Words."

Teachers can construct a set of word cards representing all of the words on the LEA chart. Then the students work in pairs to spread the word cards out on the floor and reconstruct the entire LEA chart, word-by-word.

The highlight of LEA is having each student make and illustrate a personal "book" from the text of the LEA chart. The teacher gives each student a typed copy of the LEA text, along with a construction paper book. Students cut apart the sentences from their copy of the text, paste them into the book, and add illustrations. When finished, the students read their books to the teacher and to each other.

FOR ENGLISH LANGUAGE LEARNERS

Meaningful Learning

ELL students learn best when they are engaged in activities that have personal meaning and purpose for them. When lessons are related to solving a real problem in their lives, in or out of school, ELL students (and native English users) will be more engaged, try harder, and use language in more sophisticated ways (Freeman & Freeman, 1998).

CONCLUDING THOUGHTS

Many first-grade teachers begin the school year by jumping right into formal reading instruction. Many of their students succeed. Many of them struggle. Some fail. Why do some students have a harder time learning to read and write than others?

Some teachers blame their students' struggles on the students' lack of innate ability or perhaps a developmental delay. The fact that many teachers place students in "ability groups" suggests that we tend to think of our students in terms of their IQ.

Adams (1990) has helped many professional educators change this type of thinking by associating their young students' academic performance with their level of preparedness, rather than their level of intelligence. Morris (1999) likens learning to read to running a race. Some students, through no fault of their own, begin the race far behind the other racers. Other students begin the reading race well prepared, at a distinct advantage. This focus on preparedness places more responsibility on teachers to ensure that students, especially at-risk students, possess the literacy foundations needed for success in formal reading and writing instruction.

SUGGESTED ACTIVITIES TO EXTEND YOUR LEARNING

1. Begin an oral language activities file. Collect songs, poems, tongue twisters, jokes, riddles, jump-rope rhymes, and stories that will help children delight in and develop oral language. You and your education classmates could share copies of these to further expand your file.
2. Find a beginning reader in your family or neighborhood and do some phonemic awareness activities together. Try to determine how well the child can hear speech sounds and blend them together to form spoken words.
3. Find a beginning reader in your family or neighborhood and do a language-experience lesson together. Go for a walk, bake cookies, or do some other fun

activity and then follow the steps outlined in this chapter to help the child generate a brief "story" about the experience. Help the child learn to read the story and do some follow-up teaching.

 *REFERENCES*

Adams, M. J. (1990). *Beginning to read: Thinking and learning about print*. Cambridge, MA: MIT Press.

Adams, M. J., Foorman, B. R., Lundberg, I., & Beeler, T. (1998). *Phonemic awareness in young children: A classroom curriculum*. Baltimore: Brookes.

Bradley, B. A., & Jones, J. (2007). Sharing alphabet books in early childhood classrooms. *The Reading Teacher, 60*(5), 452–463.

Bryant, P. E., Bradley, L., Maclean, M., & Crossland, J. (1989). Nursery rhymes, phonological skills, and reading. *Journal of Child Language, 16*, 407–428.

Christie, J., Enz, B., & Vukelich, C. (1997). *Teaching language and literacy: Preschool through the elementary grades.* New York: Addison-Wesley Longman.

Cooper, J. L., & Dever, M. T. (2001). Sociodramatic play as a vehicle for curriculum integration in first grade. *Young Children, 56*(3), 58–63.

Cunningham, P. M. (2004). *Phonics they use: Words for reading and writing* (4th ed.). New York: Longman.

De Regniers, B. S., Moore, E., White M. M. & Carr, J. (1988). *Sing a song of popcorn*. New York: Scholastic.

Dickinson, D. K., & Neuman, S. B. (2006). *Handbook of early literacy research* (2nd ed.). New York: Guilford Press.

Dutro, S., & Moran, C. (2003). Rethinking English language instruction: An architectural approach. In Garcia, G.G. (Ed.) *English learners: Reaching the highest level of level of English literacy*. Newark, DE: International Reading Association.

Freeman, D. E. & Freeman Y. S. (2004). *Essential linguistics: What you need to know to teach reading, ESL, spelling, phonics, and grammar.* Portsmouth, NH: Heinemann.

Gill, S. R. (2007). The forgotten genre of children's poetry. *The Reading Teacher, 60*(7), 622–625.

Hart, B., & Risley, T. R. (1995). *Meaningful differences in the everyday experiences of young American children*. Baltimore: Brookes.

Harwayne, S. (1992). *Lasting impressions*. Portsmouth, NH: Heinemann.

Juel, C., Griffith, P. L., & Gough, P. B. (1986). Acquisition of literacy: A longitudinal study of children in first and second grade. *Journal of Educational Psychology, 78*, 243–255.

Justice, L. M., & Pullen, P. C. (2003). Promising interventions for promoting emergent literacy skills: Three evidence-based approaches. *Topics in Early Childhood Special Education, 23*(3), 99–113.

Lomax, A. (1960). Folk songs of North America. Garden City, NY: Doubleday.

Maclean, M. (1987). Rhymes, nursery rhymes, and reading in early childhood. *Merrill-Palmer Quarterly, 33*(3), 255–281.

Morris, D. (1999). *The Howard Street tutoring manual: Teaching at-risk readers in the primary grades*. New York: Guilford Press.

National Reading Panel. (2000). *Teaching children to read: An evidence-based assessment of the scientific research literature on reading and its implications for reading instruction.*

Report of the subgroups. National Institute of Child Health and Human Development. Retrieved from http://www.nichd.nih.gov/publications/nrp/smallbook.cfm

Nelson, O. G., & Linek, W. M. (1999). *Practical classroom applications of language experience: Looking back, looking forward.* Boston: Allyn & Bacon.

Parr, M., & Campbell, T. (2006). Poets in practice. *The Reading Teacher, 60*(1), 36-46.

Pica, T., Young, R., & Doughty, C. (1987). The impact of interaction on comprehension. *TESOL Quarterly, 21, 4,* 737-758.

Pullen, P. C., & Justice, L. M. (2003). Enhancing phonological awareness, print awareness, and oral language skills in preschool children. *Intervention in School and Clinic, 39*(2), 87-98.

Reading, S., & Van Deuren, D. (2007). Phonemic awareness: When and how much to teach? *Reading Research and Instruction, 46*(3), 267-286.

Sekeres, D. C., & Gregg, M. (2007). Poetry in third grade: Getting started. *The Reading Teacher, 60*(5), 466-475.

Smith, J. A. (2000). Singing and songwriting support early literacy instruction. *The Reading Teacher, 53*(8), 646-649.

Stauffer, R. (1970). *The language-experience approach to teaching reading.* New York: Harper and Row.

Strickland, D. S., & Shanahan, T. (2004). Laying the groundwork for literacy. *Educational Leadership, 61*(6), 74-77.

Reading Aloud to Children

by Sylvia Read

4

Interactive Read-Aloud

Kessie: *What's this book called?*

Teacher: Julius, the Baby of the World.

Oscar: *Is it a funny book? It looks funny.*

Teacher: *Right away people are noticing this book is different from the other ones that I have read. What is different about it? Becca?*

Becca: *It's fiction.*

Teacher: *It's fiction. How can you tell?*

Becca: *Because there is no such thing as mice in clothes.*

Teacher: *Oh. So right away you can tell it is fiction because there is no such thing as mice who dress up like that. So that makes it fiction.*

The teacher begins to read aloud, stopping to discuss the events in the story when the students have questions or when she senses that they need guidance to understand what's going on. At one point the book reads, "Lilly had glorious dreams about Julius." The teacher stops to point out important information in the illustrations.

Teacher: *This is her sleeping, and this right here is her dreaming. What is happening in her dream?*

Kessie: *She is a queen.*

Teacher: *What else is happening? Michael?*

Michael: *She is a queen and she is very mean to Julius and the cat is trying to eat him.*

Teacher: *She is trying to eat him or something. Pretty scary-looking cat, huh? Sarah, do you want to add anything to that?*

Sarah: *She is chasing him because she is the wicked queen and the cat is going to obey her. And then Julius is in his pajamas and can't move fast so she is going to kill him because the cat is going to eat him.*

Teacher: *Oh. So why is this called a glorious dream? Whom is it glorious to? To Lilly, but it is not glorious to Julius, is it? Here is another dream. The book says, "And ghastly nightmares, too." So here is Lilly dreaming and this is her nightmare.*

Students: *Oh!*

Teacher: *So why is that a nightmare? What is happening in that dream? Will?*

Will: *Um, that he is trying to be a baby and eat her because she is a baby.*

Teacher: *Yeah. That's a pretty bad nightmare, huh?*

Will: *Uh huh. And he has big teeth.*

Teacher: *Yes. Julius has big, sharp teeth. Anna, what do you think?*

Anna: *It is the other way around from the other dream because she was big with sharp teeth and a kitty, and now Julius is big like the kitty with sharp teeth and she is little like a mouse.*

Teacher: *She is small and weak in this one, right? And in this one, Julius is small and weak. So what you're saying is these are the opposite of each other.*

Anna: *Yep.*

Reading aloud to students has been described as "the single most important activity for building the knowledge required for eventual success in reading" (Anderson, Hiebert, Scott, & Wilkinson, 1985, p. 23). Reading aloud increases student vocabulary and background knowledge, improves reading comprehension, and develops students' positive attitude toward reading (Lane & Wright, 2007; McGee & Schickedanz, 2007). Reading aloud to students relieves them of the decoding work for a while, allowing them to focus on meaning.

This chapter focuses on reading aloud for enjoyment and ways to make reading aloud to children a flexible and effective instructional strategy. Specifically, it discusses:

- Purposes for reading aloud
- Teaching children to respond to literature
- Reading aloud to teach comprehension
- Comprehension strategy instruction
- Types of texts to read aloud

Ms. Hsu reads aloud *Click, Clack, Moo* and then asks the students to respond to it.

Sylvia Read

PURPOSES FOR READING ALOUD

Effective teachers set aside at least two times a day for reading aloud, and many find more opportunities throughout the day. Interactive read-aloud, which is an instructional conversation about a book, helps support students' acquisition of comprehension skills and strategies, and can be especially important for introducing young children to informational books (Smolkin & Donovan, 2001). Reading aloud can also be an effective way to help students develop social skills (Doyle & Bramwell, 2006). The goals of read-aloud are to develop student enjoyment, elicit response, and foster comprehension and vocabulary development.

ENJOYMENT

Enjoyment is the most immediate purpose for reading aloud. According to Trelease, author of *The New Read-Aloud Handbook* (2003), a child's desire is the key ingredient for real success in reading. He argues that too often we teach children *how* to read but forget to teach them to *want* to read. However, when we read aloud to a child, we're sending a "pleasure message" to the child's brain (one we hope will be as strong as what they get from video games and TV). We could even say we're conditioning the child to associate books and print with pleasure (Trelease, 2003, pp. 7, 9). Thus, as teachers read aloud to students in the classroom, our first purpose is to lead them to enjoy books and enjoy being read to. It's a simple point, but a fundamental one: To hear a book read aloud is enjoyable for children (and adults), and pleasure is absolutely crucial for fostering lifelong readers.

Although teachers often read aloud books that are somewhat beyond what the students can read independently, it is important to also read aloud books that are within their independent reading range. Students will naturally want to read for themselves the books we read aloud to the class, and by encouraging this natural impulse, we can help them warm up their reading muscles.

Creating the Moment

Calkins (2001) points out that sometimes "children consider the read-aloud as a time to doze, dream, fiddle, and snack" (p. 63). I want my students to take teacher read-alouds seriously, so I prefer to have my students sitting on the floor, gathered together in our meeting area. If I'm reading a novel, I invite them to close their eyes, not only to encourage them to ignore the possibly distracting behaviors of other students, but also to give them that movie screen in their minds on which they can play their vision of the book. I make this idea explicit at certain moments: "Are you making a picture of this in your mind? Can you see it? Can you hear it? Can you taste it, smell it, feel it?" Later in the day, when they're reading independently, I remind them that they can be making movies in their heads.

Young children need to hear novels such as *The Tale of Despereaux, Tales of a Fourth Grade Nothing*, and *Ramona the Brave* read aloud. Teachers should also read and reread favorite picture books such as *Julius, the Baby of the World*. Poetry, both silly and serious, should be part of the read-aloud diet, along with informational books, magazines, newspaper articles, textbooks, dictionaries, and encyclopedias. Students' and teacher's writing also deserves to be read aloud, pondered, and honored, along with the writing of professional authors.

Teachers need to take their time with the read-aloud; depth of reading is more important than breadth. As teachers, we need to read not with the goal of finishing a book, but with our full attention on the moment of the story, wherever it is. Students can better hear and savor the language and the rhythm when we slow down a bit. With picture books, we often read "sideways" so that students can see the illustrations. But with the book in our lap, we can read slowly, dramatically, and with gestures. Then we can turn the book and show the illustrations. Text talk, discussed later in this chapter, is a strategy in which the illustrations in a picture book are not shown until after the text on a particular page has been read. We may read fewer books this way, but the experience will be richer, deeper, and more memorable.

RESPONSE

Pleasure is fundamental, but important learning opportunities would be wasted if reading aloud didn't have instructional value, too. So we also use the read-aloud time to encourage and develop our students' responses to literature. Personal response is an important strategy used by proficient readers to make meaning from what they read. Our students need to talk to us and to each other about books.

Students need to understand that readers' responses to stories are unique, that their individual interpretation of a passage may differ from that of their classmates. We should encourage them to make connections to events in their own lives, to other books they've read or heard, to events of the world, to things they've learned from watching TV or movies. Why is personal response important? Research is clear that we comprehend texts more easily when we connect what we hear to something we know, feel, understand, or believe already. We learn by building new knowledge onto *schema* for knowledge that we already have (Anderson & Pearson, 1984). Although K–3 students are newcomers to the academic world, they have a wealth of personal experience, and when we encourage their personal response to read-alouds, we help them connect what they hear to their own schema. Through read-aloud discussions we can add to students' background knowledge and vocabulary. We can draw, discuss, or explain words and concepts that will be new to them. Our students have a network of words and ideas already in their heads; we add to that network every time we read and discuss books.

We want them to experience a wide variety of genres (historical fiction, biography, poetry), but to build background knowledge, we especially need to read aloud informational texts. Also, students will be reading and writing informational texts extensively as they move up through the grades and into "real life" and informational texts predominate in many school and work settings.

Encouraging Personal Response

Of course, there are useful responses and not so useful ones. We can teach students to ask key questions of the text, of the author, of the other listeners.

Why do you think Fudge swallowed Peter's turtle?
What do you think about how Peter's mom reacted?

We can teach them to find the most relevant connections to their own lives by searching their own experience.

When have you experienced adults apologizing to you and admitting they were wrong?

How do you think Fudge is feeling in the hospital? What do you think of Peter worrying about the turtle instead of his brother? How would you react?

Asking students about their favorite parts of stories helps to develop their evaluative skills. My students often finish a book and begin to reread it immediately—though not necessarily the whole book. Usually, they tell me, they're going back to reread the parts they liked best.

The talk can happen as a whole group with everyone listening as one child makes a comment or it can happen through a think-pair-share (Lyman, 1981) where students think about what they have just heard, pair up, and share those thoughts with a partner.

COMPREHENSION AND VOCABULARY DEVELOPMENT

Finally, we read aloud to teach students comprehension strategies and build their vocabulary. The research on proficient readers (Pearson, Dole, Duffy, & Roehler, 1992) suggests that we teach comprehension through a focus on making connections, questioning, visualizing and inferring, determining importance, and synthesizing. *Reciprocal teaching* (Palincsar & Brown, 1984)—a proven strategy for building comprehension—focuses on predicting, clarifying, questioning, and summarizing. The National Reading Panel's report (NRP, 2000) concluded that the use of graphic organizers in content-area reading, vocabulary instruction, questioning, and summarizing are effective comprehension strategies. We teach and model all of these strategies when we read books aloud to and discuss books with our students.

As we read aloud, we need to keep in mind these important purposes: enjoyment, response, and comprehension and vocabulary development. We will discuss them in more detail in the rest of this chapter. Although this chapter treats them separately, remember that these purposes are not discrete. In the daily give and take of a classroom, they overlap constantly. We should allow them to blur and cooperate, as we discover ways to apply them flexibly with the particular needs of our current students in mind.

 ## TEACHING CHILDREN TO RESPOND TO LITERATURE

Readers respond to books very differently. Reader reviews of books on Amazon.com demonstrate this well. For example, some readers of *My Heart Is On the Ground: The Diary of Nannie Little Rose, A Sioux Girl* by Ann Rinaldi found that they learned a lot about American Indian culture, and that it was sad, but beautifully written. Others found it an offensive and inaccurate portrait of an important part of Native American history. These readers read the same book, but they came to it with different background knowledge and different attitudes and, ultimately, came away from the book with widely different experiences of it.

Louise Rosenblatt, one of the first literature scholars to study the importance of reader response to literature, discusses reading in terms of a transaction involving the reader, the text, and the reader's experience of the text (1936/1978). According to reader-response theory, in a sense the literary work doesn't really exist until it's experienced in the mind of the reader. This is how reader-response theory explains why one reader's understanding of a text can be different from every other reader's understanding of the same text. Many of us have experienced the traditional kind of literature teaching in which there is one correct interpretation, one that is supposed to be right there in the text, if only you read it carefully enough. We may have had to face literal, inferential, and even evaluative questions for which there were predetermined answers, and it was our job to figure out these "right" answers. Reader-response theory has, in many ways, liberated the experience of literature so that each person's personal response to a text has legitimacy. That doesn't mean we aren't accountable to the text, but it is acceptable to have divergent responses.

Responding with Feelings

Teachers need to encourage children to respond to texts authentically, so that they can understand how their reactions differ from their peers' and how they are similar. When reading a work of fiction, for example, one child might focus on the characters whereas another might focus on the action and not even remember characters' names. Children need to learn that many different responses to the same book are valid.

In addition, we want children to try to understand why they respond to texts the way they do. What is it in their own experience that makes them respond a certain way? What is the source of the feelings that a book may draw from them? We also want them to learn about themselves as they listen to stories. They learn vicariously through events in characters' lives. They will identify with certain characters and not with others. We say to ourselves, "Oh yes, I remember how hard it was for me when I did that" or "I hope I can be more understanding if I ever go through that experience." We want our students to feel free to respond this way too. We stifle their natural responses, however, when we ask questions to which we already know the answers. We need to ask authentic open-ended questions such as:

What do you think of this character?

What would you do if you were that person?

What do you think will happen next?

What were you thinking when . . . ?

How did you feel when . . . ?

Responses may also be as simple as laughing, gasping, groaning ("Oh no . . ."), sitting up straighter and widening your eyes, making wondering noises ("Hmmm . . ."), snorting in disbelief or disgust, or applauding. I have often found that when children are talking as I read aloud, they're talking about the book. I ask them to share what they're saying, without making them feel guilty for talking. These are often the most honest responses because they're spontaneous.

Teachers can ask children to respond in other ways, too, such as through writing, drawing, dramatizing, and so on. For some books and some children, these activities work well. But having an extension activity for every book is unnecessary because then we promote the idea that a book is always followed by an assignment of

Sylvia Read

Miss Cook asked the students for their personal responses after reading *Owl Moon*.

some sort. Also, it seems that many extension activities take longer than reading the book itself. If we fill up our time with puppet making, we steal that time from reading. Writing in response to reading takes less time, but because writing can be laborious for primary-grade students, it can kill the love of reading and should be used judiciously. Even at age 99, my grandfather reads voraciously. He keeps track of what he has read on index cards by recording the title, author, summary, and short critique of each book. He admits, "Some of them are really short. I'm anxious to get it written so I can start reading the next book." And isn't that the most natural response to reading a good book? We want to read another one!

RESPONDING WITH CONNECTIONS

As we read aloud, our students will make connections between what we're reading to them and their own lives, other books, poems, movies, television shows, and what they already know about the author or the topic. Keene and Zimmerman's book *Mosaic of Thought* (2007) introduces the idea of explicitly teaching students about text-to-text, text-to-self, and text-to-world connections.

Schema theory suggests that these connections are very important. Our schema, simply, is everything we know about the world and how we cluster that knowledge into a network of related ideas. When we read, we rely on that knowledge to make sense of the text.

Teachers can model the way to make connections while reading aloud. We can invite students to voice their connections, but we need to make sure they can explain what part of the text they've connected with and why. This is sometimes called *accountable talk*:

> Accountable talk is not empty chatter; it seriously responds to and further develops what others in the group have to say. Students introduce and ask for knowledge that is accurate and relevant to the text under discussion. They use evidence from the text in ways that are appropriate and follow established norms of good reasoning. (New Standards Primary Literacy Committee, 1999, p. 25)

When I read aloud to my students, they often make connections with other books they've read or heard. When we were previewing the cover of *Duncan and Dolores*, Regina noticed that Dolores was pushing Duncan around in a stroller and it reminded her of *Charlotte's Web* when Fern pushes Wilber around in a stroller. Also, when I was reading aloud *A River Ran Wild*, I emphasized how the White people took over the Indians' land. Brock pointed out, "That's kinda like Stonefox because Stonefox got kicked off his land in Wyoming."

In the classroom we like to read aloud lots of folktales. We read a few and then begin to make connections. "Hmm. . . . Three wishes. I've noticed that things tend to happen in threes in folktales. Three bears. Three billy goats. Three pigs." The children began noticing threes in subsequent stories, especially European folktales. (Four is the magic number for some cultures.)

The connections that children make with their own lives can be the most powerful for cementing the love of reading, for when we see ourselves in a story, the story is all the more meaningful and memorable. When I read aloud *Tales of a Fourth Grade Nothing* to my group of second graders they connected with Peter more than Fudge. When Peter's mother gets angry at him after Fudge swallows Peter's turtle, she later apologizes. I stopped to ask the students if an adult had ever apologized to them before. Many had stories; some had never had that experience. Much later in the year, at the end of a rough day during which I had been crabby with the students, I apologized to them for my behavior. We remembered together our discussion of adults saying they were sorry. They were quick to forgive me, just as Peter forgave his mother. *Tales of a Fourth Grade Nothing* also allowed the students to reminisce about their own hospital experiences, bad accidents, and difficulties with siblings.

RESPONDING WITH QUESTIONS

Teaching our students to generate questions during reading is perhaps the most effective means of raising their level of comprehension. It is our curiosity about a story or topic that propels us forward as we read; voicing that curiosity as questions during a read-aloud lets students explore the possibilities of meaning. However, framing a question about what they read—and framing a meaningful one—is something that primary-grade students have to learn. Effective teachers find moments to model questioning for their students.

Young students may not feel that having a question is appropriate. Teachers often seem to have all the answers, and we often ask students inauthentic questions, ones to which we already know the answer. There may sometimes be good reasons for this, but when we model questioning as a response to literature for students, we must ask real questions, questions that we truly wonder about. Some of these questions may be factual; for example, they may have concrete answers in the text we're reading. But others may remain in the realm of speculation. We want our students to ask both kinds of questions, but most of all, we want them to know that having questions about a text is a good thing, that it means we're interested in what we're reading, and that we're learning.

With younger students, we have to teach the difference between a question and a statement or comment. We might find ourselves saying, "You're telling us something; you're not quite asking a question. Sometimes questions begin with *who, what, where, why*, or *when*. Other times they begin with "I wonder . . ."

Inevitably, students will try to begin a statement with *when* and think that they've created a question. For example, Ryan said, "When baby chicks are born, they stay in the nest and tweet." He was sure this was a question because it began with *when*! I explained by saying, "You are telling us something. If you say, 'When do we go to lunch?' that's a question. If you say, 'When we go to lunch, we always wash our hands,' that is not a question, even though it starts with the word *when*. With questions, you need to be asking something, not telling."

We need to model for our students the kinds of questions that clarify meaning, the kinds of questions that cause them to wonder about the puzzling parts of books. For example, when reading *Make Way for Ducklings,* we might wonder aloud about duck behavior. "How do baby ducks know about staying in line? And how do they know what to do when they dive for food?" Students might wonder how Mrs. Mallard would know when to meet Mr. Mallard in the park.

Students Ask Authentic Questions

When reading How Animals Care for Their Babies, *I invited the students to focus on questions that came up in their minds. I read, "Some animals, like these monkeys, live together in large groups. Grownups and older brothers and sisters often share the job of protecting the babies."*

Shannon asked, "Why do the brothers and sisters have to guard the babies and not the mom and dad?" Shannon's question is particularly good because it develops directly from the text. "Many creatures make nests for their babies," I continued. "Are those rabbits?" asked Jaren, genuinely curious, and anticipating what comes next. I read on:

"[T]here are many nests you can't see. . . . A European rabbit collects grass for her underground nest. The grass makes a soft bed for her babies."

Students' questions also often refer to the illustrations. "The Northern Flicker, a woodpecker, makes its nest inside a tree," I read. Brock wondered, "Is that a male or a female woodpecker [in the picture]?" This is fine, but when reading and writing is our instructional purpose, we want them to focus primarily on the ideas and words. Sometimes I deliberately don't show the pictures when I read aloud so that the students have to think about the words they hear.

My students and I discuss the possible answers to their questions and, whenever possible, I help them look back to the text for the answer. I will say, "Sometimes we can figure out the answer by reading it again. Sometimes we can figure out the answer by looking at the pictures. And sometimes, we can't figure out the answers, and that's okay." I try not to set myself up as the keeper of all knowledge. It's okay to say, "I don't know. Where could we find out the answer?" Sometimes another student is the expert—such as when Bethany was able to explain to Evan why male birds are more colorful than female birds. When we can't find the answer, I suggest that we just don't have enough information, but invite the students to speculate or discuss ways they could go about finding the answer. Most of all, it's important to have the students think of themselves as flexible meaning-makers.

Students' questions will generate more questions. As they hear each other's thoughts, new questions will often arise in their minds. That's the beauty of using the read-aloud for teaching questioning—everyone gets to hear everyone else's questions.

RESPONDING WITH FAVORITE PARTS

When teachers ask students after a read-aloud to tell what their favorite parts were, we are fostering their critical or evaluative levels of thinking. First of all, we're asking them to *have* a favorite part—that is, to evaluate the story. Second, we want them to be able to explain *why* it was their favorite. Younger children often say they "liked it all" and explain their favorite part by saying "it was funny." This is a great reason, of course, especially if they can explain why it was funny. But through modeling, we can show them how to go beyond that. These second-grade children responded to *Ox-Cart Man* by Donald Hall by telling about their favorite parts:

- I like the part where it tells the details about what he bought.
- I like the part when he sold the cow and all the things because he was making more money for his family and how he gave the presents to his kids.
- I like the maple tree part—how they made the maple honey.
- I like the part where he sells his cow because I think that would be hard.
- I like the part where it told how long it took him to get there.
- I like the part where he kisses his ox on the nose because it reminds me of how my brother and sister sometimes kiss my dog and cats on the nose.

When they responded to *Rumpelstiltskin*, Emma said, "I like the last page where it says, 'The devil told you that. The devil told you that,' but the maid actually spied on him and he looks all grumpy on that page and he's like, oh you know my name! How could you find that out?" Dakota liked it when "she teased him because then he wouldn't be exactly sure that she knew it and because if she said it first then he would know that someone told her."

Because teachers also want students to be able to discuss a book's use of language, we can combine purposes and ask the students to find their favorite sentence or a powerful sentence. This encourages them to begin thinking about writing in terms of its style or craft.

Modeling Response

Before reading aloud Taro Yashima's picture book Crow Boy, *Mrs. Gonzales started four columns on the whiteboard: Feelings, Connections, Questions, and Favorite Parts. She then explained:*

> Feelings *means how the book makes you feel as you listen to it.* "I feel happy because. . . ." I feel angry because. . . . "I feel anxious because. . . ."
>
> Connections *means what the book reminds you of. Connections can be to your own life, to other books, or to things in the world.* "This part reminds me of something that happened to me. . . ." "This part reminds me of something I saw on the news. . . ." "This part reminds me of another book I read. . . ."
>
> Questions *are about parts of the book that make you curious.* "Why did the character do that?" "What is a moat?" "Why did the author make the book end that way?"
>
> Favorite Parts *could be your favorite events from the book, favorite characters, or your favorite snippets of the author's writing. I sometimes call these power sentences.*

Mrs. Gonzales read Crow Boy *aloud in its entirety and then went back to the whiteboard and modeled her own responses, connections, questions, and favorite parts. For example, she said, "I felt angry during the first part of the book because of how Crow Boy was treated by his classmates and teachers. I also felt happy at the end when the townspeople recognized and applauded his wonderful talent." She wrote these comments on the board in the Feelings column. Then she asked the students for their responses and wrote these on the board under her own responses.*

Moving to the Connections column, Mrs. Coonzales told the students the true story of Mark, a student in one of her elementary school classes years ago who had trouble getting along with others and, consequently, had no friends. She described her repeated attempts to help Mark make friends rather than antagonize his classmates—to no avail. She wrote the words "Mark, no friends" in the Connections column and asked students for their own connections to Crow Boy. *She repeated this modeling and eliciting process for Questions and Favorite Parts.*

It is important to realize that just one modeling lesson will not be enough to ensure that students understand how to respond to literature or that they will incorporate this into their own listening. You may need as many as half a dozen such lessons with brief powerful books. Students respond strongly to books such as *Alexander and the Terrible, Horrible, No Good, Very Bad Day,* by Judith Viorst; *Too Many Tamales*, by Gary Soto; *Amazing Grace*, by Mary Hoffman; *My Rotten Redheaded Older Brother*, by Patricia Polacco; *Marianthe's Story*, by Aliki; and *Chester's Way*, by Kevin Henkes.

 ## READING ALOUD TO TEACH COMPREHENSION

In the early grades, when students are reading texts to themselves or in a small-group lesson, the focus of the instruction is often decoding. But even young children need to begin thinking about books as something to be understood, not just words to be said. Reading aloud to young children gives teachers a perfect opportunity to teach comprehension. The teacher is doing the decoding work, so all students can participate in meaning making. You can read aloud books that are more difficult than what students could read for themselves, which will allow you to read books that have meaty issues to discuss, puzzles to ponder, characters to analyze.

BUILDING BACKGROUND KNOWLEDGE

Even if teachers never stopped to discuss and wonder about what has been read aloud, students would still benefit. Of course, we should stop and discuss texts as we read aloud, but the reading aloud itself will develop students' background knowledge like nothing else can. Think about it. No one alive today has ever seen a live wooly mammoth, but we know about them because we've read about them. We know about many things we will never see—black holes, the mantle of the earth, the passenger pigeon—because we have read about them. We can give this kind of content knowledge to our students too, by reading aloud to them.

The discussions about texts before, during, and after read-alouds can increase students' background knowledge in important ways. Students learn from each other as they interact in partners, small groups, or as a whole class. When reading aloud a book about snakes, for example, one student may be able to explain to the whole class how a snake unhooks its jaws in order to eat food larger than its head. As adults, we can quickly explain the meanings of words such as *reeds* or *rushes*, discuss why the author used those words instead of *grass*, and thus enlarge our students' background knowledge and vocabulary about swamps or marshes.

Developing Content Schema

As we read aloud books, we can often provide a student's very first encounter with a concept such as "black hole," but they probably already have a concept of "star" or "stuff in space." As we read aloud to them, they attach this new idea to their existing schema for space and all things associated with space. Rumelhart (1980) calls this *accretion*. Students may have a concept of mammal that includes dogs, cats, and bears, but when we read aloud a book about whales and learn that whales also are mammals because they give birth to live babies and nurse their offspring, students experience what Rumelhart calls *tuning* as their schema for mammal alters given this new information. Less often, people's schemas are restructured. For children, this happens when they learn that spiders are not insects. Acceptance of this idea requires that learners' schemas are dramatically rearranged.

We don't build students' background knowledge from nothing—they are not blank slates. They come to us knowing a little bit about a lot of things. Our job is to capitalize on the connections they make and build from their background knowledge through those connections.

Readers take their existing knowledge or schema and put it together with new information encountered in a text to construct meaning from the text. The meaning does not reside solely within the text nor is meaning totally formed by the reader (Pearson & Stephens, 1998). Students may not naturally draw on their prior knowledge, which is why we must teach students to consciously activate their prior knowledge by asking questions such as "What do you already know about how spiders are born?" before reading aloud a book about the life cycle of spiders. Modeling and practicing this through read-aloud sessions gives children the opportunity to see how powerful the strategy can be for enhancing their understanding and enjoyment of a text. When a student is actively constructing meaning, he or she is becoming a reader in the truest sense of the word.

Developing Genre Schema

Students come to school knowing quite a bit about stories, perhaps because parents and teachers tend to emphasize narrative texts when they read aloud to young children. Stories are wonderful, of course, but K–3

FOR ENGLISH LANGUAGE LEARNERS

ESL Learners and Activating Schema

Maria likes to stop frequently while reading to look at the pictures, point to objects and talk about them, or share a story about her sister that relates to the story. These are important side trips for Maria to take on her journey to becoming a proficient reader. Even simple texts with few words give her opportunities to build vocabulary as we stop to talk about the pictures. When we were reading a book about a boy who was scared to climb down a pole on a jungle gym, she encountered the word *ladder* which she was able to decode but didn't understand. The picture that accompanied the text gave her an efficient way to connect her knowledge of playground equipment and the new word *ladder*. Often second language learners have only phonetic clues to use when figuring out words. Their sense of English syntax may not be developed enough to help them figure out what the word could be and the semantic clues may also be missing. All emergent readers benefit from books where pictures support the text, but English language learners especially need quality texts and illustrations that will help them develop not just their decoding skills, but also develop their sense of natural English syntax and build their vocabulary and storehouse of concepts.

The rest of the classroom library is organized into baskets labeled by author topic.

students also need experience with poetry, nonfiction, folktales, biography, and specific fiction genres such as historical fiction, realistic fiction, and fantasy and science fiction (see Figure 4.1). Through the read-aloud, teachers can introduce the structures and conventions of these genres. When students have a schema for a particular genre, they can recognize it in unfamiliar text, and they can draw on informed expectations for that genre. For example, when reading fairy tales, a subgenre of folktales, students begin to see the important role of magic elements in this genre. When they approach a new text knowing it is a fairy tale, they expect to find magic. Similarly, if they're instructed in other genres, they learn what to expect as they encounter those in the future. Their informed expectations strengthen their understanding of the text.

Each year, as we read aloud a number of folktales and fairy tales, I started a labeled basket with a wide variety of folktales and fairy tales from my own and the school library's collection. When I taught the class about biographies, I added a basket for those. Gradually, as needed, our system for organizing our books became more refined. Though you might begin the year by sorting the books yourself and teaching the students to put the books back where they were found, throughout the year you can teach them how to distinguish genres from each other. Soon, when you check out

Figure 4.1   Some Common Genres and Their Definitions

Folktales: traditional stories that are passed along orally, some of which eventually become part of printed literature

Fantasy and science fiction: imaginative stories that explore an alternate reality

Realistic fiction: plausible stories about people and events that could actually happen

Historical fiction: imaginative stories grounded in the facts of our past

Nonfiction: books of information and fact

Poetry: compressed language, arranged in an interesting form, often with rhythm and rhyme and other techniques to enhance the sound of the language

Biography: tells the story of a person's life and achievements and is embedded in the time and culture of the person

a new stack of books from the school library, the students themselves can decide where the books belong.

Not surprisingly, students often find that certain books could be categorized in more than one way. The *Magic School Bus* volumes, for example, are a blend of fiction and nonfiction. Having noticed this uniqueness for themselves, my students often suggested that they deserve a basket to themselves.

Format Versus Genre

It's useful to distinguish between *genre* and what we might call *format*. A picture book, for example, may contain fiction, nonfiction, an illustrated poem, a song; the picture book format spans the genres. *Owl Moon*, for example, is an award-winning picture book, but its genre is poetry. *Make Way for Ducklings* is also an award-winning picture book, but its genre is fiction, specifically fantasy, because the animals talk. Robert Frost's "Stopping by a Wood on a Snowy Evening" is a poem that has been published in a number of formats, including as a picture book.

Genre refers to the literary structure of the text. Poetry is a genre; so is biography, folktale, novel, and so on. In contrast, *format* is a choice made about the published features in which the text is packaged. The picture book, the chapter book, the "big book," the pop-up book, the CD-ROM, are formats; they are not literary genres.

This is not to say that formats are unimportant; they can be very influential in learning. The picture book format is a unique combination of text and illustration, in which the illustrations either balance or dominate the text. In the best picture books, the text and illustrations fit together so seamlessly that one would be diminished without the other. How the illustrations support the text and how the text elaborates on the illustrations can be usefully discussed with students. For example, *The Tale of Peter Rabbit* (Beatrix Potter) is the quintessential picture book. In one text and picture spread, Mrs. Rabbit is saying to her three daughters and Peter, who is turned away, "Now, my dears, you may go into the field or down the lane, but don't go into Mr. McGregor's garden: your Father had an accident there; he was put in a pie by Mrs. McGregor." The text gives us part of the story, but the fact that Peter is turned away and his eyes are looking away from his mother suggests something about his character that the text doesn't tell us. Without the illustrations, we wouldn't know as much about Peter.

BUILDING VOCABULARY

Language learning, too, is enhanced by the daily classroom read-aloud because children internalize the language patterns they hear even without explicit instruction. In *Tale of Peter Rabbit*, the sparrows "implored him to exert himself." In "Where Go the Boats," Robert Louis Stevenson wrote, "Dark brown is the river, golden is the sand." These are examples of literary language that are generally encountered only in stories and poetry. Exposure to language this highly refined empowers children not only to develop their vocabulary, but to understand how words can be put together in varying ways to make meaning and to make language beautiful.

Young children naturally mimic the language of books. At age 8, my son reported to his grandmother that, while he was trying to feed a prairie dog, it "crept cautiously forward," imitating language he had heard in *Battle for the Castle*, by Elizabeth Winthrop, in which "the cat crept cautiously forward." While standing in a checkout line, I heard an older woman compliment a young boy on his big, beautiful eyes—to which he replied, "the better to see you with." He obviously had experience with the story *Little Red Riding Hood* and had recognized the woman's comment as similar to the language of that story. He responded with more storybook language. You, of course, have your own favorite examples of amazing things children say. This literary language is not the same as the everyday spoken language students hear in conversation. Developing students' background knowledge of literary language not only helps them when they encounter it in all kinds of literary texts, but it also develops their own facility in making meaning through language.

Building Vocabulary While Reading Aloud

Vocabulary is best taught with young children through books that teachers have read aloud, rather than books that students have read independently (Beck, McKeown, & Kucan, 2002). When students are first learning to read, the words they encounter in books they read independently can be quite simple words such as *friend* or *house* because these are the words that are already in students' oral vocabulary, which makes them ideal words for early reading material, but not very useful for building vocabulary. Books that teachers read aloud, however, can be an incredibly rich source of words for vocabulary instruction.

Tier One, Two, and Three Words

One approach to vocabulary instruction is to think of the world of words as having three tiers or levels (Beck et al., 2002). Tier One words are basic words that are used frequently by most children; they don't need to be directly taught. Examples include *clock, baby, nice, jump, ball, up.* Tier Two words are used frequently by *mature language users* and are useful words to know in a variety of situations. Examples are words such as *coincidence, absurd, industrious, fortunate, required, maintain, envious, delighted, forlorn.* They can also be thought of as "general, but sophisticated" words (Beck et al., 2002, p. 19). They are often fairly easy to explain in basic language that most children can understand. Tier Three words are somewhat rare and are usually used only in specific knowledge domains. Examples are *isotope, lathe, peninsula, refinery.* These words are important to understand in informational texts or in stories where they are important to the plot. But if the word is used only once and does not need to be understood to get the meaning of a text, then Tier Three words can go unexplained and untaught.

Read-aloud is a good way to teach Tier Two vocabulary words. The words can be chosen ahead of time from a particular book, but with young children, the teaching of the words should occur after the book has been read aloud. That way, young children have a rich context for understanding the new word. If you choose 3 words per book, and do this with one read-aloud each school day, you will have taught 540 words. (Beck et al. [2002] recommend teaching about 400 words per year.) Figure 4.2 lists some criteria for Tier Two words.

The following excerpt comes from a trickster tale of the Ojibwe people:

> On the shore of Old Meshikee's lake, across the water from his island, lives a whole village of little Shagizenz, or sand crabs. Now, the Shagizenz are industrious little animals, always building something, making something, always busy; not always too smart, however. (Spooner & Taylor, 1996)

Figure 4.2   Some Criteria for Identifying Tier Two Words

Importance and utility: Words that are characteristic of mature language users and appear frequently across a variety of domains

Instructional potential: Words that can be worked with in a variety of ways so that students can build rich representations of them and of their connections to other words and concepts

Conceptual understanding: Words for which students understand the general concept but provide precision and specificity in describing the concept

Source: Beck et al., 2002, p. 19.

Notice how in this passage, *Shagizenz,* the Ojibwe word for sand crabs, is explained. *Industrious* is also explained. But *island* and *village* are not explained. In the story, it's important to understand that Old Meshikee, the trickster turtle, has his own little island where he lives that separates him from the sand crabs, but that doesn't stop them from hearing him play his noisy drum every night. The idea that these sand crabs work as a group, a village, is also important to the story. So *island* and *village* are Tier Two words that would be worth teaching after reading this story aloud.

When teaching the words, it's best to explain their meanings in everyday terminology. For example, you could tell students that an island is land that has water all around it. It can be helpful to ask students to use the word in a sentence: "Hawaii is an island." "I've been to the island in the middle of Salt Lake. It's called Antelope Island."

Text Talk

Text talk (Beck & McKeown, 2001) is a way to help children not only improve their comprehension of texts, but also develop their use of language because it takes advantage of the "sophisticated vocabulary" found in picture books. In order for Text Talk to be effective, the stories should have a series of events and enough complexity so that children can explore and explain ideas. Through open-ended questions, the teacher asks children to talk about ideas rather than recall specific words from the text. For example, using the story *Julius, the Baby of the World,* the teacher might ask, "Why do you think Lilly changed her mind about Julius?" rather than "Who criticized Julius this time?" Using students' initial responses, the teacher forms new questions encouraging students to elaborate on what they've already said.

With Text Talk, the teacher waits to show the pictures until after the students have heard the text and talked about it. Often children respond to the pictures, rather than the text, so in order for them to develop their ability to construct meaning from decontextualized language, it is important to reserve the pictures until after discussing the text. Students' background knowledge is not stressed except when it might be involved in a student's elaboration on an initial response. As with pictures, sometimes students focus too much on their background knowledge when responding to a text and this can distract them from the work of constructing meaning from the text.

Text Talk has a strong vocabulary component: Certain words are targeted for special attention. The words should be somewhat unfamiliar to the children, yet ones they can understand and possibly use in normal conversation. Between two and four words are discussed after the story has been read aloud. The teacher asks the students to bring to mind the word as it was used in the story and then briefly explains its meaning. The students are asked to say the word aloud, to respond to its meaning, or to use the word in a sentence. For example, after explaining the meaning of *reluctant*, from *Corduroy* by Don Freeman, the teacher asks students to verbally finish the sentence: "I might be reluctant to _____." Words taught in this way should be used again and again in order for them to become part of students' vocabularies. The "word wizard" chart can be used to tally how often target words are seen, heard, or used by your students, or the covers of the books read aloud can be displayed on a bulletin board along with the chosen vocabulary words. When opportunities occur for the teacher or a student to refer back to the previously discussed words, the teacher can put a tally mark next to the word. This way, students' vocabulary awareness can be tangibly tracked and rewarded with specific praise and allows the class to have a bank of "favorite words." The teacher can maintain the understanding of the focus words by referring back to them frequently and apply previously learned words to new books and use the words in other reading and writing contexts throughout the day: "Let's be sure to walk to lunch calmly, not *frenetically*!"

COMPREHENSION STRATEGY INSTRUCTION

When teachers read aloud with students we are able to teach them about responding to literature and build their background knowledge, but we are also able to teach them comprehension strategies that they can apply to all types of reading. There are many terms used in comprehension research, some of which are interchangeable. We will focus on the comprehension strategies that researchers agree (Duke & Pearson, 2002; Pearson, et al., 1992) are effective and teachable: predicting, inferring, clarifying, monitoring comprehension, questioning, summarizing or retelling, and evaluating.

PREDICTING AND INFERRING

We naturally make predictions. Some people are so good at predicting a plot that they can take all the fun out of going to a movie. Some people are very good at predicting how others will behave in certain situations. We want our students to predict, to make hypotheses about what the author will discuss next in a text, or how a character will react to an event, or what event will happen next. Sometimes students don't have enough background information to make a prediction or they don't access this background information if they do have it. For example, as I was reading aloud *The Golden Compass* (by Philip Pullman) with Isaac, who was 9 years old at the time, one of the characters poured a powder into a glass of wine that another character was going to drink. I asked Isaac, "What do you think the powder is?" He said, "I don't know." When we'd finished the chapter, I asked him, "Have you ever seen any movies or cartoons where someone pours powder into a glass?" "Yeah," he recalled, "in *The Princess Bride*, a guy poisons both glasses, but he's been building up his immunity to the poison, so only the other guy dies." "Did you think of that when we read that part in the book?" "No."

As teachers, we need to model making predictions and show how we use our background knowledge to do that. We can then ask our students to make predictions, ask them what they know about the situation and how that helps them guess what might happen next. When we're thinking about the kinds of predictions we want our students to make, we're also thinking about how to ask the questions that will solicit those predictions. These questions will, of necessity, be inferential. When we ask, "What do you think Sally will do when she sees Mark go into the cave?" there is no literal answer. There can only be a rational guess, or inference. Readers constantly make predictions, conjectures, and inferences based on what we know, even while knowing we could be wrong. Of course, there are reasonable predictions and inferences, and there are not so reasonable ones. This is why we must be accountable to the text and make our students accountable to the text. "What did the book say that made you think that?" "What do you base that idea on?" "Tell me or show me where in the story you began to think that this would happen."

When teaching children about predicting and inferring, predicting is easier to explain. "What do you think will happen next?" is the logical question to ask, followed by "Why do you think that?" Teaching inferencing is a little harder, but kids do it naturally all the time. A little boy stood in a parking lot, in the blazing sun, waiting for his mother to get out of the car. I heard him say, "So this must be why you told me to wear shorts!" That's inferring!

You can also show kids that they are always inferring by doing a little demonstration. Ask a child to stand next to you. Pretend to whisper in her ear while also looking at one of the children. Ask the students to tell you what they think you were whispering. They will tell you that you were whispering about the child you were looking at. They'll also tell you that it was probably something secret, or mean. Otherwise you wouldn't need to whisper! You can harness your students' natural instinct to make inferences while reading fiction. Posing why questions about characters' behaviors is a good way to get students to use their inferencing skills.

Directed Listening–Thinking Activity (DLTA)

Read aloud a story and stop at predetermined points to ask children to make predictions about what will happen next. With most stories, it works to stop after the title, shortly after the story begins, at one or two places of high interest during the story, and just before the story's problem is resolved. The questions you ask to elicit student predictions should be open-ended. For example, "What do you think will happen next?" Students should be able to justify their answers and be accountable to the text when you ask, "Why do you think that? What in the story made you think that?" Here's an example from my own classroom:

 After reading part of Eve Bunting's The Wednesday Surprise, *I paused and asked my students, "What do you think the surprise will be [the one that they're working on for Anna's dad]?" "They're going to surprise the dad with a party," answered Megan.*

 "They're going to give the dad a book, and they're trying to figure out which one to give him," said Ryan.

 Lincoln said, "Anna might want to give him a birthday present that she knows how to read."

 After we finished reading the book, I asked the class if they knew any older person who couldn't read. Only one student had known of an adult who couldn't read. They didn't have the background knowledge they needed for predicting that the surprise was Grandma learning to read from 7-year-old Anna.

With both predicting and inferring, students need to put their background knowledge together with information from text and develop an informed guess about what's happening or is about to happen. Background knowledge is also important when readers monitor their understanding by stopping to clarify what they've read.

Model of Effective Comprehension Instruction

Duke and Pearson's model (2002) of comprehension connects and integrates instruction in specific comprehension strategies with reading and discussing texts. They identify five components of effective comprehension instruction. The five components are listed below along with examples of teacher talk that model the strategies.

1. **An explicit description of the strategy and when and how it should be used.** "Predicting is making guesses about what will come next in the text you are reading. You should make predictions a lot when you read. For now, you should stop every two pages that you read and make some predictions."

2. **Teacher and/or student modeling of the strategy in action.** "I am going to make predictions while I read this book. I will start with just the cover here. Hmm . . . I see a picture of an owl. It looks like he—I think it is a he—is wearing pajamas, and he is carrying a candle. I *predict* that this is going to be a make-believe story because owls do not really wear pajamas and carry candles. I predict it is going to be about this owl, and it is going to take place at nighttime. The title will give me more clues about the book; the title is *Owl at Home*. So this makes me think even more that this book is going to be about the owl. He will probably be the main character, and it will take place in his house. Okay, I have made some predictions about the book based on the cover. Now I am going to open up the book and begin reading."

3. **Collaborative use of the strategy in action.** "I have made some good predictions so far in the book. From this part on I want you to make predictions with me. Each of us should stop and think about what might happen next. . . . Okay, now let's hear what you think and why."

4. **Guided practice using the strategy with gradual release of responsibility.** Early on:
   "I have called the three of you together to work on making predictions while you read this and other books. After every few pages I will ask each of you to stop and make a prediction. We will talk about your predictions and then read on to see if they come true."
   Later on:
   "Each of you has a chart that lists different pages in your book. When you finish reading a page on the list, stop and make a prediction. Write the prediction in the column that says 'Prediction.' When you get to the next page on the list, check off whether your prediction 'Happened,' 'Will not happen,' or 'Still might happen.' Then make another prediction and write it down."

5. **Independent use of the strategy.** "It is time for silent reading. As you read today, remember what we have been working on—making predictions while we read. Be sure to make predictions every two or three pages. Ask yourself why you made the prediction you did—what made you think that. Check as you read to see whether your prediction came true. Jamal is passing out Predictions! bookmarks to remind you." (Duke & Pearson, 2002, pp. 208–209)

Throughout these five phases, Duke and Pearson emphasize that strategies are not to be used in isolation from the other strategies. They may be introduced one at a time, but the best strategy instruction asks students to use multiple strategies constantly. Although the previous sample of a strategy lesson focuses on teaching one particular strategy, other strategies should also be referenced, modeled, and encouraged once they have all been introduced.

CLARIFYING AND MONITORING COMPREHENSION

When reading aloud, teachers can model for students how they should be monitoring their comprehension by stopping periodically to ask, "Is this making sense?" "Click or clunk" is a simple self-prompt students can learn (Anderson, 1980) as a way to monitor their comprehension. After each sentence, students ask themselves, "Did that sentence make sense?" If it did, they quietly say "click." If it did not, they say "clunk." At that point, they can reread the sentence, read on, or ask someone for help in understanding.

This is where clarifying comes in. Clarifying is what readers do when they notice that what they've read didn't make sense. Perhaps they read a word wrong and the sentence didn't sound right. Good readers will go back and reread to see if they can figure out what went wrong. Or maybe they read every word correctly, but didn't know the meaning of a word or words and so the sentence didn't make sense. Again, good readers might reread several sentences and see if they can figure out the meaning from the context or ask someone else to help. There are also times when they read too quickly and realize they weren't paying attention to the meaning. Or they read aloud or in their heads with the emphasis on the wrong words and the meaning breaks down. Rereading is the most frequent remedy good readers choose when a text doesn't seem to make sense.

Clarifying also happens when readers have completely understood a passage, but stop to explain it to themselves to cement that understanding and perhaps attempt to store new ideas in their memory. Especially with nonfiction, I tell my students that it is important to stop and restate the ideas to myself. Then I show them how I monitor my comprehension and clarify what I've read. I ask myself aloud, "Do I understand what I've just read? Let's see. . . . It says here that 'not all of these seeds will grow into plants. . . . A seed may not land on good earth. It may land on a rock or in your house.' Hmm . . . it may not land on 'good earth.' That's a funny way to say it. I think that means it might not land on real dirt, because then it says it could land on a rock or in your house, and that's not dirt so it won't grow." I tell the students that what I just did was clarifying—making sure things were clear to me.

Clarifying Frog and Toad

Even with a text as seemingly simple as Frog and Toad Are Friends, *I can take the opportunity to stop and model clarifying. "So there he is on the rock sticking his feet into the swimsuit."*

"No, he doesn't wear a swimsuit," Jordan reminds me.

"Oh, that's right. He's taking off his clothes. Oh that must be Frog, because Frog is just gonna go swimming in his frog skin."

"Yeah," reply several kids at once.

"You know what we're doing? We're clarifying. I'm making sure that I understand before I read more. I always get Frog and Toad mixed up."

"Frogs are green and toads are brown," says Jordan, helpfully.

"Well that helps me!"

If the students see that even an adult can be mixed up about a book like Frog and Toad, *then they understand how important it is to stop and clarify for themselves. We can also forgive them when they don't understand, and it seems obvious to us. Jordan thought it was obvious which was Toad and which was Frog, but she didn't make me feel dumb—she just reminded me how to tell the difference. She clarified for me.*

QUESTIONING

Questioning is a way of having students respond to texts, but it is also a powerful comprehension strategy. In fact, according to the National Reading Panel (NRP, 2000), "The strongest scientific evidence was found for the effectiveness of asking readers to generate questions during reading (p. 4-45). Proficient readers ask themselves questions before they read, while reading, and after they have read. Teachers need to model for students how to ask questions that clarify meaning and questions that speculate about what has not yet been read. Questions can also be about what the author intended to mean, about the style of the writing, about the content of the writing, and about the format of the writing. Questions might also be literal questions that have specific answers in the text, or inferential questions, or even "wonderings"—questions that are not explicitly answered by the text.

During any kind of modeling, whether it's questioning, clarifying, or predicting, we need to be sure that the students can see when we're reading the actual text and when we've stopped to discuss it. When we're thinking aloud, the students might think we're reading aloud unless we signal to them that we've stopped reading. For example, after reading aloud several pages of *Galaxies, Galaxies* by Gail Gibbons, stop reading, lower the book, and ask, "What was important about these first few pages? Let me think. Well, I think Gail Gibbons wants me to know that people have been studying the stars for a long time. They have also named them and made maps of the stars." Using a think-aloud such as this demonstrates how to self-question, which improves comprehension more than being questioned by the teacher. We can demonstrate through think-aloud how to self-question by using phrases such as "I wonder. . . ." "Why does it say that. . . .?" "The part I don't understand is. . . ." "It confused me when it said. . . ."

SUMMARIZING OR RETELLING

Summarizing offers both the reader and the teacher a view of the reader's thinking process while reading. The reader learns to identify the most important ideas in a story or piece of text. The research on summarizing shows that when students are taught to summarize the quality of their summaries improves, their recall of the text improves, and they are better able to answer questions based on the text (NRP, 2000, p. 4-92).

When primary-grade students summarize, it often sounds like retelling, which is the logical place to begin teaching summarizing. After reading aloud a text to students, we can begin the retelling and then hand it off to one of the students. "Okay, now it's your turn, Kimberly." If Kimberly leaves out an important portion of the story, we can prompt her to go back or to ask another student to fill in what's missing. If she retells story events in the wrong order, we can ask her or another student to try again. Retelling with informational texts should follow a sequence if the informational text has a chronological structure. If it is descriptive, details might be listed in any order without affecting the quality of the retelling (see the list of text structures in the following section "Informational Texts").

EVALUATING

Effective teachers encourage students to be critical readers on several levels. The first level is personal. Did they like the text and why? Was the sequel better than the first book and why? Who is their favorite author? What is their favorite genre? Rank this

myeducationlab

Comprehension

Go to MyEducationLab, "Comprehension," to watch the videos *Before Reading, During Reading,* and *After Reading.*

After watching the videos, you should be able to:

- Describe techniques that a teacher can use to motivate students to read informational text.
- List the strategies that a good reader uses before reading informational text.
- Discuss the importance of giving students time to discuss a text with peers.
- Identify how a teacher guides students through visualizing and monitoring.
- Identify how a teacher assists students in their understanding of expository text.
- Identify how a primary teacher might conduct a summary lesson.
- Identify the value of a word sort.

book on a scale of 1 to 10. Is the main character one we can sympathize with? For example, after reading a book during small-group reading instruction, Melissa said, "I liked it. I liked how it told how she had to get the water and it was heavy and then she would help her mom make breakfast. The best part was that she wrote 'Happy New Year' at the end." About the same book, Regina said, "I liked it because she put a lot of detail in like she put the date like 1866. I liked the drawings too. It kinda looks like a little kid drew it. I liked the writing [the font] too because it looks like a kid wrote it."

The second level is literary. Why did the author begin the story this way? Is there a better way that the story could have begun? Were there places that seemed confusing? Were there places where the action was too slow? Do long descriptive passages help you enjoy the story or do they get in the way?

Finally, we want our students to read texts on a social or political level. Why does a character describe Native Americans as savages? What can we do to help the homeless now that we understand what their lives are like? Is it okay for a boy to want a doll?

TYPES OF TEXTS TO READ ALOUD

When choosing what to read aloud to students, it's important to include a variety of texts. Teachers traditionally have read lots of fiction or picture storybooks, and should continue to do so, but informational texts give students a chance to build background knowledge and get them acquainted with different expository text structures. Poetry is also ripe for reading aloud, especially because much poetry depends on devices such as rhyme, rhythm, or alliteration, devices that are highlighted when poetry is read aloud. Without time devoted to reading aloud texts of various kinds, students will not have a chance to learn to comprehend texts of various kinds. Teachers should make a conscious effort to include informational texts, narrative texts (children's novels, picture storybooks), and poetry in their daily read-alouds.

INFORMATIONAL TEXTS

myeducationlab

Comprehension

Go to MyEducationLab, "Comprehension," to read the articles "The Sweet Work of Reading" and "The Case for Informational Text."

After reading the articles, you should be able to:

- Explain the need for students to set purposes for reading.
- Demonstrate reading comprehension strategies for a variety of grade levels.
- State reasons why teachers at every grade level should model strategies for using informational texts.

The world of informational texts includes series books such the *Eyewitness Juniors* series, which includes books such as *Amazing Bats.* It also includes one-of-a-kind books such as *Construction Zone,* an Orbis Pictus honor book that documents the construction of a Frank Gehry building on the MIT campus.

Magazines and newspapers are a common form of informational text made available to young children in the form of classroom magazines such as *Scholastic News* or children's magazines such as *Ranger Rick* and *Cobblestone.*

Informational texts are written using text structures that students need to be familiar with (Dymock, 2005). Four easily understandable text structures can be taught to students during a read-aloud and discussion of informational texts. They should be taught explicitly, one at a time.

🐿 Description: A major idea is supported by a list of details or examples.

🐿 Chronological/sequential order: A main idea is supported by details that must be in a particular sequence.

🐿 Comparison/contrast: The supporting details of two or more main ideas indicate how those concepts are similar or different.

🐿 Cause/effect: The supporting details explain the causes of a main idea or the supporting details explain the results produced by the main idea.

Explicit Instruction Lesson on Descriptive Text Structure

Concept or Objective: Identify descriptive text structure   Date: _____

Lesson Steps	Activities	Materials
Introduction • Review previous lesson • Connect today's lesson to previous lessons • give a purpose for today's lesson	"Yesterday we read *Polar Bears* by Gail Gibbons and we noticed that the book described polar bears. It described what they looked like, where they live, and what they eat. Many books describe things in detail. Today we are going to read another book by Gail Gibbons and we're going to look carefully at how it is organized. It has a descriptive text structure. Say that, "descriptive text structure." [*Children repeat*]. Great! First let's read *Owls* all the way through."	*Owls* by Gail Gibbons
Explicit teacher explanation and demonstration	Before the lesson, prepare a web that looks like the one shown below: Say, "This book by Gail Gibbons mostly tells about these five things. It has a descriptive text structure. Each of these five areas has more detailed descriptions or lists of features of owls; that's why it's called a descriptive text structure. I'll do the first one, then you'll help me do the next one. Here on page 6 it says there are 21 different kinds of owls in North America. So, I'm going to add a smaller bubble to our map that comes off the bigger bubble that says 'different kinds of owls.'"	Chart paper or overhead Markers

Lesson Steps	Activities	Materials
	Draw a smaller bubble and a connecting line. Inside the bubble write, "21 kinds." Do this again for a few more details such as smallest owl and largest owl. Pages 6–7 of this book list all 21 names. Emphasize that in order to understand the book, you don't need to write down all the names.	
Interactive guided practice	"Now we're going to do the next one together. Let's look again at page 10. It says, 'The eyes of an owl cannot move in their eye sockets to watch for prey. Instead, owls have flexible necks that can twist almost completely around. They can even turn their heads upside down.' So, we can add a smaller bubble to the bubble that says 'owls' bodies.' What do we know about their bodies from this page?" Many children will say things like, "can't move their eyes" and "flexible neck." Each of these can be added as a smaller bubble attached to the larger bubble that says "owls' bodies." Continue in this manner, adding smaller bubbles to the larger bubbles. Use the terms *descriptive text structure* and *description* and *describe* frequently. It may take two sessions to finish a chart, but be aware that every detail does not need to be listed in order for students to understand the structure of the text.	
Monitored independent practice	This kind of modeling and interactive guided practice needs to occur several times with different books before students are asked to make a bubble chart for descriptive text structure on their own. When they are asked to complete one independently, it should be in the context of small-group reading instruction as a follow-up to an informational text. This allows you to monitor their understanding of descriptive text structure and their use of the bubble chart.	
Assessment	Assess your own efforts to allow and encourage all students to participate during the interactive guided practice portion of this lesson. Assess students' independent work by examining their bubble charts to see if they have categorized descriptive details correctly.	
Accommodations for struggling readers and writers	Struggling readers and writers should work with a teacher or more able peer to complete a bubble chart for descriptive text structure.	

Biographies are written in a narrative mode, rather than an expository mode, which can make them sound more like a story with its chronological sequence. Excellent biographies written with a child audience in mind are widely available. When reading aloud biographies, be sure to include a variety of subjects: women and men; scientists, musicians, politicians and athletes; White people and people of color; people who lived in the past and people who are still living; famous and ordinary people.

FICTION

The world of fiction includes realistic fiction, historical fiction, fantasy or science fiction, and traditional literature such as fairy tales. The main comprehension strategy to use with fiction is story mapping, which research has shown to improve students' reading comprehension and story recall (Bauman & Bergeron, 1993; Boulineau, Fore, Hagan-Burke, & Burke, 2004).

A basic story map is shown in Figure 4.3. Using chart paper or an overhead, write down the story elements, leaving room to write beside or below them. As you read aloud, stop to explain each element. For example, when reading *Lilly's Purple Plastic Purse*, Lilly is introduced on the first page. Stop and say, "Lilly is a character in this story. We'll list her name here where the chart says characters." The first setting in the story is school, so explain that school is a place, which is another word for setting, and list "school" next to setting. As each element is revealed, stop to talk about what the terms mean. What is a problem? What is a solution? What are events? Though there are usually more than three events in a story, by limiting the number of events to three or four, students are encouraged to focus on the main events, the ones that drive the plot.

A story mapping activity should be done with a book that has been read straight through on an earlier occasion. Reading stories without interruptions allows students to experience the flow of the story as it was written by the author, but stopping to discuss what's going on, to clarify, to ask questions, is *not* going to ruin the story. Students need to know that readers stop to wonder aloud, to marvel at a character's antics, to reread parts that didn't make sense, or to gasp at surprise endings.

Figure 4.3 Story Map

Characters:	
Setting:	
Problem:	
Solution:	
Events:	1. 2. 3.

Figure 4.4

> *Alliteration:* the repetition of consonants such as the *s* sounds in "Sally sells seashells by the seashore"
>
> *Assonance:* the repetition of vowels such the *o*'s and *ou* in "Bob bought hot dogs"
>
> *Onomatopoeia:* words whose sound matches their meaning: *boom, hiss, flutter, tinkle, splash*

POETRY

Poetry, more than any other kind of text, should be read aloud. When poetry is read aloud, students can hear the rhythm, rhyme, alliteration, assonance, and onomatopoeia (see Figure 4.4). Students can and should be taught these terms so that they have a common language for discussing the fun things that poets do with words. Poems also use imagery and figurative language. Familiarity with poetic language can encourage students to speak and write in ways that are beyond the level of casual conversation with their peers, parents, and teachers (Sekeres & Gregg, 2007).

Children love poetry that is funny or has silly or nonsense words, such as *hickety pickety, higglety pigglety* or *diffendorfer*. But they also need to hear poetry that is thoughtful, reflective, or serious. They need to hear poetry that is very short and makes its point quickly, but also poetry that is long and tells a story. Children enjoy poetry that has a concrete shape that repeats or supports the ideas in the poem. The world is full of wonderful poetry that isn't written by Shel Silverstein or Jack Prelutsky. Students read and hear plenty of these two poets' work; but they also need to get to know poetry by Robert Louis Stevenson, Valerie Worth, Karla Kuskin, Nikki Grimes, Christina Rosetti, Michael Strickland, Douglas Florian, and many others. Bilingual poetry, by authors such as Francisco X. Alarcón, is another type of poetry that students should read and hear.

Building Fluency with Choral Reading and Read-Alouds

Choral reading of poetry can be an effective way to improve students' oral reading fluency, and ESL students respond very positively (McCauley & McCauley, 1992). Fluency is a combination of speed, accuracy, and intonation or expression (Rasinski, 2006). When reading poetry aloud to children, be sure to use the most natural intonation and inflection that you can so that children don't come to expect poetry to sound either monotone or sing-song. Even poems with a strong rhythm should be read in a way that emphasizes the meaning. Reading aloud is also a good time to model both fluent and nonfluent reading. When the teacher reads a sentence word by word or in a monotone, students are usually able to describe why that just doesn't sound right and give the teacher "advice" on how to improve her fluency.

 ### CONCLUDING THOUGHTS

Through reading aloud and discussing what was read, teachers encourage students to be critical, effective, and comprehending readers. It sounds simple, but of course it's not. Perhaps the hardest thing is keeping a balance between reading and discussing. The next hardest thing is making sure that the talk is accomplishing one of the goals we've addressed here: responding to literature, increasing background knowledge, or improving comprehension skills. We want students to love literature, to love reading, and to grow intellectually from the encounters with literature that we create with them.

SUGGESTED ACTIVITIES TO EXTEND YOUR LEARNING

1. Read aloud Taro Yashima's picture book *Crow Boy* (or any high-quality children's book) and write these four columns on the whiteboard: *Feelings, Connections, Questions*, and *Favorite Parts*. Model your responses to each of these categories. On another day with another book, invite students to model their responses to these categories.

2. Examine a book for Tier Two vocabulary words to teach during a read-aloud. Determine student-friendly definitions.

3. Collect examples of children's poetry that would be appropriate for choral reading. Be sure to include poems that do and don't rhyme; that contain alliteration, assonance, or onomatopoeia; that have a strong rhythm; that are silly; and that are thoughtful. Choose poems by both men and women poets, and look for bilingual poetry to include.

4. Read aloud a book to a small group of children. Plan questions to activate students' background knowledge before reading. Plan three places in the text to stop and ask students to make predictions and/or inferences. After reading, have students retell the story.

REFERENCES

Anderson, R. C. , Hiebert, E. H., Scott, J. A., & Wilkinson, I. A. G. (1985). *Becoming a nation of readers: The report of the Commission on Reading.* Champaign–Urbana, IL: Center for the Study of Reading.

Anderson, R. C., & Pearson, P. D. (1984). A schema-theoretic view of basic processes in reading. In P. D. Pearson (Ed.), *Handbook of reading research.* White Plains, NY: Longman.

Anderson, T. (1980). Study strategies and adjunct aids. In R. Spiro, B. Bruce, & W. Brewer, (Eds.), *Theoretical issues in reading comprehension.* Hillsdale, NJ: Erlbaum.

Bauman, J., & Bergeron, B. (1993). Story map instruction using children's literature: Effects of first graders' comprehension of central narrative elements. *Journal of Reading Behavior, 25,* 407–437.

Beck, I. L., & McKeown, M. G. (2001). Text talk: Capturing the benefits of read-aloud experiences for young children. *The Reading Teacher, 55*(1), 10–20.

Beck, I. L., McKeown, M. G., & Kucan, L. (2002). *Bring words to life: Robust vocabulary instruction.* New York: Guilford Press.

Boulineau, T., Fore, C., Hagan-Burke, S., & Burke, M. D. (2004). Use of story-mapping to increase the story-grammar text comprehension of elementary students with learning disabilities. *Learning Disability Quarterly, 27*(2), 105–121.

Calkins, L. (2001). *The art of teaching reading.* New York: Longman.

Doyle, B., & Bramwell, W. (2006). Promoting emergent literacy and social–emotional learning through dialogic reading. *The Reading Teacher, 59*(6), 554–564.

Duke, N. K., & Pearson, P. (2002). Effective practices for developing reading comprehension. In A. E. Farstrup & S. Samuels (Eds.), *What research has to say about reading instruction* (pp. 205–242). Newark, DE: International Reading Association.

Dymock, S. (2005). Teaching expository text structure awareness. *The Reading Teacher, 59*(2), 177–181.

Harste, J., & Burke, C. (1996). *Creating classrooms for authors and inquirers.* Portsmouth, NH: Heinemann.

Keene, E. O., & Zimmerman, S. (1997). *Mosaic of thought: Teaching comprehension in a reader's workshop.* Portsmouth, NH: Heinemann.

Lane, H. B., & Wright, T. L. (2007). Maximizing the effectiveness of reading aloud. *The Reading Teacher, 60*(7), 668–675.

Lyman, F. (1981). The responsive classroom discussion. In A. S. Anderson, (Ed.), *Mainstreaming digest.* College Park: University of Maryland College of Education.

McCauley, J. K., & McCauley, D. S. (1992). Using choral reading to promote language learning for ESL students. *The Reading Teacher, 45*(7), 526–533.

McGee, L. M., & Schickedanz, J. A. (2007). Repeated interactive read-alouds in preschool and kindergarten. *The Reading Teacher, 60*(8), 742–751.

National Reading Panel. (2000). *Teaching children to read: An evidence-based assessment of the scientific research literature on reading and its implications for reading instruction. Report of the subgroups.* National Institute of Child Health and Human Development. Retrieved from http://www.nichd.nih.gov/publications/nrp/smallbook.cfm

New Standards Primary Literacy Committee. (1999). *Reading & writing grade by grade: Primary literacy standards for kindergarten through third grade.* Washington, DC: National Center on Education and the Economy and the University of Pittsburgh.

Palincsar, A. S., & Brown, A. L. (1984). Reciprocal teaching of comprehension—fostering and monitoring activities. *Cognition and Instruction, 1,* 117–175.

Pearson, P. D., Dole, J. A., Duffy, G. G. & Roehler, L. R. (1992). Developing expertise in reading comprehension: What should be taught and how should it be taught? In J. Farstrup & S. J. Samuels (Eds.), *What research has to say to the teacher of reading* (2nd ed.). Newark, DE: International Reading Association.

Pearson, P. D., & Duke, N. K. (2002). Comprehension instruction in the primary grades. In C. C. Block & M. Pressley (Eds.), *Comprehension instruction: Research-based best practices* (pp. 247–258). New York: Guilford Press.

Pearson, P. D., & Stephens, D. (1998). Learning about literacy: A 30-year journey. In C. Weaver (Ed.), *Reconsidering a balanced approach to reading* (pp. 77–100). Urbana, IL: National Council of Teachers of English.

Rasinski, T. (2006). Reading fluency instruction: Moving beyond accuracy, automaticity, and prosody. *The Reading Teacher, 59*(7), 704–706.

Rosenblatt, L. M. (1978). *The reader, the text, the poem: The transactional theory of literary work.* Carbondale: Southern Illinois University Press. (Original work published 1978.)

Rumelhart, D. (1980). Schemata: The building blocks of cognition. In R. J. Spiro, B. C. Bruce, & W. F. Brewer (Eds.), *Theoretical issues in reading comprehension* (pp. 33–58). Hillsdale, NJ: Erlbaum.

Sekeres, D. C., & Gregg, M. (2007). Poetry in third grade: Getting started. *The Reading Teacher, 60*(5), 466–475.

Smolkin, L. B., & Donovan, C. A. (2001). The contexts of comprehension: The information book read aloud, comprehension acquisition, and comprehension instruction in a first-grade classroom. *The Elementary School Journal, 102*(2), 97–122.

Spooner, M. & Taylor, L. (1996). *Old Meshikee and the little crabs: An Ojibwe story.* New York: Henry Holt.

Trelease, J. (2003). *The new read-aloud handbook* (5th ed.). New York: Penguin.

Word Study

by John A. Smith

5

Tickle Words

It's a Monday morning in mid-November in Paul Boehme's first-grade classroom. Paul's 23 students are seated together on the rug placed in front of the white-board. His spelling pattern instruction task this day is to introduce the spelling pattern CVCe, where the final silent e makes the preceding vowel say its name, or "long" sound. Behind him, written on the board, is a list of eight CVCe words.

time	*same*
made	*side*
Pete	*hope*
bone	*dude*

Paul points to the list of words and explains, "Notice that all of these words end with the letter e." Paul and his students look at the eight words together and notice all of the final letter es. He points to each of the example words and reads them aloud to his students. Paul explains to his students how the final silent e makes the initial vowel in each of the words say its name or "long" sound.

He then demonstrates or models to his students how the final silent e spelling pattern works. He points to the first example word time, covers up the final e, and asks, "What's this word now?" "Tim," his students reply.

Paul continues the demonstration, "this final e reaches over the letter m, tickles the letter i, and makes it say its name." At this point Paul very expressively pronounces a long i sound, as if he were being tickled. This gets his students' attention and makes the lesson memorable. He repeats this dramatic demonstration with each of the seven remaining example words.

Paul follows up the explanation and demonstration of the final silent e pattern with a guided practice activity designed to reinforce the final silent e pattern for his students. He sends his students back to their desks, gives each of them a set of final silent e word cards and asks his students to spread the word cards out across their desks. He pronounces the final silent e words one at a time and asks his students to find the applicable word card on their desk and hold it up to show him that they know it.

After leading his students in finding and holding up silent e word cards for a few minutes, Paul extends the guided practice activity. He shows his students how to fold back the final e on the word cards to make the word into a beginner word (e.g., pane into pan). Immediately his 23 students fold back the final e on each of *their word cards to change the words into beginner words. Paul then alternates pronouncing long and short vowel words* (Tim, made, hop, side, pet, same, Sam, dude) *and asks his students to hold them up.*

Paul concludes this introductory final silent e spelling pattern lesson with a third guided practice activity. He uses the overhead projector to project a paragraph that contains a large number of final silent e words onto the writing board. He reads the paragraph aloud, then models finding a few silent e words in the paragraph and underlining them. He asks his students, "who can come to the writing board and underline some silent e words?" Hands shoot up as the students can't wait to come to the board, take marker in hand, and underline one of the final silent e words. Paul's students easily identify and underline all of the final silent e words in the paragraph.

The next morning, Paul begins his word study lesson with a review of the final silent e pattern and then provides a monitored independent practice activity. He gives each of his students a piece of paper, has them open their reading program books, and invites them to work with a partner to make a list of all the final silent e words they can find throughout the book. He circulates among them, observes how well each pair of students can identify and write final silent e words, and provides helpful guidance as needed. After a few minutes Paul leads the class in writing a master list of final silent e words on the board that his students have found in the book.

As an assessment *activity, Paul displays 10 to 12 final silent e word cards to his students during small-group instruction time. As he displays the word cards to each group, he notes in his roll book which individual students will need more instruction and practice with the final silent e spelling pattern.*

The purposes of this chapter are to present and describe the most common and useful spelling patterns and high-frequency words that teachers must be familiar with to teach reading effectively, and to provide an explicit instruction procedure for teaching students to recognize and use spelling patterns and high-frequency words in their reading. Additionally, this chapter describes guided practice word identification activities that can be used interchangeably to teach spelling patterns and high-frequency words. Major topics of this chapter include:

- Understanding word identification
- What to teach: common spelling patterns
- Teaching spelling patterns: an explicit teaching model
- Sample explicit instruction lesson for spelling patterns
- Building students' sight vocabularies
- Teaching Multisyllable Words
- Additional guided practice words study activities

 UNDERSTANDING WORD IDENTIFICATION

In all of education, no single word may be as controversial and politically charged as the word *phonics*. Some people associate phonics with worksheets, meaningless drill-and-kill exercises, and generations of students who have been turned off to reading. Others genuinely believe that phonics is all that is really needed to read, and that more phonics instruction in elementary schools will raise test scores, reduce the prison population and teen pregnancies, and secure forever America's place at the top of the world economy. The truth is, phonics is one necessary component of a comprehensive reading instruction program; it can be taught in an enjoyable, effective manner; and it must be linked to the meaningful aspects of reading.

What Does Research Tell Us About Word Identification Instruction?

A tremendous amount of educational research has been devoted to beginning reading instruction, and specifically to the role of phonics. Three major conclusions from this research guide the word identification perspectives and instructional recommendations presented in this chapter:

1. Phonics instruction must be explicit and systematic.
2. Phonics instruction must be connected to meaningful reading.
3. Phonics instruction must be simple, flexible, and enjoyable.

Phonics Instruction Must Be Explicit and Systematic

The cumulative findings of decades of beginning reading research support teaching word identification skills explicitly and systematically (Mesmer & Griffiths, 2005). Explicit phonics instruction means that phonics concepts are presented clearly and concisely. Explicit phonics instruction is characterized by teacher explanation and demonstration of concepts, guided practice activities, independent practice activities, and ongoing assessment. Systematic instruction refers to teaching decoding concepts in a specific sequence. Students learn the simplest decoding concepts first, then move to more complex concepts that build on and reinforce previous learning. Blevins (1998) describes the importance of a sequenced cumulative system for presenting spelling patterns.

> Systematic instruction follows a sequence that progresses from easy to more difficult. Systematic instruction includes constant review and repetition of sound-spelling relationships, applications to reading and writing, and focus on developing fluency through work with reading rate and decoding accuracy. Just because a program has a scope and sequence doesn't mean it is systematic. The instruction must be cumulative. (p. 91)

Research studies continue to describe the benefits of explicit systematic decoding instruction. Pressley, Rankin, and Yokoi (1995) state that "explicitly teaching phonemic awareness, phonics, and letter–sound analysis have promoted improved performance on standardized tests and have proven superior to programs emphasizing meaning-making, such as whole language" (p. 3). The National Reading Panel's (NRP, 2000) meta-analysis (combining and reanalyzing data from many studies) of reading research data "provided solid support for the conclusion that systematic phonics instruction makes a more significant contribution to children's growth in reading" than do reading programs that provide unsystematic or no phonics instruction (p. 2-132).

Struggling Readers Need the Same Reading Skills

Because struggling readers, particularly special education students, are often taught by resource personnel who frequently use reading instruction programs that are less familiar to classroom teachers, there is a tendency for some classroom teachers to think that there may be a special set of struggling reader skills and instructional methods. This is not the case. All readers progress through the same set of basic reading skills beginning with learning the alphabet letter names and sounds and the concept of blending sounds together to form words (phonemic awareness), recognizing and blending printed letters and spelling patterns (phonics), reading accurately and fluently, building vocabulary, and learning to employ comprehension strategies. Some readers struggle because they have not mastered one or more of these skills. In such cases, teachers need to focus on these basic skills through providing additional instructional time for systematic teaching, assessing, and reteaching. Speaking of struggling readers, Torgesen (2004) writes,

> Perhaps the most important conclusion to draw from recent intervention research is that intervention instruction should focus on the same major dimensions of knowledge and skill that are taught in the regular classroom but must be more *explicit* and *intensive* than regular classroom instruction to prevent or remediate reading difficulties. (p. 363)

myeducationlab

Fluency

Go to MyEducationLab, "Fluency," and read the article "Why Reading Is Not a Natural Process."

As you read this article, notice how explicit instruction in phonics skills must be linked to meaningful reading including authentic children's literature and a print-rich classroom environment.

- What is the alphabetic principle?
- How does fluency influence reading comprehension?
- Why do some children have difficulty learning to read?

Phonics Instruction Must Be Connected to Meaningful Reading

Although word identification instruction is a very important part of a comprehensive reading instruction program, it must be kept in proper perspective. Sometimes word identification instruction is presented only as an isolated independent curriculum with little or no connection to the meaningful aspects of reading. Members of the NRP (2000) wrote:

> Phonics teaching is a means to an end. . . . Programs that focus too much on the teaching of letter–sound relations and not enough on putting them to use are unlikely to be very effective. In implementing systematic phonics instruction, educators must keep the *end* in mind and ensure that children understand the purpose of learning letter–sounds and are able to apply their skills in their daily reading and writing activities. (p. 2-135)

The point is that phonics is only one aspect of reading instruction and that it must be integrated with other instructional components to provide comprehensive reading instruction (Anderson, Hiebert, Scott, & Wilkinson, 1985; Duffy, 1998). Adams (1990b) did an exhaustive review of two decades of beginning reading research and concluded that "approaches in which systematic code instruction is included along with the reading of connected text result in superior reading achievement overall, for both low-readiness and better prepared students" (p. 125). A survey of highly effective reading teachers from across the country (Pressley et al., 1995; Pressley, Yokoi, Rankin, Wharton-McDonald, & Mistretta, 1997) suggests that effective teachers used instruction that is "multifaceted rather than based on one approach or another." Rayner, Foorman, Perfetti, Pesetsky, & Seidenberg (2002), in their research summary for the journal *Scientific American,* concluded that "indeed, recent work has indicated—and many teachers have discovered—that the combination of literature-based instruction and phonics is more powerful than either method alone" (p. 91).

Phonics Instruction Must Be Simple, Flexible, and Enjoyable

Phonics instruction must be kept simple so that beginning readers will not be overwhelmed with an overabundance of meaningless and sometimes conflicting rules. Many phonics rules are inconsistent (Clymer, 1963/1996; Johnston, 2001) or else apply to words that seldom appear in beginning reading texts. For example, one first-year teacher wasted half of a teacher workday making a board game (suggested by the adopted reading program) to help students decode three words: *gnu, gnome,* and *gnat.* The next section of this chapter presents common spelling patterns that will help beginning readers identify over 1,400 words. Anderson and colleagues (1985), in their national report *Becoming a Nation of Readers,* provided a great philosophy for phonics instruction: "Do it early. Keep it simple" (p. 43).

Reading instruction needs to be flexible. Some reading programs leave instructional decision making to the teacher, whereas other programs script out virtually every word the teacher is supposed to say. Such scripted programs run the risk of "reducing teachers' motivation to teach phonics" (NRP, 2000, 2–135), and focus on teaching the program rather than teaching students. Teaching reading is not a one-size-fits-all endeavor. Students vary tremendously in their ability, maturity, background knowledge, interests, and preparation and support from home. Teachers must be able to balance the need for instructional consistency with the need to adapt their instruction to meet individual students' needs.

Finally, word identification instruction needs to be enjoyable for both teachers and students. A national survey found that student motivation is far and away the biggest concern for classroom teachers (Pressley, 2002). When students are enjoying instructional activities, they will be more involved in the activities. The NRP (2000) suggests that instructional activities should be "as relevant and motivating as possible to engage children's interest and attention to promote optimal learning" (p. 2–137).

FOR ENGLISH LANGUAGE LEARNERS

Phonics Instruction

The best way to develop English language learners' beginning reading skills is through a combination of extensive and varied interactions with meaningful print and systematic and explicit instruction in phonemic awareness and phonics. Systematic phonics instruction can help English language learners develop word recognition and decoding skills to a high level even though their general knowledge of English is limited. However, the ability to decode does not automatically carry over into comprehension.

WHAT TO TEACH: COMMON SPELLING PATTERNS

Many reading programs and reading methods textbooks include lists of up to 200 or more phonics skills that beginning readers should be expected to learn or memorize. That is a rather daunting task for 6- and 7-year-olds. Adams (2001), on the other hand, suggests that we condense the amount of word identification concepts "from zillions of little things that must be rote memorized to relatively few big ones that the child can be reasonably asked to understand and think about" (p. 75).

Happily, there is a reasonably sized set of common spelling patterns that appear over and over in published reading programs, professional texts, and research studies. These nine spelling patterns appear frequently in texts, are generally reliable and consistent, and will help students unlock many words.

Beginning with simple three-letter CVC words (consonant–vowel–consonant: *cat, Ted, big*), these nine spelling patterns build on each other cumulatively (Blevins, 1998) to help students develop decoding automaticity and fluency. Familiarity and practice with these nine spelling patterns will enable beginning readers to recognize over 1,400 single-syllable words and also to recognize parts of many multi-syllable words. Although there is no universally accepted instructional sequence for teaching spelling patterns, a sequence is important so teachers will have a place to start and a

Table 5.1 Nine Common Spelling Patterns

Spelling Pattern	Classroom Name	Examples
Short Vowel Spelling Patterns		
1. Consonant–vowel–consonant	Beginner words	dad, ten, dig, mop, bus
2. Consonant blends	Blends	<u>pl</u>an, <u>sl</u>ed, te<u>nt</u>, <u>fr</u>og, ru<u>st</u>
3. Consonant digraphs	Digraphs	<u>ch</u>at, fi<u>sh</u>, <u>th</u>at, <u>wh</u>en
Long Vowel Spelling Patterns		
4. Final silent *e*	Tickle words	cake, pipe, rode, cute
5. Vowel digraphs	Vowel teams	r<u>ai</u>n, pl<u>ay</u>; t<u>ea</u>m, f<u>ee</u>d; g<u>oa</u>t, sn<u>ow</u>
Varient Vowel Spelling Patterns		
6. *R*-controlled vowels	Bossy-*R* words	c<u>ar</u>, f<u>or</u>; h<u>er</u>, s<u>ir</u>, f<u>ur</u>
7. Vowel diphthongs	Diphthongs	b<u>oy</u>, p<u>oi</u>nt; l<u>ou</u>d, c<u>ow</u>; ch<u>ew</u>, str<u>aw</u>
Spelling Patterns for Identifying Multisyllable Words		
8. Open syllables	Open syllables	be, go, hi, me, no
9. Consonant-*le*	Consonant-*le*	a<u>ble</u>, unc<u>le</u>, pad<u>dle</u>, waf<u>fle</u>, mug<u>gle</u>, ap<u>ple</u>

place to go next with confidence that no important spelling patterns are being overlooked.

Table 5.1 provides an overview of the nine common spelling patterns. Appendix B provides a list of over 1,400 words that can be identified from these nine spelling patterns. Some teachers make wall charts of the spelling patterns as an overview and reference for students. The following sections of this chapter describe each of the nine common spelling patterns and suggest instructional procedures for teaching them. Several lesson plans are included to show how these common spelling patterns can be taught using explicit instruction.

A "Spelling Patterns We Use" chart provides students with an overview.

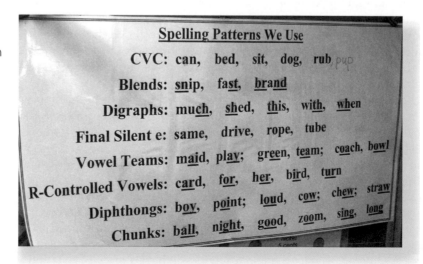

John A. Smith

Table 5.2 Beginner Words

a	e	i	o	u
dad	bed	did	job	cub
had	red	hid	rob	rub
ban	den	big	dog	bug
can	men	pig	fog	hug
map	bet	pin	hop	gum
nap	get	tin	mop	hum

SPELLING PATTERN 1: CONSONANT–VOWEL–CONSONANT (CVC) WORDS

The spelling pattern that many teachers begin with is the CVC (consonant–vowel–consonant) pattern. This pattern provides the conceptual and instructional foundation for students learning how to blend the sounds of printed letters together to form words. The CVC pattern includes the CVC short vowel word families for all five vowels. Some reading teachers and students refer to CVC words as "beginner words" because the other spelling pattern build on this foundation. Table 5.2 is a brief list of common CVC or beginner words. Complete lists of words that contain all of the nine spelling patterns is provided in Appendix B.

The ability to blend the sounds of printed letters is dependent on two of the foundation concepts discussed in Chapter 3: knowledge of letter names and sounds, and phonemic awareness. Learning to blend the sounds of printed letters into CVC words is quite easy if students know the sounds associated with the printed alphabet letters and understand the principle that sounds can be blended to form spoken words.

The principle of blending the letter sounds is the same within and across vowels, so once the students have learned this principle and the letter names and sounds, with practice they should be able to read all of the possible CVC combinations equally well.

SPELLING PATTERN 2: CONSONANT BLENDS

A consonant blend occurs when two consonant letters appear side-by-side in words such as *flat* and *sand*. In a consonant blend, you can hear both of the consonant letter sounds. Be aware that consonant blends occur only within a single syllable. For example, in the word *Batman*, the *t* and *m* do appear side-by-side, but they do not constitute a consonant blend because they are in separate syllables.

Teaching students to recognize words with consonant blends is not difficult. Once students have mastered the principle of blending three letter sounds to form CVC words, then simply adding a fourth letter sound in the words is easy. For example, if students can blend three letters (*f-a-t*), then by applying the same blending principle, they can easily blend four letters (*f-l-a-t*) or (*f-a-s-t*).

Some reading programs teach consonant blends as distinct spelling patterns such as the *cr* blend or the *sl* blend. This approach to teaching blends as individual units is overly complicated and unnecessary. When students come to understand the principle of blending the letter sounds they'll be able to produce the pronunciation of any consonant blend simply by applying the blending procedure.

Table 5.3 is a brief list of words with consonant blends.

Students chant "beginner words" in the first step of a word study lesson.

Steven Von Niederhausern

Table 5.3 Blend Words

a	e	i	o	u
ba<u>nd</u>	<u>Fr</u>ed	<u>f</u>ist	<u>gl</u>ob	<u>st</u>ub
pa<u>st</u>	<u>sl</u>ed	<u>br</u>im	bo<u>nd</u>	<u>sp</u>ud
<u>br</u>an	be<u>lt</u>	<u>g</u>ift	<u>fr</u>og	must
<u>pl</u>an	fe<u>lt</u>	<u>l</u>ift	<u>dr</u>op	<u>pl</u>us
pa<u>nt</u>	be<u>nd</u>	<u>cr</u>ib	po<u>nd</u>	du<u>nk</u>
la<u>nd</u>	ne<u>xt</u>	<u>sp</u>in	<u>sp</u>ot	<u>tr</u>ust

SPELLING PATTERN 3: CONSONANT DIGRAPHS

There are approximately 44 sounds in the spoken English language. However, these 44 sounds are represented by only 26 alphabet letters. This means that 18 English speech sounds don't have a letter. These must be represented by letters that make more than one sound (e.g., vowels) and also some combinations of letters. Consonant digraphs (*ch, sh, th, wh*) help fill this need.

Unlike consonant blends where you hear both of the letter sounds, you do not hear the letters make their sounds in consonant digraphs. For example, *ch* doesn't sound like *c* or *b*. It makes an altogether different sound /ch/ that we hear at the beginning and end of the word *church*. The digraph *tb* makes two sounds: /th/ as in *this* and /th/ as in *think*. Students must simply memorize the sounds of these four consonant digraphs and be able to blend them with the sounds of the other letters and spelling patterns to form words.

Table 5.4 is a brief list of words that contain consonant digraphs.

Table 5.4   Digraph Words

a	e	i	o	u
than	shed	thin	chop	much
chap	them	chip	shop	such
bash	then	whip	gosh	thud
cash	when	dish	shot	hush
math	Beth	itch	shock	shut
chat	check	wish	moth	crutch

SPELLING PATTERN 4: FINAL SILENT E

At this point in the sequence of spelling pattern lessons, the focus switches from short vowel concepts to two long vowel concepts: *final silent e* and *vowel teams*. The final silent *e* spelling pattern (CVCe) is one of the most reliable spelling patterns. The final silent *e* pattern also works when an ending is added to a final silent *e* word (*shines*, *shined*). However, the pattern usually works only when there is one consonant between the final *e* and the preceding vowel.

Many teachers and students refer to final silent *e* words as "tickle words," learning how the silent *e* on the end of the word reaches backward over the consonant and tickles the first vowel, making it say its name.

Table 5.5 is a brief list of common final silent *e* or tickle words. Notice that there are very few single syllable final silent *e* words when the first vowel is an *e* (*Pete*). Notice also the cumulative effect of the spelling patterns as some of the tickle words also contain consonant blends (*place*) and digraphs (*shade*).

Table 5.5   Tickle Words

a	i	o	u
face	dice	robe	cube
safe	hide	joke	dude
lake	life	home	mule
base	dime	note	tune
place	slice	smoke	prune
shade	while	choke	flute

SPELLING PATTERN 5: VOWEL TEAMS

Technically known as vowel digraphs, vowel teams refer to the old rule "When two vowels go walking, the first does the talking." The first of the two vowels says its name or "long" sound, the second vowel is silent. Clymer (1963/1996) found that the "when two vowels go walking" rule is in fact not very reliable. For example, *ie* and *ei* can be very confusing. *Oi* and *ou* don't follow the rule. *Ow* makes the long *o* sound as in *show* but also makes the vowel sound you hear in the word *cow*.

There are six vowel teams that are the most common and reliable: *ai, ay; ea, ee; oa, ow*. Some teachers refer to *ai* and *ay* as the A Teams, *ea* and *ee* as the E Teams, and *oa* and *ow* as the O Teams. Table 5.6 is a brief list of common vowel team words. Notice that some of them also contain consonant blends and digraphs.

Table 5.6   Vowel Team Words

A Teams		E Teams		O Teams	
maid	bay	bead	seed	load	mow
nail	day	leaf	meet	soak	low
gain	play	seal	seem	coal	tow
wait	stay	heat	jeep	boat	blow
brain	may	speak	fleet	coast	grow
chain	way	peach	teeth	throat	show

SPELLING PATTERN 6: R-CONTROLLED VOWELS

The five spelling patterns described so far have contained short and long vowel sounds. Patterns five and six contain vowel sounds that are neither short nor long. The first of these is the *r*-controlled vowel spelling pattern. The letter *r* often follows a vowel, and when it does, it usually changes or eliminates the sound of the vowel. For example, in the word *bar* we hear only the sounds of *b* and *r* blended together.

Like consonant digraphs, the *r*-controlled vowel sounds must simply be memorized. Some teachers and students refer to these as "bossy-*r*" words. It is interesting to note that *ar* and *or* make distinct sounds (as in *far* and *for*), whereas *er*, *ir*, and *ur* all make the same sound (as in *her*, *sir*, and *fur*). Many beginning readers will mistakenly think of *r*-controlled vowel words (e.g., *bar, car, her, fur*) as CVC words because they look like CVC words. Students must learn that these *r*-controlled vowel words cannot be CVC words because there is no short vowel sound from the vowel. Table 5.7 is a brief list of common *r*-controlled vowel or bossy-*r* words. Notice that some of them also contain consonant blends and digraphs.

SPELLING PATTERN 7: VOWEL DIPHTHONGS

Vowel diphthongs (*oi, oy; ou, ow; aw, ew*) are additional vowel combinations that produce sounds different from the actual sound of either letter. Notice that *oi* doesn't make either an *o* or an *i* sound. These diphthong vowel combinations are different

Table 5.7   Bossy-*R* Words

		Same Vowel Sound		
a	**o**	**e**	**i**	**u**
b<u>ar</u>	f<u>or</u>	h<u>er</u>	f<u>ir</u>	f<u>ur</u>
c<u>ar</u>	m<u>ore</u>	j<u>er</u>k	b<u>ir</u>d	s<u>ur</u>f
st<u>ar</u>	sn<u>ore</u>	g<u>er</u>m	g<u>ir</u>l	b<u>ur</u>n
sp<u>ar</u>k	p<u>or</u>ch	cl<u>er</u>k	f<u>ir</u>st	n<u>ur</u>se
ch<u>ar</u>m	h<u>or</u>se	s<u>er</u>ve	th<u>ir</u>st	h<u>ur</u>t

from vowel teams where you hear the first vowel's name or long sound (*rain, say, seat, soap*). Diphthongs make two additional sounds /oy/ (also spelled *oi* as in *boil*) and /ow/ (also spelled *ou* as in *proud*) and also additional spellings of the existing sounds short *o* (*aw*) and long *u* (*ew*). When introduced to the diphthong *ow*, students often point out that *ow* is also a vowel team. They must come to understand that *ow* is a vowel team when it makes a long *o* sound as in *blow* and *grow*, and *ow* is a diphthong when it makes the /ou/ sound as in *cow* and *flower*.

If this seems complicated, imagine how beginning readers feel when they have to learn it. This complexity is the reason to focus on teaching the most common and useful spelling patterns.

Notice that some of the vowel diphthong words in the list in Table 5.8 also contain consonant blends and digraphs.

Table 5.8   Vowel Diphthong Words

<u>**oi**</u>	<u>**oy**</u>	<u>**ou**</u>	<u>**ow**</u>	<u>**aw**</u>	<u>**ew**</u>
oil	boy	ou<u>ch</u>	how	<u>dr</u>aw	few
boil	joy	loud	now	saw	new
soil	toy	ro<u>und</u>	cow	hawk	<u>bl</u>ew
voice		house	<u>br</u>own	<u>cr</u>awl	<u>ch</u>ew
poi<u>nt</u>		<u>sh</u>out	<u>cl</u>own	lawn	<u>dr</u>ew

SPELLING PATTERN 8: OPEN SYLLABLES

When a word ends with a vowel (*be, hi, so*) the vowel generally says its name or "long" sound. The same holds true for syllables. When a syllable ends with a vowel (*pilot, spoken, music*), the vowel often says its name. Syllables that end with a vowel are called open syllables. As with almost all phonics concepts, there are a few exceptions to the open-syllable spelling pattern. Although a few words such as *do* and *to* look like open-syllable words, they are not because the vowels do not say their name or long sound.

A spelling pattern chart can serve as a useful reference.

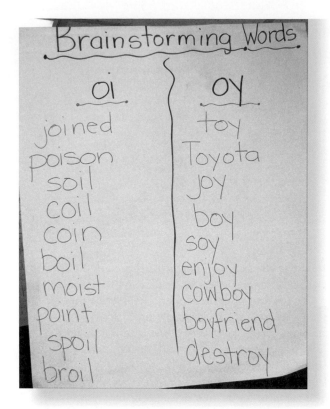

John A. Smith

The concept of open syllables is especially important as students begin to read multisyllable words. As students begin to segment multisyllable words into prefixes, word roots, base words, and suffixes they will learn that some prefixes follow the open-syllable spelling pattern. For example, the prefixes *de* (*department, describe*), *pre* (*prevent, predict*), *pro* (*productive, projector*), and *re* (*refreshment, remainder*) follow the open-syllable spelling pattern.

The list of words in Table 5.9 contains open syllables.

Table 5.9   Open-Syllable Words

a	e	i	o	u
baby	be	hi	go	human
nature	he	silent	no	bugle
favorite	me	final	so	humor
bacon	we	giant	donate	lunar
paper	between	hibernate	local	pupil
later	destroy	library	moment	super
staple	secret	rifle	robot	tuba

SPELLING PATTERN 9: CONSONANT-LE

Many multisyllable words end with the consonant-*le* spelling pattern. Being able to recognize this pattern will help students segment multisyllable words into their constituent parts more quickly. Examples of words containing the consonant-*le* spelling pattern are listed Table 5.10.

Table 5.10   Consonant-*Le* Words

adora<u>ble</u>	an<u>kle</u>	ap<u>ple</u>	bub<u>ble</u>	cir<u>cle</u>
comforta<u>ble</u>	crac<u>kle</u>	gig<u>gle</u>	hand<u>le</u>bar	incredi<u>ble</u>
horri<u>ble</u>	impossi<u>ble</u>	invisi<u>ble</u>	mum<u>ble</u>	peo<u>ple</u>
pud<u>dle</u>	puz<u>zle</u>	rat<u>tle</u>	remarka<u>ble</u>	terri<u>ble</u>
trem<u>ble</u>	tur<u>tle</u>	vegeta<u>ble</u>	hus<u>tle</u>	wig<u>gle</u>

ADDITIONAL WORD CHUNKS

There are some additional spelling patterns that many teachers refer to as word chunks (*all*, *ank*, *ing*, *ink*, *ight*, and *old*). These additional word chunks are drawn from Adams's (1990a) list of the 38 most common phonograms (word endings) and which were not included within the nine common spelling patterns. These chunks cannot be sounded out and must be memorized. For example, the *all* chunk actually makes the same short *o* sound heard in *Bob*, *dog*, *doll*, and *fox*. The *ing* chunk is common both as a word part (*sing*) and as an ending (*ending*), yet it makes a long *e* vowel sound rather than a short *i* vowel sound. The *ink* spelling pattern also makes a long *e* rather than a short *i* vowel sound. Students must also learn to recognize the *ight* chunk with its silent *gh* and long *i* vowel sound. The *o* in *bold* makes a long *o* sound rather than the short *o* sound you would get if you applied phonics rules. Examples of chunk words are listed in Table 5.11.

Table 5.11   Common Word Chunks

<u>all</u>	<u>ank</u>	<u>ing</u>	<u>ight</u>	<u>ink</u>	<u>old</u>
ball	bank	king	light	ink	bold
call	sank	sing	might	pink	fold
hall	tank	bring	tight	wink	gold
mall	thank	swing	slight	blink	told
wall	shrank	thing	fright	think	scold

TEACHING SPELLING PATTERNS: AN EXPLICIT INSTRUCTION MODEL

As described in Chapter 2, explicit phonics instruction can refer to both the overall structure of a lesson as well as the instructional language that teachers use to explain and demonstrate concepts. Mesmer and Griffith (2005) describe five characteristics of explicit phonics instruction that are common to effective phonics programs and approaches. First, phonics instruction is appropriate to students' developmental levels. Second, there is a set of phonics concepts that is to be taught in a specific sequence. Third, phonics instruction language is direct and precise. Fourth, phonics instruction activities provide opportunities for students to practice applying phonics concepts in reading words. Fifth, phonics instruction includes assessment and student accountability.

The explicit phonics lesson format described in this chapter follows a five-step sequence that incorporates these five characteristics.

1. INTRODUCE THE LESSON

Education research is very clear that students retain new information more effectively when they can connect it to previously learned information. An explicit phonics lesson begins with the teacher helping students recall previously learned information about letters, sounds, and spelling patterns. The teacher introduces each lesson by connecting it to previous instruction and providing a purpose for today's instruction. Reading consultant Dr. Deb Glaser suggests using the following instructional language for introducing an explicit phonics lesson:

> *Yesterday we learned about _____.*
> *Today we are going to learn about _____.*
> *We are going to learn about _____ because. . . .*

For example, to introduce a lesson on vowel teams, the teacher might say:

> *Yesterday we were studying long vowel words with the final silent e spelling pattern. Today we will begin learning about another spelling pattern that makes vowels say their names, or long sounds, in words. This new spelling pattern is called a vowel team and you will learn about it because being able to recognize the sounds of vowel teams will help you read many words that you will see in the stories and information books we'll be reading soon.*

2. EXPLAIN AND MODEL

The teacher explains the concept and models (or demonstrates) with a few examples of how the phonics concept or spelling pattern works. One way to begin is to display a list of five or six words that contain the spelling pattern. For example, to continue the lesson on vowel teams, the teacher would write the example words *tail, say, team, seem, boat,* and *grow* on the whiteboard. Then the teacher very directly explains to the students that each of these words contains a vowel team—a spelling pattern in which two vowels appear side-by-side in a word and the first vowel says its name (long sound) and the second vowel is silent. After the explanation, the teacher models reading each of the example words by underlining each vowel team, then points to the consonants and vowel teams while pronouncing and blending the sounds together to pronounce each word.

3. PROVIDE INTERACTIVE GUIDED PRACTICE

The teacher provides instructional guidance and feedback as students work through additional examples of the concept. To continue the vowel team lesson example, the teacher displays 10 to 12 additional vowel team example words on a whiteboard or overhead transparency. These could include *maid, leaf, road, say, mow, seem, snail, coach, steep, toast, sheep,* and *stay.* The teacher then launches into a simple, fast-paced call-and-response routine that reinforces the process of recognizing consonant and vowel team letter sounds and blending them together to pronounce words. The teacher brings students' attention to the first word (*maid*), points to the first letter and says, "sound?" The students reply /m/. The teacher then points with two fingers (to indicate two letters) to the vowel team *ai* and says again, "sound?" The students reply /ai/. The teacher points to the final letter and again says, "sound?" to which the students reply /d/. Then the teacher points to the entire word and says, "word?" to which the students reply "*maid*." The teacher quickly repeats this process with the other example words.

4. PROVIDE MONITORED INDEPENDENT PRACTICE

The teacher monitors students and provides feedback as they work through additional examples on their own or with a partner. Having introduced, explained and modeled, and provided guided practice with vowel team spelling patterns, the teacher provides an opportunity for students to practice reading words with vowel teams on their own. The teacher tells the students they will work together with a partner, gives each pair of students a piece of paper, and instructs them to go on a vowel team word hunt. The students look through books from the classroom and school libraries, examine their core reading program books, and also scrutinize the many posters on the classroom walls looking for and noting words with vowel teams. As the students find and record words with vowel team spelling patterns, the teacher circulates among the students checking to see that the lists are accurate and asking students to read their lists aloud. After 7 to 8 minutes, as students have compiled their lists, the teacher goes back to the board, invites the student pairs to read their words aloud to the class, and as they read the words makes a master list on the board of vowel team words.

5. ASSESS STUDENT LEARNING

During and after instruction, the teacher notes which students have mastered the concept and which will need additional instruction and practice. Instruction should always be linked to assessment to ensure that concepts being taught are appropriate to students' developmental levels and also to monitor how well and how quickly students are learning. At the conclusion of this example five-step explicit phonics instruction lesson on vowel teams, a teacher could prepare 10 vowel team word cards that were not part of the guided and independent practice activities and at a later time, perhaps at the end of each small-group differentiated reading lesson, quickly display the 10 word cards for each student and record how well each student was able to identify the words. Those students who demonstrated difficulty identifying the words could be grouped together for subsequent small-group follow-up vowel team instruction.

The following three lesson plans are examples of how to incorporate the five steps of explicit phonics teaching across various spelling patterns. It is intended that teachers will feel free to modify and supplement these lesson plans in actual practice to best accommodate the instructional needs of their students. What is important is that teachers develop a lesson planning mindset so that they will always remember to include an introduction, followed by clear teacher explanation and modeling of concepts. This lesson planning mindset will remind teachers to plan appropriate, effective interactive guided practice and monitored independent practice activities that will be followed by assessment of student learning.

Explicit Instruction Phonics Lesson Plan 1:

Consonant–Vowel–Consonant Spelling Pattern Lesson

Concept or Objective: Understanding the concept of blending individual letter sounds to form CVC words

Date: _____

Lesson Steps	Activities	Materials
Introduction • Review previous lesson • Connect to today's lesson • Give a purpose for today's lesson	"Students, you have been learning the sounds that each letter makes. Today we will begin putting the letter sounds together. We will do this because blending letter sounds is how people learn to read."	
Explicit teacher explanation and modeling	1. Explain that alphabet letters make sounds, and that reading begins by blending the sounds of the letters together to identify words. 2. Demonstrate blending letter sounds "the slow way, then the fast way" with a pocket chart and letter cards to make the short *a* CVC words (*mat, sat, bat, hat*).	Pocket chart Letter cards (*a, t, m, s, b, h*) for teacher modeling
Interactive guided practice	1. Do Making Words together. Dictate more at-family CVC words for students to make at their desks with individual letter sets. Circulate, monitor, and help students as needed. Show correct CVC word spellings on the pocket chart. 2. CVC phoneme-grapheme matching activity: Give each student a copy of the chart. Draw one on the teacher's whiteboard for Teacher's whiteboard modeling. Begin by pronouncing a CVC word. Ask students to identify the first sound and corresponding letter. Have them write the letter in the first cell, first row of their individual chart. Repeat with the second and third sounds. Then lead students in blending the three letter sounds to read the CVC word. Repeat with four more CVC words in rows 2–5.	Student individual at-family letter sets for guided practice Pocket chart CVC phoneme-grapheme matching chart for each student Teacher's whiteboard

Lesson Steps	Activities	Materials
Monitored independent practice	At/ad word sort: Write the words *bat, bad, cat, dad, fat, hat, had, lad, mat, mad, pat, pad, rat, rad, sat,* and *sad* on the teacher's whiteboard. Make two columns labeled "at" and "ad" on the board. Model sorting the first few words into the two columns. Have students sort the remaining words into the two columns on their individual papers. Circulate, monitor, and help as needed. While circulating, help students blend the CVC words they've sorted and written on their papers.	Teacher's whiteboard Individual student two-column word sort papers
Assessment	Meet with students individually or in small groups. Display 8–10 *at* and *ad* word family CVC word cards. Record how well each student is able to read the word cards and note how much reteaching will be needed.	8–10 *at* and *ad* word family CVC word cards

CVC PHONEME-GRAPHEME MATCHING CHART

Explicit Instruction Phonics Lesson Plan 2:

Consonant Blends Spelling Pattern Lesson

Concept or Objective: Extending students' CVC blending ability to words containing consonant blends

Date: _____

Lesson Steps	Activities	Materials
Introduction • Review previous lesson • Connect to today's lesson • Give a purpose for today's lesson	"Students, you have been learning to blend letter sounds in CVC words. Today we will begin learning a new spelling pattern called blends that builds on the CVC spelling pattern. Learning to read words with consonant blends is the first step to going beyond CVC words to learn to read bigger and longer words."	
Explicit teacher explanation and modeling	1. Explain that a consonant blend is two consonants side-by-side where you hear both consonant letter sounds. 2. Demonstrate consonant blends by writing 6–8 examples of blend words on the teacher's whiteboard (*crab, slap, sled, rest, swim, drip, frog, hunt*). Underline the blends and pronounce the blend sounds and then the whole word.	Teacher's whiteboard
Interactive guided practice	1. Project an overhead transparency containing 8–10 consonant blend words onto the teacher's whiteboard. Point to the first blend word and ask students to study the word and find the blend. Then ask a student to come to the board to underline the blend letters and pronounce the word. Have students copy the blend words onto their own papers and underline the blends. 2. Do a "backward spelling test" activity with blend words. Pronounce 5–6 blend words, sound-by-sound. Have students write the letter corresponding to each sound. Have students blend the letter sounds they have written to pronounce the word.	Blend overhead transparency and overhead projector Teacher's whiteboard Blank paper for students Spelling test paper
Monitored independent practice	Have students work individually or in pairs to find and list blend words in connected texts found in the classroom. Circulate, monitor, and help as needed. List student-located blend words on chart paper for display.	Connected texts, paper, and pencils Chart paper
Assessment	Meet with students individually or in small groups. Display 8–10 blend word cards. Record how well each student is able to read the word cards and note how much reteaching will be needed.	8–10 blend word cards

Explicit Instruction Phonics Lesson Plan 3:

Introducing Syllables Lesson

Concept or Objective: Making students aware of the concept of syllables, preparatory to studying multisyllable words

Date: _____

Lesson Steps	Activities	Materials
Introduction • Review previous lesson • Connect to today's lesson • Give a purpose for today's lesson	"Students, you have learned a lot of spelling patterns found in one-syllable words. [Review the patterns]. Many big words are made up of spelling patterns we have already learned. When studying big words, we call these parts syllables. Today we will learn how to count how many syllables are in a big word because that will help us find the spelling patterns and read the word."	
Explicit teacher explanation and modeling	1. Begin by clapping and counting the syllables in familiar words. Point out that *car* has one syllable, *hotdog* has two syllables, and *basketball* has three syllables. Have students clap and count additional multisyllable words with you. 2. Go to the teacher's whiteboard and write the word *woman*. Make a dot beneath each of the two vowels. Explain to students that each syllable has one vowel sound and by counting the dots beneath each of the vowels we can tell how many syllables are in a big word. Write the words *octopus, pepperoni,* and *refrigerator* on the board. Place and count dots beneath the vowels in each word. Have students, clap and count the syllables with you. Note: Vowel teams and diphthongs get one dot together.	Teacher's whiteboard
Interactive guided practice	Prepare an overhead transparency with 15-20 multisyllable words on it. Give each student a copy of the same page of words. Use the overhead to model making and counting dots beneath the vowels in the first 2-3 words. Then do the next 5-7 words together with the students. Have students come to the board to make and count the dots.	Overhead transparency and student copies of page with 15-20 multisyllable words Teacher's whiteboard
Monitored independent practice	When students appear to have grasped the concept, have them work individually or in pairs to make and count the dots beneath the vowels on the remaining words on the page. Circulate, monitor, and help as needed.	
Assessment	Later in the day provide each student with a slip of paper containing five multisyllable words and ask them to place dots and tell you how many syllables are in each of the five words. Record which students will need reteaching.	Slip of paper containing five multisyllable words for each student

BUILDING STUDENTS' SIGHT VOCABULARIES

When teachers speak of sight vocabulary or sight words they are generally referring to *high-frequency words* such as *a, for, of, some, that, the,* and *very*—words that appear in virtually every sentence. A reader's sight vocabulary consists of high-frequency words that he or she has come to recognize instantly, usually through seeing the words over and over again in print.

Many high-frequency words are phonetically regular (*and, for, with, each*) and can be easily identified using phonics spelling patterns. However, other high-frequency words (*a, because, come, does, give, of, said, was*) are known as *irregular words* because they don't follow the "phonics rules," can't be sounded out, and simply must be memorized.

High-frequency words appear in print so regularly that it makes sense for students to learn to recognize them by sight. For example, 10 words—*the, of, and, a, to, in, is, you, that,* and *I*—make up nearly 25% of the words in print (Cunningham, 2004). It would be cumbersome and counterproductive to have to sound out these words every time they show up. However, because these and other high-frequency words show up so often, most beginning readers learn to recognize them automatically simply from the sheer amount of repetition.

A second reason for helping students quickly increase their sight vocabulary is that good readers use words in their sight vocabulary to help decode unfamiliar words (Brown, 2003; Cunningham, 2004). For example, a student who can automatically recognize the familiar word *big* will have an easier time recognizing the less familiar word *jig*. The unfamiliar word *shank* is less problematic for a student who can already recognize the word *bank* and who also knows the *sh* digraph. Sight words are generally learned through two avenues: wide reading and direct teaching (Cooper, 2000; NRP, 2000).

BUILDING SIGHT VOCABULARY THROUGH WIDE READING

It has been estimated that high school seniors have vocabularies of about 40,000 words (Cooper, 2000). Based on this figure, a minute or two with a calculator suggests that students are learning 3,333 new words per school year, or about 92 new words per week (assuming 36 weeks in a school year). How many teachers can teach 92 new words per week, and have students remember them all? So, where do college-level readers learn all of those words? They learn them from seeing these words over and over during reading in meaningful, connected texts.

Wide reading is the most powerful way for beginning readers to increase the size of their sight vocabulary. Nagy (1988) states that "increasing the volume of students' reading is the single most important thing a teacher can do to promote large-scale vocabulary growth" (p. 32). Anderson et al. (1985) concluded from their review of the research that "the best way to get children to refine and extend their knowledge of letter–sound correspondences is through repeated opportunities to read" (p. 38). Most classroom teachers have had the experience of helping a student decode a word during a reading lesson, and then noticing that the student correctly identified the word the next time it appeared in the reading passage. Large amounts of meaningful reading give students the opportunities to encounter and scrutinize many words over and over, thus increasing their sight vocabulary.

DIRECT TEACHING OF SIGHT VOCABULARY

Teachers commonly use direct teaching of sight vocabulary to ensure that students can recognize high-frequency words quickly and accurately. Many primary-grade teachers use the Fry Instant Words List of the most common 300 words in print during their word identification instruction. The Fry Instant Word lists may be downloaded at: http://connwww.iu5.org/cvelem/RR/Fry_Words.html. Following are several activities for directly teaching high-frequency words.

Incremental Rehearsal

One effective technique for directly teaching high-frequency words is incremental rehearsal (Joseph, 2006). In incremental rehearsal, the teacher prepares a set of 9 word cards that students have already mastered (known words) and also a set of 10 new words (unknown words). To begin, 1 new word card is interspersed with the set of 9 known words. The new word is shown repeatedly along with the known words until it is learned to mastery. Then one of the known words is dropped out of the set, the newly mastered new word becomes one of the known words, and the next new word is added. This cycle of incrementally adding new words to the set and deleting known words is repeated until all 10 new words have become known words. Joseph (2006) lists six steps in the incremental rehearsal procedure.

1. Present the first unknown word, orally read it to the student, and then have the student read it orally.
2. Present the first known word and have the student read it orally.
3. Present the first unknown word; have the student read it orally and then have the student read the first and second known words.
4. Present the first unknown word; have the student read it orally; and then have the student read the first, second, and third known words.
5. When the first unknown word becomes a known word, it remains in the stack and the ninth known word is removed.
6. Continue the procedure until all 9 new words have been introduced. (p. 804)

Preteaching Sight Vocabulary

When examining reading passages prior to using them for instruction, many teachers often notice words that students might not recognize. Rather than risk interrupting the flow of the reading lesson, a few of these potentially unfamiliar words are pretaught during the introduction to the passage. This is very common practice when using a basal or core reading program. Preteaching potentially unfamiliar sight words is especially important when introducing informational texts that contain content-specific vocabulary.

Preteaching sight vocabulary usually includes writing the words on the board, pronouncing the words, underlining or highlighting familiar spelling patterns in the words, and then telling students what the word means.

Word Wall

A word wall (Cunningham, 2004; Wagstaff, 1999) is a very useful resource that many teachers and students use daily to study spelling patterns and also use as a reference during writing workshop. A word wall is an effective device for teaching students to recognize irregular words that don't follow the phonics rules.

To construct a word wall, many teachers write high-frequency or other selected words on index cards and attach them to the word wall in alphabetical columns. Rather than display all the words at once, some teachers add about 5 or 6 words to the word wall each week, so that by the end of the school year there are about 200 words displayed.

Teachers should do a word wall activity each day so that students will be familiar with the word wall and use it regularly. Activities can include chanting a column of words each day; top-to-bottom, bottom-to-top, and in random order to help them become sight words. Teachers often connect word wall words to daily word study instruction. Many teachers enforce the classroom rule that word wall words must be spelled correctly on writing workshop drafts.

Cunningham (2004) suggests a word wall activity she calls "Be a Mind Reader" in which the teacher chooses a word from the word wall and gives students five hints to see how quickly they can determine the selected word. The hints are:

1. *It's on the word wall.*
2. *It has _____ (number of) letters.*
3. *It begins with the letter _____.*
4. *The vowel letter is _____.*
5. *It finishes the sentence _____.*

 ## TEACHING MULTISYLLABLE WORDS

Although multisyllable words may be daunting to some primary-grade students, the study of multisyllable words can be done in a systematic fashion to help young readers begin to see multisyllable words as merely combinations of familiar spelling patterns. Most multisyllable instruction revolves around three major steps: (1) identify prefixes and suffixes, (2) break the word root or base word into syllables, and (3) reassemble all of the word parts and read the word. The following four-step procedure combines steps from two well-known multisyllable instruction resources (Gleason, Vachon, & Archer, 2006; Honig, Dimond, Gutlohn, & Mahler, 2000).

1. *Circle any prefixes and suffixes.* Write the word on the board. Circling the prefixes and suffixes isolates these word parts from the word root or base word, yet leaves them in view for easy recombining after all word parts have been identified.

2. *Put dots under the vowels.* As described in Lesson Plan 3, there is a one-to-one correspondence between vowel letters and syllables. Placing dots beneath the vowels in the word root or base word will help students determine the number of syllables in the root or base and also help make the division into syllables easier. Remember that vowel teams and vowel diphthongs get one dot together.

3. *Divide the word root or base word into syllables.* With dots placed beneath the vowel letters, the next step is to divide the word root or base word into syllables. Most teachers will make a slashmark between the syllables. For example, after steps 1–3 the words *development* and *determination* would look like this:

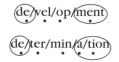

4. *Blend the word parts together*. At this point the teacher points to each of the word parts on the board and leads students in pronouncing each word part, then blending the word parts together to pronounce the word.

The study of multisyllable words is not an exact science. There will be questions about specifics of certain words. Experience will help provide clarification. What is important is that the process of examining multisyllable word parts, segmenting them, and blending them back together will increase students' familiarity with print patterns and their ability to identify unfamiliar words they will encounter in their reading.

ADDITIONAL GUIDED PRACTICE WORD STUDY ACTIVITIES

So far, this chapter has focused on common spelling patterns that students should learn, an explicit instruction model with several lesson plan examples, tips on how to help students build sight vocabulary, and steps for teaching multisyllable words. The following pages present additional word study activities that are appropriate for the guided practice portion of an explicit phonics teaching lesson. Bear in mind that some of these activities will work well across various spelling pattern lessons.

SAY IT SLOW, SAY IT FAST

Many teachers introduce the concept of blending together the sounds of printed letters using the "say it slow, say it fast" explicit instructional language. Write a CVC word (for example, *cat*) on the board, say to students "Let's say it the slow way," and point to each letter individually, inviting the students to join in pronouncing each sound in turn. After pronouncing the third sound, say, "Now, let's say it fast" and sweep your hand left-to-right beneath the letters as the students pronounce the word. Some teachers like to begin teaching the blending concept with two-letter words including *ad, an, at, Ed, if, in, it, on*, and *up*.

BLENDING LETTER SOUNDS WITH STICKY NOTES

Write each alphabet letter on a sticky note and display the notes on the board. Then take three of the letters (*m, a, t*), make a CVC word, and invite the students to "say it slow, then say it fast." Replace the initial letter with other sticky note letters to form a variety of word family words. Invite students to come to the front of the class and change the sticky note letters to make words you dictate. When students become proficient at manipulating the initial consonants (*mat* to *hat*), the focus can shift to final consonants (*run* to *rug*), then to manipulating both initial and final consonants (*dog* to *fox*).

MAKING WORDS

Making words is a popular activity developed by Cunningham (2004) in which the teacher provides each student with a set of letter cards that form a "mystery word" and then dictates words that the students form at their desks with the letter cards. Begin by determining the subsets of words that can be formed from the mystery word letters and then, one by one, dictate these words to the students and help them

Post-It® notes for
teacher modeling
and guided practice.

John A. Smith

form the words at their seats. Many teachers use a pocket chart to display the letters at the front of the class so that students can check to see if they've made the words correctly. After students have formed a number of dictated words, some teachers invite students to write a list of how many two-letter, three-letter, four-letter, and so on words they can make using the letter cards from the mystery word.

MAKING BLEND WORDS WITH AN OVERHEAD PROJECTOR

This activity is a variation of the sticky note activity described earlier. After explaining and demonstrating the consonant blend spelling pattern with the list of example words, move the overhead projector to the front of the classroom and shine it on the board. From a set of plastic alphabet letters, gather the letters *a, e, u, b, c, d, l, m, n, r, s, t, t* and place them on the projector. Begin by demonstrating how to select and use the plastic letters to form a few blend words, then ask for student volunteers to come to the projector and select and use the letters to form blend words. For example, model the blending process with the words *slab* and *crab*, then ask students to make the words *bend, lend, blend*, and *bust, dust, must, rust*, and *trust*.

BACKWARD SPELLING TESTS

A favorite guided practice activity is what some teachers and students call a "backward spelling test." Veteran teachers may know this activity as "sound spelling." In a backward spelling test, the teacher pronounces the *sounds* of a word's letters, one sound at a time, and the students write the letter that makes each sound. For example, to further reinforce the concept of consonant blends, begin by distributing spelling test paper (see Appendix F) to the students. Select a consonant blend word such as *flip* and provide the letter sounds in the following manner:

1. *Word number one; the first sound is /f/. Write the letter that says /f/.*
2. *The second sound is /l/. Write the letter that says /l/.*
3. *The third sound is /i/. Write the letter that says /i/.*
4. *The last sound is /p/. Write the letter that says /p/.*

At this point the students look at the letters they've written, blend the letter sounds together, and on cue from the teacher, pronounce the word aloud together.

DIGRAPH WITH EVERY-PUPIL-RESPONSE CARDS

Prepare 5 × 7-inch index cards with the four consonant digraphs arrayed on each card as shown in Figure 5.1.

Pronounce some words that contain consonant digraphs and instruct students to rotate the index card so that the digraph contained in the pronounced word is upright on the card. This is called an every-pupil-response activity (Cunningham, 2004) because every student participates. Every-pupil-response activities allow teachers to quickly observe which students have mastered the concept and which students have not.

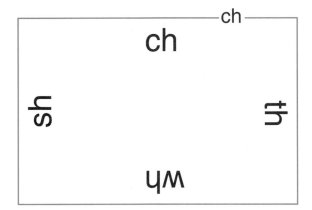

Figure 5.1
Pupil Response Cards

DICTATION

Dictation activities are a natural follow-up to the spelling tests. After introducing and explaining a spelling pattern using a list of example words, dictate a few sentences that contain the spelling pattern. For example, dictate a few sentences such as *Chuck thanked Shelly in church* or *The white whale chased the shark*. Students write the sentences on their writing paper. Then the teacher can write each sentence on the board and have students check their own sentences for accuracy.

CONCENTRATION

This is a very versatile activity. After introducing and explaining final silent *e* words with a list of example words, teachers and students can play Concentration using a piece of posterboard with 18 library pockets rubber-cemented to the front side. Index cards with final silent *e* words are inserted into nine of the library pockets. Nine other index cards with the CVC version of the final silent *e* words (*tap–tape, dud–dude, mad–made*) are inserted into the other nine library pockets.

Students explore "tickle words" in a word study lesson.

Steven Von Niederhausern

Many teachers introduce this game first as a whole-class activity and then later let students use it as a small-group or center activity. One word of caution is important here. Games like Concentration can be very time-consuming. Teachers need to think of the learning:time ratio and decide if the learning from an activity justifies the amount of time that it takes.

Final Silent E Flashcards

As described in the vignette at the beginning of this chapter, students enjoy using final silent *e* word cards to further explore the final silent *e* spelling pattern. (Appendix D shows final silent *e* words that can be made into CVC words by folding back the final *e*. The first step is to pronounce the final silent *e* words as students find and hold them up until the students can easily recognize them. Then after the students have folded back the final *e* on each word card, alternate pronouncing the short vowel and long vowel version of the words while students find and hold up the correct word.

Long Vowel Pattern Sort

After introducing and explaining the vowel team spelling pattern using lists of example words, teachers can reinforce the vowel team spelling pattern, and other ways of spelling long vowel sounds, with an activity known as a long vowel pattern sort. For example, begin by asking students to brainstorm as many words as they can with the long *a* sound (*main, game, freight, day, whale, bait, same, sleigh, stay, scale, paid, great, play*, etc.). List these words on the board and bring their attention to the various spelling patterns represented among the words. Then guide the students in sorting the words into columns on the board. One long vowel pattern sort yielded the pattern categories shown in Table 5.12.

Table 5.12   Long *A* Spelling Pattern Sort

ae	ai	ay	ei	ea
date	bait	day	freight	great
made	main	play	sleigh	
late	sail	stay	neighbor	
skate	straight	away		
game	braid	say		
whale	chain	runway		
space	main			

Notice that the first column is comprised of final silent *e* words. Columns two and three are vowel team words. Columns four and five are patterns that are very infrequent and may need to be mentioned only as they appear. Many teachers like to do the long vowel pattern sort on a large piece of chart paper so that they can use the charts for a follow-up word hunt activity to add to the list of words sorted into spelling pattern columns.

SPELLING PATTERN BINGO

Teachers can occasionally give students a list of 24 vowel team words, along with a blank personal Bingo card (five rows and five columns, with the center cell labeled FREE). Students write the vowel team words in random order on their Bingo cards. Each student's list of the 24 words can serve as a check-off sheet to help them avoid forgetting some words or writing other words twice on their Bingo cards. As the teacher pronounces each vowel team word from the list, students use math manipulatives, soda bottle twist-off caps, or other objects to cover the words on their Bingo page. After the first student has called "Bingo," teachers may call out another two or three words to keep the game going a little longer. Like Concentration, Bingo is quite time consuming, so use it judiciously.

WORD SORTS

Word sorts are popular activities for giving students hands-on practice in identifying word families and spelling patterns (Bear, Invernizzi, Templeton, & Johnston 2008; Morris, 1999). Simply put, individuals or small groups of students sort a deck of 12 to 15 words printed on index cards into two or three word families or spelling patterns. For example, the following 15 *r*-controlled vowel words were sorted into three spelling pattern columns.

bar	*for*	*her*
car	more	germ
star	snore	jerk
yard	storm	clerk
smart	sport	serve

A word sort.

John A. Smith

Word sorts teach students to do what teachers want them to do all the time as readers: use parts of familiar words (*for*) to help identify unfamiliar words (*sport*). Cunningham (2004) calls this reading by analogy.

Spelling can serve as an effective word sort follow-up activity. Each student receives a sheet of paper divided into three columns labeled with three spelling patterns. The teacher pronounces one of the spelling pattern words and asks the students to determine which column it belongs in and to write the word. This combination of both recognizing and writing word families and spelling patterns is especially effective in helping students understand the reading and writing connection.

Bear et al. (2008) provide a sequential list of 117 word sorts. These include various short vowel sorts, spelling pattern sorts, and a variety of additional sorts including sorts of inflections, multisyllable words, word roots, and word concepts.

I WIN–YOU WIN

This is a simple word card game that can be used to help reinforce students' familiarity with spelling patterns and high-frequency words. After teaching students about *r*-controlled vowels with example word lists, prepare a deck of word cards with words containing *r*-controlled vowels. Show the first word card, and if the student correctly recognizes the word, he or she keeps the card. If the student misreads the word, it goes back into the deck to be shown again. Teacher and student continue until the student has all of the word cards.

DIPHTHONG WALL CHART

An effective activity for exploring vowel diphthongs is to have students construct a diphthong wall chart. Hang a long piece of colored butcher paper on a classroom wall and across the top in big letters print the sentence *The boy pointed as the loud cow chewed straw.* This sentence contains the six diphthongs. Next, brainstorm on the board all the words students can think of that make the /oy/ and /ou/ sounds.

Invite students to print a favorite diphthong word on an index card and tape the diphthong card to the diphthong wall chart below the corresponding diphthong word in the sentence. Finally, send students on a diphthong hunt to look for additional diphthong words in their reading books and other print. The next day, write the words they found on index cards and add them to the appropriate columns of diphthong words growing on the diphthong wall chart. Leaving the chart displayed prominently in the classroom helps maintain students' awareness of diphthong words and provides a valuable reference tool for reteaching when necessary.

OPEN–CLOSED SYLLABLE DOOR

Honig et al. (2000) suggest a simple activity for teaching the concept of open syllables. Prepare a strip of paper where the last part is folded over to make a "door" (see the illustration). Print the letters *h* and *i* on the first part of the paper strip, and the letter *t* on the door. Explain to the students that when a vowel comes at the end of a word or syllable it is "open" and usually says its name or long sound. However, when a consonant comes after the vowel, it "closes" the vowel so the vowel can't say its name and has to make some other sound.

Demonstrate with the paper strip that when the door is closed the students read the CVC, closed-syllable word *hit.* When the door is open, they read the open-syllable word *hi.* Repeat the teaching process with the words *men, sob, hen,* and *got.*

An open–closed syllable word sort provides an effective follow-up activity for helping students learn that when decoding an unfamiliar multisyllable word, they may need to try a word both ways (open or closed). For example, students may need to try the word *music* as a closed syllable (*mus-ic*) and as an open syllable (*mu-sic*) to see which way makes sense. Honig et al. (2000) suggest the following words for an open–closed syllable sort: *music, goblin, begin, helmet, open, traffic, student, basket, total, silent, hidden, bottom, basic, rabbit, pilot, muffin, baby, forest, always, silent.*

CONCLUDING THOUGHTS

Although every published core reading program has its own unique scope and sequence of decoding skills, the spelling patterns and procedures described in this chapter are common to all programs. Many teachers closely follow the sequence of decoding skills specified in the core reading program teacher's manual. Other teachers use a supplemental decoding program to provide additional decoding instruction. What is important is to identify a sequence of word identification skills that covers these major spelling patterns and to follow it carefully.

Once a sequence of skills has been identified, explicit instruction should be provided so that students are not left to guess how letter sounds and spelling patterns work. Teachers need to link new concepts to previously learned concepts, making the instructional purpose clear to students. Teachers should explain and demonstrate new concepts and then provide guided practice and independent practice activities to help students gradually assume ownership of the skills. And of course, instruction should always be linked to assessment data.

Although word identification instruction has often been associated with skills and drills, effective reading teachers know that word identification instruction can be gamelike and enjoyable. Effective decoding instruction makes use of the specificity of teaching spelling patterns systematically and explicitly, along with the functionality of applying spelling patterns in meaningful reading.

SUGGESTED ACTIVITIES TO EXTEND YOUR LEARNING

1. Interview a local first- or second-grade teacher about his or her philosophy toward teaching phonics. Do the spelling patterns to be taught come from the basal reading program, the state core curriculum, a supplemental phonics program, or some combination of these? To what extent does the teacher use the five steps of explicit instruction: introduce, explain and demonstrate, provide interactive guided practice, provide monitored independent practice, and assess student learning?
2. Find a child in your family or neighborhood and try a simple phonics lesson. (1) Select a spelling pattern such as blending CVC words or final silent *e*, and *explain* the pattern to the child using a list of example words. (2) Engage the child in one or more of the *exploration* activities described in this chapter. (3) Help the child find examples of the spelling pattern in meaningful print.
3. Get a copy of the book *Words Their Way* (2008) by Bear, Invernizzi, Templeton, and Johnston. Use the lists of word sorts in the Sample Word Sorts by Spelling Stage appendix to create your own file of words sorts on index cards organized in zipper-type snack-sized plastic bags.

REFERENCES

Adams, M. J. (1990a). *Beginning to read: Thinking and learning about print*. Cambridge, MA: MIT Press.

Adams, M. J. (1990b). *Beginning to read: Thinking and learning about print (summary)*. Urbana–Champaign, IL: Center for the Study of Reading.

Adams, M. J. (2001). Alphabetic anxiety and explicit, systematic phonics instruction: A cognitive science perspective. In S. B. Neuman & D. K. Dickinson (Eds.), *Handbook of early literacy research*. New York: Guilford Press.

Anderson, R. C., Hiebert, E. F., Scott, J. A., & Wilkinson, I. A. G. (1985). *Becoming a nation of readers: The report of the Commission on Reading*. Washington, DC: National Institute of Education.

Bear, D. R., Invernizzi, M., Templeton, S., & Johnston, F. (2008). *Words their way: Word study for phonics, vocabulary, and spelling instruction* (4th ed.). Upper Saddle River, NJ: Merrill/Prentice Hall.

Blevins, W. (1998). *Phonics from A to Z: A practical guide*. (1998). New York: Scholastic.

Brown, K. J. (2003). What do I say when they get stuck on a word? Aligning teachers' prompts with students' development. *The Reading Teacher, 56*(8), 720–733.

Clymer, T. (1996). The utility of phonic generalizations in the primary grades. *The Reading Teacher, 50*(3), 182–187. (Original work published 1963)

Cooper, J. D. (2000). *Literacy: Helping children construct meaning* (4th ed.). Boston: Houghton Mifflin.

Cunningham, P. M. (2004). *Phonics they use: Words for reading and writing* (4th ed.). New York: Longman.

Duffy, G. G. (1998). Powerful models or powerful teachers? An argument for teacher as entrepreneur. In S. Stahl & D. Hayes (Eds.), *Instruction models in reading.* Mahwah, NJ: Erlbaum.

Gleason, M. M., Vachon, V., & Archer, A. L. (2006). *Rewards reading excellence: Word attack & rate development strategies: Multisyllabic word reading strategies*. Longmont, CO: Sopris West.

Honig, B., Dimond, L., Gutlohn, L., & Mahler, J. (2000). *Teaching reading sourcebook: Sourcebook for kindergarten through eighth grade*. Novato, CA: Academic Therapy Publications.

Johnston, F. P. (2001). The utility of phonics generalizations: Let's take another look at Clymer's conclusions. *The Reading Teacher, 55*(2), 132–143.

Joseph, L. M. (2006). Incremental rehearsal: A flashcard drill technique for increasing retention of reading words. *The Reading Teacher, 59*(8), 803–807.

Mesmer, H. A. E., & Griffith, P. L. (2005). Everybody's selling it—but just what is explicit, systematic phonics instruction? *The Reading Teacher, 59*(4), 366–376.

Morris, D. (1999). *The Howard Street tutoring manual: Teaching at-risk readers in the primary grades*. New York: Guilford Press.

Nagy, W. E. (1988). *Teaching vocabulary to improve reading comprehension*. Newark, DE: International Reading Association.

National Reading Panel. (2000). *Teaching children to read: An evidence-based assessment of the scientific research literature on reading and its implication for reading instruction. Report of the subgroups.* National Institute of Child Health and Human Development. Retrieved from www.nichd.nih.gov/publications/nrp/smallbook.cfm

Pressley, M. (2002). *Reading instruction that works: The case for balanced teaching* (2nd ed.). New York: Guilford Press.

Pressley, M., Rankin, J., & Yokoi, L. (1995). *A survey of instructional practices of primary teachers nominated as effective in promoting literacy* (Reading research report no. 41). Athens: Universities of Georgia and Maryland, National Reading Research Center.

Pressley, M., Yokoi, L., Rankin, J., Wharton-McDonald, R., & Mistretta, J. (1997). A survey of instructional practices of Grade 5 teachers nominated as effective in promoting literacy. *Scientific Studies of Reading, 1*(2), 145–160.

Rayner, K., Foorman, B. R., Perfetti, C. A., Pesetsky, D., & Seidenberg, M. S. (2002, March). How should reading be taught? *Scientific American.* 84-91.

Torgesen, J. K. (2004). Lessons learned from research on intervention for students who have difficulty learning to read. In P. McCardle & V. Chhabra (Eds.), *The voice of evidence in reading research.* Baltimore: Brookes.

Wagstaff, J. M. (1999). *Teaching reading and writing with word walls: Easy lessons and fresh ideas for creating interactive word walls that build literacy skills.* New York: Scholastic.

Differentiated Small-Group Reading Instruction

6

by John A. Smith

Meredith's Low-Middle Reading Group

*I*t's early October in Meredith Bush's first-grade classroom. Meredith has just finished her whole-class teacher read-aloud and a word study lesson. In preparation for her differentiated small-group reading lessons, Meredith reviews with her students the procedures for what will take place during the next 60 to 70 minutes. She reminds her students that when they are not meeting with her in their reading group they will be reading silently to themselves, rereading leveled reading books together with a partner, completing an assignment, writing, or working productively at one of several learning centers Meredith has set up in the classroom. When everyone is clear about what to do, Meredith excuses her students to their seats and centers.

As the students settle into their tasks, Meredith heads to the kidney-shaped small-group reading instruction table and gathers the books and word cards she had ready for the first group from a small plastic tub and places them on the table. She calls for the low-middle group and they quickly set aside what they are doing and join her at the table. Each of Meredith's 15-minute small-group reading lessons follows a pattern of (1) beginning with a quick review of high-frequency word cards, (2) a word study lesson, (3) connected text reading, and (4) a fluency-building activity.

Knowing that she has a lot to cover with this group in just 15 minutes, Meredith picks up a stack of 10 high-frequency word cards. These cards are words 31 to 40 from the Fry Instant Word List. She briefly displays each word card, noting how well it is recognized by the group members. Less-recognized words are reinserted into the stack. After going through the stack of words twice, Meredith determines that the students still need more practice with these words and that it will be good to review the same words again tomorrow.

Although Meredith's whole-class word study lesson this morning was on the vowel teams ai and ay, Meredith knows that this group of lower-reading students still needs to master recognizing words with consonant blends. Meredith distributes small whiteboards and markers to each student and picks up one for herself. She writes the word fog on her board and asks the students to do the same. She leads the students in reading the word fog the slow way, then the fast way. Then she changes fog to frog on her board and again leads the students in blending the letter sounds and reading the word. After writing and reading five or six blend words with her students, Meredith quickly distributes decodable books that feature blend *words. She reads the first few pages aloud together with her students and then instructs them to finish reading softly to themselves so she can listen to each student individually and provide guidance as needed.*

As her students finish reading the decodable books, Meredith gives each student a copy of one of the leveled books that accompanies her classroom core reading program selection for that week. She gives a brief introduction to the leveled book that includes activating her students' relevant background knowledge, and providing some information about the story's setting and characters as she and the students examine the illustrations on the first few pages. Meredith and her students generate a few predictions together, she reminds them to note any unfamiliar words in the text and think of questions about the text, and then she assigns them to begin reading the text quietly to themselves. She alternately taps her students on the wrist as a signal for them to read aloud softly so she can listen in and either give word identification support or briefly discuss the story.

In between listening to her students, Meredith glances at the wall clock and realizes that she's already 18 minutes into her lesson with this group. She gathers the leveled books from her students, telling them that they'll finish the story tomorrow. Her final instruction to the group is to pair up and reread the blend words decodable book before reading independently and participating in center activities. Meredith replaces the materials back into the plastic tub, picks up the tub for the next reading group, and takes a deep breath.

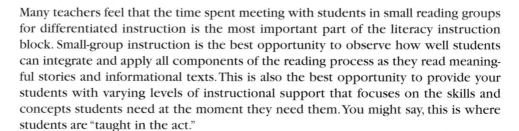

Many teachers feel that the time spent meeting with students in small reading groups for differentiated instruction is the most important part of the literacy instruction block. Small-group instruction is the best opportunity to observe how well students can integrate and apply all components of the reading process as they read meaningful stories and informational texts. This is also the best opportunity to provide your students with varying levels of instructional support that focuses on the skills and concepts students need at the moment they need them. You might say, this is where students are "taught in the act."

This chapter provides information about the differentiated small-group reading instruction strand of the literacy instruction framework and specifically information about the following topics:

- Issues associated with small-group instruction
- Placing students in differentiated reading groups
- Differentiated small-group reading lesson components

 ## ISSUES ASSOCIATED WITH SMALL-GROUP INSTRUCTION

The practice of providing reading instruction to students in small groups is a compromise between whole-class instruction and individualized instruction. Whole-class instruction may be appropriate for students functioning at grade level, but can be a waste of time for advanced students and frustrating for slower students. Individualized instruction is ideal for targeting lessons exactly to a student's specific learning needs, but is impractical for a class of 20 to 30 students. Small-group instruction brings together students with similar instructional needs.

Differentiated small-group reading instruction focuses on word study, comprehension, and oral reading fluency depending on the needs of the students in each group by using different materials and activities. For example, second-grade students in the lowest reading group may be working on blending individual letter sounds in CVC words such as *sat, bed*, and *hid*. Students in the low-middle reading group may be working on long-vowel spelling patterns such as *sail, beat*, and *roam*. Students in the middle-high reading group may have mastered most spelling patterns and will focus on building oral reading fluency through repeated readings and performance reading. Students in the high reading group may be solid in their phonics and fluency and will focus instead on discussing a chapter from a novel or an informational text.

An important characteristic of differentiated small-group reading instruction is its flexibility. Flexible grouping is similar to traditional ability grouping in that it involves pulling together groups of students with common instructional needs. However, flexible grouping is different in that it is more fluid. Students are not locked in to the same group for months, if not the entire school year. Rather, differentiated small-group membership changes on a regular basis. For example, a student may meet with three to five classmates in a reading group to solidify his or her knowledge of vowel patterns, but the following week join a different reading group to begin studying multisyllable words. This fluidity and flexibility allows students to better progress through reading instruction concepts at their own rate.

PLACING STUDENTS INTO DIFFERENTIATED READING GROUPS

Teachers use data from a variety of reading assessments to place students in reading groups. Early in the school year teachers use data from screening assessments to identify their students' reading ability levels and make initial group lists. Then, throughout the remainder of the school year teachers use data from progress-monitoring assessments to switch students from group to group depending on how quickly they are progressing. Teachers may also use data from diagnostic assessments to pinpoint exactly which reading concepts are problematic for struggling readers, and form reading groups of students with similar reading problems. Teachers strive to place students into groups where reading texts are at their instructional level. This is the level where the text is "just a little over their heads" and where the students' reading ability will stretch and grow with teacher instruction and support.

SCREENING ASSESSMENTS

Screening assessments are given at the beginning of each school year in order for teachers to determine which students are at or above grade level, a little below grade level, or substantially below grade level. This information is used to determine the levels of instructional support each student will receive to catch up or stay on track to successful reading achievement.

Teachers can give screening assessments in a variety of reading areas, depending on grade level. For example, kindergarten teachers will want to screen their students in the areas of print awareness, alphabet knowledge, and phonemic awareness. First-grade teachers will want to screen students in the areas of phonemic awareness, phonics, and recognition of high-frequency words. Second- and third-grade teachers will want to screen their students in the areas of phonics, fluency, and recognition of high-frequency words. Teachers at all grade levels may want to give screening assessments to identify students' levels of oral language, spelling, vocabulary, and comprehension.

One example of a screening assessment is the Dynamic Indicators of Basic Early Literacy Skills (DIBELS) test (Good & Kaminski, 2002; Good, Simmons, & Kame'enui, 2001; Kaminski & Good, 1996). DIBELS provides a series of quick, one-minute assessments commonly used in the areas of alphabet knowledge, phonemic awareness, phonics, and fluency. For each assessment there are nationally normed benchmarks so that teachers can tell immediately where each student stands in comparison to grade-level standards at the beginning of the year and throughout the remainder of the year.

Another common screening assessment procedure is for teachers to get a copy of the school's comprehensive reading program books at each grade level. Then, during the first several days of school, invite students to read aloud individually from appropriate-level books and take notes on each student's reading ability. Many teachers begin by having each student read a page from the middle of a book one level below grade level and then make a judgment that this particular level was either too hard, too easy, or just right for teaching (instructional level). If the level was too hard, select easier levels until finding the student's instructional level. If the initial level was too easy, move up through the levels until finding the student's instructional level.

With screening assessment data in hand, teachers can set about the task of assigning students to beginning-of-year differentiated small groups. Teachers also use screening data to determine initial instructional objectives, materials, and activities for each group.

PROGRESS-MONITORING ASSESSMENTS

Whereas teachers in years past often had to wait until the end of the school year to learn how well their students achieved in reading, teachers now can progress monitor their students' rate of reading achievement on a weekly, monthly, or quarterly basis and adjust instruction accordingly. Progress-monitoring assessments are designed to give teachers a continual stream of reading achievement data on each student. Once teachers have used screening data to make initial reading group placements, they use progress-monitoring data to continually check the appropriateness of those group placements and make adjustments as needed.

The frequency of progress monitoring will vary from student to student. It is common practice in many schools across the country to progress monitor the "at or above grade level" students only three times each school year—in fall, winter, and spring. Students that are slightly below grade level may be progress monitored on a monthly basis. Students who are substantially below grade level generally receive a progress-monitoring assessment each week. This model of differentiated assessment saves time by gathering student reading assessment data on the basis of need.

Grade-level teacher teams frequently meet together to review progress-monitoring data on their students, plan instruction, and make adjustments in the membership of differentiated reading instruction groups. Progress-monitoring data allow teachers to identify which students are not keeping up with the instructional pace and need more instructional time during which they will be retaught below-grade-level and at-grade-level reading skills in order to catch up.

Because the DIBELS assessments described earlier can be given quickly, they also work well for monitoring students' progress throughout the school year. Most commercial comprehensive reading programs include in-program assessments. These assessments are given several times throughout the school year and provide teachers with data on how well students are learning the concepts and skills covered in the comprehensive reading programs.

Many teachers use data from running records (Clay, 1993, 2000) to monitor students' progress and place them into reading groups. A running record is a quick procedure wherein a teacher listens to a student read aloud and records the student's oral reading errors (or miscues) on a scoring sheet. From the number of errors, the teacher calculates the percentage of words read correctly. This percentage allows the teacher to determine whether the student is reading that particular text at an independent, instructional, or frustration level (see Chapter 10).

It is important to remember that student placements in reading groups should always be seen as temporary. After placing students into initial reading groups at various levels of difficulty, teachers should always "try out" the placements for a couple of weeks by observing how well each student does with the instructional materials and activities, then fine-tuning the placements by moving students to small groups at other reading levels as needed.

Diagnostic Assessments

Diagnostic assessments are designed to identify, on a skill-by-skill basis, a student's reading strengths and weaknesses. Because diagnostic assessments typically take longer to administer, most teachers give them only to students who are reading below grade level.

One example of a diagnostic assessment is the CORE Phonics Survey (Gutlohn, 1999). This survey contains a series of subtests beginning with alphabet letters and sounds and also phonemic awareness. The survey then assesses students' knowledge of consonant blends and digraphs, short vowels, and various long vowel spelling patterns. The survey concludes with a subtest assessing students' ability to decode multisyllable words.

Data from diagnostic assessments can be very helpful for struggling readers who need the most focused and intensive instruction. Rather than grouping students by achievement levels as is often done with screening and progress-monitoring data, teachers can use diagnostic assessment data to group students for instruction based on the exact reading skills they need at any given time.

DIFFERENTIATED SMALL-GROUP READING LESSON COMPONENTS

How teachers spend those precious 10 to 20 minutes in each small-group differentiated reading lesson depends on what mix of reading skills instruction a particular group of students needs most. Instruction for lower-level readers focuses primarily on alphabet knowledge, phonemic awareness, phonics, and high-frequency word recognition skills. Readers who are more advanced may need more instruction in oral reading fluency in order to consolidate reading skills and build automaticity. Higher-level readers who have mastered word reading skills and fluency benefit most from an instructional focus on vocabulary, comprehension, and building content knowledge.

Teachers with a firm understanding of the components of reading, the progression of reading skills, and students' instructional levels and needs will be able to determine how to allocate instructional time among four differentiated small-group reading lesson components: high-frequency word review, word study, text reading, and oral reading fluency.

The following sections of this chapter describe many instructional activities for differentiated small-group reading lessons. There is not enough time for teachers and students to complete all of these activities in the 10 to 20 minutes available each day for small-group reading lessons. It is expected that teachers pick and choose from among these activities based on students' instructional needs and the amount of instructional time that is available.

High-Frequency Word Review

It is important to be clear that high-frequency word review is meant to help students *recognize* printed words that occur often in the stories and texts they read. For example, the first 300 Fry Instant Words (Fry, 2006) appear in about 65% of texts. This is different from helping students understand the meaning of selected vocabulary words chosen from reading program stories and teacher read-aloud texts. High-frequency word review is intended to help students build reading automaticity so that they instantly recognize commonly occurring words and thus avoid having to sound out such words each time they appear.

Teachers generally select words to review from one of several sources. Many teachers select words from generic lists of common words such as the Fry Instant Words list. Other teachers may select review words from lists that accompany each lesson in the comprehensive reading program teacher manuals.

For example, many teachers teach their students to recognize the 300 most common words. First-grade teachers often focus on teaching their students to recognize the first 100 words by the end of the school year. Second-grade teachers focus on making sure their students recognize both the first and second 100 words. Third-grade teachers will try to ensure that their students will recognize all 300 common words.

Most teachers create sets of 10 high-frequency word cards and introduce them to their students in small-group reading lessons by displaying a word card, pronouncing the word, bringing students' attention to the letters in the word, and inviting students to pronounce the word again in unison with the teacher. Then a second word is similarly introduced and the first word is reviewed. Words are introduced and reviewed cumulatively in this manner until students easily recognize all 10 words. Then another set of 10 words is introduced. Teachers keep track of the high-frequency words students have learned until all the high-frequency words recommended for that school year have been learned. Recognition of high-frequency words is an important complement to decoding words by recognizing and blending letter sounds and spelling patterns.

Word Study

These brief lessons are an opportunity for teachers to reteach or provide extra practice to students on word study skills at their instructional level. Whereas whole-class word study lessons often follow the scope and sequence outlined in the comprehensive reading program teachers manuals and lessons, differentiated small-group word study lessons topics frequently derive from screening, progress monitoring, or diagnostic assessment data that identify the specific set of reading skills that a particular group of students needs to learn. For example, the popular program *Words Their Way* (Bear, Invernizzi, Templeton, & Johnston, 2008) has an assessment component that determines each student's developmental level of word knowledge. These developmental levels are correlated to a wide range of instructional activities. Many teachers use the phonics component of supplemental programs such as *Read Well* published by Sopris West or *Fundations* published by Wilson Language Basics in their differentiated small-group reading lessons.

Like whole-class word study lessons, differentiated small-group word study lessons should be very explicit and systematic, following the explicit teaching steps outlined in Chapter 5: introduction, teacher explanation and modeling, interactive guided practice, monitored independent practice, and assessment. However, because the amount of time available for word study lessons during differentiated small-group instruction is very limited, the focus of these lessons is on teacher explanation, modeling, and interactive guided practice. The independent follow-up portion of the word study lesson may become part of the students' activities during independent reading and center time.

Most small-group word study lessons consist of the teacher explaining and modeling a spelling pattern using a small whiteboard and then leading students in interactive guided practice by having them write and read additional examples of the same spelling pattern on their individual whiteboards. For example, a teacher may begin a lesson on the long vowel spelling patterns *oa* and *ow* by reminding students that they have already studied the *ai*, *ay*, *ea*, and *ee* vowel team spelling patterns. The teacher then writes examples of *oa* and *ow* words in two columns on the whiteboard:

boat	grow
loan	slow
soap	mow

The teacher reads the words to the students and underlines the vowel team in each word, points out how each vowel team makes the long *o* sound, and has the students read the list of words aloud in unison. The teacher models blending the letter sounds and vowel teams together to pronounce each of the words (*b–oa–t*: *boat*).

The teacher then writes additional examples of *oa* and *ow* words on the board and invites the students to write the words on their boards and find and underline the vowel teams.

road	blow
toast	show
coach	grown

The teacher monitors and helps as the students write the words and underline the spelling patterns on their whiteboards. The teacher and students then blend and read the words aloud together.

The teacher concludes the small-group word study lesson by giving each student a copy of a decodable reader featuring vowel teams. Because the students are familiar with the vowel team spelling pattern the teacher expects that they should be able to read the words in the decodable successfully. For independent practice, the teacher

Word Study

Word study group lessons are particularly appropriate for struggling readers. These lessons give you an opportunity to provide additional focused instruction to those students who need it. The word study group lessons may be a review of instruction provided earlier or they may present the word study concepts in a different way that may help your struggling readers better connect the new concepts to prior understandings.

assigns the students to partner-read the decodable reader with a group member after the small-group lesson, then find and write a list of vowel team words—found in the decodable—on a piece of paper.

TEXT READING

There are two purposes for the text reading component of differentiated small-group reading lessons—comprehension and fluency—and teachers may choose to focus on one or both of these purposes depending on the students' instructional needs. For example, the text may be a leveled book that is part of the comprehensive reading program and covers the same theme or content as the selection from the whole-class lesson presented earlier in the day. In this case the teacher may focus on reinforcing vocabulary, building background knowledge, and helping students apply comprehension strategies as they read the text to focus on its content. This option is generally more appropriate for advanced readers who already have a strong foundation in word reading skills.

The other option is to use the text to focus on building students' oral reading fluency. This option is best suited for lower-functioning readers who are still working to solidify their knowledge of spelling patterns and their ability to read words quickly and accurately. In this case the teacher may begin by giving a very quick overview of the text's content. The teacher would then model fluent oral reading by reading a paragraph from the text aloud to the students as they follow along or read along in their copies of the text. Then the teacher would assign the students to read the remainder of the text softly to themselves while "listening in" and providing guidance and support as needed. The following section of this chapter describes small-group text-reading instruction that focuses on comprehension and oral reading fluency.

Focusing on Reading Comprehension

Just as small-group word study instruction mirrors and builds on whole-class word study lessons, small-group text reading instruction that focuses on comprehension mirrors and builds on the text reading comprehension lessons provided during the whole-class part of the daily 3-hour literacy instruction block. Comprehension instruction is generally addressed in three steps: what to do before, during, and after reading. Bear in mind that in the limited amount of time available during differentiated small-group reading instruction, it is likely that only one of these aspects of comprehension instruction may be addressed in one day's lesson.

Before Reading

There are several major before-reading activities that are effective in preparing students to read and comprehend a text successfully. First, teachers build students' meaning vocabulary and background knowledge. Second, teachers alert students to text structure. Teachers also lead students to predict the content of the texts they will read. Again, because of the limited amount of time available during differenti- ated small-group reading lessons, before-reading instruction activities are quick and concise.

Preteaching meaning vocabulary prior to text reading can focus on Tier Two or Tier Three vocabulary words (Beck, McKeown, & Kucan, 2002). Tier Two words are general vocabulary words such as *savor* and *impressive* that may be unfamiliar to students but are words that students will more frequently encounter and want to use as they progress as readers. Teachers generally want to focus on identifying and teaching Tier Two words when using narrative texts. Tier Three words are content- specific words such as *metamorphosis* and *immigration* that teachers want to identify and teach when students are reading informational texts. Teachers should limit the number of preteaching vocabulary words to two to four per text selection.

Steps for explicitly and quickly preteaching vocabulary words include the following:

1. Bring students' attention to the word by pronouncing the word, showing it to them in the text selection, and reading the sentence that contains the word aloud to the students.
2. Provide a quick meaningful explanation and an example or two of the word's meaning.
3. Invite students to use the word in a meaningful sentence.

Vocabulary words should also be displayed on word cards or on a vocabulary chart to facilitate reviewing the words on a regular basis to ensure that the words remain familiar to the students.

In the fast-paced context of small-group instruction, background-knowledge activation and building usually takes the form of a brief discussion. The teacher usu- ally introduces the topic and provides a brief elaboration, depending on students' existing familiarity with the topic. When the topic is less familiar to students, using the whiteboard can be effective in focusing the discussion. For example, to develop background knowledge about classifications of animals the teacher can write the names of familiar animals on the whiteboard and lead students in categorizing them as shown in Table 6.1.

Table 6.1 Classifying Familiar Animals

Mammals	Reptiles	Birds	Insects
cow	snake	chicken	beetle
horse	lizard	eagle	mosquito
pig	chameleon	robin	tick
deer	tyrannosaurus	duck	bee

Hanging vocabulary charts.

John A. Smith

Animal vocabulary.

John A. Smith

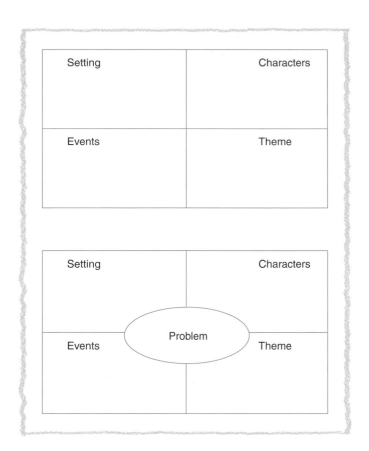

Figure 6.1
Two Narrative Text Graphic Organizers

Any classification or webbing activity should reflect the content of the passage as closely as possible.

After preteaching selected vocabulary and building students' background knowledge, many teachers focus briefly on text structure to help students set up a mental framework to organize the information that they will be reading. One very effective way to focus on text structure is to use graphic organizers. A graphic organizer is a chart or graph that the teacher displays on the whiteboard with space to fill in information from the text either at a few stopping points during reading or after the text has been read entirely. To use a graphic organizer the teacher must preview the text, determine how the information is organized, and either choose or design the graphic organizer. The first step is to determine whether the text is narrative or informational. If the text is narrative, the two graphic organizers shown in Figure 6.1 would work, depending on whether or not there is a problem that is central to the story.

If the text is informational, one of the graphic organizers illustrated in Figure 6.2, or an adaptation, should work to help students see the relationships among the major information points in the text. In addition, some informational

myeducationlab

Vocabulary

Go to MyEducationLab, "Vocabulary," and watch the video *Introducing Words to Young Readers*.

As you view the video, notice how the teacher introduces two new words during the before-reading portion of a small-group lesson.

- What criteria might the teacher have used to select the two words she chose to teach?
- How did the teacher redirect a student's attention during the lesson?
- What other activities might the teacher use to introduce new words?

Figure 6.2
Informational Text
Graphic Organizers

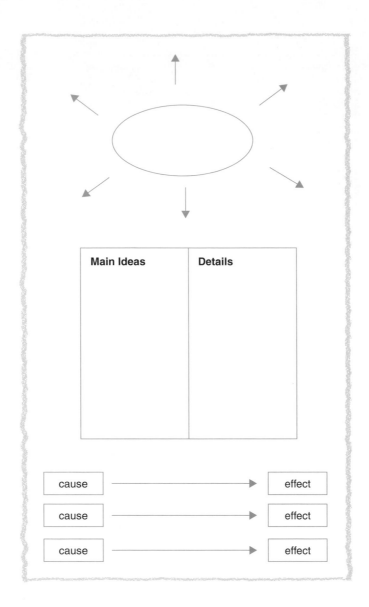

texts have a table of contents that can help students understand the structure of the texts.

Before reading the text, the teacher displays the graphic organizer, explains the parts of the graphic organizer, and then alerts students to be on the lookout for pieces of information that would help fill in the graphic organizer. The filling-in process may take place at stopping points during reading or after the entire text has been read. Figure 6.3 is an example of a completed graphic organizer that helps students recognize the text structure of Arnold Lobel's story *The Great Blueness and Other Predicaments*, about a wizard living in an all-gray world who invents color.

Notice how the graphic organizer in Figure 6.3 fits into the before-reading portion of the graphic organizer lesson plan form. Teachers may have students fill in the graphic organizer at preselected stopping points during the reading or fill in the graphic organizer after the reading is completed.

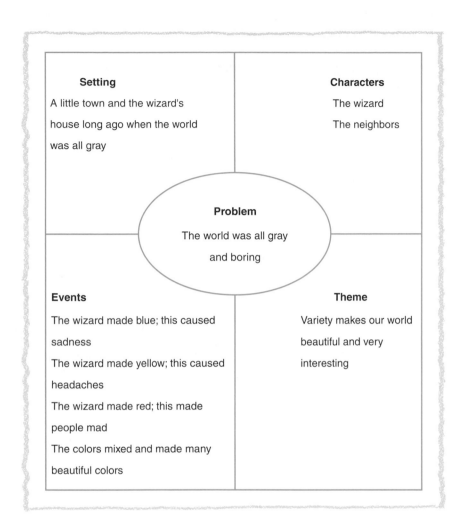

Figure 6.3
Completed *Great Blueness* Graphic Organizer

A fourth before-reading activity that teachers often include is predicting the text content. Predicting is a commonly used comprehension strategy that guides students to use their existing background knowledge to set a purpose for reading. When the text is narrative, students generally predict what they think will happen. With informational texts, students predict what content the text might cover. Rather than simply guessing, prediction uses background knowledge to make informed predictions.

Because explicit teaching begins with teacher explanation and modeling, teachers often model for their students how to make informed predictions. For example, in preparing students to read *The Great Blueness and Other Predicaments*, the teacher would provide introductory information about setting and characters and then model and justify a prediction before asking students to contribute predictions of their own. The teacher might say:

> *I predict that the people will paint the whole world blue* because *the title says "The Great Blueness."*

After the story has been read, the teacher and students return to the predictions to see how accurate they were. As students determine whether or not each prediction

Explicit Instruction Graphic Organizer Lesson Plan

Concept or Objective: Using a graphic organizer to represent the organization of information in students' reading

Date: _____

Lesson Steps	Activities	Materials
Introduction • Review previous lesson • Connect to today's lesson • Give a purpose for today's lesson	Review with students the characteristics of narrative and information texts. "Today we'll begin learning how to organize information from narrative texts according to narrative text characteristics because organizing information helps us understand and recall information more effectively."	
Explicit teacher explanation and modeling	1. Display the graphic organizer on the teacher's whiteboard. Remind students of the five parts. Explain that almost all stories have these parts. 2. Read a *Frog and Toad* story aloud to the students and fill in the five parts of the graphic organizer as you go.	Teacher's whiteboard Narrative text structure with problem graphic organizer (see the second example in Figure 6.1) A *Frog and Toad* story
Interactive guided practice	1. Display a blank version of the graphic organizer on the whiteboard. Also, distribute a handout copy of the blank graphic organizer to the students. 2. Read another *Frog and Toad* story. Guide the students in identifying the five parts of the story and filling them in on the graphic organizer on the whiteboard. As you do so, instruct the students to fill in the information on the handout copies of the graphic organizer at their seats.	Narrative text structure with problem graphic organizer (see the second example in Figure 6.1) Handouts of the graphic organizer for the students A *Frog and Toad* story
Monitored independent practice	1. Distribute another handout copy of the blank graphic organizer to the students. 2. Have them work in pairs to fill in the handout graphic organizer using a story from the comprehensive reading program. Circulate, monitor, and assist as students complete the task.	Another handout copy of the blank graphic organizer for the students Story from the core reading program books
Assessment	As students work to complete the graphic organizer, note which students will need reteaching and practice.	
Accommodations for students	Repeat the filling-in process one step at a time. Stick with each part until the student demonstrates understanding of that part.	

was accurate, they can be asked to cite sentences from the text to support their assertions.

During Reading

During reading is the time when teachers typically teach the comprehension strategies of clarifying and question generating. Many teachers, when focusing on comprehension, instruct students to look for words and concepts they don't understand (clarifying) as they read and also to think of questions they have about the text (questioning).

Clarifying, also referred to often as monitoring, leads students to pay close attention to whether or not the text is making sense to them. For example, *The Great Blueness and Other Predicaments* contains the words *potion* and *afternoon teas.* These words are likely to be unfamiliar to many early readers and are good candidates for clarifying. To explain and model clarifying, the teacher would say:

> *I've found a word that I think we should clarify. The word is* potion. *This sentence says, "The wizard made many wonderful magic potions and spells." In this story the word* potion *means medicine. Back in the wizard days there were no drugstores. Wizards would mix together and cook plants and other ingredients to make potions, like medicines, that could help sick people get better.*

Following the modeling of clarifying with a word or two, the teacher asks the students to suggest other words they have found in the text that they didn't understand. This activity can be very motivating for slower readers because now it is desirable not to know what some words mean.

Carr (1985) and Reutzel and Cooter (2007) describe a strategy called click or clunk that helps students monitor whether or not a text makes sense. At the end of each sentence or paragraph, the teacher or students can ask if that text "clicked" or "clunked." If the text clunked, then a follow-up discussion is held to clarify exactly where the meaning broke down and what comprehension strategies might be employed to fix the problem.

Many teachers use another comprehension-monitoring activity known as Knew–New–Q (see Figure 6.4). During and after reading, students complete the three-column Knew–New–Q chart by writing down (1) what information they already knew, (2) what information was new, and (3) what questions they still have about the text.

Question generating is the other major comprehension strategy that takes place during reading. The National Reading Panel (NRP, 2000) compared the effectiveness of the major comprehension strategies and found that teaching students to generate questions about text content is the most powerful. There are a couple of activities that are effective in teaching students to generate questions. One activity is paragraph-by-paragraph teacher modeling. The teacher and students read a text together, one paragraph at a time, either aloud together or silently. At the end of the paragraph the teacher models generating a question, then asks students to generate questions. For example, after the teacher and students read a paragraph in *The Great Blueness and Other Predicaments* in which the wizard invents the color blue and the neighbors paint everything blue, the teacher says:

> *My question is, why did the neighbors paint everything blue instead of leaving some things gray so there would be two colors?*

Figure 6.4   Knew–New–Q

Knew	New	Questions
		Name _____

The teacher and students discuss their answers to the question, then the teacher invites students to contribute their questions. After the discussion, the teacher and students read the next paragraph and the teacher again models generating a question. The teacher monitors how well the students are catching on to generating their own questions and then gradually begins to fade out the modeling and allows students to generate more of the questions on their own.

Another question-generating activity is to teach students to generate questions before, during, and after reading (see Figure 6.5).

The teacher begins to teach this process to students by modeling with a short story or informational passage. The teacher projects a copy of the Questions: Before, During, and After form onto the whiteboard. The teacher scans the title, illustrations, and enough information from the passage to generate a before question about the text. Then the teacher reads the passage and models generating one or two during reading questions. After reading the passage, the teacher models generating an after-reading question. To complete the activity, the teacher and students answer the questions. After modeling this activity a few times, the teacher can provide the form to students as a handout and begin having the students generate questions on their own. As students become proficient at using the form to generate questions, they can complete the form after small-group reading time as an independent reading or center activity.

After Reading

After reading is the time to tie all of the information together and ensure that students understood the text content. The most common way of doing this is summarizing passage content. Summarizing is one of the best-known and most difficult

Figure 6.5   Questions: Before, During, and After

Name _____

	Questions	Answers
Before		
During		
After		

comprehension strategies for students to learn. The difficulty lies in the fact that many students are unable to distinguish main ideas from details. There are several effective activities that help students learn to summarize. The Main Ideas and Details graphic organizer presented earlier in this chapter (Figure 6.2) lends itself well to teaching students to summarize informational texts. The teacher models by filling in information in both the Main Ideas and Details columns, explaining why some ideas are main ideas and others qualify only as supporting details. When the graphic organizer is complete, the teacher models how to link the main ideas together to compose a summary. List, Group and Label is another popular summarizing activity for informational texts. The teacher leads students in listing important information, grouping the information in categories, and then labeling each group. List, Group, and Label charts make effective outlines for follow-up informational writing.

A similar activity for narrative text is to use the information that the students have recorded in the Setting, Characters, Events, and Theme graphic organizer (see Figure 6.3, for example) to compose a summary. Returning to *The Great Blueness and Other Predicaments* example, the teacher would lead students in combining information from the graphic organizer to generate a summary such as:

> *A wizard living in a boring gray world invented blue, yellow, and red. The colors made people sad, then achy, then angry. The colors mixed and made many beautiful colors. Variety makes life interesting.*

This activity can also work for informational texts. The teacher simply leads the students in using the information recorded on any graphic organizer to compose a summary.

PEARSON
myeducationlab

Comprehension

Go to MyEducationLab, "Comprehension," and watch the videos *Before Reading, During Reading,* and *After Reading.*

As you view the videos, pay particular attention to the comprehension strategies the teachers use before reading to prepare students to read successfully, the strategies used to guide students during reading, and the strategies used after students read a meaningful passage.

- Video #1: How does the teacher prepare and motivate the students to read the selection successfully?
- Video #2: What strategies did the teacher use to build students' comprehension during reading?
- Video #3: What activities did the teacher use to build students' comprehension after reading the selection?

Figure 6.6   Somebody Wanted But So

Somebody . . .	Wanted . . .	But . . .	So . . .

A "List, Group, and Label" graphic organizer.

John A. Smith

Another activity for teaching students to summarize stories that contain problems is called "Somebody Wanted But So." Using the Somebody Wanted But So format (Figure 6.6), the teacher reads a short story to the students, then models listing the main character in the first column, what that character wanted in the second column, the problem to be overcome in the third column, and the character's actions to overcome the problem in the fourth column. Horizontal lines can be drawn across the form to create two or three sections for completing the form with multiple characters from the story.

Somebody	Wanted	But	So	S
Crocodile	to eat Mrs. Chicken	Mrs. Chicken said they were sisters	Crocodile didn't eat her yet	
Mrs. Chicken	to see how beautiful she is	Crocodile grabbed her leg	Mrs. Chicken had to wait to see herself.	
Mrs. Chicken	not be eaten by Crocodile	Crocodile said I'll fatten you up then eat you	Mrs. Chicken got fatter and Crocodile got thinner and hungrier	
Crocodile	to eat a-fat Mrs. Chicken	traded eggs with Crocodile	Crocodile believed they were sisters	

John A. Smith

A "Somebody Wanted But So" graphic organizer.

Focusing on Oral Reading Fluency

For many students, particularly struggling readers, differentiated small-group reading lessons should focus on building oral reading fluency. Oral reading fluency is defined as reading quickly, accurately, and with good expression (NRP, 2000). Fluency is critically important to early readers because it is the link between phonics and comprehension. As students learn to read words quickly and accurately their attention is freed from the demands of decoding and made available for attending to comprehension, the meaning of what they read.

The NRP describes two major approaches to building students' oral reading fluency: wide reading (described in Chapter 7) and guided oral reading practice. The research literature on fluency revolves around four kinds of fluency-building activities: teacher modeling, performance reading, repeated reading, and assisted reading.

Teacher Modeling

As with all good teaching, fluency instruction begins with teacher explanation and modeling. Teacher modeling activities that focus on the expression aspect of oral reading fluency include teacher think-aloud, good–bad reading cards, and shared reading. In teacher think-aloud (Osborne & Lehr, 2003) the teacher reads a few sentences aloud, then explains to the students the thought processes that lead to the teacher's expressive oral reading of the text. Osborne and Lehr provided the following example of a teacher think-aloud using the popular children's book *The Paperbag Princess* (p. 6):

> Teacher reads from text: *"The Prince should have been happy, but he wasn't."*

> Teacher Think-Aloud: *Did you hear how I grouped the words "The prince should have been happy"? That's because the words go together. And then I paused a little before I read the words "but he wasn't." This comma (points to the comma) told me to do that.*

Explicit Instruction Quotation Marks Fluency Lesson Plan

**Concept or Objective: Using quotation marks effectively
to help improve expression in students' reading**

Date: _____

Lesson Steps	Activities	Materials
Introduction • Review previous lesson • Connect to today's lesson • Give a purpose for today's lesson	"Students, we have been studying fluency, ways to read more smoothly. Most stories include dialogue (characters talking to each other), and good readers make dialogue in stories sound like real talking. Quotation marks tell us when characters in printed stories are talking. We learn about quotation marks because they help us read dialogue with more expression."	
Explicit teacher explanation and modeling	1. Write 3–4 sentences that contain quotation marks on the teacher's whiteboard. Point out to students the quotation marks in each sentence. Explain to students the purpose of the quotation marks. In each sentence, underline who is talking in one color and what is being said in another color. 2. Read the sentences together with the students, emphasizing expression in the dialogue.	Teacher's whiteboard
Interactive guided practice	1. Invite students to make up and contribute sentences with dialogue. Write the sentences on the teacher's whiteboard and invite students to come to the board and underline the speaker and the dialogue. 2. Read the sentences together with the students, emphasizing expression in the dialogue.	Teacher's whiteboard
Monitored independent practice	1. Give each student a handout with 10–12 sentences containing dialogue. Assign the students to underline the speaker with one color and the dialogue with another color. 2. Instruct students that when they have finished underlining the sentences on the handout, they are to find a partner and read the sentences on the handout to each other, emphasizing expression in the dialogue. 3. Optional: Photocopy a page containing dialogue from this week's reading program story. Assign students to underline speakers and dialogue in each sentence and then read the page to a partner, emphasizing expression in the dialogue.	Handout with 10–12 dialogue sentences Photocopy a page containing dialogue from this week's reading program story
Assessment	Listen to students reading dialogue from the reading program story and note how well each student recognizes and uses dialogue. Note which students will need reteaching and further practice.	
Accommodations for students	Repeat the explicit teacher explanation and modeling step with the student until he or she understands the concept of quotation marks.	

Third-grade teacher Tami Zirker uses good–bad reading cards to model for her students how to read with good expression, along with several ways not to. Tami writes the terms *Robot Reading, Messed-Up Punctuation, Over the Top*, and *Good Fluent Reading* on four index cards. With a small group of students seated by her at the kidney-shaped table, Tami puts the first card, Robot Reading, on the table and reads a few sentences from the students reading text in a monotone voice, as the students follow along in their copies of the text. Then she and her students discuss whether or not that sample of reading sounded good, and why or why not. Then she repeats the process with the Messed-Up Punctuation card, ignoring all punctuation so that the oral reading is totally unintelligible. Again, Tami provides a discussion of the quality of the oral reading and the importance of attending to punctuation. The Over the Top demonstration is too fast and overly expressive. Finally, Tami displays the Good Fluent Reading card and models how good readers sound. After the discussion, Tami shuffles the cards and gives the students a turn at reading poorly and reading fluently. The juxtaposition of good and poor reading makes it all the more clear to Tami's students what they need to do in order to read fluently. For a detailed example of a punctuation fluency lesson, see the Explicit Quotation Marks Fluency Lesson Plan.

Shared reading is a very common four-step early reading practice in which teachers model fluent reading. Teachers, often using a big book, will first introduce a text with a quick picture walk to familiarize students with the text content. Teachers conduct a picture walk by pointing to objects and characters in the illustrations or photographs, and generating quick clarifying discussions by asking and discussing questions such as, "What's this called?" "What can you tell me about this?" "Who's this person?" "What do think this person might do?" The next step is for the teacher to read the text aloud *to the students*, pointing to the words and modeling good expression. Then the teacher reads the text aloud *with the students* in unison as he or she teacher continues to point to the words and students follow the model of fluent reading. This step may happen several times until the students are able to read the text confidently with the teacher's support. Finally, when the students have demonstrated that they are ready, the teacher invites them to read the text aloud *on their own*, though the teacher continues pointing to the words to keep the group together in their oral reading.

Many teachers engage students in a number of shared reading follow-up activities to build word recognition and fluent reading skills. Teachers may note which words were most troublesome to students during the successive readings and come back to these words and focus on the applicable spelling pattern. For example, students may have trouble reading the word *sing* during shared reading, so afterward the teacher writes the word *sing* on the whiteboard and explains the sound of the *ing* chunk and then provides a few more examples of *ing* words such as *wing, bring*, and *thing*. The teacher then asks students if they can think of any additional *ing* words to add to the list on the board. When the list is complete, the teacher and students read the list of *ing* words together several times and then return to the text and reread the sentences that contain *sing* or other *ing* words.

Perhaps the most effective shared reading follow-up activity is for the teacher to put the students into pairs and have them partner-read the text using small, regular-sized copies. As the students partner-read, the teacher circulates, listens in, and provides additional modeling and instructional support.

Whereas shared reading is commonly done with big books, teachers can also use the shared reading procedure with other text formats including texts projected

PEARSON
myeducationlab

English Language Learners

Go to MyEducationLab, "English Language Learners," and watch the video *The Second Rereading in a K–3 Multilingual Classroom.*

As you view the video, notice how the teacher modeling and peer support associated with shared reading helps ELL students develop fluent oral reading skills.

- The video example takes place in a whole-class setting. How might shared reading be adapted for ELL students in small groups?
- What is the teacher's role in this shared reading lesson?
- What features of the big book support students' fluency development?

on the whiteboard with an overhead projector, texts written on chart paper, and in small groups with regular-sized texts.

Performance Reading

Like teacher modeling, performance reading also focuses on the expression aspect of oral reading fluency. One popular form of performance reading is readers' theater. Readers' theater is highly motivating and is an excellent way to get students to read narrative texts multiple times in order to build fluency. Creating a readers' theater is simply a matter of identifying narrative texts that are rich in dialogue, excerpting important dialogue, and writing a few "narrator" parts to tie the dialogue together.

A quick way to convert a text into a readers' theater is with overhead transparencies. A text such as a *Frog and Toad* story can be put onto overhead transparencies and students can be taught to read the story through shared reading. After the students have learned to read the text well, the teacher underlines each character's dialogue in a different colored overhead marker. Dialogue markers such as "said Toad" and "she cried" are also underlined with another color. The nondialogue parts become the narrator parts and are not underlined. Thus a *Frog and Toad* story would result in four parts: Frog's dialogue underlined in green, Toad's dialogue underlined in blue, the "said" dialogue markers underlined in red, and the narrator parts that are not underlined. The class is divided into four groups, each group is assigned one of the parts, and soon a readers' theater is under way.

Rasinski (2003) has adapted readers' theater for informational texts in an activity he calls radio reading. In radio reading, an informational text is converted into a two-part script that imitates a two-person newscast. Students enjoy trying to imitate the evening news anchors as they read the informational script with as much expression as they can muster. The radio reading script shown in Figure 6.7 was created from the informational book *Mummies Made in Egypt* (Aliki, 1979).

Repeated Reading

Repeated reading (Samuels, 1979) involves students reading a text multiple times in order to build reading rate and accuracy. Unlike performance reading that focuses on building expressive reading, the purpose of repeated reading is to get students to process a large number of words in connected text repeatedly to build recognition of spelling patterns and high-frequency words.

Many teachers use a stopwatch to time students' successive reading of a text. The timing of repeated readings provides an element of suspense and progress monitoring that many students find highly motivating and that makes students more willing to read a passage multiple times.

One common version of repeated reading is for teachers to have the students work in pairs. Each member of the class has a copy of the same text, usually a grade-level text. The teacher says "go" and clicks a stopwatch. In each pair, Student A reads the text aloud while Student B follows along. After 1 minute, or sometimes 2 minutes, the teacher calls time and Student B notes how many words Student A had read when time was called. Then the process is repeated as Student B reads the text for 1 or 2 minutes while Student A notes how many words Student B has read.

Figure 6.7   Mummies Made in Egypt

by Aliki

Performers: News-person #1 and News-person #2

News-person #1	We are here to report some very important information about mummies.
News-person #2	We have learned that ancient Egyptians believed that a person would start a new life after they died. They believed that the person's soul would travel back and forth to a new world.
News-person #1	They believed that the person's soul needed their body to come back to, so that is why Egyptians preserved dead bodies as mummies.
News-person #2	A mummy is a dead body, or *corpse*, that has been dried out so it will not decay. The earliest mummies were dried out naturally in the hot dry sands of Egypt's deserts.
News-person #1	Later, the Egyptians wrapped the mummies in cloth, and buried them in wooden coffins and put them in tombs made of brick and stone.
News-person #2	It took 70 days to prepare a mummy. First they took out the dead person's inner organs. They cut a hole in the mummy's side to remove the *intestines*. They pulled the dead person's brains out through the nose with metal hooks.
News-person #1	The inner organs were kept in jars with a chemical called *natron* that dried out the body parts. After the inner organs were removed the *embalmers* also put natron inside the body to dry it out.
News-person #2	After 40 days the *natron* was removed from the body, and the body was cleaned with oils and spices.
News-person #1	The body was packed with new chemicals to keep it dry. The mummy's eyes were closed, and the nose was stuffed with wax.
News-person #2	The hole in the mummy's side was sewn up and the mummy was carefully wrapped with long strips of cloth.
News-person #1	After the *embalmers* finished wrapping the mummy, they painted it to look like the person and then covered it with *resin*, a sticky substance that dried into a hard covering.
News-person #2	When the mummy was finished, they made a coffin to put the mummy in for burial. The coffin was decorated with pictures of gods and magic spells to protect it. Jewels and other treasures were also put into the coffin.
News-person #1	Finally, the mummy and its coffin were placed in a tomb made of brick and stone. The Egyptian *pyramids* are large tombs that are burial places for powerful Egyptian rulers.
News-person #2	There would be an elaborate funeral parade. The mummy would be placed in the tomb, sometimes in a secret chamber, then the tomb would be sealed shut for the mummy's eternal resting place.
News-person #1	Thank you very much, and now back to our teacher.

Source: Radio reading script by John A. Smith, Department of Elementary Education, Utah State University. Based on *Mummies Made in Egypt*, by Aliki, 1979, New York: HarperTrophy.

In some classrooms the student who is following along also checkmarks any words that are omitted or misread and subtracts them from the total number of words read. The practice of counting off students' oral reading errors during repeated reading maintains a focus on accuracy so that students aren't reading unnecessarily and unnaturally fast. A single passage may be read three or four times by each student before the teacher and students move on to another passage. Students often record their total number of words read across successive readings on a personal chart. Many students find this activity highly motivating as they continually try to improve their reading speed. It is important to remind students that they are competing against themselves, not against other students.

Assisted Reading

Assisted reading happens when a reader reads along with another reader, often a stronger reader, in order to receive support and build fluency. Perhaps the most commonly used version of assisted reading is partner reading.

Partner reading can be organized in various ways. Partners can be friends, self-selected by the students. Teachers can pair struggling readers with stronger-reading classmates. Teachers at different grade levels can pair younger readers with older readers. Adults can serve as reading partners. The intent is that partners support each other in reading, helping with difficult words and other challenges.

In many classrooms, teachers pair students for partner reading and each pair designates who is Student A and Student B. The teacher says, "Student A, begin reading" and each Student A begins reading softly aloud while each Student B follows along and helps as needed. After 3 to 5 minutes the teacher says, "Student B, read" and each Student B immediately picks up where Student A left off and continues the reading. After another 3 to 5 minutes the teacher announces, "Student A, read" and the process continues until both Students A and B have had several turns to read aloud.

During this partner reading time the teacher circulates, listens in, and provides guidance and feedback. The best way to improve students' oral reading fluency is to provide them with many opportunities to practice reading aloud while receiving feedback (NRP, 2000). This form of partner reading is a very effective way to provide large amounts of oral reading practice and feedback.

Listening centers are another common way of having readers read along with a model of fluent oral reading. Five to six copies of a text are placed at a table in the back of the classroom. An audio recording of the text is played on a tape recorder or CD player and students read along with the recoding while listening on headphones. Listening center recordings are often commercially produced tapes or CDs of the stories from the comprehensive reading program. However, many teachers create their own listening center recordings of favorite teacher read-aloud books.

Although this activity can be very productive, there are several cautions that should be noted. Students might waste time at the listening center, goofing with the technology or simply not reading along with the recording and staring off into space. A good practice is to build an accountability component into the listening center. One way to provide accountability is to inform students that after they have spent time at the listening center, they will be expected to read the text aloud to the teacher.

 ## CONCLUDING THOUGHTS

Differentiated small-group instruction is an opportunity to provide instruction that is carefully focused on students' shared reading instruction needs. Teachers have many instructional options as they meet with small groups for instruction. The membership of differentiated small groups should be based on screening, progress monitoring, and diagnostic assessment data. Group membership should be reviewed and adjusted on a regular basis according to students' levels of progress.

It is clear that many more activities were presented in this chapter than teachers would have time to do in the 10 to 20 minutes available each day for each group's differentiated small-group reading instruction. Teachers need to pick and choose activities based on the instructional needs of the students in each group. Some activities may stretch over several days. Other activities may be introduced during the small-group time and completed during independent reading and center time.

SUGGESTED ACTIVITIES TO EXTEND YOUR LEARNING

1. Have class members share recollections and impressions of ability grouping from their own primary-grade years. What was it like to be assigned to the "low" group? Were there opportunities to move from group to group? Were there group-to-group differences in the quality of reading materials? Was that an effective way to manage reading instruction?

2. Find a beginning reader in your family or neighborhood and teach him or her a shared reading lesson. Gather a selection of picture books at the child's level and let the child choose one. Do a picture walk of the cover and inside illustrations. Read the story aloud to the child and then again aloud with the child in unison. Then ask the child to read the story aloud to you. Finish with some follow-up teaching activities.

3. Meet with a small group of education classmates, select a story from a basal reading program, and develop a lesson plan for the story. Generate a list of *before-reading* activities including building background knowledge, introducing vocabulary, identifying and teaching a spelling pattern, and setting a purpose for reading. Prepare activities for the *during-reading* portion of the lesson including identifying stopping points for discussions and a list of questions to discuss and words and concepts that might need clarification. Finally, develop some *after-reading* activities including summarizing the story content, following up on spelling pattern instruction, and extending student learning through writing, dramatizations, projects, research, and other curriculum integration activities.

REFERENCES

Aliki. (1979). *Mummies made in Egypt*. New York: HarperTrophy.

Bear, D. R., Invernizzi, M., Templeton, S., & Johnston, F. (2008). *Words their way: Word study for phonics, vocabulary, and spelling instruction* (5th ed.). Upper Saddle River, NJ: Merrill/Prentice Hall.

Beck, I., McKeown, M. G., & Kucan, L. (2002). *Bringing words to life: Robust vocabulary instruction*. New York: Guilford Press.

Carr, E. (1985). The vocabulary overview guide: A metacognitive strategy to improve vocabulary comprehension and retention. *Journal of Reading, 28*(8), 684–689.

Clay, M. M. (1993). *An observation survey of early literacy achievement*. Portsmouth, NH: Heinemann.

Clay, M. M. (2000). *Running records for classroom teachers*. Portsmouth, NH: Heinemann.

Fry, E. B. (2006). *The reading teacher's book of lists*. San Francisco: Jossey-Bass.

Good, R. H., & Kaminski, R.A. (2002). *Dynamic indicators of basic early literacy skills* (6th ed.). Eugene, OR: Institute for the Development of Educational Achievement.

Good, R. H., Simmons, D. C., & Kame'enui, E. J. (2001). The importance and decision-making utility of a continuum of fluency-based indicators of foundational reading skills for third-grade high-stakes outcomes. *Scientific Studies of Reading, 5*(3), 257–288.

Gutlohn, L. (1999). CORE phonics survey. In *Assessing reading: Multiple measures*. Novato, CA: Arena Press.

Kaminski, R.A., & Good, R. H. (1996). Toward a technology for assessing basic early literacy skills. *School Psychology Review, 25*, 215–227.

National Reading Panel. (2000). *Teaching children to read: An evidence-based assessment of the scientific research literature on reading and its implication for reading instruction. Report of the subgroups.* National Institute of Child Health and Human Development. Retrieved from www.nichd.nih.gov/publications/nrp/smallbook.cfm

Osborne, J., & Lehr, F. (2003). *Focus on fluency.* Honolulu: Pacific Resources for Education and Learning.

Rasinski, T.V. (2003). *The fluent reader: Oral reading strategies for building word recognition, fluency, and comprehension.* New York: Scholastic.

Reutzel, D. R. & Cooter, R. B. (2007). *Strategies for reading assessment and instruction: Helping every child succeed* (3rd ed.). Upper Saddle River, NJ: Merrill/Prentice Hall.

Samuels, S. J. (1979). The method of reported reading. *The Reading Teacher, 32*, 403–408.

Children's Literature

Anderson, H. C. (1999). *The ugly duckling.* New York: Morrow Junior.

Coerr, E. (1986). *The Josephina story quilt.* New York: HarperTrophy.

Cowley, J. (1980). *Mrs. Wishy Washy.* Auckland, New Zealand: Shortland Publications.

Cowley, J. (1987). *Just this once.* San Diego: The Wright Group.

Dr. Seuss (1960). *Green eggs and ham.* New York: Random House.

Lobel, A. (1979). *Frog and Toad are friends.* New York: HarperCollins.

Lobel, A. (1983). *Fables.* New York: HarperTrophy.

Lobel, A. (1987). *The great blueness and other predicaments.* New York: HarperCollins.

MacLachlan, S. (1987). *Sarah, plain and tall.* HarperTrophy.

Rylant, C. (1996). *Henry and Mudge: The first book.* New York: Aladdin.

Turner, A. (1985). *Dakota dugout.* New York: Macmillan.

Independent Activities

by John A. Smith

7

Becky's Small-Group Lesson

*I*t's mid-morning, and Becky Monhardt's first-grade classroom is humming like a beehive. Becky is seated at her small-group reading instruction table with five students working their way through a decodable book. Becky leans in and listens briefly to each of them, reminding Jacob to look at each of the letters in the words rather than just looking at the first letters and guessing at the words. The students handle the decodable book well because it features spelling patterns that Becky has already taught them.

The remainder of Becky's 23 students are working in small groups at five differentiated activity centers she has set up to provide practice on the reading skills and strategies she teaches in her small groups. Allie, Emma, and Michael, three of Becky's emerging readers, are completing a picture sort to strengthen their phonemic awareness skills. Madison and Hannah, and Parker and Anthony are partner-reading the leveled reading book from their small-group lesson to increase their oral reading fluency. Elena, Marcus, Ethan, and Sebastian are tracking print with their fingers in copies of a prerecorded Frog and Toad book Becky has placed in the listening center. These four readers know that they'll soon be reading this book aloud to Becky when it's time for their reading group lesson.

Danny, Drew, and Kylie are seated at the writing center, illustrating pages for their soon-to-be published books about their families and pets. Ahmad, Shanise, Emily, and Samantha, four of Becky's most capable readers, are working together to complete a Main Ideas and Details graphic organizer page following their reading of an informational book on reptiles. Shanise makes sure that they note that iguanas sometimes eat other iguanas.

As Becky again reminds Jacob to look at all the letters in a word, she scans across her classroom and notes that, for now, all of her students seem productively engaged. She hopes that the upcoming transition to the next round of center activities will go as smoothly as the last.

A question that teachers frequently ask when they are preparing to implement differentiated small-group reading instruction is,"What do I do with all of the other students while I am meeting with a small group?" The simple answer is to provide students with opportunities to practice the reading skills and strategies that they are being taught in their small-group lessons (Diller, 2003; Guastello & Lenz, 2005).

In many classrooms, students receive 10 to 20 minutes of differentiated small-group instruction from the teacher and then spend 45 to 60 minutes working on their own while the teacher meets with other students in small groups. In other words, students are working on their own for up to three-fourths of the small-group instruction time. The extent to which these 45 to 60 minutes each day are used effectively will greatly influence how quickly and well students learn to read. Teachers cannot afford to waste three-fourths of their small-group instructional time. In describing ways to help students use their independent reading, writing, and center time effectively, this chapter address the following topics:

- Preparing students to work independently
- Three options for independent work time

PREPARING STUDENTS TO WORK INDEPENDENTLY

Explicit teaching focuses on teacher explanation and modeling, interactive guided practice, and monitored independent practice. Small-group lessons are the time for teachers to provide explanation, modeling, and interactive guided practice. The time students spend working on their own, when the teacher is working with other students in small-group lessons, is a natural time for students to engage in the monitored independent practice component of explicit instruction. Students receive instruction in reading skills and strategies in their small groups, then reinforce and apply these skills and strategies during independent practice activities.

Just as students need explicit instruction in reading skills and strategies, they also need explicit instruction in how to work independently when the teacher is occupied teaching other students in small groups. Students need to become familiar with independent practice materials and activities. Students need to know classroom routines for transitioning from one activity to another. Students need to learn how to manage themselves for an extended period of time so they can complete activities and make decisions without interrupting the teacher's small-group instruction. There are some important preliminary steps teachers can take to prepare students for independent work so that this time is used effectively and productively.

INTRODUCING ROUTINES

Teacher Explanation and Modeling

Teaching students how to work independently is very similar to teaching them how to recognize spelling patterns or use comprehension strategies. It begins with lots of teacher explanation and modeling. Much of the first few weeks of each school year will be spent in whole-class activities while the teacher and students get to know each other. During this time the teacher becomes familiar with each student's reading and writing abilities. The students become familiar with basic classroom routines such as moving from place to place in the classroom, locating and returning instructional materials, when and how much talking is appropriate, and how to line up for recess and other out-of-class activities. The third week of the school year, as teacher and students are settling in, is a good time for teachers to get their students together and explain that it will soon be time to begin small-group reading instruction. Teachers further explain that students will begin to spend much of reading instruction time working on their own.

Many teachers begin teaching students to work independently by calling the class together and bringing their attention to the small-group table, telling them that soon they will each begin having reading lessons at the table with four or five of their classmates. The teacher explains to students the reasons for small-group instruction and also begins to explain what they will be doing when they are not meeting with the teacher. This is a good time to introduce the classroom workboard, the signal that the teacher uses to announce transition times (a small bell), and any other procedural rules associated with working independently. Many teachers teach students that the bell will ring two times for each transition. The first bell tells students to stop what they are doing and listen to the teacher's instructions. The second bell tells students to make the transition.

After explaining the procedures for small groups and independent work, the teacher should demonstrate the procedures for students. The teacher selects five to seven students to come to the small-group table to show students what a small-group lesson looks and sounds like. Students can view the letter cards, word cards, word lists, decodable texts, leveled books, core reading program books, and the writing boards and other instructional materials that they will use in small-group lessons. The other students are invited to return to their seats, get out a book, and begin reading independently. The teacher then tells students that when the transition signal is sounded, the small-group students return to their seats and five to seven more students take their places at the table.

Guided Practice

As students catch on to the idea of small-group lessons and independent work, the teacher involves them in several guided practice opportunities to participate in making the transition. Using sets of colored index cards, (the teacher gives blue index cards to five to seven students, red index cards to five to seven students, and so on. All students begin by reading silently at their seats and then the teacher calls for the blue group to come to the small-group table, then the other color groups one-by-one. The teacher guides students in making the transitions between the table and their seats several times. This is the time for providing specific teacher guidance and feedback about proper ways to make the transitions and also about transition behaviors to avoid. Teachers may want to be as specific as to point out to students the need to push their chairs under their desks or tables, which route to take to the small-group table and back, and how to avoid interrupting other students during the transition.

Independent Practice

At this point in teaching students how to work independently, the teacher gets all students reading silently at their seats then takes his or her place at the small-group table. The teacher rings the bell and makes sure that all students have stopped reading and are listening for instructions. The teacher announces which group will come first to the small-group table, asks if everyone is clear about what to do, then rings the bell the second time and observes how well students make the transition. The teacher repeats this process until all students have made the transition at least once.

It is recommended that teachers guide students through practicing this transition routine daily for at least a week before assigning students to their actual reading

Explicit Instruction Learning Center Workboard Lesson Plan

Concept or Objective: Working independently at learning centers   **Date:** _____

Lesson Steps	Activities	Materials
Introduction • Review previous lesson • Connect to today's lesson • Give a purpose for today's lesson	"Students, most classroom activities to date have been for the whole class. A few activities have included independent seatwork. Today we will begin adding another way of learning in our classroom: working together in small groups. This is important because the teacher needs to begin teaching small groups, so students will need to work by themselves and in small groups each day. This workboard will help us work together in small groups."	Workboard
Explicit teacher explanation and modeling	1. Show students the four centers: small-group instruction area, rereading for fluency area, word study area, and the writing area. Tell them that you will show them each area in detail over the next few days. 2. Show students the top part of the workboard that show the names of students in each of the four groups. Invite students in each group to stand when their group name is called. 3. Next, show the lower part of the workboard that shows the four centers and the rotation through them. Invite students to point to each of the four center areas as you name it. 4. Show the first row of activities. Ask each group where they go first during small-group instruction time. Have each group show you, one group at a time, that they know where to go by going there.	Workboard
Interactive guided practice	1. Point to the first row of activities again. Tell students that when you give the signal (a bell, etc.) you want to see all students stand up and go with their group to their first center. Practice this one or two times. 2. Repeat this with rows 2–4.	Type of signal (bell, etc.)
Monitored independent practice	1. Tell the students that when you give the signal they should go to their first center. Then when you give the signal again, they should go to their second center, then their third and fourth centers. 2. Practice this several times.	
Assessment	Note which groups or students have caught on to the process, and which will need reteaching and more practice.	
Accommodations for students	Some students still may not understand how to use the workboard. Assemble them as a small group and repeat the explicit teacher explanation and modeling step.	Workboard

groups and beginning small-group differentiated reading instruction. (see Lesson Plan for Introducing the Learning Center Workboard). When the transition process is running smoothly, teachers may begin the process of introducing students to working independently at teacher-made seatwork assignments and at learning centers (Florida Center for Reading, Research [FCRR], 2005; Reutzel & Cooter, 2008).

It is important to recognize that just because students are able to make transitions smoothly does not mean that they will always do so. Expect that on occasion procedures will break down. Students may get sloppy in their transition, independent work, and learning center behaviors. When this happens it is very important to stop everybody immediately, explain the problem, reteach correct behaviors, and then practice correct procedures several times. Maintain high teacher expectations for correct transition and independent work and learning center behaviors, and follow through with reteaching and practice as needed.

SCHEDULING

There are two major ways of organizing student activities during independent reading—writing and center time (FCRR, 2005). Some teachers prefer to have their students remain together in their groups during this time, transitioning together as groups from one activity to another (Guastello & Lenz, 2005). Other teachers prefer to provide a menu of independent activity options and allow students to choose how they spend much of their independent work time. Each model has its own advantages and disadvantages. The point is that students must spend their independent work time actively engaged in genuine reading and writing activities.

The Group Model

In the group model, the students rotate together in their groups through independent and center activities when they are not with the teacher receiving small-group instruction. For example, a teacher with 60 minutes of small-group instruction time and four groups to work with will have each group rotate together as a group among the small-group lesson with the teacher and three additional independent or center activities in 15-minute intervals. The teacher keeps watch on a timer at the small-group instruction table and every 15 minutes rings a bell or provides a signal that it is time to transition to the next activity.

Many teachers use a "workboard," a chart or poster that lists the members of each group and the sequence of activities for each group, to help keep students organized and working effectively during small-group instruction time (Fountas & Pinnell, 1996; Reutzel & Cooter, 2008; Tyner, 2004). A workboard shows each of the groups with the names of students in each group. The workboard also lists each of the centers and shows the order of rotation through the centers—where each group goes first, then to each center in order afterward. The small-group instruction is listed as one of the center activities and is part of the rotation. Figure 7.1 shows a typical workboard for a classroom with four small groups.

Helping Student Groups Move from One Center Activity to Another

As teachers finish the whole-class word study lessons, many keep the students together and use the next few minutes to display the workboard for the day and

Helping Students Transition Among Centers

Second-grade teacher Cinthya Saavedra is seated with the Rockets reading group at the horseshoe table she uses for her small-group reading lessons. She glances at her timer, notices that the allocated 15 minutes for rotation 1 is up, and rings the small bell she keeps at this table. Immediately her students know to "freeze" and listen for her instructions. Cinthya refers to the classroom workboard for today and reminds her students where to go for the next rotation.

"When I say the word go," *Cinthya reminds her students, "put away the materials you are using, move quietly to your next center, and quickly resume working. You're doing great!* Rockets, *you'll reread the decodable books we've just finished, with a partner. When you've finished the decodable, you may choose a book from the browsing basket to read silently on your own.* Tigers, *you are coming to the table to read with me.* 49ers, *you'll be working on your writing workshop stories. Make sure to include dialogue in your stories the way I've been showing you in the mini-lessons this week.* Sharks, *you'll be at your seats doing the a, ai, ay, and a_e word sort."*

"Now," she says, "Are there any questions? Do you all know where to go?" When Cinthya is satisfied that all of her students are ready for the transition, she says the word "go." Most of Cinthya's students move quickly to their next center activity. Cinthya's "teacher look" reminds Carson, James, and Ella that now is not the time for chatting and they move quickly to their seats to begin the word sort. Because the students are rotating together as groups, the number of students participating in any activity at any given time never grows too large.

make sure that all students are familiar with the tasks at each center and the order of rotating through the centers. When all students are ready to go, the teacher gives the first signal and the students disperse to their first centers. The teacher makes sure that everyone is getting to work, then goes to the small-group instruction area to meet the students in that group and begin small-group instruction. To facilitate student groups transitioning from their first center activity to subsequent center activities, the teacher gives the signal, reminds students where each group is scheduled to go next, asks if everybody is ready, then gives the signal for the next rotation (see Helping Students Transition Among Centers).

The Independent Model

As students become more capable of working independently, many teachers transition to an independent model for reading, writing, and center time. This model involves the teacher writing several independent activity options on the board for students to do when they are not with the teacher for small-group instruction.

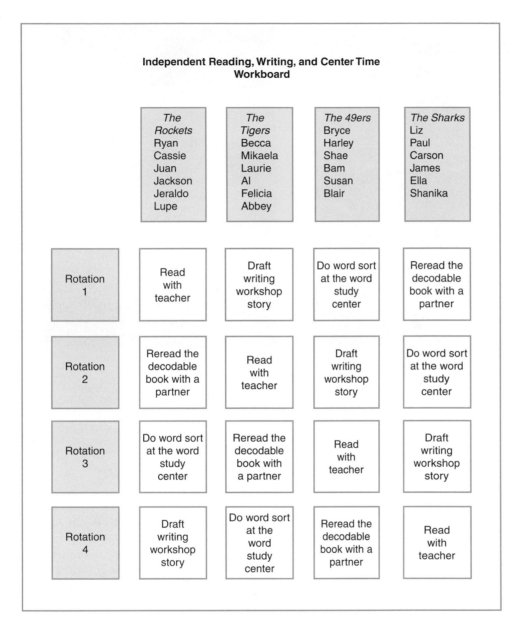

Figure 7.1

An Independent Reading, Writing, and Center Time Workboard

After whole-class word study, the teacher keeps the students together for a moment and ensures that they are familiar with all of the options and that each student knows what he or she plans to do. When the teacher is convinced that the students are ready, the signal is given and students head to their chosen activities. After a minute or two, when all students are busily engaged, the teacher goes to the small-group instruction table, gets the instructional materials ready, and calls for the first group to come to the table. When the first group lesson is finished, the teacher often gives the students a follow-up assignment, such as rereading the text for fluency, then excuses the first group. After scanning the class to ensure that all students are productively engaged, the teacher calls for the second group to come to the table for their small-group lesson.

Sylvia Read

Shannon leans against the wall while reading *Junie B. Jones* by Barbara Park.

Sylvia Read

Bethany has couch privileges today!

Helping Students Work Independently

Third-grade teacher Troy Jorgensen has just finished his morning's teacher read-aloud and the whole-class word study lesson. It's time to begin his daily small-group differentiated reading instruction. With his students seated together on the classroom rug Troy begins describing for his students what they are expected to accomplish during the next 60 minutes.

"We're having a very good morning, so far," Troy begins. "Let's keep up the good work. When I say the word dinosaur, *these are the things for you to do while I meet with the reading groups. First, I want each of you to reread the* Animal Camouflage *story from our reading book on your own."* *Troy steps to the teacher's whiteboard and writes in the upper right corner: 1. Reread* Animal Camouflage.

"When you have finished rereading Animal Camouflage," *Troy continues, "get a piece of writing paper from the basket and make a two-column animal–camouflage chart. In the left column, list the animals from the story and in the right column list what kind of camouflage each animal has."*

Troy holds up a sample chart he has prepared and lists the first animal from the text: walking-stick. He demonstrates for the students how to find the walking-stick page and a description of its camouflage. On the right column of his chart Troy writes, "looks like a twig." When Troy is sure that all students understand the task he returns to the whiteboard and writes: 2. Animal–camouflage chart.

Troy continues this process of describing the morning's independent reading activities and listing them on the board. When he is finished, the upper right corner of the teacher's whiteboard reads as follows:

1. *Reread* Animal Camouflage
2. *Animal–camouflage chart*
3. *Writing workshop*
4. *Prefixes and suffixes word sort*
5. *Sight word flashcards 2x with a partner*
6. *SSR*

Troy asks, "Does everybody know what they're going to do? Mariel, what are you going to do first? Trevor, what are you going to do first? LaShaun, what are you going to do first? Is everybody ready? Okay—dinosaur."

As Troy's students move to their seats and begin working, he circulates around the classroom, listens to a few students read aloud to him, and helps a few other students get started with their camouflage chart and word sort page. After about 5 minutes, when all students are working effectively, Troy calls for the Blue group to meet him at the small-group table.

As Troy works with the students in the Blue group, he continually scans the classroom, making sure that all students are on task. After 15 minutes, Troy excuses the Blue group to return to their seats to begin rereading Animal Camouflage. *Troy takes another 3–4 minutes to circulate around the classroom and monitor his students' productivity. Some students are finishing the rereading and beginning to work on the camouflage chart. Troy calls the Green group back to the small-group table.*

Fifty-five minutes later, most of Troy's students are reading silently at their seats or adding to their writing workshop stories. He tells them to get ready for recess, after which he'll finish the morning literacy block with a writing workshop mini-lesson, more writing time, and authors' chair.

THREE OPTIONS FOR INDEPENDENT WORK TIME

Many teachers provide a variety of instructional activities for students during independent reading, writing, and learning center time. Some students will be at their seats reading independently or with a partner from self-selected books. Other students will be completing an activity that was assigned to them during their small-group lesson such as writing a personal response to the reading selection. Groups of students may be working together at one of several learning centers such as sorting words according to their spelling patterns at the word study center. Whatever the tasks, they should not be busywork, but should instead be opportunities for students to practice the important reading and writing skills and strategies that are being taught.

INDEPENDENT READING AND WRITING

Research repeatedly confirms that there is a strong positive relationship between the amount of reading that students do and their reading achievement (National Assessment of Educational Progress [NAEP], 2005; National Reading Panel [NRP], 2000; Taylor, Frey, & Maruyama, 1990).Time spent reading and writing independently, with careful teacher guidance, can also be effective in helping students master important reading skills and concepts. Independent reading has also been shown to improve the reading achievement of second language learners and English language learners (Elley, 1991; Flippo, 1999; Morrow, 1992).

Independent reading is important for developing students' positive attitudes for reading. Beyond offering choice and increasing motivation, independent reading is also a time for applying what has been learned during whole-class and small-group literacy instruction.

Procedures for Independent Reading

Independent reading time needs to be just as structured as other parts of the school day. Too often during independent reading, precious time is wasted as students stare at books that are too difficult, talk to their classmates, and stand at the bookshelf looking for something to read.To be effective, students need guidelines and expectations for independent reading time. Procedures for teaching students to select appropriate

Daily independent reading is one part of a comprehensive literacy program.

Sylvia Read

Sylvia Read

Mrs. Navarro listens to Susana read.

level books for independent reading were described in Chapter 2. Teachers must help students find books that are of personal interest and are also at the student's independent reading level.

Students should select books for independent reading at the very beginning of each school day, during those minutes between walking in the classroom door and when class business actually begins. They can each place a small stack of two to four books, at their independent reading level, on their desks so that when independent reading time arrives they won't spend reading time wandering around the classroom looking for something to read.

Many teachers hold a few individual teacher–student reading conferences in between small-group lessons to help keep track of the quantity and quality of students' independent reading. Teachers often begin these conferences by asking students how and why they chose their independent reading book, to gather information about students' reading interests. The student then reads a paragraph from the book aloud to the teacher who may take notes on the student's oral reading fluency. The teacher and student then discuss the book's content as a way for the teacher to gather information on the student's reading comprehension. The conference may conclude with the teacher giving the student guidance on word identification, comprehension, or book selection.

FOR STRUGGLING READERS

Volume of Reading Is Critical

In addition to effective reading instruction, students need opportunities to practice and apply what they've been taught. This means opportunities for long periods of uninterrupted reading of meaningful texts. Struggling readers need more instruction and they need more practice. The latest National Assessment of Educational Progress (NAEP, 2007, p. 17) shows that students who received two or more hours of reading instruction per day scored three times higher on the reading test than students who received only one, or slightly more, hour of reading instruction per day. In addition, students who read 20 or more pages per day in school and for homework scored 50% higher than their classmates (p. 18) and students who read weekly for fun scored almost two to three times as high as their classmates who read only one or two times per month for fun (p. 19). These NAEP trends have been consistent year after year. Teachers need to ensure that their struggling readers receive effective instruction and generous amounts of time to practice reading.

Bethany and Shannon partner read *The One in the Middle is the Green Kangaroo* by Judy Blume.

Sylvia Read

Partner Reading

After meeting with groups and after the students have spent 25 to 30 minutes reading independently, many teachers provide time for students to read with a partner. Sometimes they can choose their own partner and sometimes the teacher provides them with a partner.

Teachers can enhance the effectiveness of partner reading by following a few guidelines. One suggestion is that students should read from one book (which means they must sit closely together and therefore are more likely to listen attentively while the partner reads) and they must trade off pages. Trading off pages generally works well because students' attention may wander while listening to longer sections, and trading off chunks of less than a page makes the reading too choppy and ruins the flow.

Many teachers pair students with partners who are somewhat equal in their reading ability. However, other teachers may want to have better readers partner with and listen to and coach struggling readers. Some students are very good at this; they are attentive, patient, and don't interrupt to provide words too quickly. Other readers are not good at this and are better off with a partner who reads at basically the same level so that they can share the reading and keep each other engaged. It all depends on the students.

myeducationlab

English Language Learners

Go to MyEducationLab, "English Language Learners," and watch the video *Peer Scaffolding*.

As you view the video, notice the teacher's role in supporting these two ELL students during their partner reading.

- What effect did the teacher's intervention have on both children?
- In what ways did the older student help the younger student with reading comprehension?
- In what ways did both ELL students benefit from partner reading?

ASSIGNMENTS

It is very common, at the end of a small-group reading lesson, for the teacher to provide students with an assignment to complete during independent reading, writing, and center time. These assignments generally are an extension of the instructional activities provided in the small-group lesson. Students complete the assignments independently, then move on to the next task, as in the independent model.

For example, a teacher may teach a lesson on *r*-controlled vowels during the small-group lesson in which he or she explains the *r*-controlled vowel spelling pattern, reads a list of example words with *r*-controlled vowels, then begins an interactive guided practice activity where the students sort *r*-controlled vowel words across the five vowels on a workpage. A follow-up assignment could be to complete the *r*-controlled vowel sort at their seats before reading independently or spending time at a learning center.

Another follow-up assignment may focus on students' comprehension or response to the small-group reading text. For example, second-grade teacher Gloria Bell reads a leveled reader with her students in small group, then at the end of the group lesson Gloria provides students with a "big question" about the book. The big question may have to do with the students' opinions about the book's characters, how the students might solve a problem the characters are facing, or perhaps the big question may focus on personal connections the students may have to the text. After the small-group lesson, the students return to their seats and write their answers to the big question in their reading journals. The next day, the students bring their reading journals to the small-group lesson and share and discuss what they have written. This procedure of receiving a big question, writing and answer in the reading journal, then discussing it the next day is an effective and predictable day-to-day routine. A consistent and predictable daily routine is desirable because it allows students to contextualize their activities in the daily schedule, know when current activities will finish, and mentally prepare for what comes next. Students who don't know what's going on are more likely to be confused and fidgety.

A few additional follow-up assignments that students may complete during independent reading, writing, and center time include:

- Writing sentences that contain one or more spelling or vocabulary words.
- Completing a response project (writing, drama, art, artifact, research) that relates to a text read in the small group.
- Completing a workpage where students sort a list of words according to a spelling pattern taught in the small group.
- Going on a word hunt to find spelling pattern words in any classroom books or print displays.

Tyner (2004) reminds us that follow-up assignments need to be at students' instructional or independent levels in order to avoid student confusion and frustration. When students complete the assignment they should move quickly to the next activity rather than wait for a timer or signal that it's time to change, as in the group model. Students should also know where to turn in the completed assignments before moving to the next activity.

LEARNING CENTERS

Learning centers are classroom locations where students can extend skills and concepts taught in whole-class and small-group lessons. Learning centers should not be used for initial instruction in reading concepts, but rather as opportunities for students to practice what has already been taught to them by the teacher.

Learning centers range from the very formal, such as a physical arrangement at a table with instructional materials and a poster outlining the center's purpose and procedures, to the very informal, such as a plastic basket containing an activity that students would select and complete at an empty space somewhere in the classroom. Many primary-grade teachers like to provide learning centers that correspond to the essential elements of reading (NRP, 2000). For example, a classroom may feature centers that focus on alphabet letter names and sounds center, phonemic awareness, phonics, fluency, vocabulary, comprehension, and writing. Some teachers also include content-area centers so that students can practice reading and writing skills while reviewing content-area concepts.

Researchers at the Florida Center for Reading Research (FCRR, 2005, p. 11) have described steps for implementing and managing learning centers. The first steps involve teacher advance planning. The final steps are for implementing and managing centers.

Teachers begin planning for centers by using screening and progress-monitoring data to form flexible groups for small-group differentiated reading instruction. Groups should not be larger than seven, and no larger than five for students who struggle with reading. Groups should be formed with specific reading skills and concepts in mind. Next, plan activities based on learning objectives, not instructional products. Learning center activities should be within each student's zone of proximal development so that the activities challenge students rather than boring or frustrating them. Always plan to have additional instructional materials on hand for those students who finish center activities more quickly.

FCRR suggestions for implementing and managing learners begin with a workboard (management board). Workboards should be large and simple enough so that students can see and use them from anywhere in the classroom. Teachers should start early in the school year with just one center rotation. As students become familiar with how to use a center, introduce a second center and gradually build up as students learn how to manage themselves at a center. Before students are permitted to go to a center, they should be well enough prepared so that they know (FCRR, 2005, p. 26) what to do when they don't understand an activity, what to do when they complete an activity, whom to go to for help, how to clean up, and how to decide who goes first.

In preparing students to function at learning centers, teachers should always explain and demonstrate for students how to complete center activities before expecting students to complete center activities on their own (Reutzel & Cooter, 2008). Additional suggestions for making learning centers run smoothly are to keep the classroom well organized. Make sure that all materials are easily accessible and clearly labeled. Teach students to make transitions among learning centers quickly and efficiently by modeling for them where to go and what to do when they arrive at a learning center. Finally, learning centers should have an accountability component so that students understand that learning center work is serious business. Teachers should review students' learning center work regularly and provide feedback in a timely manner.

Because learning centers are meant to provide students with opportunities to practice the skills they have been taught in whole-class and small-group reading lessons, teachers should develop reading centers that focus on the reading skills they teach. Summaries of thousands of research studies (NRP, 2000; Snow, Burns, & Griffin, 1998) in the field of reading instruction have identified the essential elements of reading that include alphabet letter name and sounds, phonemic awareness, phonics, fluency, vocabulary, comprehension, and writing. Therefore learning centers should be developed around these topics. Many teachers establish three to five consistent learning centers based on the essential elements of reading and simply switch specific activities within each center. Table 7.1 provides

PEARSON
myeducationlab)

English Language Learners

Go to MyEducationLab, "English Language Learners," and watch the video *Planning for Management Learning Centers.*

As you view the video, notice the many different learning centers this teacher has set up and how well the classroom environment is organized to support instruction.

- What are some of your favorite centers? What is the instructional purpose of each of these learning centers?
- How does the teacher introduce and explain each learning center to her students?
- How does the teacher build accountability into her learning center activities?

Table 7.1   Sample Learning Center Activities

Centers	Activities
ABC	• Students copy alphabet letters from an alphabet poster or chart onto writing paper. • Students match printed alphabet letters to pictures that begin with the same sound. • Students try to match a set of plastic alphabet letters to an alphabet letter chart in 3 minutes or less. • Students use rubber alphabet letter stamps to stamp alphabet letters on an alphabet handout. • Working in pairs, one student shines a flashlight on individual letters from an alphabet chart while the other student names the letters. • Students place alphabet cards face down on the floor or table, start a timer, and see how long it takes to turn over and name the letter on each of the cards. • Students will use a timer to see how long it takes to match a set of lowercase alphabet cards to a set of uppercase alphabet cards.
Phonemic awareness	• Students sort wallet-sized pictures into columns based on the pictures' initial sounds. • Students turn over picture cards, say the name of the picture, then say the picture's beginning sound. • Working in pairs, one student turns over a picture card and says the name of the picture. The second student says a word that rhymes with the picture. • Students cut out pictures, group them, and glue them onto a separate page according to initial sounds or rhyming sounds. • Students are given a page with familiar pictures on it. Have students count the number of phonemes in the word represented by each picture and write the number next to the picture.
Word work	• Students sort words according to spelling patterns or number of syllables. • Students are given cards with onsets (initial consonants, blends, and digraphs) and rimes (common ending phonograms). Students mix and match to see how many words they can make. • Teacher prints some multisyllabic words on strips of paper, cuts them apart syllable-by-syllable, and places the pieces in a Ziploc™ plastic bag. Students take out the pieces, reform the words, write them on a list, then read the words to partners and to the teacher. • Teacher chooses 7–10 high-frequency words, makes two word cards for each word, and spreads the cards on the floor or table upside down for the students to play memory. • Teacher prepares a set of 5–10 word cards with a common spelling pattern. Student one reads the words to student two who must write the words. Then students switch roles.

Table 7.1 Continued

Centers	Activities
Fluency	• Students listen to prerecorded books-on-tape or CD while following along with a print copy of the text at the listening center.
	• Students partner read a decodable or leveled text to each other.
	• Student pairs time each other reading a text and record the time. Then both reread the text three times, timing each other again and recording times.
	• Student groups practice rehearsing a reader's theater script and then perform the script for the rest of the class.
	• Students pairs time each other reading high-frequency phrases. Phrases are available at http://www.uen.org/k-2educator/downloads/FryPhrases12.pdf
Vocabulary	• Students match words to student-friendly definitions.
	• Students illustrate vocabulary words.
	• Students play memory with contraction pair word cards (*I am—I'm; will not—won't; she is—she's*).
	• Students play memory game with pairs of antonym word cards.
	• Students write sentences with multiple vocabulary words.
	• Students create Word Expert Cards. These are 5 × 7-inch index cards on which students (1) write a vocabulary word, (2) write a sentence from a book containing the word, (3) write a student-friendly definition of the word, (4) write the word's part of speech, and (5) draw a picture representing the word. Students use their cards to teach classmates the word meanings.
	• Students play memory game with pairs of word cards listing words and their abbreviations (*mister—Mr.; misses—Mrs.; captain—capt.; et cetera—etc.*).
Comprehension	• Students complete a setting, characters, problem, events, theme, graphic organizer about a previously read narrative text.
	• Students list important facts contained in a previously read expository text.
	• Students complete a character weave about characters in a previously read narrative text (see Figure 7.2)
	• Students draw a picture showing the beginning, middle, and ending parts of a story.
	• Students receive a set of story events (in scrambled order) written on sentence strips. Student pairs reassemble the story in proper order.
	• Students make a list of words or concepts that they don't fully understand and questions they have about the text. Teacher and students use these lists in follow-up discussions of the text.
Writing	• Students add to ongoing pieces of personal writing.
	• Student pairs swap drafts, read, and circle words that may be misspelled.
	• Students brainstorm lists of three or four potential topics for their next piece of writing.
	• Students use crayons, colored markers, or other drawing tools to illustrate a text that they are publishing.
	• Students practice previously taught letter forms.

Figure 7.2 Character Weave

Character	Appearance	Actions	Personality

Name _____ Date _____

sample learning center activities commonly found in primary-grade classrooms, organized according to the essential elements of reading. Many of these activities are adapted from comprehensive descriptions of center activities found at the FCRR website (http://www.fcrr.org/Curriculum/StudentCenterActivities.htm).

 ## CONCLUDING THOUGHTS

Teachers provide daily instruction to students in small groups to differentiate reading instruction concepts and materials and ensure that instruction is at the right level for each student. To do this, students must spend part of their literacy instruction time working independently while the teacher works with other students in small groups. This independent reading, writing, and learning center time can provide valuable opportunities for students to practice and reinforce critical reading and writing skills and strategies.

A smoothly running classroom often has a variety of activities to keep students productively engaged during independent reading, writing, and center time. These include having students read appropriate-level books independently and with a partner, completing teacher-given assignments that reinforce concepts learned in small-group instruction, and participating in learning center activities that may focus on literacy skills and strategies and also on integrating literacy and content-area learning.

SUGGESTED ACTIVITIES TO EXTEND YOUR LEARNING

1. Visit a local classroom that provides both whole-class and differentiated small-group instruction. Observe what the students do while the teacher is with small groups. Note the activities and how productively the students are engaged. Interview the teacher to learn how he or she determines what activities the students will do independently. How well do these activities support the small-group instruction rather than simply keep students busy?

2. Collaborate with classmates to develop a list of learning center activities and possibly prepare instructional materials for the centers.

3. Observe a classroom during independent reading time. Notice what percentage of the time students are actually reading texts at their independent reading level. How much time is wasted as students look for more books to read, talk to classmates, or otherwise waste instructional time? If independent reading time is inefficient, what could be done to improve it?

REFERENCES

Diller, D. (2003). *Literacy work stations: Making centers work*. Portland, ME: Stenhouse.

Elley, W. B. (1991). Acquiring literacy in a second language: The effect of book-based programs. *Language Learning, 41,* 375–411.

Flippo, R. F. (1999). *What do the experts say?: Helping children learn to read.* Portsmouth, NH: Heinemann.

Florida Center for Reading Research. (2005). *Implementing and managing student centers in the classroom*. Retrieved from http://www.fcrr.org/Curriculum/StudentCenterActivities.htm

Fountas, I. C., & Pinnell, G. S. (1996). *Guided reading instruction: Good first teaching for all children*. Portsmouth, NH: Heinemann.

Guastello, E., & Lenz, C. (2005). Student accountability: Guided reading kidstations. *The Reading Teacher, 59*(2), 144–156.

Morrow, L. M. (1992). The impact of a literature-based program on literacy achievement, use of literature, and attitudes of children from minority backgrounds. *Reading Research Quarterly, 27*(3), 251–275.

National Assessment of Educational Progress. (2007). *Reading report card*. U.S. Department of Education. Retrieved from http://nationsreportcard.gov/reading_2007

National Reading Panel. (2000). *Teaching children to read: An evidence-based assessment of the scientific research literature on reading and its implication for reading instruction. Report of the subgroups.* National Institute of Child Health and Human Development. Retrieved from http://www.nichd.nih.gov/publications/nrp/smallbook.cfm

Reutzel, D. R., & Cooter, R. B. (2008). *Teaching children to read: The teacher makes the difference*. Upper Saddle River, NJ: Merrill/Prentice Hall.

Snow, C. E., Burns, M. S., & Griffin, P. (1998). *Preventing reading difficulties in young children*. Washington, DC: National Academy Press.

Taylor, B. M., Frey, B. J., & Maruyama, G. (1990). Time spent reading and reading growth. *American Educational Research Journal, 27,* 351–362.

Tyner, B. (2004). *Small-group reading instruction: A differentiated teaching model for beginning and struggling readers*. Newark, DE: International Reading Association.

Effective Writing Instruction

by Sylvia Read

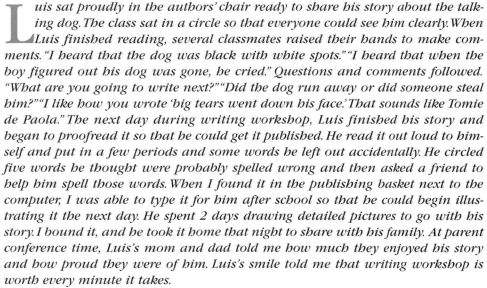

The Power of Writing Workshop

Luis sat proudly in the authors' chair ready to share his story about the talking dog. The class sat in a circle so that everyone could see him clearly. When Luis finished reading, several classmates raised their hands to make comments. "I heard that the dog was black with white spots." "I heard that when the boy figured out his dog was gone, he cried." Questions and comments followed. "What are you going to write next?" "Did the dog run away or did someone steal him?" "I like how you wrote 'big tears went down his face.' That sounds like Tomie de Paola." The next day during writing workshop, Luis finished his story and began to proofread it so that he could get it published. He read it out loud to himself and put in a few periods and some words he left out accidentally. He circled five words he thought were probably spelled wrong and then asked a friend to help him spell those words. When I found it in the publishing basket next to the computer, I was able to type it for him after school so that he could begin illustrating it the next day. He spent 2 days drawing detailed pictures to go with his story. I bound it, and he took it home that night to share with his family. At parent conference time, Luis's mom and dad told me how much they enjoyed his story and how proud they were of him. Luis's smile told me that writing workshop is worth every minute it takes.

A comprehensive literacy program includes a healthy dose of writing instruction. Writing is a lifelong skill worth teaching for its own sake, but its value in supporting children as they learn to read should not be underestimated. This chapter discusses the importance of writing instruction for children who are learning to read. Specifically, it addresses the following:

- The reading–writing connection
- Writing workshop
- Writing in many genres

THE READING–WRITING CONNECTION

Many children write before they read. They play with writing using scribbles and perhaps random letters to represent "real" writing. Drawings are also an early form of writing. When asked to tell about a drawing, many children tell an elaborate story. Indeed, oral language is how writing begins (Casbergue & Plauché, 2005). Eventually, their drawings are accompanied by letters representing the beginning sounds of words. *ILMM* represents "I love my mom." They can read their own writing long before they read words written conventionally. Children tend to use temporary spellings such as *M* for *mom, MK* for *milk*, or *PICSHR* for *picture* (see Figures 8.1 and 8.2). Although writing is important on its own, it is also a natural way to begin the process of learning to read (Harste, Woodward, and Burke, 1984; Schulze, 2006).

When they write, children learn how print works, and what they write shows us what they've noticed and internalized about print. Writing is a complex task—children must look and think carefully about the specific features of letters; write words, one letter at a time; place letters spatially on a page; think about how to place letters in a specific order; and pay attention to the smallest details of forming letters while also keeping in mind the words and sentences they create (Clay, 1991; Spandel, 2007).

Figure 8.1 Kristen wrote *SSW: Spiders spin webs.*

Figure 8.2 B.J. wrote *SPMKWB: Spiders make webs.*

Effective writing instruction supports children as they learn to read because reading and writing processes are similar:

> Readers, to read words, must learn to deal with letter and phonemes and how they combine. Writers, likewise, must learn about letters and sounds if they are to spell accurately. (Fitzgerald & Shanahan, 2000, p. 40)

The National Research Council's report *Preventing Reading Difficulties in Young Children* (Snow, Burns, & Griffin, 1998), recommends the following about writing:

> Once children learn to write letters, they should be encouraged to write them, to use them to begin writing words or parts of words, and to use words to begin writing sentences. Instruction should be designed with the understanding that the use of invented spelling is not in conflict with teaching correct spelling. Beginning writing with invented spelling can be helpful for developing understanding of phoneme identity, phoneme segmentation, and sound–spelling relationships. Conventionally correct spelling should be developed through focused instruction and practice. Primary-grade children should be expected to spell previously studied words and spelling patterns correctly in their final writing products. Writing should take place on a daily basis to encourage children to become more comfortable and familiar with it. (pp. 323–324)

Writing is a personal and active way for students to strengthen their knowledge and use of phonics.

Phonics knowledge is acquired through the process of becoming a reader and writer (Schulze, 2006; Weaver, 1996). Young children often begin writing using scribbles to represent letters and words. If young children are writing every day, they can think deeply about sound–letter relationships as they use phonetic, transitional spellings to record their thoughts and stories. As they learn to read, they use the same understanding of letter–sound relationships to decode unknown words. Young children begin to spell sight words such as *was* or *they* as they have seen them repeatedly in the books they read. By writing, children learn how print works. Through reading their writing back to themselves either as part of the writing process or during the sharing time of writing workshop, students learn to decode their own writing. They quickly learn that they can't read what they've written if they haven't left themselves enough phonetic or contextual clues to figure out a word. At the end of first grade, children sometimes look back at their writing from the beginning of the year and wonder what it says and why they ever wrote it that way!

As the number of words they can spell conventionally grows, they continue to need to use phonetic spellings for less frequently used, but important, words. If they felt comfortable using temporary spellings early in their writing history, they will feel comfortable using them later for difficult words such as *exciting* or *Disneyland*. Students need to know that although spelling is important, it is more important to get their ideas down first and worry about the spelling of difficult words later. They learn to circle words they think are misspelled as they write and look them up later during the editing and proofreading phases of the writing process. They begin to gradually phase out their use of temporary spellings of frequently used words while they write and use phonetic spellings only for words they know they'll want to look up later. They learn to judge what kinds of words they should know how to spell and what kinds of words can be represented phonetically.

The research on invented spelling shows that if students are reading and writing a lot and also thinking and learning about spelling patterns, they will advance through stages toward conventional spelling (Henderson, 1990). The words they write most frequently are the ones they need to learn correctly because it is possible to get them embedded incorrectly (Cunningham, 2004). Children need to know that we expect them to spell phonetically irregular words such as *they* correctly after they have had some teaching and practice with those words.

SUPPORTING STRUGGLING SPELLERS

The best way to help students who are struggling with spelling is to assess their spelling knowledge and provide instruction that matches their needs. *Words Their Way* (Bear, Invernizzi, Templeton, & Johnston, 2008) provides spelling assessments that diagnose which spelling elements students need to learn. Once the teacher has determined the students' spelling levels, students work with words containing the spelling elements they need to learn. Word sorting is the main instructional activity in the *Words Their Way* approach to spelling instruction. Through sorting and classifying words according to the sounds, patterns, or meanings they contain, students begin to make sense of spelling. This approach does not rely on rote memorization as many traditional spelling programs do.

THREE INSTRUCTIONAL STRATEGIES THAT CONNECT READING AND WRITING

When children are learning to read, they are first of all trying to differentiate the sounds they hear. This phonemic awareness can be fostered through writing activities such as language-experience approach, interactive writing, and scaffolded writing. Each of these methods also helps students understand the concept of word and sentence, both of which are crucial to beginning reading and writing.

Language-Experience Approach

Although children are capable of using phonetic spellings to write independently, taking dictation from children through the language-experience approach (LEA; Allen, 1999; Cramer, 2000) is an efficient way to teach children about the conventions of language they might not yet be using. Dictation takes advantage of the relationships among thought, oral language, reading, and writing. Students quickly and easily see that what they think can be said, what they say can be written down, and what has been written can be read. This can be an inspiring discovery to a young child! Students who may not understand or value writing when they come to school will quickly see how writing is a powerful tool for expressing themselves. For a more in-depth description of the language-experience approach, see Chapter 3.

Interactive Writing

Interactive writing is a technique developed and named by McCarrier, Pinnell, and Fountas (2000). With small groups or the whole class, the teacher engages the children in composing and constructing a written message on chart paper. Many aspects of writing can be addressed in a typical interactive writing lesson:

- Deciding on a topic
- Spelling individual words
- Forming letters
- Spacing between words
- Constructing a sentence
- Punctuating
- Paragraphing
- Adding interesting words to jazz up a sentence
- Deciding on a title
- Formatting a friendly letter

Once the teacher and the students have decided on the first sentence of the writing, the teacher selectively invites students to come up and "share the pen." Students write anything from single letters to whole words. While one student is writing a letter or word on the chart paper, other students write it on individual whiteboards or paper, which keeps them attending to the lesson and makes it more likely that the learning will transfer to their individual writing.

Interactive writing can consist of a short daily message. Miss Roundy and her bilingual class wrote "Today is pajama day."

Sylvia Read

Example of interactive writing.

Sylvia Read

Part of the goal of interactive writing is to produce a text suitable for students to read, so the writing needs to be as conventional and legible as possible. That means formatting mistakes, such as backward or incorrectly formed letters, are corrected using correction tape or "Band-Aids®" made from computer labels. During the production of the text, the teacher has children refer to the many writing tools in the room: labels, name chart, alphabet chart, word wall, and any other writing displayed in the room.

It takes several days to produce a complete text. Children must come up to the chart paper to write, and each contribution they make can take awhile to write. It's important to know that the children *do not* need to have a turn to write every day, nor should they write every word of the text. Instead, the teacher selects the focus of the lesson carefully, choosing to have students write those parts that they're just beginning to have control of. Anything they've already mastered can be written quickly by the teacher, which will keep the lesson flowing more smoothly and keep the pace brisk. The teacher can also write words or word parts that students do not need to know yet.

Here are some steps for teaching an interactive writing lesson on clouds:

1. Read aloud *The Cloud Book* by Tomie de Paola.
2. Observe the clouds outside.
3. Gather students on the rug in front of an easel. Each student should have an individual whiteboard or a piece of paper on clipboard so they can write what's being written on the chart. This keeps everyone engaged.
4. Explain that you're going to write a book together about clouds. Ask students for a title. Invite students to come to the easel to write sounds they hear or letters they know are in the words of the title.
5. Negotiate and compose sentences, inviting students to write sounds or words. The teacher writes words that everyone already knows (e.g., *and*) or words that none of them should be expected to spell yet (e.g., *cumulus*).
6. Remind students to say the words slowly and connect them to names on the class name chart or words on the word wall. The teacher models, "*Cloud* starts with *C* just like *Calvin*," or "We have the word *are* on the word wall."
7. An alphabet strip is posted near the easel so that children can refer to it when they're unsure about how to form a particular letter or when the teacher needs to correct their formation of a letter.
8. Reread the message so far.
9. The next day, reread the previous day's text. Add more text until you and the students are satisfied.
10. Post the text in the classroom. Students can add illustrations to make a bulletin board about clouds. Students should be encouraged to read the text during "read around the room."

Scaffolding Emergent Writing

Scaffolded writing (Bodrova & Leong, 1998) is a method for supporting emergent writers so that their writing moves from one developmental stage to the next more quickly. The theory is based on Vygotsky's idea of the zone of proximal development, which Vygotsky (1978) defined as "the distance between the actual developmental level as determined by independent problem solving and the level of potential development as determined through problem solving under adult guidance, or in collaboration with more capable peers" (p. 86). In other words, the zone of proximal development is the gap between what a child can do independently and what he or she can do with assistance.

Here's how it works. The teacher asks the child to say aloud the message she wishes to write, and then the teacher repeats the message so that the child can confirm its accuracy. Next, the teacher and the child repeat the message together as the teacher draws a highlighted line to stand for each word in the message. The highlighted lines are placeholders for the words. The child and teacher repeat the message together while pointing to each highlighted line. The child then writes the message by writing the word on each line drawn by the teacher in whatever form he or she can: a letterlike form, a letter, or a combination of letters. While the child is writing, the teacher may help the child with "sounding out" the words or encourage the child to use the class name chart and alphabet chart or word wall to aid in figuring out how to write the word (see Figure 8.3). The teacher–child interaction can happen in a brief one-to-one interaction or when working with a group of four to six children. Eventually, the children use this strategy on their own as they transition to independence. Scaffolded writing is a temporary tool that, like training wheels on a bike, is eliminated when it's no longer needed.

READING LIKE A WRITER AND WRITING LIKE A READER

Beyond noticing spellings as they read and incorporating those into their writing, students will notice, borrow, and imitate literary language from what they read. "I like how you said 'it was a frightful noise.' That sounds like a book!" remarked Jordan. Sitting in the authors' chair during sharing time which ends writing workshop every day, Megan looked pleased that Jordan had pointed this out. Now other children begin to experiment with dialogue to make their writing sound more like the books they read. Their use of dialogue ranges from "Where is Ryan?" in a simple mystery story about a missing classmate to taunting jibes back and forth between sibling characters Sam and Samantha in Brock's new spy story. Sometimes the dialogue advances the plot and sometimes it helps develop a character, but whether or not the student is consciously crafting his or her writing at age 7 depends on the development of that

Figure 8.3   Example of Scaffolded Writing

I HV A DOG

HR NM IZ CORKY

SHE DOST HV A

TAL.

Luis gets help with his writing from Mrs. Bilbao.

Sylvia Read

student as a writer. Sometimes students decide to use dialogue just because others are trying it out, which is why building a community of writers who are willing to share their writing with each other can help all of them grow and develop.

These second-grade students have begun to notice word choices in each other's writing; their comments reflect the discussions during read-alouds about specific word choices authors have made.

Brock: I like how you put the word *suffocated.*
Evan: Thank you.
Braden: I like how you said that Frodo was furious.
Teacher: Did you like the word *furious?*
Braden: Yeah.
Teacher: It's a much more descriptive word than *mad,* isn't it? (*Braden nods.*)
Sydney: I like how you said Frodo was getting the creeps.
Evan: That's 'cause he gets scared easy.
Teacher: What do you like about that, Sydney?
Sydney: I just like how it says "getting the creeps."
Teacher: You like the phrase "getting the creeps."
Sydney: Yeah.

Sydney and Braden's comments sound much like the kinds of comments students make during read-alouds of professionally written books. Teachers should encourage students to make these connections between what they have read and what they write.

Jared made his reading–writing connections clear in a writing conference.

Teacher: Tell me what you're working on.
Jared: Well, it rhymes. I wanted to try writing something that rhymes.

His text was titled "The Mountains," and the teacher noticed that he was writing descriptive nonfiction about the animals and plants in the mountains, but writing in the form of rhyming couplets.

Teacher: Wow, Jared! How did you decide to do that?

Jared: Well, my mom and I were reading Shel Silverstein and I thought I'd like to try writing something that rhymes but something more serious.

Jared had been reading like a writer at home with his mom. Now he was writing like a reader at school.

Kids borrow from literature and from each other (Graves, 1983). For example, Megan, a second grader, wrote a *Magic Tree House* mystery (e.g., Osborne, 1998) using the same characters, Jack and Annie, but she created a new adventure for them. Stevie, a first grader, used the word *impertinent* in her writing after hearing *The Tale of Peter Rabbit* read aloud. Teachers should call students' attention to these connections; it shows that their writing and reading lives are interwoven. What teachers read aloud in class and what students read to themselves will have a direct impact on what students write during writing instruction.

 WRITING WORKSHOP

Writing workshop is a structure for teaching writing. During writing workshop, students are supported as they write meaningful texts every day. Each writing workshop begins with a short lesson, or "mini-lesson," that teaches students about a procedure, skill, strategy, or craft related to writing. This is followed by a time for students to write, with the teacher monitoring and guiding them through continuously conferencing with students individually. Writing workshop ends with a time for sharing works in progress or finished pieces. Students learn how to respond thoughtfully to each other's writing during this sharing time, and teachers model appropriate responses and reinforce mini-lessons previously taught.

Writing workshop takes between 30 and 60 minutes a day, every day, preferably at the same time. When students know that they will write every day, they come mentally prepared to do that. The predictability of the routine makes them feel safe and secure; they know what to expect and they know what is expected of them. Students rarely run out of ideas to write about because they know that when one piece is finished, they are expected to write another and they usually have a list of ideas written down or ideas lurking in their minds that they're eager to begin writing about. They think about writing when they're home and they come to school prepared to write more.

Writing instruction should emphasize both the process of writing and the product. When writing instruction focuses on process, teachers give students support as they prewrite, compose their first drafts, and revise and edit at a level appropriate to their age and ability. The products of writing workshop are the finished pieces of writing, which can be published formally or informally through students reading aloud their writing to their peers during authors' chair.

Elements of effective writing instruction include:

- Explicit teaching of the writing process, writing skills and strategies, and genres
- Teacher-directed and student-chosen writing topics
- Guidance during writing practice
- Response from an audience through sharing
- High expectations

🐑   Predictable routines and procedures

🐑   Evaluation

Effective writing instruction includes *explicit teaching* in the form of explanations and demonstrations of all phases of the writing process, of writing skills and strategies, and of genres. The lessons, often called mini-lessons, that begin each writing workshop are when these explanations and demonstrations occur.

Some writing topics will be *teacher directed*, some will be entirely *student chosen*. When students make choices about their writing, they can take ownership of their writing (see Figures 8.4 and 8.5). Teachers may limit the range of choices, for example, by asking them to focus on writing in a particular genre, but teachers should never remove the element of choice entirely because choice and motivation are inextricably tied.

Teachers must be available to students during their daily writing time to provide them *guidance* in the form of conferences. During conferences, they provide additional explanations and demonstrations of skills and strategies.

Students need *response* to their writing from both the teacher and their peers. Without an audience, many students will not be motivated to write. The main forms of response occur during peer conferencing and sharing. Many times the students and teachers respond to a student's writing with wonder and delight. Sometimes they are confused and need the author to clarify for them. Other times they have suggestions

Sylvia Read

Shaylee chooses to write while sitting on the floor.

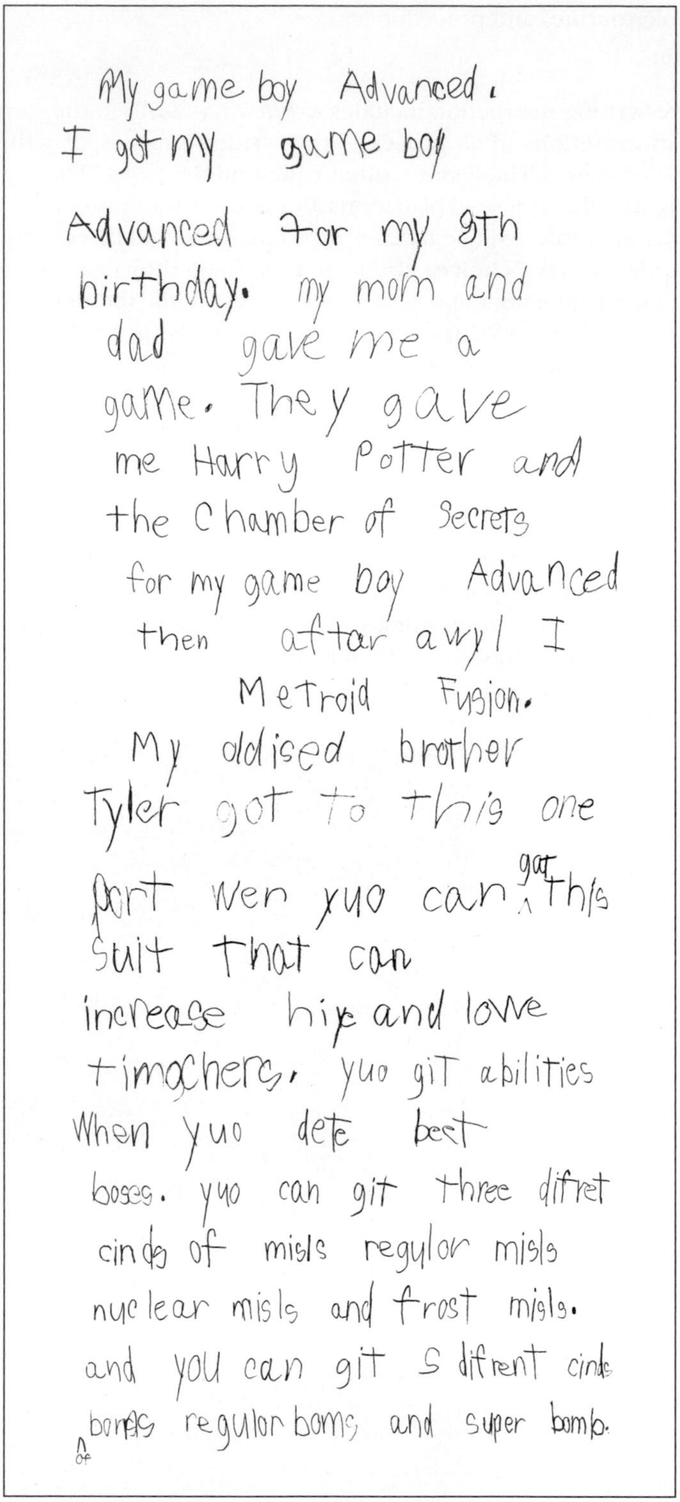

Figure 8.4 Talan chose to write about his Game Boy Advanced.

My game boy Advanced.
I got my game boy
Advanced for my 9th
birthday. my mom and
dad gave me a
game. They gave
me Harry Potter and
the Chamber of Secrets
for my game boy Advanced
then aftar awyl I
Metroid Fusion.
My oldised brother
Tyler got to this one
part wen yuo can got This
suit that can
increase hip and love
timochers. yuo git abilities
When yuo dete best
boses. yuo can git three difret
cinds of misls regulor misls
nuclear misls and frost misls.
and you can git 5 difrent cinds
bomes regulor boms and super bomb.

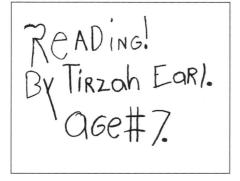

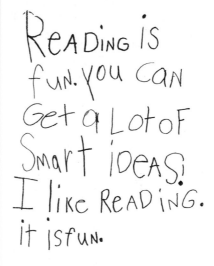

Figure 8.5 Tirzah chose to write a little book called *Reading!*

for the author to consider. Always, responses occur within the safety of the classroom community. The teacher's presence and guidance is crucial. Teachers teach students how to respond in ways that are helpful to the writer.

Teachers foster students' writing growth by having *high expectations*, and communicating this repeatedly through all interactions with students. For example, let kindergartners know that their drawings need to be accompanied by a form of writing. These expectations grow incrementally through the years. Along with higher expectations for writing conventions, teachers also expect that students' thoughts will be explained more thoroughly, that they will be making some decisions about word choice, that their writing will have some organizing features, and that they will have some sense of their own voice in their writing.

Predictable procedures and routines allow the teacher to focus on teaching effective writing lessons and allow the students to focus on writing. Students need to be taught how to plan for their writing time, get their writing folders, what to do when their pencil breaks, what to do when they finish a piece of writing, and what to do when they need a bathroom break. This room structure pervades the day, which is what makes it work during writing instruction. When students know what to do and what to expect, they are free to learn and grow as writers.

For years, *evaluation* was the teachers' job only. But lately, through evaluation procedures like collecting writing in a portfolio and reflecting on the writing, students have become part of the process. Much of students' time is spent alone with their writing, and they need to be taught early on to self-assess: How is my writing going? Am I accomplishing what I set out to do? Will my readers understand me? These self-assessing habits are taught through many interactions with students during conferencing and sharing. Consider teaching your students the language of the six traits (Spandel, 2001), as Spandel recommends, so that they are able to think about their writing in those terms. The six traits are ideas and content, organization, voice, word choice, sentence fluency, and conventions. With older students, each trait has a rubric with numbers for scoring writing, but Spandel recommends not using the numbers of rubric scoring with young children: "[There is] plenty of time for

Figure 8.6 Students can have words they want to use in their writing added to their dictionary cards by the teacher or by looking up the correct spelling in a dictionary.

Dictionary Card

Aa	Bb	Cc	Dd	Ee	Ff	Gg	Hh
a	baby	came	Dad	eat	father	get	had
after	back	come	day	each	for	girl	have
all	be	can	did	every	found	go	he
am	because	could	do	enough	friend	going	her
and	big	cousin	down		from	good	him
are	boy	can't	didn't		favorite	got	his
Aunt	brother	chapter	don't			Grandpa	home
any	but		dedicated			Grandma	house
animal							
away							
again							

Ii	Jj	Kk	Ll	Mm	Nn	Oo	Pp
I	jump	know	like	made	no	of	people
if	just	knew	little	me	not	on	place
in	joke	king	look	mother	now	one	play
into			love	Mom	never	our	put
is				my	night	out	
it					neighbor	over	
						off	
						other	

Qq	Rr	Ss	Tt	Uu	Ww	Xx	Zz
queen	ran	said	that	Uncle	was	x-ray	zoo
quickly	run	saw	the	up	we		zipper
quiet	rabbit	school	them	us	went		
	really	see	then		were	**Yy**	
		she	there		when	yes	
		sister	they		will	you	
		so	this	**Vv**	would	your	
		some	to	very	who	yellow	
		should	threw	volcano	where	yesterday	
		surprise	through		why	year	
					write		
					writing		

that beginning in third or fourth grade" (p. 324). Spandel's book *Creating Young Writers: Using the Six Traits to Enrich Writing Process in Primary Classrooms* (2007) contains a wealth of primary-grade specific advice and demonstrations. She also advocates focusing on ideas and voice primarily, then on conventions. As children experiment with conventions, they will make mistakes, sprinkling apostrophes and quotation marks, and teachers should be glad to see this. Celebrate children's use of new conventions, however inexpertly they apply them, because it is a sign of growth. Just like a baby's first steps are wobbly, so are children's first steps in each new literacy skill or tool. So, although evaluation is important, it should be used gently and judiciously with young children's writing.

I am going TO MY COUSINS.
HOUSe. Her Name is
Alexa. Yesterday Was
her Birthday.
I'm giring her a
surprise. The
surprise is
a water Gun.
I PLd tag
I said to my sister
to GOTO the zoo

Figure 8.7 "I am going to my cousin's house" was written by Lorena, an English language learner. She liked to use her dictionary card to help her spell as she wrote.

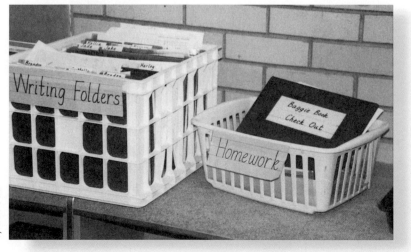

Writing folder crate.

THE ROUTINE

The daily writing workshop routine consists of a mini-lesson, time for writing (during which conferences occur), and sharing time; this is consistent with how workshop was originally defined by Graves (1983), Calkins (1994), and Atwell (1987). A daily ritual for writing workshop has certain repetitive aspects. For example, the lesson lasts for 5 to 10 minutes, and then the students tell the teacher what their writing plans are for the day. This allows the teacher to know where students are in the writing process. The teacher keeps a record of what students are working on by using a "status of the class" chart (Atwell, 1987). For the few children who aren't sure what they will write about, it helps to hear others' plans. Students will answer in various ways: "I'm working on my story about our trip to Yellowstone." "I'm editing my story so it can get published." "I'm thinking of a new story today." As the teacher asks, "what are your writing plans today?" he or she conveys to students the importance of having a plan. Everyone is swept along in the tide of getting down to the important work of writing.

Children are dismissed one at a time from the group area after telling the teacher their writing plans. Then they get their writing folder and find a good place to write (at a table, on the floor, on the couch, in the rocker) and begin to write for 20 to 30 minutes. During this time, the teacher conferences with individual students. This time is quiet, but by no means silent, because students need to be able to talk about their story ideas or ask each other how to spell words.

After they have been taught how to peer conference through modeling and guided practice, students can engage in peer conferences to discuss their writing with each other to get ideas or other kinds of help. One system for regulating conferences uses laminated cards that students take when they want to conference with another student. On one side of the card are listed the reasons to have a peer conference and on the other side are the steps to follow when conducting a peer conference.

Quinten and Lincoln having a peer conference.

Sylvia Read

Writing center.

Sylvia Read

Some reasons to have a peer conference may include:

1. To get encouragement.
2. To get ideas.
3. To get help so your story will be more interesting.
4. To get help with spelling or punctuation or capital letters.
5. To see if your story makes sense.

Steps for having a peer conference should include:

1. Only two people can have a conference.
2. Tell your partner why you need to have a conference.
3. Read aloud your writing to your partner.
4. Ask for questions or comments.
5. The other person gets a turn to read aloud and get comments.
6. Get back to writing!

WRITING LESSONS

Through writing lessons, the teacher explains and models a wide variety of writing skills and strategies and various genres and forms of writing that young writers need to try out. These are often called mini-lessons because they are short, focused lessons that occur just prior to guided writing time. Here are the steps to follow:

1. Introduce and explain the skill, strategy, or genre. Connect to previous lessons.
2. Demonstrate the skill or strategy or share an example of the genre. Interactive or shared writing can be used as the context for these demonstrations.
3. Ask students to use the skill or strategy or genre during guided writing.
4. Reflect on learning. Did the students use what you taught them that day? During sharing time, ask students to report on their use of what was taught in the lesson. Be aware that not all students will be ready to use what you taught. Lessons are repeated as necessary for the whole class or through individual conferencing or small-group instruction.

myeducationlab

Writing

Go to MyEducationLab, "Writing," and watch the video *Writing Workshop Minilesson in 2nd Grade.*
   After watching the video, you should be able to:

- Describe ways in which teachers can model the writing process for their students.
- Explain the parts of a multiple paragraph composition.
- Explain the ways in which students can use the *Drawing Out* technique to plan their writing.

Students need to be explicitly taught how to behave during writing workshop; this is addressed through procedural mini-lessons. Mini-lessons also cover writing skills, writing strategies, and writing craft.

Procedural Mini-Lessons

At the beginning of the school year, it's important to teach procedural mini-lessons, which are crucial to establishing predictable routines. You teach lessons that help students establish good work habits like dating their writing, numbering pages, writing on one side of the paper, and skipping lines. You also teach them where to store their writing folders, what to do when their pencils need to be sharpened, what to do when they need more paper, or how to organize their writing folders so that precious pages of writing are not destroyed or lost. The following are some suggested procedural mini-lesson topics:

- Writing name and date on pieces of writing
- Getting writing folders
- Stapling finished pieces
- Handing in pieces of writing
- Using one side of the paper and skipping lines on lined paper so that revision is possible
- Conducting a peer conference
- Finding a quiet place to work

Skill Mini-Lessons

Skill mini-lessons should grow out of the needs you perceive among your students and your district's or state's core objectives for your grade level. For example, kindergartners and beginning first graders will need skill lessons focusing on how to orient print on a page and how to put space between words, whereas second graders will need to see you model how to insert punctuation. Skill lessons are effectively taught through modeling or interactive writing where the students participate in the creation of a shared text. Skills mini-lesson topics might include:

- Orienting print top-to-bottom and left-to-right
- Putting spaces between words and concept of "word"
- Using capital letters at the beginning of sentences and for proper names
- Using quotations marks to indicate character talking out loud (use your own writing or let a student teach this lesson using his or her writing)
- Adding *ing* and *ed* to verbs
- Learning the concept of sentence and listening for where punctuation goes (role-play putting periods at the end of lines)
- Writing left to right, top to bottom (role-play the wrong way)
- Learning how and when to use various spelling resources such as a word wall, dictionary card (see Figures 8.6 and 8.7), book, or peer or adult

Strategy Mini-Lessons

Writers sometimes have tricks or strategies they use during the writing process. Teachers can demonstrate these in strategy mini-lessons. Strategies include simple behaviors like lining out words instead of erasing. We want to teach students to line out words both because it is faster than erasing and because it allows the writer and the teacher to see the changes that have been made. Sometimes writers decide to restore their original text. Strategies can also be more complex and abstract, such as learning to narrow the focus of a piece of writing. Some suggested strategy mini-lesson topics are:

- Selecting topics
- Brainstorming new topics
- Prewriting strategies such as listing, webbing, and charting
- Using a caret to insert words
- Lining out instead of erasing when you want to make a change
- Rereading your own writing at the beginning of writing time
- Rehearsing ideas at home or with friends through talk
- Figuring out the important part of your writing and concentrating on that

Craft Mini-Lessons

Craft mini-lessons teach students how to improve the quality of their writing. Though students need to write fluently and produce lots of writing, they also need to learn ways to make their writing better or more interesting. It's important to talk positively with young children about their writing, but you can tell them you are confused by what they have written, or suggest that they might add or change words that could help readers better understand their writing. Teachers are clearly writing experts compared to students and should not overwhelm them with all the growth they have ahead of them or make them feel as if they will never measure up. So, while introducing ways that authors make their writing more effective, don't expect that students will use the ideas immediately. First, make students aware of the qualities of good writing; before they can produce writing of that quality, they need to be able to recognize it. Craft mini-lessons do not teach discrete skills that we expect them to master in a finite period of time; these are ideas, techniques, and strategies that they will eventually use to enhance their writing. Figure 8.8 provides high-quality book titles and possible craft mini-ideas.

Writing

Go to MyEducationLab, "Writing," and watch the videos *Minilesson: Teaching Students to Add Detail* and *Editing Conference*.

After watching the videos, you should be able to:

- Explain the structure of a writing conference.
- Identify the ways in which samples of a student's writing can form the basis for diagnostic instruction.
- Explain the ways in which checklists can be used to help students monitor and maintain ownership of their writing.
- Discuss the use of positive reinforcement in a writing conference.
- Discuss the ways in which literature can be used to help students improve their writing.
- Identify a system for monitoring students' work during writing workshop.

For example, *Voices in the Park* by Anthony Browne (1998) is written from the point of view of four different characters. Using this book, you can show students how point of view changes the story. Young children can see how this works even if they aren't ready to write from different points of view.

Craft mini-lesson topics could include:

- Making a picture in the mind of the reader
- Considering the effective leads in familiar books

Katie enjoys writing poetry.

Sylvia Read

- Using words to advance a story (other than *and then*); for example, use phrases such as "the next day," "2 weeks later," "later that night," and so on
- Considering how point of view affects the way a story is told
- Letting the writer's personal voice come through
- Using your senses when adding description

Figure 8.8   High Quality Literature to Teach the Craft of Writing

Aliki. *Fossils tell of long ago.* Use of sequenced drawings in information text to visually explain a process.

Berger, M. *Do all spiders spin webs?: Questions and answers about spiders.* Using a question-and-answer format for writing informational text.

Brown, M. *Arthur's computer disaster.* All the Arthur books have great examples of dialogue and alternate words for *said.*

Browne, A. *Voices in the park.* Great for showing multiple points of view of the same event.

Casely, J. *Bully.* Problem and resolution structure of fiction.

DuTemple, L. *Polar bears.* Using a table of contents to organize informational text.

Guiberson, B. *Cactus hotel.* Using chronological narrative structure to relay information.

Henkes, K. *Julius, the baby of the world.* Effective word choice for characterization.

James, S. *Dear Mr. Blueberry.* Letter writing between characters as a narrative structure.

Lester, H. *Author: A true story.* Various strategies authors use.

Lowery, L. *Martin Luther King day.* Elements of a good biography.

Nixon, J. *If you were a writer.* Various writing strategies.

Pallotta, J. *The icky bug alphabet book.* Pallotta's series of alphabet books are all useful for modeling the alphabet book as a nonfiction writing structure.

Spooner, M. *A moon in your lunch box.* Good examples of concrete poetry, free verse, and subtle rhyming verse.

Steig, W. *Sylvester and the magic pebble.* Word choice for description.

Viorst, J. *Alexander and the terrible, horrible, no good, very bad day.* Using a repeating phrase to add humor to a story.

Conferencing During Independent Writing

Almost all experienced writers discuss their writing with others at some stage in the writing process. Adult writers often belong to a writing group that meets face-to-face to respond to pieces written by members of the group. During these meetings, they talk about the writing, tell the author what worked and what was confusing, and offer suggestions. Adults benefit from bouncing ideas off each other, getting feedback, before deciding how to proceed. Children can also benefit from getting feedback and encouragement from their peers.

Some children need to talk through their stories, rehearsing them aloud, before they can write them down. Other children find they have so much more to say after they've explained what they're writing. When conferencing, try to focus mostly on the content. Spelling, punctuation, or other conventions are legitimate concerns that children have and teachers can offer them help while their writing is in process, but mostly we need to save discussions of conventions for the editing phase of the writing process.

Listen as much as possible in a writing conference, but try to end a conference by helping a child in some specific way. For example, if the text has a confusing sentence, encourage the writer to add a word or sentence that clarifies the meaning. Or, read aloud the student's writing and help her to hear the pauses so that she can determine where periods go. Here is an example of a conference during which the teacher helped a student brainstorm titles.

Teacher: You were saying that you were trying to think of a title? Is that right?

Ryan: Uh huh.

Teacher: Can I show you a strategy for thinking up titles?

Ryan: Okay.

Teacher: Okay. What's your story about?

Ryan: It's a story about a detective.

Teacher: Uh huh. A detective story? And what's the problem in your story?

Ryan: Um, he gets a phone call and he goes and tries to find her cat and he finds her cat. It was in the. . . . I forgot where it was.

Teacher: Okay. So, it's a lost cat story. It's a detective story. It's a mystery?

Ryan: (*Nods head*)

Teacher: Okay, let's think of about three different titles and then you could probably choose one of those. Let's just think of one first. It doesn't have to be interesting.

Ryan: The Case of the Missing Everything?

Teacher: The Case of the Missing Everything. Why do you say everything?

Ryan: 'Cause everybody's calling me and all their stuff is lost.

Teacher: Oh, okay. There's one idea. Let's think of another one. (*Pause*) Does your detective have a name?

Ryan: Mmm, no.

Teacher: What if he did? Let's call him Detective Ryan. That could be a title. (*I left Ryan to think of a third title, which he did, and came back a few minutes later.*) You don't have to decide which title you like now, but is there one you like better than the others? Which one do you like best?

Ryan: The Deep Dark Night.

Teacher: Hey, good, I'm glad 'cause that's one you thought of. Great!

When conferencing with students, don't overload the writer with advice; young writers can usually attend to only one teaching point. If you keep conferences brief, then you can touch base with as many students as possible during writing time; it helps to keep track of who you've conferenced with so that across several days you can be sure to conference with everyone. Often several students need something at the same time. When students have been taught what to do about pencils, bathroom, and other routine tasks, they don't need to interrupt a writing conference. If they have questions about writing, ask them to check with other students first, then raise their hand for help. Circulate continuously among the students; proximity keeps many students on task and allows the teacher to be available to as many students as possible.

Prompts to begin and extend writing conferences may include:

- How's it going?
- How can I help you?
- What's going to be the most important thing?
- Tell me about the most important part.
- How do you do that?
- What's happening in this piece?
- What are you writing about?
- What was the best part?
- Are you going to write about that?
- What are you going to say about it?
- Tell me what you're going to do.
- Tell me about the picture in your head.
- Are you going to write all this?
- What are you going to write next?
- What do you particularly like?
- Any surprises in your writing?

During writing conferences, children talk about their topic and as they talk, they discover what they have to say, and then they are able to write, or elaborate on what they have already written. Through conferencing, the teacher validates their ability to think and solve their own writing problems (soon they may be able to have a conference with themselves). We must really listen and be genuinely interested in what our students have to say. Really listening means being open to the child's agenda. You show the child you've listened well when you try to restate what he or she has said before you offer your response.

Teacher: What's happening in your story?

Shannon: They came home and they're like going to eat supper.

Teacher: Mm hm.

Shannon: Then they're going to bed. Then wake up.

Teacher: Okay, so what are you going to write right now?

Shannon: I can't decide.

Teacher: So you're trying to make a decision. Tell me what you're trying to decide.

Shannon: If they're going to set the table or if it's all set and they're going to eat.

Teacher: So you're trying to decide how much detail to put in?

Shannon: (*Nods*)

Teacher: Like whether to have the characters set the table or have it all set and not worry about that?

Shannon: (*Nods*)

Teacher: Which do you think would keep your audience more interested? Do you think they want to hear about setting the table or would they rather get going farther along in the story?

Shannon: Get going in the story.

Teacher: Did that help you make a decision?

Shannon: Yeah.

Teacher: Okay.

Try (and this is difficult) to teach your students not to interrupt a writing conference; ignore those who try to interrupt and focus on the writer. If students know the procedures in your classroom, most routine matters can be taken care of independently, without adult intervention. There are times when they truly do need you, such as when someone feels sick and needs to call home. You don't want to coldly ignore the genuine needs of all your students, but you do want the writers you are conferencing with to know they are important.

SHARING WRITING

Writing workshop ends with a sharing session that lasts for 10 to 15 minutes. A few students read part or all of their writing and take comments and questions from their classmates. Young writers need to share their writing. Knowing they will have an audience is very motivating. Also, their peers are an authentic audience for their writing. Writing for the teacher's eyes only is a sure way to develop writing that meets only minimal standards of quality. When students are reluctant to share, we can encourage them to have a friend read their writing with them, which can make the situation seem less intimidating. If many students are reluctant to share, this may indicate that the classroom climate is threatening.

Author Concerns

Who should share? Someone who's had a good writing day. Someone who's tried something new. Someone who hasn't shared recently. It's a good idea to keep track of who has shared their writing in any given 1- or 2-week period so that everyone has a fair chance to share during that time. Limit the numbers of students who share each day because, if more than two to four writers share, the focus becomes too fragmented and students' attention spans reach their limit. Choose how many students share based on the length of writing to be shared, the length of time available, and an estimate of students' ability to listen attentively at that point in the school year.

During sharing, the author sits in a chair, sometimes labeled the authors' chair, and reads his or her piece of writing loudly and clearly enough to keep the audience engaged. Afterward, the students and the teacher ask questions or make comments. If authors have received useful suggestions, write them on a sticky note so that they can use them the next day. Ultimately, the author decides whether or not to make changes.

Listener Responsibilities

At the beginning of the year, teach students to listen intently to those who share. When students are required to respond with "I heard. . . ." or "I learned. . . ." it teaches them to listen for the meaning and lets writers know if their writing is clear. When the audience listens carefully, the students feel valued.

Later in the year, after careful listening has been established, students are ready to begin their responses with questions or comments, and sometimes suggestions for the writer.

Shannon: Are you gonna describe, like, what color the unicorn is?

Author: White with a gold mane and a silver horn.

Jared: What's the unicorn's name?

Author: Good question. Maybe I'll name it Audrey.

Brock: I like that one sentence.

Author: You mean, "through brambles, across little streams, under low branches of trees, finally the two found what was making the noise."

Teacher: That *is* an amazing sentence. It is very descriptive.

Questions for the author should clarify meaning. "I was wondering. . . ." "I was confused when you said. . . ." "I want to know. . . ." Sometimes we have to steer students away from focusing on unimportant details that would not improve the writing. Of course, this means modeling and discussing which kinds of details are important and which are not. Good questions can help the author generate ways to extend the writing the next day.

Comments for the author about the writing should be specific. "I liked your story" is too vague and not helpful. Comments should focus on the author's story, not the person who's commenting (many children have a tendency to want to tell their own experience that is similar to what the author has written).

Shannon: Where did you get the idea that Bessie got sucked into the book? (*Shannon asked this about the author's time travel historical fiction, "Bessie the Colonial Girl."*)

Author: Um, I got it from *Scooby Doo and the Cyber Chase* and I also got the colonial idea from *If You Lived in Colonial Times*.

Bethany: What does Bessie look like?

Author: I'll probably add that in here. She has long, to her shoulder length, dark brown hair. And she has kind of a stubby nose, which means small. She has big eyes, like me. She wears this yellow dress with an apron and a bonnet. Oh, and just to tell you, they're 10 years old.

Regina: I'm excited for your story.

Lincoln: What's gonna happen next?

Author: They're gonna meet Helen and then Maria doesn't hate Helen and then Bessie and Maria aren't friends anymore, but then Bessie has to rescue her father from jail because he was arrested. And so Maria calls Bessie her hero because Bessie's dad is Maria's great-, great-, great-, great-, grandmother's son.

Sharing time often needs its own mini-lessons. The following is an example of a sharing session where the teacher began by establishing a clear purpose for listening. (The students had been asking less helpful questions such as "When did you start writing this?" and "What's going to happen next?")

Teacher: I want you to be listening for things that you like about Alex's writing, about the way he wrote it or the information that he included. That's what I'd like you to make comments about. *(Alex reads aloud.)*

Jaren: I liked the sentence where you used the word *smaller*.

Teacher: So he used comparison words, *smaller than*?

Jaren: Yeah.

Lincoln: I liked how you said *than* instead of *then*. (*The difference between* than *and* then *was difficult for some of the students earlier in the year and I had worked hard with a few of them to impress on them that* than *was used when comparing things.*)

Teacher: Yes, we've talked about that, haven't we? Alex did a good job with that.

Braden: I like how you put in descriptive words like *Mercury is smaller than Earth* and *Pluto is smaller than Mercury*.

In some ways, sharing is more important than formal publishing because students get more feedback that helps them improve the piece they're working on or write differently the next time. But publishing is also important, because students gain the satisfaction of creating a finished product that they can share with their parents and then place in the classroom library.

PUBLISHING

Publishing can take many forms. The simplest is when students read their writing aloud to the class. More permanent forms of publishing include bulletin board displays, letters (i.e., when they are actually sent to the recipient), student-written classroom newsletters, posters, books, single poems, and class anthologies of poetry. Figure 8.9 shows a published poem, which was displayed on a bulletin board and later bound in a class anthology.

Each student should have several pieces of writing published during the school year. We must teach young children to proofread their own writing the best they can and then an adult can keyboard their writing using conventional spellings and punctuation. The students then illustrate the pages, which can be bound using heavy card stock for the front and back covers. These books can be produced quickly using the materials and tools found in most elementary schools. Every book should have a title page as well as a cover, with optional dedication pages or about-the-author pages (see Figure 8.10). Including these "real-book" features is important because it gives their book an authentic feel—students know that "real" books have these elements. Pages are numbered for everyone's convenience. Most children want to illustrate the whole book like a picture book, but some prefer a more chapter book-like look with no interior illustrations. You might allow them to illustrate during writing workshop for a day or two, and then finish during free time or at home (illustrating can also be integrated into the art curriculum; teaching children about horizon lines, for example, improves their illustrations considerably). These books are valuable to the children; they take them home to share with their families, but you may ask that they bring the books

Figure 8.9   Dalton's
Published Poem

My Dogs
by Dalton Childs

Otis is the wild one.
He runs around the
yard chasing
his tail. He jumps on
me when I get home.
Shadow just lays around.
One time Shadow jumped on
a chair and on the counter
and slept there.
Taz look puffy.
He loves his little
basketball. He looks for
it all
the time. He knocks over couches
and lamps and knocks
over chairs.
And Romeo,
he's a weiner dog
and he jumps
high and he eats
cat food and chases the cat.
Romeo is fun.
He drinks
out of the sink.
He climbs up the drawers.
When he gets down he jumps

back to be part of the classroom collection until the end of the year (alternatively, a photocopy of the book can be included in the class library). Pieces of writing that are not published, but are finished, go into the students' portfolios.

Tips on Publishing

1. As a mini-lesson, discuss what they need to do before they can publish their work. First, they must have at least three pieces to choose from. They must read all three of them in their entirety and then choose which one they want to publish. Then they need to proofread according to a proofreading checklist that they've been taught how to use.

2. Before keyboarding their writing, check to see if they have proofread to the best of their ability. If they haven't, ask them to check again. For spelling, you can pair students with a parent volunteer or with a more advanced speller. Then an adult can keyboard the student's writing, fixing the remaining spelling and punctuation errors. "Real" authors have editors too.

3. With more advanced writers, ask yourself what they are ready to do in terms of revising and editing their own writing:

    🐾 Are they ready to find some correct spellings in a picture dictionary?

    🐾 Are they ready to add periods and capital letters?

    🐾 Are they ready to add quotation marks?

About the aułher

Tirzah EarL lives in Utah. aShe has a baby brother, & her mom is going to have a baby girl. I am the oldest. My baby brothers name is Micah. My mom's name is Robyn. My dad's name is Bryan. I was born in Logan, Utah. I am eight years old. I go to school at North Park Elementry.

Figure 8.10 Tirzah wrote an About the Author page for one of her published books.

Writing portfolios.

🐾   Are they ready to change the sequence of their writing?

🐾   Are they ready to cut extraneous material?

🐾   Are they ready to figure out where paragraphs should go?

As students become more fluent writers, their writing pieces get quite long. Teachers shouldn't publish everything they write. Students must decide which piece they want to submit for publication, realizing that as their "publisher," the teacher has the right to "reject their manuscript." This is why it helps to ask students to wait until they have three pieces of writing before they publish. They must reread these three pieces carefully and consider which one is their best or favorite. If they've followed these steps, publish their chosen piece as a meaningful reward. Parent volunteers can be very useful in the publishing process. They can be taught to edit students' work alongside the students, to type edited pieces, and to bind books.

Teachers should also publish shorter pieces of writing: class books about field trips, interactive writing pieces, New Year's resolutions, poems, biographies of classmates, and book reviews, to name a few. Writing in these other genres is important to the overall development of writers.

WRITING IN MANY GENRES

EXPLICIT INSTRUCTION MODEL

Effective writing instruction for different genres must be based on a model of explicit instruction (see the Explicit Instruction Writing Lesson Plan). Most students come to school unfamiliar with academic genres such as the report and informal genres such as the friendly letter. With explicit writing instruction, teachers need to first immerse students in examples of the genre.

After students have developed some familiarity with the genre, the next step in explicit instruction is to provide a clear explanation of what you want students to do and then model that for them. If your teaching objective is to have students write a friendly letter, you must explain what it is, show them examples, and then demonstrate or model writing a friendly letter while students watch.

The third step in explicit instruction is to provide interactive guided practice. Using letter writing as the example again, you would lead the students in writing a group-authored letter, perhaps a letter thanking the school's custodians for their hard work.

The fourth step is to provide students with time to practice writing in the chosen genre, while continuously monitoring them through conferencing.

Assessment is the last step. While conferencing with students and after they have finished a particular piece of writing, you must assess the effectiveness of your instruction. What have students understood, what areas need improvement, what objectives were they unable to achieve? From this assessment, you can decide which objectives need to be retaught. You can also revise your instruction so that students better understand the task the next time you teach the lesson.

Explicit Instruction Writing Lesson Plan

Lesson Steps	Activities
Introduction • Connect today's lesson to previous lessons • Give a purpose for today's lesson	Immersion in examples of writing through read-aloud of teacher-written texts, children's literature, environmental print, and students' writing
Explicit teacher explanation and modeling	Mini-lessons in which procedures, skills, strategies, or craft are explained and modeled
Interactive guided practice	Interactive writing, shared writing
Monitored independent practice	Students compose texts alone or with a partner while teacher provides support through conferencing
Assessment	Conferencing Observation/field notes Six traits, developing writer's continuum

Explicit Instruction Notetaking Lesson Plan

Concept or Objective: *Notetaking from informational books using dash facts*

Lesson Steps	Activities	Materials
Introduction • Connect today's lesson to previous lessons • Give a purpose for today's lesson	"Students, we've been reading some informational books this year like *Owls* by Gail Gibbons. To write a book like that, Gail Gibbons had to do some research. She probably read books, watched videos about owls, and talked to experts. She kept track of everything she learned by taking notes. Today we're going to take notes together from a book called *Weird Friends*. It's a book that explains how animals sometimes help each other out in strange ways. And we're going to learn to write dash facts."	*Weird Friends: Unlikely Allies in the Animal Kingdom* by José Aruego

Lesson Steps	Activities	Materials
Explicit teacher explanation and modeling—Day 1	1. Say, "Dash facts are short phrases that help us remember important ideas. I'm going to show you how to write a dash fact and then you're going to help me write some." 2. Begin by writing at the top of the chart paper: "This information came from *Weird Friends: Unlikely Allies in the Animal Kingdom* by José Aruego." 3. Say, "It is important to write down where your information came from so that you can tell your readers. That way your readers know you aren't just making it up." 4. Read aloud the first two pages. Draw a dash for each important idea or phrase. 5. Close the book when writing the idea and explain to students that closing the book helps you remember the idea and stops you from copying the whole sentence.	Chart paper Markers *Weird Friends*
Interactive guided practice	1. Read aloud the next two pages. Close the book and have students say the phrase or idea they think was important. 2. Continue in this manner for a few more pages.	*Weird Friends* Chart paper Markers
Monitored independent practice	Provide students with informational books that are at their independent reading level. Students can work in pairs. Conference briefly with all students providing support with reading of text and observing their writing of dash facts.	Informational books written on students' independent reading levels. Paper and pencils for each student
Assessment	Assessment occurs through conferencing and observation.	Conferencing checklist to ensure that all students are monitored (anecdotal records of observations can be collected on the checklist)
Accommodations for students	Struggling readers can be paired with readers working on or above grade level or with an aide or classroom volunteer. Some students may need a scribe for writing the dash facts.	

PREWRITING STRATEGIES FOR DIFFERENT GENRES

Of all the phases of the writing process, prewriting is the most neglected. Students are often asked to plunge into drafting without any preparation. We need to teach students not only about different genres, but also to use prewriting strategies that will help them generate and organize ideas. For each of the genres discussed in the following text, a specific prewriting strategy is provided.

Letters

Letter writing instruction should happen within an authentic context. For example, when a visitor makes a presentation at the school, it makes sense to write thank-you letters. Get-well cards, farewell letters, and letters requesting information all have an authentic purpose that students understand. Before asking students to write letters, show them examples of letters in picture books and from your own life.

A simple, yet highly useful prewriting strategy for letter writing is listing. The explicit instruction sequence should also be followed when teaching prewriting strategies. Explain the purpose for the strategy and model it. Before engaging in interactive guided writing of a letter, use the listing strategy. During independent writing, provide separate paper for students to use for prewriting and monitor their use of the prewriting strategy. Figure 8.11 illustrates a prewriting list and an interactive guided writing of a thank-you letter.

Figure 8.11   Listing Strategy and Thank-You Letter

Prewriting List of Ideas to Include in a Thank-You Letter to the Local Fire Department

- Learned about stop, drop, and roll
- Learned about checking doors for hotness
- Smoke house was the most fun
- Thanks for visiting, keeping homes safe, rescuing people

Interactive Guided Writing of Thank-You Letter

Dear firefighters,

We had so much fun when you brought your trucks to our school last week. We learned that if we catch on fire, we should stop, drop, and roll. We also learned that if there's a fire in our house, we should touch our door to see if it's hot before we open it. Most of us thought the smoke house was the most fun, but the smoke smelled funny.

Thank you for visiting our school. Thank you for keeping our houses safe and for rescuing people who are in danger.

Sincerely,

Ms. B's class

Figure 8.12   Book Review Prewriting Strategy

Information to include in a book review
Character:
Setting:
Some events:
Conclusion:
Good book/not good book, and why:

Book Reviews

Unlike traditional book reports, book reviews have a definite purpose beyond fulfilling a teacher's requirement. Book reviews are meant for other students to read to get recommendations for good books to read. Begin by sharing examples of reviews of familiar picture books from Amazon.com, book blogs, or from newpapers or magazines.

As students are immersed in the book review genre, explicitly teach them what a book review is and its purpose. Then, model writing a book review, and show students that a book review usually has a short summary of the book (though the ending isn't always revealed) and a statement or two of evaluation.

Before engaging in an interactive guided writing of a book review, teach a prewriting strategy. For book reviews, the prewriting strategy can be a modified story map (Figure 8.12).

Autobiography and Biography

Writing autobiographies is a great way to begin the school year. It allows students to get to know each other as they share or publish their autobiographies. Later in the year, students can be paired to write biographies of each other. Both are forms of nonfiction that do not require reading any source materials but allow students to draw on their own knowledge of themselves as they write about themselves or tell a peer about themselves.

Read aloud examples of autobiography and biography, and create a chart that lists the features of autobiographies and biographies (see Figure 8.13). This will become the framework for prewriting before writing a first draft. Figure 8.14 shows the rough draft of a biography written by a second grader.

Figure 8.13   Features of Autobiographies and Biographies

- Where and when born
- Childhood
- Family members
- Likes and dislikes
- Hobbies and work
- Big events in life

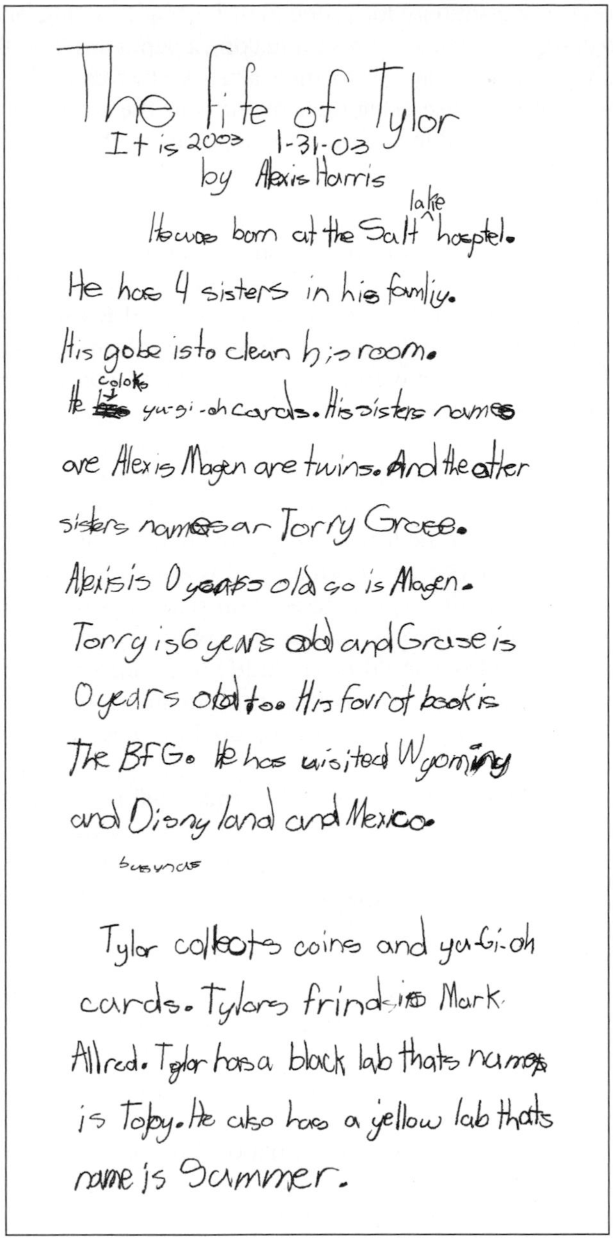

The Life of Tylor
It is 2003 1-31-03
by Alexis Harris

He was born at the Salt lake hosptel. He has 4 sisters in his famliy. His gobe is to clean his room. He colokts yu-gi-oh cards. His sisters names are Alexis Magen are twins. And the ather sisters names ar Torry Grace. Alexis is 0 years old so is Magen. Torry is 6 years old and Grase is 0 years old too. His favrot book is The BFG. He has visited Wyoming and Disny land and Mexico.

busnas

Tylor colkots coins and yu-Gi-oh cards. Tylors frinds is Mark Allred. Tylor has a black lab thats names is Toby. He also has a yellow lab thats name is Sammer.

Figure 8.14 The Life of Tylor by Alexis Harris

Procedural/How-to Writing

Begin by showing students how-to books and other procedural texts (cookbooks, craft books, board game instructions, etc.) and by explicitly explaining the purpose of procedural writing. Then, in addition to modeling how to write a procedural text, it helps to carry out the activity being described. For example, if you plan to model writing a recipe, you could model making a sandwich. Afterward, ask the students to explain each step in the sandwich-making process. As they explain the steps, reenact the sandwich making, following their instructions literally. Usually, students leave out details, which become apparent as you follow their instructions.

The best prewriting strategy for procedural writing is acting out the process. If students want to describe the procedures for making a paper airplane, they will need to fold paper as they write, carefully noting their actions. They can also write the procedures for their areas of expertise using their memory as the source of steps to follow: babysitting, making friends, making a favorite food, cleaning their room, and so on.

Informational Reports

Before asking students to write informational texts, they need to become familiar with the features of these kinds of texts through read aloud. Through reading aloud, you can introduce students to the topics, structures, and features of informational books. This understanding will help them as they write informational reports.

Once students are familiar with informational texts, you can prepare them to write an informational report. You should begin by explicitly explaining and modeling how to write an informational report using a prewriting tool. Regardless of how students learned the information they are going to write about (teacher read-aloud, independent reading, video, life experience), the nuggets of information they want to include in their reports should be listed before they begin to write a first draft.

The next step is to write an informational text together. If you plan to have students write from their life experiences, then choose a topic that everyone is familiar with, such as school. Through shared or interactive writing, create the list of items that the students think should be included in an informational report about school. Use the list as the basis for writing the informational report. Figure 8.15 shows how Kaylee used listing as a prewriting tool before writing her informational book *I Love Soccer*.

If you plan to have students write an informational report using sources (like books, videos, experts), then you must teach them a notetaking strategy as a prewriting tool. 'Dash facts" are a way to teach notetaking to young children. Dash facts are words or phrases that summarize a smaller piece of information that the writer wants to remember and include in an informational report. Putting a dash in front of the words and phrases helps signify that the words and phrases they've written down are *NOT* sentences and therefore not the writing itself, but rather a way to prepare for writing. Figure 8.16 is an example of a first grader's list of dash facts and the final draft of his informational book. Also see Explicit Instruction Notetaking Lesson on p. 205.

Once students have seen you explain and demonstrate how to write an informational report and participated in the creation of a group-written informational report, they are ready to try writing an informational report on their own.

Poetry

Any attempt to teach children to write poetry must begin with reading and hearing lots of poems read aloud. Poems should include those written for children, but also classic and contemporary poems that appeal to a broad range of readers.

The prewriting tool that you use for poetry very much depends on the kind of poetry that students will write. A descriptive poem in free verse (nonrhyming, nonrhythmic poetry) benefits from a stimulus of some kind: students' drawings, a photo or piece of artwork, a piece of music, a location or object. By brainstorming descriptive words and using the senses, students are able to gather the ideas they need to form a poem.

Formula poetry can be a helpful support to some students, though overusing formula poetry risks leading students to think that poetry is overly rule-bound. Acrostic, diamante poems, haiku, cinquain, and bio-poem are common examples of formula poems.

Figure 8.15   Kaylee used this list as a prewriting strategy when writing *I Love Soccer.*

Soccer

- Rules*
- The stuff you wear*
- Goalie*
- Dribbling the ball and passing the ball*

*Kaylee used stars to mark the items in her list as she finished writing about them.

I Love Soccer
by Kaylee Carlsen

Rules

The rules in soccer are you have to keep the ball in bounds. If the other team kicks the ball out of bounds, you get to throw the ball in bounds. There is a certain way to throw the ball. Your feet have to stay on the ground. If they come up you have to throw the ball again. After you throw the ball, you can't be the first one to touch the ball.

You wear shin guards. They protect your shins. And you wear long socks so you can't see your shin guards. There is a soccer shirt you have to wear. It is yellow or blue. If you come with the yellow and your team is blue, you have to turn your shirt over. The goalie has to guard the ball from going into the goal. If the other team gets the ball in the net, they get a point.

How You Start the Game

You put the ball in the circle and kick it.

Dribbling

When you dribble, you have to kick the ball back and forth. And when you get close to the goal, you kick it and score for your team. My team won every game last year. My team's name is Lightning Bugs and we won.

Figure 8.16   Tyler took notes from a book using "dash facts." He then turned these dash facts into sentences for his book *Mammals Are Great.*

All About Mammals
This information came from *Mammals* by Paul McEvoy

- Warm-blooded
- Covered with fur
- Same body temperature all the time
- Baby feeds on milk from its mother
- The only mammals that can fly are bats
- Mammals are animals that have a backbone and are warm-blooded
- Mammals eat more food than cold-blooded animals

Mammals Are Great
by Tyler Brown

Mammals are warm-blooded animals that live on land and in water. Most mammals have fur or hair. They have the same body temperature all the time. The baby drinks milk from its mother. Bats are the only mammals in the world that can fly. Mammals eat more food than other animals, like reptiles.

This information came from *Mammals* by Paul McEvoy.

Figure 8.17   Prewriting strategies vary, depending on the type of poem.

Type of Poem	Prewriting Strategies	Lesson Plan
Free verse—nonrhyming, non-rhythmic poetry	Oral brainstorming of topics; visual or auditory stimulus, listing descriptive words using five senses	*Kids' Poems* by Regie Routman http://content.scholastic.com/browse/article.jsp?id=4414 and *Kids' Poems: Teaching Second Graders to Love Writing Poetry* by Regie Routman
Acrostic—first letter of each line of the poem spells a word	Listing of words that begin with each letter of the alphabet for students to use as a word bank	*Acrostic Poems: All About Me and My Favorite Things* by Renee Goularte at http://www.readwritethink.org/lessons/lesson_view.asp?id=309
Found poem—words found in texts shaped into poetry	Read-aloud of several books, other poems, listing of interesting words and phrases	*A Bear of a Poem: Composing and Performing Found* Poetry by Carolyn Wilheim http://www.readwritethink.org/lessons/lesson_view.asp?id=835

Once you have determined the kind of poetry that students will write, you must explain what it is and model it, using the prewriting strategy that matches (see Figure 8.17). This should be followed by a shared or interactive writing of a poem by the whole class. Once students have seen you write a poem (and heard you think out loud while prewriting and drafting the poem) and then participated in a whole-class poetry writing experience, they are ready to try out poetry writing independently.

Fiction

As with every other genre, when teaching fiction writing, you must begin by immersing students in fiction. Teachers read fiction aloud frequently, but to prepare for writing fiction, it's important to read fiction and also study its structure. As you read aloud several stories, work together as a class to complete a story map for each one. Short stories like those found in *Frog and Toad* (Lobel, 1970) or *Henry and Mudge* books (Rylant, 1987) work well because the elements of fiction are easy to identify, which keeps the task of analyzing story structure simpler. The same story map that you use to identify the elements of a *Frog and Toad* story will later serve as the prewriting tool that students use to plan their fiction stories.

Also, in keeping with the explicit instruction model, after examining several stories and mapping the elements, you should explicitly explain and model how to use the story map to plan a story and write a first draft (see Figure 8.18). Then, you should engage the students in a shared or interactive writing lesson using the story map to plan and draft a group-written story. With this preparation, students will be ready to plan a story using the story map and begin writing their own fiction story (see Figure 8.18). Figure 8.19 shows an example of second-grade fiction writing.

Figure 8.18   Story Map for "A Lost Button" from *Frog and Toad Are Friends* by Arnold Lobel

Characters: Frog, Toad

Setting: meadow, woods, river, home

Problem: Toad loses button

Solution: Search for button

Events:

1. Take long walk
2. Return home and notice button is gone
3. Search for button in places where they walked
4. Return home and find button

Figure 8.19   Page 13 of Emily's Five-Chapter Fiction Piece Called *The Secret Shortcut*

CONCLUDING THOUGHTS

Writing workshop needs to take place every day. It works best when teachers make writing part of the daily classroom schedule, preferably at the same time every day. Children thrive on the structure and predictability of writing workshop. They know what to expect and are prepared for it.

Effective writing instruction begins by immersing students in examples of a genre, then following an explicit instruction model that begins with explicit explanation and modeling of how to use a prewriting tool and how to write in the chosen genre. Then students should participate in a shared or interactive writing using the prewriting tool to create a class-written piece. Through this careful scaffolding, teachers prepare students to write in a variety of genres on their own.

SUGGESTED ACTIVITIES TO EXTEND YOUR LEARNING

1. Observe in a classroom where writing workshop happens on a daily basis. Take note of the management routines and the nature of the mini-lessons. If possible, talk to the students about their writing and look at writing samples.
2. Select two or three pieces of high-quality children's literature that would be useful examples of a genre.
3. Develop an interactive writing lesson plan based on a content area topic from your state's curriculum and a high-quality nonfiction children's book. See the steps for teaching an interactive writing lesson on clouds presented earlier in the chapter for an example.

REFERENCES

Allen, R. V. (1999). Using language experience in beginning reading: How a language experience program works. In O. Nelson & W. Linek (Eds.), *Practical classroom applications of language experience.* Boston: Allyn & Bacon.

Atwell, N. (1987). *In the middle: Writing, reading, and learning with adolescents.* Portsmouth, NH: Heinemann.

Bear, D. R., Invernizzi, M., Templeton, S., & Johnston, F. (2008). *Words their way: Word study for phonics, vocabulary, and spelling instruction* (4th ed.). Upper Saddle River, NJ: Merrill/Prentice Hall.

Bodrova, E., & Leong, D. J. (1998). Scaffolding emergent writing in the zone of proximal development. *Literacy Teaching and Learning, 3*(2), 1–18.

Calkins, L. M. (1994). *The art of teaching writing.* Portsmouth, NH: Heinemann.

Casbergue, R. M., & Plauché, M. B. (2005). Emergent writing: Classroom practices that support young writers' development. In R. Indrisano & J. R. Paratore (Eds.), *Learning to write, writing to learn: Theory and research in practice.* Newark, DE: International Reading Association.

Clay, M. (1991). *Becoming literate: The construction of inner control.* Portsmouth, NH: Heinemann.

Cramer, R. (2000). *Creative power: The nature and nurture of children's writing.* Boston: Allyn & Bacon.

Cunningham, P. M. (2004). *Phonics they use: Words for reading and writing* (3rd ed.). Boston: Allyn & Bacon.

Fitzgerald, J., & Shanahan, T. (2000). Reading and writing relations and their development. *Educational Psychologist, 35*(1), 39–50.

Graves, D. (1983). *Writing: Teachers and children at work*. Portsmouth, NH: Heinemann.

Harste, J. C., Woodward, V. A., Burke, C. L. (1984). *Language stories and literacy lessons*. Portsmouth, NH: Heinemann.

Henderson, E. (1990). *Teaching spelling*. Boston: Houghton Mifflin.

McCarrier, A., Pinnell, G. S., & Fountas, I. C. (2000). *Interactive writing: How language and literacy come together, K–2*. Portsmouth, NH: Heinemann.

Routman, R. (2000). *Kids' poems: Teaching second graders to love writing poetry*. New York: Scholastic.

Schulze, A. C. (2006). *Helping children become readers through writing: A guide to writing workshop in kindergarten*. Newark, DE: International Reading Association.

Snow, C. E., Burns, M. S., & Griffin, P. (1998). *Preventing reading difficulties in young children*. Washington, DC: National Academy Press.

Spandel, V. (2001). *Creating writers through 6-trait writing assessment and instruction* (3rd ed.). New York: Addison-Wesley Longman.

Spandel, V. (2007). Creating young writers: Using the six traits to enrich writing process in primary classrooms (2nd ed.). Boston: Pearson.

Vygotsky, L. S. (1978). *Mind and society: The development of higher psychological processes*. Cambridge, MA: Harvard University Press.

Weaver, C. (1996). Facts on research on the teaching of phonics. In C. Weaver, L. Gillmeister-Krause, & G. Vento-Zogby (Eds.), *Creating support for effective literacy education*. Retrieved from http://www.heinemann.com/shared/onlineresources/08894/08894f2.html

Children's Literature

Aruego, J. (2002). *Weird friends: Unlikely allies in the animal kingdom*. New York: Harcourt.

Browne, A. (1998). *Voices in the park*. New York: DK Publishing.

De Paola, T. (1985). *The cloud book*. New York: Holiday House.

Lobel, A. (1970) *Frog and Toad are friends*. New York: HarperCollins.

Osborne, M. P. (1998). *Vacation under the volcano*. New York: Random House.

Potter, B. (1920). *The tale of Peter Rabbit*. New York: F. Warne.

Rylant, C. (1987). *Henry and Mudge: The first book*. New York: Simon and Schuster.

Reading and Writing Across the Curriculum

9

by Sylvia Read

Nonfiction in a Second-Grade Writing Workshop

It's writing workshop time in Mrs. Read's second-grade classroom. Jeff and Tony are huddled over a book about snakes. They stop to point at things in the illustrations and they talk animatedly. They turn the book face down on the floor, then Jeff dictates and Tony writes, "Snakes have jaws that can open real wide so they can swallow stuff that's bigger than their head." Taisia stands by the rack of nonfiction books looking for the one about butterflies that we read aloud yesterday. She finds it and carries it over to the chrysalis of a monarch butterfly that we have hanging upside down in a canning jar. She finds the picture of the chrysalis in the book and says to Jaime, who is drawing a picture of the chrysalis, "The real one is much more shiny than this picture. I think the author of this book should have done a better picture. She should have used real gold 'cause the real one has those dots that look like real gold." Jaime nods and keeps drawing. Jaime is drawing the life cycle of the butterfly by showing the different stages of the metamorphosis. So far, he's labeled them with numbers showing the order in which they happen.

————————   ————————

Reading and writing across the curriculum allows children to use the literacy skills they're developing to support the learning of objectives in science, math, and social studies. This chapter discusses why and how informational texts can be incorporated into every school day. Specifically, this chapter discusses:

- Reading informational texts
- Writing informational texts
- Reading, writing, and math
- Reading, writing, and science
- Reading, writing, and social studies

READING INFORMATIONAL TEXTS

Research tells us that in most primary-grade classrooms, students aren't exposed to much informational text (Duke, 2000; Kamberelis, 1998; Yopp & Yopp, 2000). In basal readers, the percentage of informational text varies from as low as 12% (Hoffman et al., 1994) to a high of 33.8% (Schmidt, Caul, Byers, & Buchman, 1984). Yopp and Yopp (2000) found that teachers reported that only 14% of read-alouds were informational text. In her study of both high- and low-socioeconomic status (SES) classrooms, Duke found that an average of only 3.6 minutes per day were spent with informational texts. In low-SES classrooms, the average was 1.9 minutes!

Interestingly, when given the opportunity, children gravitate toward informational texts, checking them out from their neighborhood library more often than fiction (Kamil, 1994). They can retell it (Pappas, 1991) and they can write about it (Read, 2001). Reluctant readers and writers often become engaged in reading and writing when they are given the opportunity to work with informational texts (Caswell & Duke, 1998). Struggling readers particularly benefit from a classroom library well stocked with informational texts, frequent read-alouds of informational text, and time to read informational texts independently (Dreher, 2003).

Often teachers assume that fiction is read for pleasure and informational text is read for information, which means the choice is pleasure versus information. The thought that information can be pleasurable is left out of the decision. But children find facts and information interesting and fun—in fact, their strong curiosity about the world is fed with informational text. Patricia Lauber, a well-known children's author of nonfiction, says she wants to show readers that "it is possible to read science for pleasure, that a good science book touches the mind, the heart, the imagination" (Lauber, 1992, p. 15).

When teachers *do* read aloud informational texts, the conversations that can occur are often better for fostering comprehension than the conversations that occur during fiction read-alouds (Smolkin & Donovan, 2001). Because students will be asked to read and write informational texts so often in the intermediate, middle school, and high school grades, it only makes sense to read aloud an abundance of informational books. Immersion in high-quality examples of informational texts is necessary for children to be able to write informational texts (Jenkins & Earle, 2006).

PURPOSES FOR READING ALOUD INFORMATIONAL TEXTS

Teachers need to read informational texts aloud to young children so they are exposed to a variety of text features and structures. Children also learn specialized vocabulary and new concepts, which builds their background knowledge (Yopp & Yopp, 2000). When students are asked to read informational texts independently, their comprehension is highly dependent on their level of background knowledge, which is why teachers need to make a special effort to build their knowledge base through read-alouds. When reading informational texts aloud to students, they often note discrepancies between different texts. Texts do not always present the "facts" the same way and may even contradict each other. The discussions about the contradictions help students become critical readers. Finally, informational texts can be a catalyst for literacy (Caswell & Duke, 1998), drawing in reluctant readers and writers because the content is interesting to them.

Mrs. Kendrick is reading aloud *Bats* by Gail Gibbons (2000) to her kindergarten class.

Sylvia Read

INFORMATIONAL TEXTS IN SHARED READING AND INTERACTIVE READ-ALOUDS

Shared reading is a way to read books aloud with students that allows the students to participate interactively. Rather than read aloud a book straight through, an interactive read-aloud (Smolkin & Donovan, 2001) allows for discussion to take place during the reading. If charts, big books, basal anthologies containing informational selections, or photocopies of articles are used, students can also read aloud along with the teacher.

Students will have questions, comments, and connections with other media (books, magazine, television programs) as the informational text is read. An effective teacher will use an interactive style of reading and discussion that capitalizes on students' curiosity and wonderings to make the experience of the text deeper and more complete. This is how students will be able to build their vocabulary and background knowledge, which is crucial to their comprehension of all kinds of texts.

When reading aloud informational texts, there are many opportunities to model how to learn new vocabulary words, how to summarize, how to use the features of nonfiction such as headings and bold print, how to visualize information, how to make inferences about texts, and how to "fix up" students' understanding when they don't understand a text.

For example, during an interactive read-aloud, the teacher should be modeling and scaffolding an understanding of how new vocabulary can be understood in context because texts have links between and within sentences. In the text *Quest for the Tree Kangaroo* (Montgomery, 2006), the author is describing the lush landscape of the cloud forest. She uses links within sentences. For example, "Whole bushes—rhododendrons with pink and red flowers—grow on tree branches" contains an example of a link within a sentence. The teacher can stop and explain briefly that "rhododendrons" and "bushes" are linked in this sentence and that "bushes" provides the meaning for "rhododendrons."

Teachers can also model summarizing. The following is an example of modeling summarizing using *Quest for the Tree Kangaroo*. "Everything is clothed in moss. The moss is studded with ferns. The ferns are dotted with lichens, liverworts, and fungi. Life piles on life. Whole bushes—rhododendrons with pink and red flowers—grow on tree branches. In a cloud forest, more than three hundred different species of plants might be growing on a single tree." Before summarizing, signal to the students that you are not reading anymore, but rather, you are now thinking aloud. You might put the book in your lap, or put your hand over the text. Then say something like, "Okay, I see. Trees in the cloud forest are covered with lots of different kinds of plants that grow right on top of each other. It's good to stop and make sure you understand what you've read by telling it back to yourself in your own words."

By pointing out the features of the informational text you're reading aloud, you give students a chance to see how those features can be used to understand the ideas in the text. For example, if a book has pictures with captions, you can point out which captions go with which pictures and how the captions give you information about the picture. Headings and subheadings are also useful features to point out. Once students understand that headings and subheadings tell them the main idea or topic of the text that follows, they will be more likely to read them and use them to help themselves focus on the important parts.

Creating mental imagery and using analogies are two strategies for promoting comprehension that can be modeled during an interactive read-aloud. Kate Petty's book *Pandas* shows a close-up of a newborn panda and the text says, "The babies are the size of kittens." You can help students better understand how small newborn pandas really are by saying, "Hold out your hands and cup them together. Imagine a baby panda nestled in your hands. That's how small they are when they're born. Amazing, isn't it?" Later the book says, "The young panda is fully grown toward the end of its second year. It is over 220 lb in weight and about five and a half feet tall when it stands upright." Here you can show students how tall five and a half feet is by telling them how tall you are and making the analogy or by showing them on a wall chart that you use for measuring the students' height.

Inferring or inferencing can be modeled when the text and what you already know can be put together into a hypothesis. In Gail Gibbons's (1984) book *Fire! Fire!* the text says, "A man is trapped. A ladder tower is swung into action. The man is rescued quickly." The illustration shows a six-story apartment building. You might say, "I think that if the building is too tall, the ladder might not reach the person who is trapped. That must be when they use those trampoline things. Let's see if the text tells us." In this case, the text doesn't tell what happens with taller buildings, but the hypothesis can be pursued by finding and reading other resources that might answer the question.

Teachers also need to model using fix-up strategies when comprehension breaks down. For example, sometimes when you're reading aloud, you may make a mistake. It's good to acknowledge that mistake aloud and explain how you're going to go back and reread so that you can be sure the text makes sense. Also, when you've read aloud a fairly complex passage, stop and think aloud about your comprehension process. "Did I understand that right? Let's see. . . ."

All these comprehension strategies should be modeled, though not in every read-aloud. Eventually, your students will interrupt the reading to make similar sorts of comments. Your job then is to validate their use of the strategies and praise them for their efforts to make sense of what is being read. You also want to ask them to reflect on their comprehension in a similar fashion during guided reading sessions and independent or partner reading. You need to be sure to expose your students to a variety of types of informational texts as well.

Because there are different kinds of informational texts, it is important to read aloud from a variety of them so that you can demonstrate the different features they have and the different ways they can be read. Short magazine articles can be read in their entirety. Books with indexes and tables of contents can be read selectively, depending on the kind of information you're looking for, or they can be read cover-to-cover if you're hoping to get some background knowledge on a subject you don't know much about. Encyclopedic kinds of books especially lend themselves to selective reading. Question-and-answer books such as *Do Stars Have Points? Questions and Answers About Stars and Planets* (Berger & Berger, 1998) can be read selectively also. Informational alphabet books such as *Amazon Alphabet* (Jordan & Jordan, 1996) lend themselves to cover-to-cover reading because it can be great fun to predict what the featured subject of each letter will be. Later alphabet books can be used selectively to go back and reread the parts the class is most interested in hearing again.

Reading aloud across the curriculum allows students to make connections between pictures in books and learning in content areas such as math, science, and social studies (Laminack & Wadsworth, 2006). Choose books that allow you to teach content-area vocabulary and concepts, and in discussions with students, help them use the language in the book as they explore its ideas as well as their own connections and insights. Students should also be encouraged to express their confusion about a book's language or concepts as well as their desire to learn more about a topic or idea.

Different books also use different expository text structures. As you read aloud, you can point out the places where the books use these text structures to achieve their purposes.

Expository Text Structures

Description: Authors provide lists and examples to describe the characteristics, features, or traits of a person, place, or thing. Metaphor and simile are also used to describe. Seymour Simon, in *Whales* (1989), compares the length of a humpback whale with the length of a large bus.

Sequence: Authors write about certain kinds of phenomena sequentially when it is important to show the order in which something happens. For example, history is often written in chronological order. Life cycles of animals and plants need to be written about sequentially. *Desert Giant: The World of the Saguaro Cactus* by Bash (1989) uses sequence to describe the life cycle of the saguaro cactus.

Compare and Contrast: Authors use comparison and contrast when they want to describe the similarities and differences among people, places, or things. Sometimes visuals are used to illustrate the comparison and contrast. In her book *Frogs,* Gail Gibbons (1993) compares frogs and toads using diagrams.

Cause and Effect and Problem and Solution: Authors often use these structures together. *A River Ran Wild*, by Lynne Cherry (1992), describes in detail the causes of pollution and its effect on the river. She also describes the pollution as a problem and how the river was cleaned up as the solution.

Combination of Structures: Most texts do not use just one text structure. For example, a book describing the life cycle of a butterfly will use both sequence and description. Another common combination is description and compare and contrast. *Christmas in the Big House, Christmas in the Quarters* (McKissack & McKissack, 1994) uses both sequence and compare and contrast as it shows the ways that Christmas is celebrated by the White people in the plantation house and how it is celebrated by the slaves who worked the plantation.

Mixed genre: Some authors combine a fictional narrative with information. Children enjoy the *Magic School Bus* books by Joanna Cole and the *Magic Tree House* books by Mary Pope Obsorne, which combine a fantasy story structure with fact. Historical fiction uses historical facts to support a fictional narrative. Biography employs a narrative structure to tell the story of someone's life.

Nonlinear Structures: Books published by Dorling Kindersley often have a nonlinear structure. There are short paragraphs, extended pieces of text, pictures with captions, timelines, and diagrams combined on a page. The text can be read in any order and seems to invite the reader to skip around in an almost hypertextual sort of way. When children read this sort of text, they often concentrate on the pictures and sample the text itself in a highly selective way.

INFORMATIONAL TEXTS IN GUIDED READING

Because basal readers sometimes have little informational text (Hoffman et al., 1994), it is especially important to find and use informational texts during guided reading lessons. If your school has a guided reading book room, actively seek to have an equal number of nonfiction and fiction titles. If you collect multiple copies of books for your own instructional use, be sure to include informational texts. If your budget is limited and the basal is all you have, use magazine articles from magazines such as *Ranger Rick*. Figure 9.1 lists magazines that include informational articles written for children.

When students read informational texts in guided reading lessons, it can be helpful to use the features of nonfiction to guide the lesson. For example, to introduce the book, begin with a picture walk of the book (Duke & Bennett-Armistead, 2003), but also notice and read aloud any headings. Look at the table of contents to anticipate what the children will be reading about in the book. As a follow-up to their reading of the text, ask them to respond to the reading by using the index to find their favorite part of the book. The next day, you can revisit the book and concentrate on

In a guided reading leveled library, there should be a wide selection of books, including sets of informational texts.

Sylvia Read

Figure 9.1   Informational Magazines for Children

Click, ASK (Arts and Sciences for Kids), and *Appleseeds*, http://www.cobblestonepub.com
Kids Discover, http://www.kidsdiscover.com
National Geographic Kids, http://www.nationalgeographic.com/ngkids/
Ranger Rick, http://www.nwf.org/kidspubs/rangerrick/
Sports Illustrated for Kids, http://www.sikids.com
Time for Kids, http://www.timeforkids.com/TFK/class/index.html
Weekly Reader, http://www.weeklyreader.com
Zootles and Zoobooks, http://www.zoobooks.com

one section of the book. Talk together to determine which ideas were most important and use those ideas to form a verbal summary.

INFORMATIONAL TEXTS IN INDEPENDENT READING

Informational books need to have a prominent place in a classroom library, with an equal number of informational books as fiction. Have your students organize the books into categories that interest them. The books can then be stored in baskets with labels that the students make. This increases their ownership of the classroom library and facilitates their search for books so that they don't spend time wandering. Reorganizing the books every year gives each new group of students their own sense of ownership and also allows you to repair or replace well-used books.

Children should be encouraged to read independently in a wide variety of genres. You can model this for them by what you read aloud. This also gets and keeps them interested in informational texts because children gravitate toward those books the teacher has read aloud (Robinson, Larsen, Haupt, & Mohlman, 1997). Their literary diets can also be tracked by having them record the genre on a simple reading log. They can either color-code the book by coloring a square on the reading log or they can write *I, F, C,* or *P* for *information, fiction, combination,* or *poetry*.

Jared chose to read nonfiction for independent reading.

Sylvia Read

WRITING INFORMATIONAL TEXTS

In writing workshop, teachers encourage young children to write about what they know, which often turns out to be personal narratives about the children's lives. Personal narrative is a form of informational writing, but it is only a small fraction of the informational writing realm. Daniels (1990) states that

> the writing curriculum experienced by many American students as they go up through the grades is essentially: story, story, story, story, story, story, story, story, story, story, story, term paper. . . . A predictable outcome of this unbalanced curriculum is that today's students write much better stories than they write reports, arguments, or essays. (p. 107)

In the primary grades, teachers can balance story writing with opportunities for young children to explore informational writing. Keep in mind that most young children are not ready to learn the technical aspects of report writing like paragraphs or bibliographies, but they are full of curiosity about real things and they're definitely ready to explore them through reading, talking, writing, and drawing.

Sometimes it is the reluctant writers in the classroom who are especially drawn to informational writing. Both boys and girls find informational writing stimulating and a way to express themselves that doesn't involve writing a personal narrative. Some children are uncomfortable with writing personal narratives for various reasons and when encouraged to write informational texts, they enjoy immersing themselves in the particulars of a topic that fascinates them personally, but doesn't expose them emotionally.

For some students, exposure to informational texts and encouragement to write them just isn't enough. Perhaps stories and personal narratives have been such a huge part of their reading diet that they don't feel comfortable venturing into the writing of informational texts. However, with explicit instruction, students are not only able to write informational texts, but those texts are of higher quality than when students are only shown models of informational texts (Jenkins & Earle, 2006).

Before having young children write informational texts independently, it is important to model informational writing and explicitly teach how to write informational texts through various whole-class experiences.

WHOLE-CLASS INFORMATIONAL WRITING

You can begin a whole-class experience of writing informational text simply by choosing a topic that makes sense for your students in terms of what you're currently studying. For example, if you are studying insect life cycles, then you would model information writing with the whole class through interactive writing, language-experience approach, or shared writing. You would be modeling a basic report—a traditional kind of informational writing. The following is a process that could be used to teach students to write what they've learned from a text using their own words:

- After reading a book (or part of a book) aloud to the class, deliberately close the book and set it aside (do this in an obvious way and explain why you're doing it).
- Model writing what you learned or what was important about what you just read. For shared writing, students can also tell what they learned.
- Think aloud as you write.

🔖 Make mistakes. Draw a line through words you want to change or delete and insert revisions using a caret (^).

🔖 Add new information using a caret.

🔖 Change the order of the information using a numbering system. Circle sections of text and number them according to the order that makes the most sense.

🔖 Throughout this process, let the students tell you things to write that they learned or thought were important. This process can take several days. When you're done, you have a text that can be:

> Read as a chart
>
> Typed and copied for all the children to have as reading material
>
> Typed so that each child's contribution is on a separate page that they can illustrate, thus producing a class book
>
> Displayed on a bulletin board in the classroom or hallway

Once you've modeled this a few times (especially at the beginning of any new unit of study), the children may be ready to begin writing information individually or in pairs.

An example of this process occurred when I taught in a multiage class of 6- and 7-year-olds. We studied insects with a special focus on the praying mantises that lived in our school's native garden by observing the praying mantises closely and reading a high-quality informational book about praying mantises called *Backyard Hunter* (Lavies, 1990). I read the book aloud slowly over about a week's time. Each day we put aside the book and the children told me what was important about what we'd read that day. I wrote it down in note format, sometimes using complete sentences and sometimes not. Each day, we reviewed our notes from the day before. The day after we finished the book, we reread all of our notes. Then I turned to a fresh piece of chart paper and, through language-experience approach, each child dictated to me while the rest of the class listened (see Figure 9.2). They listened attentively so that the next sentence made sense and was connected to the previous sentence. Students raised their hands when they were ready to contribute a sentence. The children's names are written next to their contributions in the tradition of language-experience approach.

EXTENDING INFORMATIONAL WRITING TO INDEPENDENT AND SMALL-GROUP WORK

To provide children with a chance to write individually or in pairs about an information topic, it helps to choose a broad topic such as weather, animals, rocks, insects, or ocean life. Any topic in your state's core curriculum can be used as a topic. Based on the resources you have available, you can determine some subtopics for children to choose from when they write alone or with a partner. For example, if the broad topic is weather, then students could choose to write about snow, rain, clouds, seasons, tornadoes, hurricanes, floods, and so on. When you are not concerned about connecting to your state's core curriculum, you can have children choose any topic for which you have resources. For example, you might have two children who want to study knights, two children who want to study cheetahs, and so on.

When you have students work in pairs, you can choose partners or let the children choose a topic and then pair up the students based on their chosen topic.

Figure 9.2   Language-Experience Approach Text

All About Praying Mantises
Written by Mrs.Read's Class

Praying mantises look like they are praying. (Montana)

But they aren't really saying their prayers. (Isaac)

They are just waiting to catch some bugs for food. (C. C.)

They stay up all the time and never rest. (Jordan)

Praying mantises don't drink nectar like bees. (Lauren)

They eat other insects and sometimes other praying mantises. (Mrs. Read)

Praying mantises snatch their food faster than you can see. (Colin)

They don't eat big grasshoppers when they are little. (Courtney)

They don't hunt their food. They wait for it. (Brooke)

Praying mantises are good climbers. (Laura)

They crawl in your house. (Christina)

They go on top of your roof. (Celestia)

Kyle's page from our class book about praying mantises.

When the mothers make their egg case, the fathers spread their wings and the mother makes a signal back to him. (Kyle)

19

Figure 9.2 Continued

Praying mantises have an exoskeleton on the outside instead of inside like us. (Eryn)

They shed their skin as soon as they come out of the egg case. (Jessica)

They shed every bit of their exoskeleton. (Michael)

When they come out of the egg case, they have a little string, kind of like a thread, attached to them. (Lorna)

When they come out of their egg case, they are orange. (C. C.)

They have to wait for their exoskeleton to harden. (Taylor)

When the mothers make their egg case, the fathers spread their wings and the mother makes a signal back to him. (Kyle)

The girls are bigger than the boys. (Ashlyn)

They bite hard. (Jimmy)

They bite until you bleed. (Edward)

There are some kinds of praying mantises that are white. (Jonathon)

Some praying mantises are black. (Landon)

Some praying mantises are pink. (Brendan)

They have good camouflage. (Jason)

When you decide how to pair up students, keep in mind the social dynamics of your class and the academic strengths and weaknesses of your students. The advantage of pairing them yourself is that you can put good readers with less able readers or enthusiastic writers with reluctant writers. You can also make sure that a socially problematic child isn't left out. Once you pair them up, let them choose their subtopic so that it's a decision the partners make together. If you want to increase the students' ownership of the topics, then you should have them choose a topic and then pair them up.

The first day of research can be done without reading anything. The children can begin by writing what they already know about their topic. Meanwhile, you can gather library books and other materials (web pages, magazines, guest speakers, videos, etc.) that the children will need for their research. These materials, along with a folder for their writing, can be placed in hanging files, or boxes, so that the children can easily find their materials and have easy access to them. With young children, it is helpful to scaffold the research process by preselecting books, magazines, and so forth that are written at a useful readability level.

When children start using their resource materials, give them time to read and look at pictures without any pressure to write or draw anything. The goal is for them to internalize the information, become experts, and make the learning their own. Even the youngest students can glean information from pictures and draw or write about what they see.

When they begin to read their resource materials, volunteers or older students can spend time with younger students to read and reflect on source materials. You can also pair students so that strong readers are with beginning readers. If you have only a couple of students who need help reading their resources, circulate among them reading aloud a paragraph or two and leaving them to write down what they thought was important.

PEARSON myeducationlab

Emergent Literacy

Go to MyEducationLab, "Emergent Literacy," and read the article "Projects That Power Young Minds."

After reading this article, you should be able to explain how projects based on children's interests and initiative support active learning, cognitive development, and academic skills.

Figure 9.3 I-Chart on Dinosaurs

Dinosaurs	When did dinosaurs live?	Why did the dinosaurs die?	What did dinosaurs eat?	Where did dinosaurs live?	Some cool dinosaurs we like.
What we know					
The World of Dinosaurs by Melvin Berger					
My Visit to the Dinosaurs by Aliki					
The Magic School Bus in the Time of Dinosaurs by Joanna Cole					
Video on dinosaurs					

Some teachers find it useful to help students organize their writing by giving them notecards or pieces of paper that have been folded into fourths. On each card or section, the students can write one sentence. Later, these can be organized before the sentences are keyboarded or rewritten in a book or report format. Often when students use a web to brainstorm, their writing is more organized, but not all students can predict what they will find interesting or want to write about. Students could also write their ideas on sticky notes which can then be rearranged over and over again until the order is logical and pleasing to the writer. A research-proven effective organizational structure for report writing is the inquiry chart or I-chart (Viscovich, 2002). Figure 9.3 provides an example of an I-chart that students could use to organize their research on dinosaurs.

Teachers often publish students' informational texts by keyboarding it for them (correcting spelling, punctuation, and other errors of convention) and binding it as a book that they can illustrate. It's also possible to integrate art by having them produce a watercolor painting, clay figure, or other art form to go with their information.

Informational Text Written by First Graders

Figure 9.4 shows an example of informational writing done by a pair of children, both first graders. One was a proficient reader and one was reading below grade level. Over the course of 2 weeks, Isaac read several books aloud to Landon and they looked at pictures as they talked, drew, and wrote. Talking and drawing were immensely important parts of the writing process for both of them; they tended to talk and draw first and then write, with the drawings serving as the anchor for the writing. They each drew and wrote their own part and made no attempt to put the parts together in any

Figure 9.4 Page from Isaac and Landon's Published Book on Knights

Knights

by Isaac and Landon

Swords were used very often when a knight was knocked off his horse.

These are the helmets that the knights have. The helmets are made out of metal.

These are the weapons that the knights sometimes use.

Knights from stories fight dragons. . . . Well, sometimes. And save princesses.

Knights fight a lot. Sometimes on horseback and sometimes on the ground.

Knights save people from dragons in stories. In Saint George, George kills a dragon. Sir Lancelot fought good. King Arthur pulled the sword from the stone.

Charge! Many knights did tournaments. They use blunt weapons. It is a fake battle. They have feast after that. Excalibur can break rocks. Excalibur is the best sword. Excalibur can break any sword. King Arthur pulled Excalibur from the stone.

These are weapons that the knights use. But the knights still have the weapons.

These knights are fighting with each other.

One dragon is on the ground.

The kids practice being knights.

Dragons in stories have fire to kill knights.

The knights have pretend war. They sit on horses and fight each other with lances.

Knights steal money from dragons. They give it to the poor.

One guy tied up another guy but the guys' swords fell into the ground.

People tell kids dragons and knights stories. They are tales.

These are weapons that the knights use. But the knights still have the weapons. And the shield.

These knights are fighting with each other.

way. The teacher put together their separate pages of writing into a published book and they each got their own copy to illustrate and keep. Each line break indicates a page break in their published book.

INTEGRATING INFORMATIONAL WRITING INTO THE WRITING WORKSHOP

Informational writing can occur throughout the school day in math, science, and social studies. Children can choose to write informational texts during writing work-shop and information writing should always be mentioned as one of the choices during a topic brainstorming lesson. For example, you might say, "Hmm. . . . I could write about my dog and then I could write about dogs . . . or I'm really interested in knights. I have knight Legos and I like to read books about knights, so maybe I could write about that." You can also make the informational report the genre focus for a few weeks and require all students to write a brief informational report. A writing workshop unit focusing on informational report writing would form the basis for a variety of mini-lessons such as these:

- Teach the idea of informational writing as a way to teach others *what you know* and what you've learned. Some kids get stuck on the idea that they should write only the new information they've learned.
- Web as a way to brainstorm and organize information. Begin by putting a topic of interest in the center, then think aloud as you add related topics and subtopics to the web.
- Use I-charts as a way to organize information.
- Read a short passage, close the book, write what you understand, and then compare. This helps students see when they have copied word-for-word from a book. This usually happens when students haven't understood what they've read but sense that the information they've copied is important.
- Express voice issues: Does it sound like me? Does it sound like the book? Have I accidentally copied?
- Discuss features of informational texts such as pronunciation keys, captions, headings, and labels and ways to incorporate them into student writing.
- Explain how to look for books on your topic in the library, in an encyclopedia, or on the web. The younger the students you work with, the more you need to scaffold this.
- Model and explicitly teach genres of information writing such as the ABC book, informational poster, question-and-answer book, informational poetry, biography, book review, movie review, video game review, how-to texts, and so on.

When students choose to write information, I like to reinforce their decision by selecting them to share their writing, by encouraging them to publish it, and by publicly praising them for choosing to try a new kind of writing. But some students will not choose to do informational writing even though their classmates have done so and been praised for it. Thus, you must teach reluctant students how to write informational texts and require them to write them. This could be as simple as having them write about a food item. Pam Richardson's first graders participated in a shared writing that focused on pickles (Duke & Bennett-Armistead, 2003). Then each child received a card with the name of a food product on it. By not offering the students a choice of topics, the teacher is showing them that they can write about anything if they do a little research, which she shows them how to do by using the Internet, books in the classroom, discussions with their classmates, and interviews with relatives. One child wrote: "Cheese is a kind of food. It comes from a cheese factory. Cheese comes from milk. Cheese can be different shapes. Some people like to eat it" (Duke & Bennett-Armistead, 2003, p. 137).

One of the most useful sets of mini-lessons I have taught is on the conventions of informational texts. I got the idea from *Strategies That Work* by Harvey and Goudvis (2000). We began with three sheets of $8\frac{1}{2} \times 11$-inch white copy paper folded in half and stapled with a blue copy paper cover. We wrote "Nonfiction Conventions" on the cover and then we began the process of reading lots of informational books and noticing and discussing their special features. For example, we noticed right away that many informational books have a table of contents, so we began ours on the front inside cover of our book. We went on to create examples of headings, subheadings, illustrations with labels, captions for pictures, comparisons such as the Statue of Liberty next to the Great Pyramid at Giza, pronouncing clues, bold words, glossary, index, and finally, a blurb on the back cover of the book (see Figure 9.5). For nearly every feature we noticed in the books we read, we created an example of that feature in our booklets. Every child made one and I made one right along with them. Through this activity they became very conscious of these features in the books they read and also began to put them in their informational writing. One child wrote for her blurb on the back of her nonfiction conventions booklet: "This book is about different nonfiction conventions. If you know about nonfiction conventions, you can write your very own nonfiction book. You could learn a lot."

Students Choose to Write Informational Texts in Writing Workshop

The following examples were written by second graders during writing workshop. They chose to write an informational text and they chose their topic. Both of these students read multiple sources to gather information. Jaren's reading ability was below grade level, whereas Braden's was above grade level. See Figures 9.6, 9.7, and 9.8 for more examples of informational text written by young children.

"Out in Space" by Jaren

When you're in space there is no gravity, but did you know the hottest planet is Mercury?

And the coldest planet is Pluto and Pluto is the farthest planet from the Sun.

The Sun is 27,000,000 degrees F. The crust of the Sun is ten million degrees F.

That's it for today.

"What Is a Mammal?" by Braden

A mammal does not lay eggs, except the monotremes, which are platypuses, and echidnas. A mammal gives birth to its baby like we do. It gives birth to live babies.

The world's smallest mammal discovered is a bat. The bat's name is the bumblebee bat. It is the size of a jelly bean and weighs as much as a penny. Can you believe that? It must have a really small wing span.

Figure 9.5 Jade enjoyed the process of learning about nonfiction conventions.

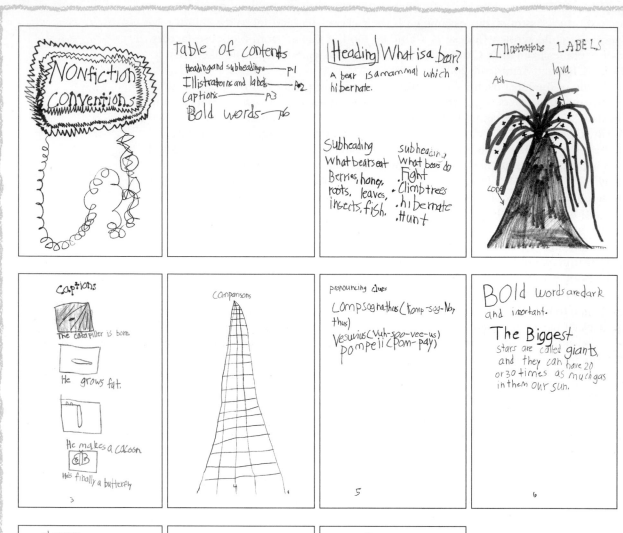

Nonfiction Conventions

Table of contents
Heading and subheadings——— p.1
Illustrations and labels——— p.2
Captions——— p.3
Bold words—— p.6

Heading What is a bear?
A bear is a mammal which hibernate.

Subheading
What bears eat
Berries, honey,
roots, leaves,
insects, fish.

subheading
What bears do
.Fight
.Climb trees
.hibernate
.Hunt

Illustrations LABELS
Ash   lava

core

Captions
The caterpillar is born.

He grows fat.

He makes a cocoon

He's finally a butterfly

3

Comparisons

4

pronouncing clues
Compsognathus (Komp-sog-Na-thus)
Vesuvius (Vuh-soo-vee-us)
Pompeii (Pom-pay)

5

BOld words are dark and important.

The Biggest
stars are called giants, and they can have 20 or 30 times as much gas in them our sun.

6

glossary
Axis The imaginary line through the center of a star, planet, or moon, around which it spins.
Core The center of a planet or star.

12

Index

Blurb
This book is about different nonfiction conventions. If you know about nonfiction conventions, you can write youre very own nonfiction book. You could learn a lot.

A volcano is so hot that it could melt a car. Hot lava can be 2100°F. The lava can flow at 6 miles per our. There are two kinds of lava pahoehoe and aa. Pahoehoe is smooth, aa is rough and Jaged

Figure 9.6   Paisley wrote about volcanoes during writing workshop.

The second smallest mammal is a pygmy shrew. I am not sure how much a pygmy shrew weighs.

The biggest mammal weighs about three hundred thousand (300,000) pounds. That means that you would have to get 27 elephants and put them on a scale. Then you will have the weight of one big blue whale. Blue whales are amazing. They're like all mammals except they don't have hair. Most mammals grow hair, but the blue whale does not. Lots of animals and mammals have hair that live in the sea.

Why are insects not mammals? Insects are not mammals because all insects lay eggs, are not homothermic, which means warm-blooded, and all insects have six legs. So there is a big difference between mammals and insects.

Mammals also have endoskeletons (end-oe-skel-uh-tuns) and insects have exoskeletons. Endoskeleton means that they have meat around their bones. And exoskeleton means the opposite—the bones are around the meat.

Is a dolphin a fish? No, a dolphin is a sea mammal. It kind of looks like a fish, but it is not because it doesn't have gills and all fish have gills. The dolphins have lungs instead of gills.

Figure 9.7 Daniel wrote about the life cycle of a snail during writing workshop.

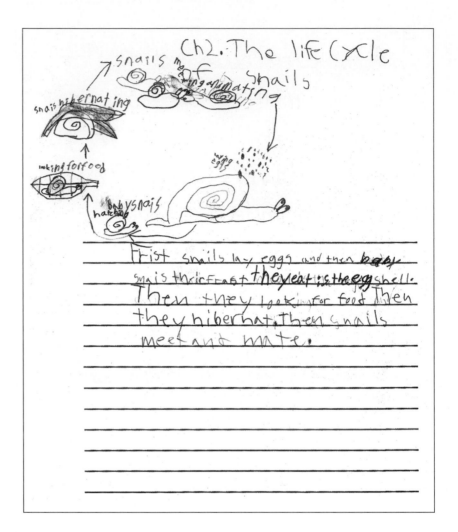

 ## READING, WRITING, AND MATH

Math is a form of communication that conveys what we are thinking about mathematical ideas. We want students to be able to actively construct their understanding of mathematics, connect new ideas to familiar ones, and develop new understandings about the interconnections among ideas. Even though we are teaching more than the abstractions of pure math in school, the curriculum often emphasizes the abstract more than the practical. When students compute problems with only numbers and mathematical symbols, they are working with only a small portion of mathematics. We need to provide them with personally meaningful contexts for using mathematical ideas and procedures. Further, they need to communicate their thinking either through talking, writing, and/or drawing. Writing, in conjunction with talking and drawing, is a powerful way to lead kids to a deeper understanding of the concepts.

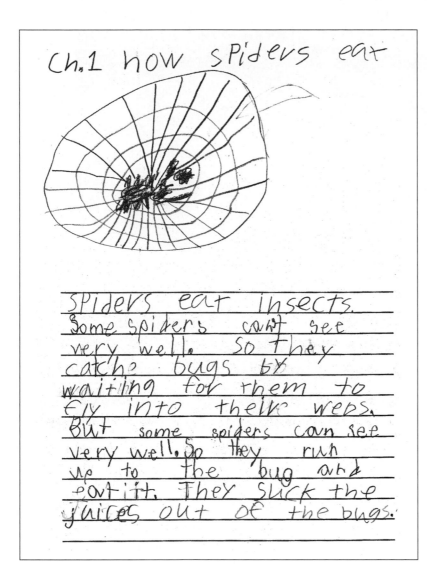

Figure 9.8 Jonathan wrote the first chapter of his book about spiders during writing workshop.

Metacognition, or thinking about our thinking, is also important for a deeper understanding of math. Writing is a way for your students to find out what they are thinking about math as a subject, about concepts they're learning, and about how they gather, organize, and clarify their thoughts. Writing is a way for the teacher to both develop and assess students' mathematical understanding. Before asking students to write for assessment purposes, though, it is important to have them write about math for a variety of other reasons.

WRITING STORY PROBLEMS

Students can write their own story problems. Not only does writing story problems make math relevant to children's lives, research has shown that it is more effective than simply solving story problems (Armbruster, McCarthy, & Cummins, 2005). For example, when exploring two- and three-digit addition, students can write story problems such

Alex chose to write informational texts during writing workshop.

Sylvia Read

as, "If I have 33 rocks in my rock collection and my best friend has 18 rocks in her collection, how many do we have together?"

Students can also be given an equation such as $11 + 15 = 26$ and asked to write a story problem to go with the equation, which is an effective way to assess students' understanding of basic operations (O'Connell, 2000). Students can then share their story problems and the rest of the class can indicate whether the story matches the equation through a whole-class response of thumbs up/thumbs down (see Figure 9.9).

FOR ENGLISH LANGUAGE LEARNERS

Content-Area Teaching

When teaching content-area objectives, English language learners benefit from the use of

- Modeling and demonstrations
- Hands-on manipulatives
- Commercial and teacher-made illustrations or photos
- Timelines, graphs, maps
- Simulations
- Vocabulary previews
- Word banks or word walls
- Connecting of concepts to students' background knowledge
- Links to previous lessons
- Regular checks for students' understanding

WRITING AS AN EXTENSION OF MATH-RELATED CHILDREN'S LITERATURE

Informational picture books can be used to introduce, support, or extend the mathematical thinking that the students are developing. For example, *The Doorbell Rang* by Pat Hutchins (1986) is a natural way to introduce division; children divide up a plate of cookies in smaller and smaller portions as more and more people ring the bell and come into the kitchen. For excellent ideas on incorporating literature into math lessons, see *Math and Literature, Grades K–3* by Burns (1992).

Figure 9.9   Fermi Questions

> Another kind of story problem that students can explore are *Fermi questions*, named for Enrico Fermi, who liked to pose impossible mathematical questions and come up with approximate, but reasonable, answers. After students have played around with ways to answer the question, they can write their answers and explain how they arrived at them. Teachers need to encourage students to come up with reasonable answers, because Fermi questions don't have set answers. Here are some examples of Fermi questions:
>
> - How many jelly beans could you hold in both your hands cupped together?
> - How many jelly beans would it take to fill a gallon milk jug?
> - How many steps will it take to walk across the classroom?
> - How many students could fit into this classroom if we took out all of the furniture?
> - How many meals will you eat in a year? (Hyde & Bizar, 1989)
>
> For more on Fermi questions, see http://www.vendian.org/envelope/dir0/fermi_questions.html.

Jon Scieszka's *Math Curses* covers a wide range of mathematical problems, but the focus is on seeing math in everyday events and using them as a basis for problem solving. Writing in response to *Math Curse*, first and second graders wrote story problems like those they encounter in real life.

> *This morning I got dressed in 5 minutes. It took me 10 minutes to eat breakfast. How many minutes did it take me to eat breakfast and get dressed?*

> *My sister is going to get a puppy and say it is 2 feet long and it grows 4 more feet. And in each foot is 12 inches. Then how many inches will he be?*

> *I am going to the dentist in 2 weeks. My cousins are coming in 5 weeks. How many days until I see my cousins?*

Figure 9.10 lists books and websites with more book lists that address mathematical concepts. Writing in response to these resources can extend the students' understanding of math concepts.

SCAFFOLDING MATH WRITING USING SENTENCE FRAMES

To support students' thinking as they venture into writing about math, sentence frames are useful. For example, during an introduction to division, you can read and discuss Pat Hutchins's (1986) *The Doorbell Rang*. To present the solution to the problem presented in the story, provide these sentence frames: "They each get _____ cookies. I figured it out by _____." The students copy the sentence frame or write their own sentence to explain their answer and, more important, how they arrived at their answer. Drawing a picture or a diagram is a great strategy that students can use before they write and include with their written explanation.

Sentence frames give many students a starting place for their writing, but it is open-ended enough to allow them to express their ideas their own way. Some children don't need the frame and need not be required to use it; however, they must

Figure 9.10 Children's Literature and Math Books and Websites

Books

Concepts	Titles	Authors
Counting, size, comparison, and ratio	*Counting on Frank* *If You Hopped Like a Frog* *Mouse Count* *Anno's Counting Book* *Ten Black Dots*	Rod Clement David M. Schwartz Ellen Stoll Walsh Mitsumasa Anno Donald Crews
Measurement	*Measuring Penny* *How Big Is a Foot?* *Twelve Snails to One Lizard: A Tale of Mischief and Measurement* *Inch by Inch* *How Tall, How Short, How Far Away?*	Loreen Leedy Rolf Myller Susan Hightower Leo Lionni David Adler
Money	*Alexander, Who Used to Be Rich Last Sunday* "Smart" from *Where the Sidewalk Ends* *A Chair for My Mother*	Judith Viorst Shel Silverstein Vera B. Williams
Counting, patterns	*I Can Count the Petals of a Flower* *One Monkey Too Many*	John and Stacey Wahl Jackie French Koller
Shapes, geometry, spatial sense	*Grandfather Tang's Story* *Architecture Shapes* *Reflections*	Ann Tompert Michael J. Crosbie Ann Jonas
Number sense	*How Much Is a Million?*	David M. Schwartz
Estimation	*Moira's Birthday*	Robert Munsch
Problem solving	*A Million Fish . . . More or Less*	Patricia McKissack
Addition and subtraction	*Annie's One to Ten* *12 Ways to Get to 11* *Rooster's Off to See the World* *Splash*	Annie Owen Eve Merriam Eric Carle Ann Jonas
Multiplication and division	*Two of Everything* *The Doorbell Rang* *A Remainder of One*	Lily Toy Hong Pat Hutchins Elinor J. Pinczes
Place value	*Number Art: Thirteen 123s From Around the World*	Leonard Everett Fisher

Websites with lists of math-related children's literature

http://www.enc.org/focus/lit/resources_v4n5/math_books/

http://www.terc.edu/investigations/resources/html/MathChildLit.html

http://illuminations.nctm.org/lessonplans/prek-2/literature-p2/

http://www2.tltc.ttu.edu/cooper/Activities/math/Children's_Literature/default.htm

http://math.youngzones.org/literature.html

http://fcit.usf.edu/math/resource/bib.html

http://www.geocities.com/Heartland/Estates/4967/math.html

explain their thinking as fully as they can. Just as in writing workshop, the teacher needs to circulate among students and hold brief conferences. Many children need to discuss their thinking aloud before they can write it down, and asking questions and reflecting their answers back to them draws out their thinking. The drawing also serves as a way to clarify student thinking and provides an anchor for their writing. They need not do a literal, representational drawing (because that can be distracting and time-consuming), but should be encouraged to use circles, squares, *X*s, or other simple symbols to represent the objects in the problem. Coloring is also unnecessary, unless the colors represent data (O'Connell, 2000).

WRITING SURVEY QUESTIONS

The students in Angie Putz's first-grade class wanted the cooks to make some other kind of soup besides tomato, so they decided to survey the students in their elementary school (Lehrer, Giles, & Schauble, 2002). Their survey question was, "What's your favorite soup?" This kind of data collection helps students realize that math doesn't always involve doing a mathematical calculation or solving a story problem.

When preparing students to do a survey, you can model the process of thinking through wording a question so that a limited number of answers are possible. When I taught second grade, I showed my student how the answers to their survey question would turn out if they asked an open-ended question, such as what is your favorite movie? Then I showed them how I could narrow the range of possible answers by either writing a question that could be answered only with a yes or a no, writing a question and providing a multiple-choice array of answers, or using a Likert-type scale of 1 through 5 or 1 through 10. Using my question, I collected my data from the student, then showed them how to take that raw data in the form of tally marks or whatever they chose to indicate answers and create a bar graph. I modeled how to create the scale, label the categories, and write a title for the graph. When I was done, I asked them lots of questions about the graph—questions that involved an overall interpretation of the graph as well as questions that focused on specific categories.

The next day they began the process of writing their questions, gathering the data from their classmates (and another class), and recording it. It's a bit chaotic to have them all asking and answering each other's survey questions simultaneously, but it's also interesting to see how they manage the problem of knowing who they have asked and who they haven't asked. They're so engaged in what they're doing that they behave very well. Sometimes I provide a class list for them so they can keep track of who they had surveyed; other times I don't because the problem-solving opportunity is so real that I don't want to jump in with my own solution.

The next day, after we reviewed the parts of a graph, I modeled how to create a bar graph. Then they took their data and created a bar graph to represent the information they had collected. I modeled and explained how to write questions based on my graph. Finally, they wrote questions about their graph for the other students to

PEARSON
myeducationlab

Content Area Reading

Go to MyEducationLab, "Content Area Reading," and watch the video *Food Survey Lesson*.
After watching the video, you should be able to:

- Describe two types of graphs that students can construct to represent data.
- Describe ways a teacher can assist students in analyzing graphs.
- Describe elements of an effective closure to a lesson.

answer. The graphs and their questions were displayed throughout the room; they then read and recorded their answers to their classmates' questions. The thinking and writing that went into this weeklong activity was invaluable.

Other forms of representing and visualizing data are frequency tables, pie charts, and line graphs, which, depending on the type of data collected, students can be taught to create and interpret (Lehrer et al., 2002). Students can also be asked to write summary statements that require them to analyze and interpret the data they gathered. If the class gathers data over a period of time, such as daily temperatures, then a line graph can be created and students can write questions or summary statements about the line graph.

The cognitive work involved in moving from experiencing data collection to interpreting data demands that students learn to see attributes of objects, events, or experiences as measurable. "A pumpkin is not just 'big,' but has width, height, and weight" (Lehrer et al., 2002, p. 26). As students' vocabularies and abilities to express ideas mathematically develop, we see the power of reading and writing across the curriculum.

Assessing Students' Understanding of Math Concepts

Writing can be used to assess students' understanding of math concepts. For example, students can be presented with a set of doubles addition facts paired with their multiplication counterpart. For example, $6 + 6$ is paired with 6×2. They then answer the question, "How are adding and multiplying alike?" Students write things such as,

> *Well, if I ask you what $6 + 6$ is then it has to be 12. So . . . it's 2 groups of six so it's $2 \times 6 = 12$.*

> *If you count 5 twice you are multiplying and you do not know it. You are working on 2×5 and $5 + 5$.*

> *Well, I know that all you have to do is add that number 2 times and you did multiplication like $5 + 5 = 10$. So that is just like doing $2 \times 5 = 10$.*

When I taught second grade, I introduced division for about a week near the end of the year. After a week in which we read *The Doorbell Rang* and played the game Dividing Cookies (Burns, 2002), I asked my students to respond to the question "What is division?" This helped me assess their understanding of division as a math concept. Here are two answers:

> *What is division? Division is dividing something equally. Division can be fractions too. It's how many times one number goes into another number. $8 \div 4 = 2$. When you divide you practically regroup. Regrouping is if you have a group of 4 and you break it into 2 groups. Division is also like splitting a pizza. If there are 4 people in your family and the pizza has 8 pieces you would first take 4 out of 8 so there are 4 left. So everybody would get 1 piece and there would be 4 more left and everybody would get one more piece. So everyone would get 2 pieces.*

> *What is division? O.K. It was after supper and my big sister was there. It was time for our 6:45 dessert. I got out the cookie jar. There were 3 cookies left and 4 of us. How could we divide the 3 cookies equally? You would cut each cookie into 4 quarters so we would each get 3 parts.*

USING WRITING TO ASSESS STUDENTS' UNDERSTANDING OF MATH PROCESSES

Writing can be used to assess students' understanding of a math process (Burns, 1995). Assessment should be ongoing, so that we can know what students understand and what we may need to reteach. Monitoring students' progress has become a regular part of reading instruction, but it's just as important in math. After a series of instructional activities, students can write their understanding of a mathematical process such as addition or subtraction with or without regrouping.

For example, when Mrs. Cook's second graders had worked on subtraction with regrouping for a couple of weeks, she asked them how they would solve the problem $63 - 35 = $ _____. One student, whose calculations were frequently off by one or two, wrote this:

> *First I checked to see if I need to borrow. I do so I cross out the six and write a 5 and I make the 3 a 13. Then I get 10 fingers and count up from 3 to 5 and I get 8. And then I go to the 5 and then take away 3 of the five and I get 28.*

Using this written explanation of her process and an observation of her backward counting, Mrs. Cook was able to determine that her errors were a result of inaccurate backward counting. The student understood the process perfectly.

READING, WRITING, AND SCIENCE

Because the main goal of science instruction is to have children understand and apply science concepts, writing can be a powerful tool. Students' use of scientific vocabulary, complex sentence structure, and organization can be developed through lessons that combine the behaviors of a scientist (observing, hypothesizing, drawing conclusions) and writing. Writing can be incorporated through the use of science notebooks (Hammerman, 2006) in which students describe their investigations, make predictions, collect data, record questions, draw or illustrate objects or processes being investigated, and develop theories.

Elementary teachers are fortunate to be able to integrate reading and writing with all areas of the curriculum. In fact, to fit everything into a packed school day, we must integrate. Writing in science can take the form of notes, lists, journals, or reports. These should not be rote activities like copying notes into a journal or completing worksheets because these activities do not stimulate student engagement or thinking (Freeman & Taylor, 2006).

The way we set up the writing moment is crucial. We cannot ask students to write in a vacuum, but if we bring in a frog or a leaf, boil a pot of water, or scrape some cheek cells onto a slide and put it under the microscope, and *then* ask our students to write, we have given them something real to focus on. That doesn't mean the writing will be easy to do or exciting to read every time, but it does mean that there is true content there to be grappled with. We want our students to be able to observe, collect data, predict, analyze, and communicate about scientific artifacts or phenomena. These processes of scientific inquiry need to be structured so that students are not left to flounder and feel frustrated. If we provide structure and guidance, then students can think about something, explain it to themselves, and communicate it to others. When this occurs, they have truly

Shannon writing
"What I Have Learned
About Rocks"

Sylvia Read

internalized that knowledge and claimed it as their own. See the Explicit Instruction Descriptive Writing Lesson Plan on p. 243 for an example of how to provide guidance and structure.

SCIENTIFIC OBSERVATION AND DESCRIPTIVE WRITING

In the early grades, we can focus on teaching students to be scientists who write from observation. We are confronted daily with the phenomena that scientists study and yet we don't often take the time to reflect on them. Learning logs provide a place for students to draw and write in response to a variety of situations that cause them to think about scientific ideas or phenomena such as these:

- Predict what they might learn from a read-aloud of *Red-Eyed Tree Frog* by Joy Cowley (1999).
- Write what they learned after hearing and seeing *Red-Eyed Tree Frog* by Joy Cowley.
- After a floating and sinking experiment, write about the process of creating a clay boat and filling it with pennies.
- Draw and write about a leaf gathered from a neighborhood walk.
- Draw and write daily over a period of a few weeks about the growth of a bean seed.

Explicit Instruction Descriptive Writing Lesson Plan

Concept or Objective: Learning to write descriptive text

Lesson Steps	Activities	Materials
Introduction • Connect today's lesson to previous lessons • Give a purpose for today's lesson	"Students, last week at the science table we had our pumpkin, which we measured and weighed every day. This week at the science table I have some seed pods from different plants. There are milkweed, sweetgum, sweetpea, sunflower, and maple seeds. Today I'm going to get you to help me write a description of one of them. Then you are going to do your own writing that describes one of them. You'll also draw the seed pod you choose."	Various seeds or other specimens for students to observe, enough for each student to take one back to his or her desk or table, if the lesson is done with the whole class together. If done at a center, you'll need enough for 5 to 7 students to have a specimen close by while they draw and write.
Explicit teacher explanation and modeling	Say, "When we write a description, we want to use words that tell about the object's color, size, weight, shape, and texture. As I show you my object, I'd like you to think of words to use to describe it." As students provide words, list them on the teacher's whiteboard or chart paper. (*Note:* Having a digital scale would be invaluable for weighing small items.)	Teacher's whiteboard or chart paper Markers
Interactive guided practice	Using this word bank, generate the first sentence of the description. Then have students generate the next sentences, prompting them to use the words in the word bank.	
Monitored independent practice	Send students in small groups to choose their item to observe. Provide blank paper for drawing and writing. As students draw and write, praise them for using specific descriptive words and details in their drawings. Use the word *description* or *describe* repeatedly during your interactions with individual students.	Blank paper Pencils, crayons
Assessment	Students share their descriptions and drawings during science meeting. If students are in third grade or above, a rubric could be used to assess the detail in their writing.	Central gathering place for science meeting where students can easily see each other's drawings and written descriptions
Accommodations for students	Add words to students' individual word banks or personal dictionaries. If necessary, take dictation from a student's oral description of an item.	Students' word banks or personal dictionaries

The artifacts and phenomena that children can observe are numerous. Simple field trips to the playground can be a site for observing, drawing, and writing. Students can draw and write about:

- Tree bark, leaves, and so on
- A hula-hooped area of grass
- Insects
- The heat of the blacktop compared to the heat of the grass
- The sky
- Shadows
- Cardinal directions (When I look north I see . . .)
- Puddles
- Heart rate after running the perimeter of the playground

Artifacts can be brought into the classroom for close observations. For example,

- Feather
- Frog, insect, spider, fish, or other creature
- Classmate's pet such as a guinea pig
- Fossils
- Shells
- Batteries and bulbs
- Electromagnet
- Magnets
- Pond water
- Onion skin

Figure 9.11 shows what Alexis wrote about one of the many rocks that were displayed for students to observe.

When students are writing, it can be helpful to provide a prompt. For example, after exploring the school grounds looking for objects of certain shapes or colors, students can finish the sentence, "I think things outside are green (or brown, or whatever color) because . . . ." After a session where students focus on using their senses of sight, hearing, smell, and feel, they might write about which sense they think is most important and why. After collecting hitchhiker-type seeds on socks that are worn over their shoes, students can write about what kinds of seeds they collected, why they think seeds are important, or what they learned about how seeds travel. Provide two or three prompts for students to choose from; choice is always crucial for keeping motivation high.

Ellen Doris, in her book *Doing What Scientists Do: Children Learn to Investigate Their World* (1991), recommends the use of worksheets that are both structured and yet open-ended. The worksheets she uses are designed by the teacher (not a publisher) to fit the nature of the activity, to help define the activity, and to provide the children with a way to approach a task. Doris says, "simply sending them off to observe can be too open-ended or vague for some children. The worksheet can suggest a way to proceed without narrowing children's responses to 'one right answer.' It can say, 'Tell your name and what you looked at. Draw what you see in this space. Notice some things and write about them here'" (pp. 31–32). Though recording their observations is important, she stresses that the finished product is only one aspect of the work of science. Because writing and drawing are demanding tasks, especially for young children, they need to

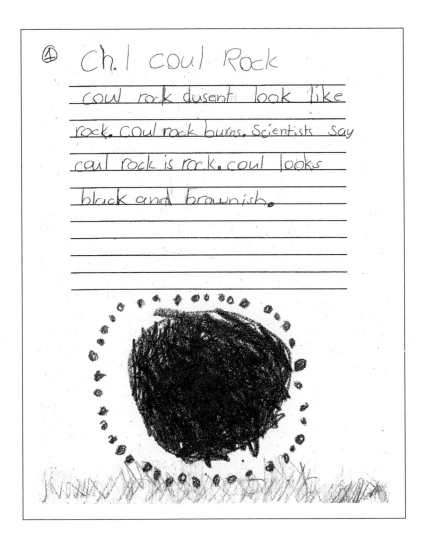

④ Ch. 1 coul Rock
coul rock dusent look like
rock. coul rock burns. Scientists say
caul rock is rock. coul looks
black and brownish.

Figure 9.11 Alexis wrote: Coal rock doesn't look like rock. Coal rock burns. Scientists say coal rock is rock. Coal looks black and brownish.

have time just to look. As teachers, we need to make sure that we provide those times for looking and sharing, free from the requirement to record, otherwise students will equate scientific observation with filling in a worksheet, which, even if the worksheet is open-ended, is not the overall message we want children to receive about science.

Scientists Share Their Work

When you do have students create a product, it is important to provide a way for students to "publish" their work through sharing or display. When they know they will be sharing their findings with an audience, students feel that there is a reason for recording their observations other than obeying the directions of the teacher. Rather than calling it sharing the way we do when it follows writing workshop, you can have a science meeting or seminar where students present their findings. This isn't just cute; it's a way to teach students that scientists have official ways that they share their research with other scientists. Doris (1991) explained it to a group of 5- and 6-year-olds this way:

> After scientists have been working on a project for a while, they might go to a meeting. Sometimes scientists work on their own or with a team and sometimes

they get together with lots of other scientists at a meeting. Sometimes the meeting has a special name, like "seminar" or "symposium" or "conference." We'll call ours a "Science Meeting." (p. 65)

Science meetings need to be actively managed by the teacher so that children understand how to behave respectfully while others share their work and how to respond appropriately. The teacher models how to do this over and over and in some ways these behaviors are more important than the content of what is shared. Having a predictable format is also important. Young children will be better able to think, talk, and pay attention when they know that the meeting won't last longer than a specified amount of time, and when they know they won't miss recess or lose any free time.

INTERACTIVE WRITING AND SCIENCE

Young children, especially kindergartners and first graders, need to have writing modeled for them frequently. A powerful way to model, while also involving the students in the writing, is called *interactive writing*. A thorough description of interactive writing can be found in Chapter 8.

Briefly, interactive writing is a form of shared writing in which students come to the easel and write letter sounds, parts of words, and whole words. "Sharing the pen" with students is the most obvious way that interactive writing differs from shared writing, but it also differs from shared writing in its emphasis on involving students in all parts of the writing process: writing the easy-to-hear sounds of our language; writing whole, memorized sight words; using left-to-right and top-to-bottom directionality; keeping handwriting proportional to already written text; deciding the purpose of a text; deciding what to write; rereading to check their writing; summarizing what was written; revisiting the text to notice particular details; and extending the writing to its intended purpose (e.g., a recipe would be used to cook with the students).

Interactive writing can be used with the whole class or with a small group of students who need to focus on particular skills. For science, whole-class interactive writing is best because through the process of creating a text using interactive writing, you build a community of learners with a common core of knowledge and the desire to explore together new ideas and concepts.

Specifically with science writing, interactive writing can be used to teach students how to take notes, label drawings, describe something in detail, organize information into charts or diagrams, and compare and contrast. Writing is also modeled as a tool for inquiry. As an example, before exploring the schoolyard for certain shapes or colors, the students can write their prediction of what they might find. While outside, they keep a tally sheet and write a few words to describe what shapes and colors they see. On returning to class, or the next day, they can create a chart that includes all the things they saw, and they

---

FOR ENGLISH LANGUAGE LEARNERS

Think, Pair, Share

"Think, pair, share" is a strategy in which the teacher poses a question or idea and gives students think time. Then each student shares with a learning partner. An optional step is to have student pairs share with other pairs. The think time allows ELL students to process their thoughts with a peer before they are expected to report to their partner, to the teacher, or to the whole class. Comprehensible input also occurs as they listen to a peer explain concepts. Vocabulary and concepts are repeated, which gives students time to absorb and remember unfamiliar words and ideas.

can also write an analytical statement about it such as, "We saw lots of green leaves because it is spring."

Writing is a flexible tool to support science inquiry. It can used in all content areas, including social studies.

READING, WRITING, AND SOCIAL STUDIES

Good social studies instruction assumes that there will be reading and writing going on as a part of instruction and assessment. However, reading an informational article or textbook chapter and writing answers to questions is not effective social studies instruction (McGuire, 2007). The subject matter for discussing and writing should be much more than a textbook. Students should be engaging in "cooperative learning, construction of models or plans, dramatic recreations of historical events, role-play and simulation, interviews of family members, and data collection in the local community" (Brophy & Alleman, 1996, p. 48). With young children especially, the writing need not be the major part of social studies learning, but it is a way to record learning, to process an idea, or to explore possibilities.

Content Area Reading

Go to MyEducationLab, "Content Area Reading," and watch the video *The Supply Chain*.

After watching the video, you should be able to:

- Explain how good children's books can help establish a historical sense of order and time.
- Clarify the role of a teacher in using selections from literature in the social studies program.
- Identify criteria that would be helpful for selecting children's books for a social studies program.

SIMULATIONS

Simulations are a powerful way for students to have a "lived-through" experience of a historical, political, economic, or social event of the past or present. Simulations are whole units of instruction in which students take on the role of actual or fictional persons and then make decisions, debate with others, carry out activities, and otherwise live the experience. As students work through a simulation, they begin to ask questions that require them to interpret the events of the past or present, rather than memorize. This in turn leads students and teachers to seek out sources of information; judge their trustworthiness and accuracy; select, organize, and interpret those sources; reach conclusions based on evidence; and explain their conclusions in written forms (Fertig, 2005).

Storypath (McGuire, 1999) is one structure for learning social studies concepts through story, dramatic play, reading, writing, talking, and listening. Each unit lasts 2 to 3 weeks, but doesn't take over the entire day. Writing workshop, reading instruction, and math continue as usual with Storypath allocated to a separate time of day. For example, in a kindergarten unit on "Neighborhood," the teacher reads a story about a neighborhood or a description of a neighborhood setting and the students adds their own ideas about what a neighborhood should be like. Then the students create a mural representing their neighborhood. They populate their neighborhood with characters, including themselves and their families, and the teacher leads them in some shared writing about their neighborhood. A social context is built through having the students experience the everyday events that might occur. Eventually, the teacher introduces a problem, or "critical incident," such as the discovery of litter in the neighborhood. The students discuss what to do about it, make decisions, and act accordingly. They can also explore ideas like what to do when a new student comes to the classroom and how to incorporate that "new neighbor" into their neighborhood. Each time a problem is encountered and solved, the teacher leads the class in shared or interactive writing about it. All these writings can be compiled into a book of writing and photographs that can be sent home with the children to share with their families. Sometime during the unit, it may be appropriate to go on a field trip or invite a guest speaker to the class to find out more about the situation. The unit ends with a positive experience such as a ceremony, festival, or parade.

Storypath can be used to explore other social studies concepts and incorporate other kinds of writing. For example, in Main Street, the setting is a Main Street business district or shopping mall, the characters are the employers and employees of the businesses, and the plot involves the problems of public safety and the needs of the workers. Writing activities include writing advertisements to persuade people to come and shop at their stores. Other language activities that can be integrated into a Storypath unit are developing word banks, writing poetry about the setting, writing descriptive paragraphs about the setting, drawing and writing postcards, writing character biographies, introducing characters to the class, writing about significant events in characters' lives, writing captions for pictures depicting events in the history of the context, creating a timeline, writing flyers or newsletters, interviewing an expert regarding the "critical incident," writing a persuasive speech in response to the "critical incident," and creating advertising flyers or invitations for the culminating event.

READING AND WRITING BIOGRAPHIES

Asking "what if" questions about people such as Ruby Bridges allows students to examine critical turning points in the life of someone important to history (Zarnowski, 2003). Rather than seeing history as facts to be memorized, looking at history as a series of choices in the lives of real people allows students to ask important questions about intentions and outcomes. Biographies written for children can be the basis for this kind of study.

Reading and writing biographies of scientists helps students understand what scientists actually do (Monhardt, 2005). Many students have a limited idea of what scientists do and usually depict them as White men wearing thick glasses and a lab coat. Reading about Dian Fossey or George Washington Carver can quickly dispel that myth. When students inquire into the activities of living scientists who study the behavior of forest fires or collect water samples in local rivers, they can write profiles of them that capture diversity of their work.

Through reading and writing biographies, students can learn that history and science—indeed any area of study—are processes of inquiry, not a collection of facts to be memorized.

 ### CONCLUDING THOUGHTS

Reading and writing can, and should, be incorporated into all areas of the curriculum. However, math, science, and social studies should not be viewed as a way to teach literacy, but rather, literate practices should be seen as ways of interacting with the powerful ideas of math, science, and social studies. Rich, engaging experiences in the content area are going to require that students, read, speak, listen, and write. The goals of literacy instruction are that students comprehend and critically think about all areas of the curriculum. Neglect of content-area learning in favor of a narrow literacy skills curriculum is not going to help our students become citizens of a thriving democracy. All students deserve rich, engaging experiences in which they interact with each other, ask meaningful questions, develop their own theories based on evidence and experience, and make decisions. Reading and writing across the curriculum are means to this end, not an end in themselves.

SUGGESTED ACTIVITIES TO EXTEND YOUR LEARNING

1. Use an informational book as the basis for a language-experience approach lesson. Develop a multiday plan for how you will read the book and how you will take notes with the students, and conclude with having the students dictate the contents of an informational "book."
2. Write down the steps for solving a word problem or doing long division. Notice your thought process as you do this and analyze the benefits for students of writing about math.
3. Bring regalia into the classroom related to a subject of study in science or social studies. Set up an observation table where students will go in ones or twos to observe and write about the objects. When everyone has observed and written, hold a "science conference" so that students can share.
4. Take students on a field trip to the playground. Have them pick a place to sit. Give them a loop of string (or a hula hoop) to define the space that they will observe and write about. Model first using your own space and hoop so that students understand how much detail they can see and write about in their defined space. Follow up with a science conference.
5. Using a persistent problem in society, develop a simulation that highlights that problem. Use your state's core curriculum to identify an area of learning. For example, the simulation might be The Neighborhood, with persistent problems such as water scarcity, speeding on residential streets, or emergency preparedness.
6. Explore the world of computer-based simulations such as The Oregon Trail, SimCity, Mars Simulation Project, or Election Day.

REFERENCES

Armbruster, B. B., McCarthy, S. J., & Cummins, S. (2005). Writing to learn in elementary classrooms. In R. Indrisano & J. R. Paratore (Eds.), *Learning to write, writing to learn: Theory and research in practice*. Newark, DE: International Reading Association.

Brophy, J., & Alleman, J. (1996). *Powerful social studies for elementary students.* Fort Worth: Harcourt Brace.

Burns, M. (1992). *Math and literature, Grades K–3, Book One*. Sausalito, CA: Math Solutions Publications.

Burns, M. (1995). *Writing in math class: A resource for Grades 2–8*. Sausalito, CA: Math Solutions Publications.

Burns, M. (2002). *Teaching arithmetic: Lessons for introducing division, Grades 3–4*. Sausalito, CA: Math Solutions Publications.

Caswell, L. J., & Duke, N. K. (1998). Non-narrative as a catalyst for literacy development. *Language Arts, 75,* 108–117.

Daniels, H. A. (1990). Developing a sense of audience. In T. Shanahan (Ed.), *Reading and writing together: New perspectives for the classroom* (pp. 99–125). Norwood, MA: Christopher-Gordon.

Doris, E. (1991). *Doing what scientists do: Children learn to investigate their world.* Portsmouth, NH: Heinemann.

Dreher, M. J. (2003). Motivating struggling readers by tapping the potential of information books. *Reading & Writing Quarterly, 19*(1), 25–38.

Duke, N. K. (2000). 3.6 minutes per day: The scarcity of informational texts in first grade. *Reading Research Quarterly, 35*(2), 202–224.

Duke, N. K., & Bennett-Armistead, V. S. (2003). *Reading and writing informational text in the primary grades: Research-based practices.* New York: Scholastic.

Fertig, G. (2005). Teaching elementary students how to interpret the past. *The Social Studies, 96*(1), 2–8.

Freeman, G., & Taylor, V. (2006). *Integrating science and literacy instruction: A framework for bridging the gap.* Lanham, MD: Rowman & Littlefield Education.

Hammerman, E. (2006). *Eight essentials of inquiry-based science, K–8.* Thousand Oaks, CA: Corwin.

Harvey, S., & Goudvis, A. (2000). *Strategies that work: Teaching comprehension to enhance understanding.* York, ME: Stenhouse.

Hoffman, J. V., McCarthey, S. J., Abbott, J., Christian, C., Corman, L., Curry, C., et al. (1994). So what's new in the basals? A focus on first grade. *Journal of Reading Behavior, 26,* 47–73.

Hyde, A. A., & Bizar, M. (1989). *Thinking in context: Teaching cognitive processes across the elementary school curriculum.* New York: Longman.

Jenkins, C. B., & Earle, A. A. (2006). *Once upon a fact: Helping children write nonfiction.* New York: Teachers College Press.

Kamberelis, G. (1998). Relations between children's literacy diets and genre development: You write what you read. *Literacy Teaching and Learning, 3*(1), 7–53.

Kamil, M. (1994, April). *Matches between reading instruction and reading task demands.* Presented to the American Educational Research Association, New Orleans, LA.

Laminack, L. L., & Wadsworth, R. M. (2006). *Reading aloud across the curriculum: How to build bridges in language arts, math, science, and social studies.* Portsmouth, NH: Heinemann.

Lauber, P. (1992). The evolution of a science writer. In E. B. Freeman & D. G. Person (Eds.), *Using nonfiction trade books in the elementary classroom: From ants to zeppelins* (pp. 11–16). Urbana, IL: National Council of Teachers of English.

Lehrer, R., Giles, N. D., & Schauble, L. (2002). Children's work with data. In R. Lehrer & L. Schauble (Eds.), *Investigating real data in the classroom: Expanding children's understanding of math and science.* New York: Teachers College Press.

McGuire, M. E. (1999). *Storypath Foundations: An innovative approach to social studies.* Chicago: Everyday Learning.

McGuire, M. E. (2007). What happened to social studies? The disappearing curriculum. *Phi Delta Kappan, 88*(8), 620–624.

Monhardt, R. (2005). Reading and writing nonfiction with children: Using biographies to learn about science and scientists. *Science Scope, 28*(6), 16–19.

O'Connell, S. (2000). *Introduction to problem solving: Strategies for the elementary math classroom.* Portsmouth, NH: Heinemann.

Pappas, C. C. (1991). Fostering full access to literacy by including information books. *Language Arts, 68,* 449–461.

Read, S. (2001). "Kid mice hunt for their selfs": First and second graders writing research. *Language Arts, 78*(4), 333–342.

Robinson, C., Larsen, J., Haupt, J., & Mohlman, J. (1997). Picture book selection behaviors of emergent readers: Influence of genre, familiarity, and book attributes. *Reading Research and Instruction, 36*, 287–304.

Schmidt, W. H., Caul, J., Byer, J. L., & Buchmann, M. (1984). Content of basal selections: Implications for comprehension instruction. In G. G. Duffy, L. R. Roehler, & J. Mason (Eds.), *Comprehension instruction: Perspectives and suggestions* (pp. 144–162). New York: Longman.

Smolkin, L. B., & Donovan, C. A. (2001). The contexts of comprehension: The information book read aloud, comprehension acquisition, and comprehension instruction in a first-grade classroom. *The Elementary School Journal, 102*(2), 97–122.

Viscovich, S. A. (2002). The effects of three organizational structures on the writing and critical thinking of fifth graders. In P. E. Linder, M. B. Sampson, J. R. Dugan, & B. Brancato (Eds.), *Celebrating the faces of literacy: The twenty-fourth yearbook of the College Reading Association.* Readyville, TN: College Reading Association.

Yopp, R. H., & Yopp, H. K. (2000). Sharing informational text with young children. *The Reading Teacher, 53*(5), 410–423.

Zarnowski, M. (2003). *History makers: A questioning approach to reading and writing biographies.* Portsmouth, NH: Heinemann.

Children's Literature

Adler, D. (1999). *How tall, how short, how far away?* New York: Holiday House.

Aliki. (1985). *My visit to the dinosaurs.* New York: Harper and Row.

Anno, M. (1977). *Anno's counting book.* New York: HarperCollins.

Bash, B. (1989). *Desert giant: The world of the saguaro cactus.* Boston: Little, Brown.

Berger, M. (1996). *The world of dinosaurs.* New York: Newbridge.

Berger, M., & Berger, G. (1998). *Do stars have points? Questions and answers about stars and planets.* New York: Scholastic.

Carle, E. (1972). *Rooster's off to see the world.* New York: Scholastic.

Cherry, L. (1992). *A river ran wild.* New York: Harcourt Brace.

Clement, R. (1991). *Counting on Frank.* Milwaukee, WI: Gareth Stevens.

Cole, J. (1994). *The magic schoolbus in the time of the dinosaurs.* New York: Scholastic.

Cowley, J. (1999). *Red-eyed tree frog.* New York: Scholastic.

Crews, D. (1986). *Ten black dots.* New York: Greenwillow.

Crosbie, M. (1993). *Architecture shapes.* New York: Wiley.

Fisher, L. E. (1982). *Number art: Thirteen 123s from around the world.* New York: Four Winds Press.

Gibbons, G. (1984). *Fire! Fire!* New York: HarperCollins.

Gibbons, G. (1993). *Frogs.* New York: Scholastic.

Gibbons, G. (2000). *Bats.* New York: Holiday House.

Hightower, S. (1997). *Twelve snails to one lizard: A tale of mischief and measurement.* New York: Simon and Schuster.

Hong, L. T. (1993). *Two of everything.* Morton Grove, IL: A. Whitman.

Hutchins, P. (1986). *The doorbell rang.* New York: Greenwillow.

Jonas, A. (1987). *Reflections.* New York: Greenwillow.

Jonas, A. (1995). *Splash.* New York: Greenwillow.

Jordan, M., & Jordan, T. (1996). *Amazon alphabet.* New York: Kingfisher.

Koller, J. F. (1999). *One monkey too many.* New York: Harcourt Brace.

Lavies, B. (1990). *Backyard hunter: The praying mantis.* New York: E. P. Dutton.

Leedy, L. (1997). *Measuring Penny.* New York: Henry Holt.

Lionni, L. (1960). *Inch by inch.* New York: Aston-Honor.

McKissack, P. C. (1992). A million fish . . . more or less. New York: Knopf.

McKissack, P. C., & McKissack, F. L. (1994). *Christmas in the big house, Christmas in the quarters.* New York: Scholastic.

Merriam, E. (1993). *12 ways to get to 11.* New York: Simon and Schuster.

Montgomery, S. (2006). *Quest for the tree kangaroo: An expedition to the cloud forest of New Guinea,* Boston: Houghton Mifflin.

Munsch, R. (1987). *Moira's birthday.* Toronto: Annick Press.

Myller, R. (1991). *How big is a foot?* New York: Dell.

Owen, A. (1988). *Annie's one to ten.* New York: Knopf.

Petty, K. (1991). *Pandas.* Hauppauge, NY: Barron's.

Pinczes, E. (1995). *A remainder of one.* Boston: Houghton.

Schwartz, D. M. (1985). *How much is a million?* New York: Lothrop, Lee & Shepard.

Schwartz, D. M. (1999). *If you hopped like a frog.* New York: Scholastic.

Scieszka, J. (1995). *Math curse.* New York: Viking.

Silverstein, S. (1974). *Where the sidewalk ends.* New York: HarperCollins.

Simon, S. (1989). *Whales.* New York: William Morrow.

Tompert, A. (1990). *Grandfather Tang's story.* New York: Crown.

Viorst, J. (1978). *Alexander, who used to be rich last Sunday.* New York: Atheneum.

Wahl, J., & Wahl, S. (1976). *I can count the petals on a flower.* Reston, VA: National Council of Teachers of Mathematics.

Walsh, E. S. (1991). *Mouse count.* San Diego: Harcourt Brace Jovanovich.

Williams, V. B. (1982). *A chair for my mother.* New York: Greenwillow.

Reading Assessment That Guides Instruction

10

by John A. Smith

Tyrone's Reading Instruction

When third-grade classroom teacher Angelina Rhees noticed that her student Tyrone was falling behind in reading, she asked her school reading specialist, Shae Hancock, to give Tyrone a reading diagnostic assessment. Shae happily agreed to help and began the testing by giving Tyrone the first-grade word list from her informal reading inventory (IRI) and asking him to read the words aloud. The first-grade list was easy for Tyrone (independent level). He missed only one word. On the second-grade list, Tyrone struggled with 4 or 5 words. This placed him at the instructional level for second-grade word recognition. When Shae asked Tyrone to read the third-grade word list aloud, he missed 11 words, placing him in the frustration level. Shae concluded that Tyrone's sight word recognition was at the second-grade level, approximately 1 year behind his classroom grade level.

Next, Shae handed Tyrone the first- to third-grade IRI reading passages and asked him to read the passages aloud to her and answer comprehension questions about them. Shae recorded the words Tyrone misread and his responses to the comprehension questions. Tyrone's performance on the reading passages was very similar to his performance on the word lists. First-grade reading was easy, second-grade reading was just a little difficult, and third-grade reading was too hard. Shae noted that Tyrone was reading at the second-grade instructional level.

Finally, Shae assessed Tyrone's listening comprehension. She read the remaining IRI passages aloud to Tyrone and reminded him to pay attention because she would ask him comprehension questions. To Shae's surprise, Tyrone easily answered the comprehension questions through the sixth-grade-level passage. Based on these IRI data, Shae created a bar graph of Tyrone's reading ability (see Figure 10.1) to share with Angelina.

After school, Shae pointed out to Angelina that Tyrone was a year below grade level in sight word recognition, oral reading fluency, and reading comprehension. Shae also pointed out that Tyrone's listening comprehension level was very high, meaning that his vocabulary and background knowledge were strong. This "profile" of Tyrone's reading abilities suggested that his reading problems centered around his lower ability to recognize and read words fluently. Additionally, Shae suggested that if Angelina worked carefully with Tyrone and his word recognition and reading fluency levels improved, his reading comprehension level

Figure 10.1 Tyrone's Informal Reading Inventory Bar Graph

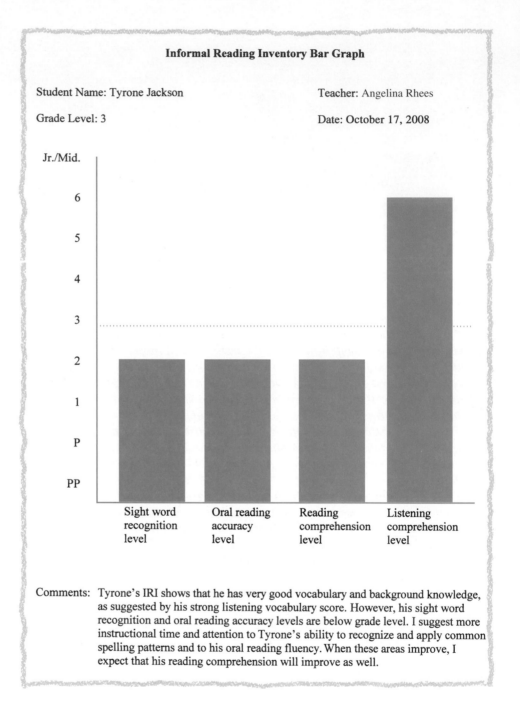

Informal Reading Inventory Bar Graph

Student Name: Tyrone Jackson   Teacher: Angelina Rhees

Grade Level: 3   Date: October 17, 2008

Comments: Tyrone's IRI shows that he has very good vocabulary and background knowledge, as suggested by his strong listening vocabulary score. However, his sight word recognition and oral reading accuracy levels are below grade level. I suggest more instructional time and attention to Tyrone's ability to recognize and apply common spelling patterns and to his oral reading fluency. When these areas improve, I expect that his reading comprehension will improve as well.

would improve because it was his word recognition problems that were constraining his comprehension.

Accordingly, Shae and Angelina worked out a plan for Angelina to (1) focus Tyrone's phonics instruction on spelling patterns he hadn't yet mastered, as identified by additional diagnostic testing that Shae will administer; (2) connect Tyrone's phonics instruction directly to his reading of connected text by having him underline spelling patterns on photocopies of his reading group texts; and (3) increase the amount of time that Tyrone received phonics and fluency instruction each day through participation in an "extra" reading skills group each day.

The data-based intervention plan that Shae and Angelina developed was successful. Tyrone was able to catch up and keep up with his classmates. He was never again referred to or needed support from the Title 1 reading program.

————————————   ————————————

For many years, elementary classroom teachers taught school for 9 to 10 months and then had to wait until the end of the school year to find out how well their students did on "the test." There were a variety of reading assessments available, but assessment was generally thought of as something you did after the teaching was over. The problem with doing the assessment after instruction was that teachers had little information about how well their students were doing during instruction. Teachers didn't have ongoing data about which students might be keeping up, falling behind, or zooming ahead.

Much has changed in recent years. Teachers now have more and better reading and writing assessment tools, a much clearer understanding of the purposes of assessment, and better-defined procedures for using reading assessment data to plan instruction. This chapter describes how to gather, analyze, and use reading assessment data in preparation for designing instruction to meet students' reading and writing instructional needs. Specific chapter topics include:

- Assessment issues
- Assessing the essential elements of reading and writing

ASSESSMENT ISSUES

ALIGNING READING GOALS, INSTRUCTION, AND ASSESSMENT

An effective educational program, in any discipline, requires a three-way alignment among (1) educational *goals*, (2) *instructional* methods and materials, and (3) *assessment* measures and practices. Once clear educational goals are established, instructional programs must be selected and implemented to help students reach those goals. Then an assessment plan must be developed and put in place to determine how well students are reaching the goals and what instructional modifications must be made to improve students' achievement if necessary.

Goals for reading instruction have always focused on teaching students to (1) recognize and read words fluently, (2) comprehend the content of what they read, and (3) enjoy reading for information and recreation. Therefore, teachers routinely provide students with instruction in recognizing and applying spelling patterns to build reading fluency, building vocabulary and applying reading comprehension strategies, and providing regular opportunities for students to enjoy discussing literature and learning from text. To monitor how effective instruction is in helping students achieve reading goals, teachers employ a variety of assessment measures including recording and charting students' reading rate and accuracy, asking questions about and having students retell what they read, and discussing with students what kinds of books they like to read and how they can broaden their reading repertoire.

The process of analyzing student reading achievement involves comparing student achievement against reading goals (Helman, 2005; Reilly, 2007). When students are making steady progress toward reaching reading goals, teachers will know that their instruction is effective. When students are not making adequate progress toward reading goals, teachers will know that instruction must be adjusted.

VALIDITY AND RELIABILITY

Any discussion of assessment must include the concepts of *validity* and *reliability* (Denton, Ciancio, & Fletcher, 2006). Validity refers to the appropriateness of an assessment. Invernizzi, Landrum, Howell, and Warley (2005) write that "a measure is valid to the extent to which it measures what it is intended to measure" (p. 611). Reliability refers to the consistency of an assessment. Reliable assessments are very straightforward in their scoring so that five different teachers, reading specialists, or teacher's aides could give the same test to a student and come up with the same score.

Some assessments may have high validity but low reliability. For example, a running record is an assessment where a teacher listens to a student read a passage aloud, mark the student's oral reading errors, and calculate the student's percentage of oral reading accuracy. This assessment is valid because it involves the student actually reading a meaningful text that is being used in the classroom. However, the reliability of a running record can be suspect because different teachers may not agree on how to score certain reading errors. The subjective nature of running record scoring can lead different teachers to come up with different percentages on a student's reading accuracy. Fawson, Ludlow, Reutzel, Sudweeks, & Smith (2006) found that it takes three separate raters rating three different passages for a single student to get a reliable running record score.

On the other hand, other assessments may have high reliability but low validity. For example, the Oral Reading Fluency (ORF) subtest of the Dynamic Indicators of Basic Early Literacy Skills (DIBELS) test (Good & Kaminski, 2002; Good, Simmons, & Kame'enui, 2001) is a very reliable assessment for monitoring students' growth in reading rate and accuracy. The scoring procedures are precise and relatively simple. If 10 teachers who are experienced in administering the DIBELS ORF subtest used it to test the same student, the likelihood is high that all 10 would get very close to the same score. However, some teachers may question the validity of the DIBELS ORF subtest for assessing students' oral reading fluency because fluency is defined as reading quickly, accurately, and expressively, but the ORF has no scale for measuring expressiveness. Although students are instructed to read ORF passages at a natural rate, many read the passages unnaturally fast, with no regard for expressiveness, in an attempt to achieve a high ORF score.

This is not to say that teachers should refrain from using running records or DIBELS assessments. They are both very good assessments, but teachers need to be aware of their strengths and limitations to correctly interpret the data. Reading assessments that are less reliable or valid for the purposes that they are being used may provide data that can lead teachers to make improper instructional decisions. When considering whether to use any form of assessment, teachers should judge the extent to which it is valid and reliable in order to know what level of trust to place in the data.

PURPOSES OF READING ASSESSMENT

To obtain useful assessment data that will guide instruction and help students reach reading goals it is important to be clear on purposes for assessment and to select assessments that are appropriate for those purposes. Teachers must be familiar with early literacy assessments that can be used for (1) *screening* students for reading problems and initial program placement, (2) *diagnosing* students' reading strengths and needs, (3) *monitoring* students' ongoing progress in reading, and (4) measuring students' reading achievement *outcomes*.

Screening

Screening assessments are given to all K–3 students at the beginning of each school year for two major purposes. First, teachers use screening data to identify students who may have reading problems and who are likely to need additional instructional support to achieve reading goals. For example, a set of widely used screening assessments is the Dynamic Indicators of Basic Early Literacy Skills (DIBELS), previously mentioned (Good & Kaminski, 2002; Good et al., 2001; Kaminski & Good, 1996). Each DIBELS subtest has benchmark scores that indicate the levels at which students should be achieving to be on track to reach or exceed grade-level reading ability. DIBELS benchmark scores also indicate levels below which students are considered to be at risk for reading difficulties. A second-grade student who reads below 26 words correct per minute at the beginning of the school year may need additional instructional support to reach the goal of reading at or above grade level by the end of the year. Teachers also use screening data to sort students into initial small groups for differentiated reading instruction. Based on screening data, teachers place students in small instructional groups, observe how well students perform in these groups, then make necessary ongoing adjustments in group membership.

PEARSON myeducationlab

Assessment, Remediation, and Diagnosis

Go to MyEducationLab, "Assessment, Remediation, and Diagnosis," and read the article "Measuring Reading At Grade Level."

As you read this article, notice how valid and reliable screening tests can help teachers make informed decisions about where to begin instruction for students.

- What are the purposes for administering screening assessments?
- What are characteristics of the oral reading fluency measures described in this article?
- What are your thoughts about the strengths and needs of the school district's three-phase oral reading project?

Diagnosing

Diagnostic assessments are more detailed tests that provide in-depth data on students' specific reading strengths and needs. For example, the Cooter/Flynt/Cooter Comprehensive Reading Inventory (Cooter, Flynt, & Cooter, 2006) begins with a student reading lists of words at successive grade levels to estimate the student's word recognition level. The student then reads a passage aloud to the teacher who is recording the words from the passage that the student misreads. Finally, the student is asked to answer comprehension questions about the passage to determine his or her level of reading comprehension.

Another example of a diagnostic reading test is the CORE Phonics Survey (Consortium on Reading Excellence [CORE], 2007). This diagnostic assessment examines students' familiarity with alphabet letters, phonemic awareness, and all of the major spelling patterns in a common instructional sequence. As teachers guide their students through this assessment, they are able to pinpoint with a high degree of certainty exactly which spelling patterns the student is, and is not, familiar with and exactly where instruction should focus.

Figure 10.2　Diagnosis of Reading Problems: Drilling Down

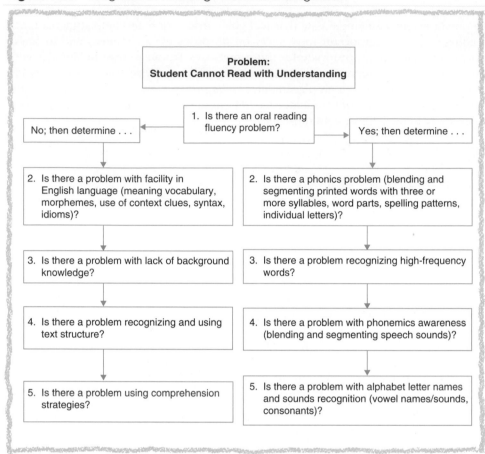

Diagnosis employs a process commonly known as drilling down to pinpoint a student's specific reading strengths and weaknesses (see Figure 10.2). Drilling down involves assessing a student's mastery of the essential elements of reading, beginning with reading comprehension and working backward through successive lower-level reading skills until the source of the student's reading problems is identified. For example, if a student is having trouble comprehending the content of a text, the teacher would assess the student's oral reading fluency to see if lack of fluency is the root of the student's reading problem. If the student is unable to read fluently, the teacher would drill down to see if the student's reading problem is a lack of ability to apply phonics skills. If the student tests poorly in phonics, then the teacher drills further down to see if the student has a problem recognizing high-frequency words, building phonemic awareness, or knowing the names and sounds of the alphabet letters. However, if the student's oral reading fluency is adequate, then the teacher would check to see if there is a problem with the student's facility with English, a lack of applicable background knowledge, a lack of ability to make use of text structure, or an inability to use comprehension strategies.

Diagnostic assessments are generally given only to students who struggle with learning to read. For example, diagnostic assessments have traditionally been given at the beginning of a school year only to students identified by the screening assessment as needing extra instructional support. Currently, however, many teachers withhold diagnostic assessment until struggling students have had a chance to receive an instructional intervention for 4 to 6 weeks to observe how well students respond to the intervention (Fuchs & Fuchs, 2006). Students who respond well to intervention and demonstrate progress will not need a diagnostic assessment. Students who do not respond well to intervention will receive a diagnostic assessment that will guide teachers in designing instruction that is tightly focused on a student's specific reading instruction needs.

Progress Monitoring

Progress-monitoring assessments are tests that are given repeatedly (weekly, monthly, quarterly) to allow teachers to track students' rates of progress to identify students who are not making adequate progress. For example, DIBELS ORF subtests, in addition to serving as screening assessments, function well as progress-monitoring assessments because they are quick, easy to administer, and because there are multiple forms of the subtest at each grade level. Teachers can give the ORF subtest often without the problem of students memorizing the passages and inflating their reading achievement scores. Students' progress-monitoring scores are routinely entered in teachers' desktop computers, sent to an Internet assessment site, and graphed by computer to create charts for teachers showing exactly how well students are progressing throughout the school year.

Progress monitoring may occur at different intervals for students of varying ability levels. For examples, students whose screening assessment data indicate that they are on track to stay at or above grade level might receive progress-monitoring assessment only three times each year. Those students who are a little below grade level might receive progress monitoring once or twice a month. Students who are well below grade level routinely receive progress monitoring on a weekly basis.

Outcome Measuring

At the end of each school year teachers, administrators, parents, and others in the education community need to know how well students did during the school year in learning to read. Reading outcome measuring assessments are the

FOR STRUGGLING READERS

Creating Case Studies of Struggling Readers

Many people who experience serious medical problems will be seen by several physicians in order to get a "second opinion." Physicians who are treating patients with serious medical problems often consult with colleagues to get the broadest perspective and develop the best informed course of action. Teachers who are responsible for students with serious reading difficulties should also consult with grade-level teammates and other knowledgeable school personnel to develop the best course of action.

One way to facilitate such consultations is to develop case studies of students with serious reading difficulties. Case studies are in-depth collections of information about the backgrounds and educational histories of struggling students. Case studies usually include the following information:

- Family background including primary language spoken at home, cultural influences, parents' occupations and levels of education, and siblings' performance in school.
- Health, including persistent medical conditions and needed medications, results of hearing and vision screening, and any evidence of nutrition and general physical condition.
- Achievement data, including standardized test scores and any informal assessment data carried over from previous years, the current year's screening and progress-monitoring data, in-depth diagnostic data such as an informal reading inventory, testing results from a school psychologist or special education teacher, and classroom teacher observations about the student's performance on routine classroom tasks.
- Instructional history, including classroom instruction and any special placements and interventions that have already been tried.

These case study data are often written up in a four-or five-page report that is distributed to and discussed by members of a school-based special services team made up of the principal, reading specialists, special education teachers, school psychologists, and other school personnel. Classroom teachers and parents are invited to attend when their students are being discussed. Special services teams review case study data on individual students and make recommendations about in-class interventions and also placements in special programs if needed.

end-of-year assessments, both standardized and informal, that provide a final indication of how well students achieved. Reading outcome measuring assessments allow teachers to determine which students excelled, achieved at grade level, or failed to make adequate progress during the year. The assessments are often end-of-year standardized tests, but the final data gathered from progress-monitoring assessments may also be used for outcome assessment.

STANDARDIZED TESTING

Types and Purposes of Standardized Tests

When educators discuss standardized testing, they're usually referring to commercially published tests that are generally given at the end of the school year to determine how well students have learned (outcome measuring). Standardized tests such as the California Achievement Test, the Iowa Test of Basic Skills, the Comprehensive Test of Basic Skills, and the Stanford Reading Test are referred to as standardized tests because they are given under standardized conditions such as (1) being given during prescribed weeks of the school year, (2) given with prescribed time limits for each test subsection, and (3) given with uniform test administration and test-taking instructions.

In many school districts around the country, standardized reading tests are given only in Grades 2 and up because kindergarten and first-grade students haven't yet had sufficient opportunity to learn to read. Additionally, many educators express concern about the emotional stress that high-stakes standardized tests may place on young students. Standardized tests are usually given in the spring as an outcome measure of students' reading achievement, but some may be given in the fall for screening and diagnosis.

Standardized tests generally come in two formats: (1) *norm-referenced* tests, and (2) *criterion-referenced* tests. The purpose of norm-referenced tests is to *compare* the academic performance of each student, school, district, and state against others taking the same test across the country. For example, the National Assessment of Educational Progress (NAEP, 2005) is designed to show how well students in Grades 4, 8, and 12 in each state perform academically compared to students in other states. Based on NAEP test scores, states are rank-ordered from highest performing to lowest performing. NAEP scores also allow for comparisons across socioeconomic and cultural groups. NAEP testing allows policymakers to see which regions of the country and which groups are doing well and which are not, and this can help them decide where precious educational resources are most needed.

The purpose of criterion-referenced testing is to see how well students are meeting educational goals or criteria. For example, in most states the state office of education creates *core curriculum* and educational objectives in each subject area. These core curriculum documents and objectives are distributed throughout the state and local districts and schools are expected to "cover the core." From their core curricula, states also create end-of-level criterion-referenced tests that are given to all students near the end of each school year to assess how well they are mastering core curriculum content and skills. Rather than placing the emphasis on comparing schools against schools and districts against districts, the scores from criterion-referenced tests reflect to what extent each student has mastered the objectives in the core curriculum. During the summer, families usually receive a letter from the local school district containing their child's criterion-referenced test scores. These scores are represented as a list of the instructional objectives and a statement that the student has achieved "mastery," "near-mastery," or "minimal mastery" for each objective. Criterion-referenced test scores are instructionally useful to teachers because they show where each student is performing well and where additional instructional support is needed.

Using Standardized Tests Appropriately

In this era of increased educational accountability, the pressure on educators to generate high test scores is intense. There are serious consequences for students attached to standardized test scores including promotion to the next grade, high school graduation, and placement in mandatory summer school programs. Likewise there are also serious consequences for educators. Under the federal government's current education initiative, No Child Left Behind, schools that don't generate acceptable levels of student progress face sanctions including paying for remedial instruction for students, paying transportation costs for students to attend other schools, and reassigning of the principal and teachers to other schools. This national obsession with standardized test scores, also known as *high-stakes testing*, has raised serious concerns among educators about the misuse of test scores.

In July 2000, the American Educational Research Association (AERA) released a position statement acknowledging the high-stakes nature of standardized testing and outlining considerations that must be addressed in order for standardized testing to be fair, accurate, and useful.

Don't Make High-Stakes Decisions Based on the Results of a Single Test

A score from a single test should always be considered together with other pertinent information about a student's academic performance including classroom teacher observations of the student in the classroom setting, scores on other tests, and, if appropriate, testing by another educator such as a resource teacher or school psychologist. If evidence exists that the low standardized test score may not represent a student's true academic ability, then other means should be made to allow the student to demonstrate his or her ability such as retaking the test or taking another similar test.

Ensure Alignment between the Test and the Curriculum

Assessment needs to be closely aligned with instructional content and objectives. It is not fair to students and teachers when students are taught content ABC during the school year and then tested on content XYZ on the end-of-year standardized test. One of the first things new teachers should do is to ask the principal for a list of the reading objectives that will be covered on the end-of-year standardized test. That list of objectives should guide instruction and help ensure that objectives are covered. There must be a seamless three-way alignment among the education objectives, the content of classroom instruction, and the assessments.

Provide Opportunities for Remediation for those who Fail

One purpose of standardized testing is to determine which students are succeeding academically and which are not. When standardized testing identifies failing students, it is incumbent on schools and teachers to provide remedial instruction and support to help those failing students "reach the bar." Chapter 11 of this text includes a description of the Three-Tier model that provides high-quality instruction for all students coupled with layers of remedial instruction for students that need extra help to succeed in reading.

Provide Appropriate Accommodations for Students with Language
Differences or Learning Disabilities

If a student who is learning English (English language learner or ELL) cannot read the instructions or the items on a standardized test, then the test results become a reflection of the student's knowledge of English rather than the student's knowledge of the curriculum. A student who reads very well in her native language may be classified as a nonreader because of her inability to read the test in English. Similarly, a student with a learning disability who has strong knowledge of science or social studies content may not be able to demonstrate his level of knowledge because of reading skill problems. In the case of students with language differences or other learning disabilities, special accommodations such as additional testing time, individual testing setting, or having portions of a test read aloud to the student may be needed.

ASSESSING THE ESSENTIAL ELEMENTS OF READING AND WRITING

There is strong consensus across the country that reading instruction needs to focus on the "essential elements of reading" identified by the National Reading Panel (NRP, 2000). These include phonemic awareness, phonics, fluency, vocabulary, and comprehension. Comprehensive reading programs also address oral language, alphabet knowledge, and writing. Commercial reading programs, professional development programs, and professional textbooks are increasingly based on these elements of reading. School districts look for and adopt reading programs that are built on these elements. Because these elements have become the focus of reading instruction, it is important to have ways to assess student progress in these areas.

Table 10.1 provides an overview of reading and writing assessments that focus on the essential elements of reading and that are commonly used in elementary school classrooms. The following pages describe these reading assessments. The list of assessments is not meant to be complete, but rather to provide a sample of reading assessments.

ASSESSING ALPHABET LETTER KNOWLEDGE

Learning the alphabet may be considered the first step in leaning to read. In assessing student alphabet knowledge it is important to learn how well beginning reading students recognize both upper- and lowercase letters and know the names and sounds of the letters.

DIBELS Letter Naming Fluency Subtest

The Dynamic Indicators of Basic Early Literacy Skills (DIBELS; Good & Kaminski, 2002; Good et al., 2001; Kaminski & Good, 1996) is a series of individually administered reading subtests for students in Grades K–6 that can be used for screening, progress monitoring, and outcome measurement in the areas of phonemic awareness, phonics, and fluency. DIBELS subtests were designed to be quick and easy to administer so that teachers can measure and analyze their students' reading achievement on a continuous basis throughout the school year. The DIBELS Letter Naming Fluency (LNF) subtest is a quick assessment that can be used for both screening and progress monitoring. This subtest begins by showing the student a page containing all upper- and lowercase alphabet letters in random order. Using a timer, the teacher records the number of

Table 10.1   Commonly Used Reading Assessments

Essential Elements	Published Assessments
Alphabet knowledge	• DIBELS: Letter Naming Fluency • CORE: Phonics Survey • PALS: Alphabet Knowledge • PALS: Letter Sounds
Phonemic awareness	• DIBELS: Initial Sound Fluency • DIBELS: Phoneme Segmentation Fluency • PALS: Rhyme Awareness • PALS: Beginning Sound Awareness • CORE: Phonological Awareness Screening • CORE: Phoneme Deletion • CORE: Phonological Segmentation • CORE: Phoneme Segmentation • CORE: Spanish Phonemic Awareness • Texas Primary Reading Inventory • Yopp-Singer Phonemic Awareness
Phonics/Spelling	• DIBELS: Nonsense Word Fluency • CORE Phonics Survey • Words Their Way: Qualitative Spelling Inventory • Informal Reading Inventories • Running Records • PALS • Texas Primary Reading Inventory • San Diego Quick Assessment of Reading Ability (CORE) • Fry Oral Reading Test (CORE) • Teacher/Student Reading Conferences
Fluency	• DIBELS: Oral Reading Fluency • Texas Primary Reading Inventory • Oral Reading Fluency Scale • PALS • Gray Oral Reading Test • Teacher/Student Reading Conferences
Oral language and vocabulary	• Critchlow Verbal Language Scale (CORE) • Critchlow Spanish Verbal Language Scale (CORE) • Peabody Picture Vocabulary Test • Picture Naming Test • In-Program Assessments

Table 10.1   Continued

Essential Elements	Published Assessments
Comprehension	• Informal Reading Inventories
	• Retellings
	• In-Program Assessments
	• Teacher/Student Reading Conferences
Writing	• Six Traits
Attitude toward reading	• Elementary Reading Attitude Survey
	• Teacher/Student Reading Conferences
	• Attitude Inventories
	• Interest Inventories

letter names the student can pronounce correctly in 1 minute. DIBELS provides benchmarks that show how many letter names a student should be able to recognize at the beginning, middle, and end of kindergarten. The LNF subtest can be given repeatedly to monitor and chart student progress in learning the alphabet. Teachers who enter their students' DIBELS scores on the DIBELS website will immediately receive a variety of electronic charts and graphs that are valuable for monitoring student progress and planning instruction. Information about DIBELS assessments can be found at http://dibels.uoregon.edu/. Whereas the DIBELS LNF subtest assesses only student knowledge of letter names, assessments such as the Letter Names and Sounds test (Figure 10.3) can assess student knowledge of both letter names and sounds.

PALS: Alphabet Knowledge Subtest

Phonological Awareness Literacy Screening (PALS) is a series of Internet-based early literacy assessments developed at the University of Virginia. PALS-K and PALS 1–3 are designed to help teachers *screen* for students who are lagging behind in reading and who would benefit from additional literacy instruction. Additionally, PALS can serve as a *diagnostic* assessment, helping teachers gather detailed information about individual students' reading strengths and instructional needs. Teachers administering the PALS-K record the number of each student's correct responses on scoring sheets provided for each PALS subtest. Individual subtest scores are summed to produce a total score that is compared to grade-level benchmarks established for both fall and spring of the kindergarten year.

The PALS *Alphabet Knowledge* subtest measures how many of the lowercase alphabet letters a student can identify. This is followed by the *Letter Sounds* subtest in which students are asked to produce the sounds of 23 uppercase letters and three digraphs. Information about PALS assessments can be found at the PALS website: http://pals.virginia.edu/.

CORE Phonics Survey

The Consortium on Reading Excellence (CORE, 2007) publishes a useful assessment handbook that contains a variety of assessments focused on the essential elements of reading. One of the assessments, the CORE Phonics Survey, contains alphabet knowledge

Figure 10.3 Letter Names and Sounds Test

Name _____ Date _____

Letter Names and Sounds Test

Step 1: Point to each letter and ask, "What is this letter called?" Write a small letter *n* beside each letter that the student is able to name correctly.

Step 2: Point to each letter (lower-case only) and ask, "What sound does this letter make?" Write a small letter *s* beside each letter for which the student is able to produce the correct letter sound.

Step 3: Group students for alphabet instruction based on the letter names and sounds they need to learn.

m	o	q	w	h	s
a	u	p	n	x	i
e	z	d	y	t	f
b	r	k	v	l	c
j	g	M	J	B	S
U	I	C	G	P	L
O	Z	X	T	W	K
H	F	E	V	Q	D
N	R	Y	A		

subtests that assess student knowledge of letter names and sounds. Further information on CORE assessments may be found at http://www.corelearn.com/.

ASSESSING PHONEMIC AWARENESS

Phonemic awareness, the understanding that individual speech sounds are blended together to form spoken words, is the foundation for understanding how phonics works. Many good tests are available for assessing phonemic awareness.

DIBELS Phonemic Awareness Subtests

DIBELS offers two assessments of student phonemic awareness: the Initial Sound Fluency (ISF) and the Phoneme Segmentation Fluency (PSF) subtests. To administer the ISF, the teacher or other examiner shows the student four pictures, names the pictures, and then asks the student to point to or say the picture that begins with the sound pronounced by the teacher. For example, the teacher shows pictures of a boat, horse, kite, and tiger, names the four pictures and asks, "Which one starts with /b/?" The teacher calculates the number of initial sounds the student can name in 1 minute and records the score. To administer the PSF, the teacher pronounces a list of words one at a time, asking the student to pronounce the individual phonemes from each word. For example, the teacher says the sounds *mud* and the student says /m/ /u/ /d/. The teacher calculates the total number of phonemes the student can pronounce in 1 minute and records the score. These tests are administered repeatedly so that student progress can be monitored and charted.

PALS Phonological Awareness Subtests

The PALS subtests for phonological awareness are Rhyme Awareness and Beginning Sound Awareness. The Rhyme Awareness subtest is administered in small groups and measures students' ability to identify which of three pictures rhymes with a target picture. Students who struggle with this task may be tested individually. The Beginning Sound Awareness subtest is similar to the Rhyme Awareness subtest; however, students are asked to identify which of three pictures has the same beginning sound as the target picture.

Other Phonemic Awareness Subtests

CORE's (2007) assessment handbook contains five phonemic awareness subtests: Phonological Awareness Screening, CORE Phoneme Deletion, CORE Phonological Segmentation, CORE Phoneme Segmentation, and CORE Spanish Phonemic Awareness.

The tests shown in Figure 10.4 were constructed based on a procedure described by Griffith and Olson (1992) to assess students' ability to recognize rhyming words, blend speech sounds, and segment speech sounds. It is important that these tests be administered in a relaxed, playful manner. Teachers may want to pronounce some of the words in sentences if needed.

ASSESSING PHONICS

Phonics, the process of blending letter sounds together to pronounce written words, is the beginning of actual reading. There are many ways to assess how well students know and can apply phonics skills. Some phonics tests assess students' ability to

Figure 10.4 Phonemic Awareness Tests

Name _____   **Date** _____

1. Rhyming Awareness

Use the two example pairs of words to explain the concept of rhyming to the student. Then pronounce each pair of words and ask the student if they rhyme. Place a checkmark in the blank beside each item the student answers correctly. The average kindergarten score is 15.

Example pairs: dog–log   mat–bed

   1. bag–tag   _____
   2. men–ball   _____
   3. same–tame   _____
   4. dime–time   _____
   5. pull–full   _____
   6. bug–mom   _____
   7. tap–him   _____
   8. sell–tell   _____
   9. bet–man   _____
10. big–pat   _____
11. seat–beat   _____
12. boat–float   _____
13. night–fight   _____
14. pot–hot   _____
15. hope–Sam   _____
16. dim–rim   _____
17. mud–sip   _____
18. put–rap   _____
19. dog–fog   _____
20. fun–bun   _____

Number Correct _____

Name _____   **Date** _____

2. Sound Blending Ability

Use the three example words to explain the concept of blending sounds to the student. Then tell the student that you will pronounce some more words sound-by-sound to see if he or she can determine the word. Place a checkmark in the blank beside each item the student answers correctly. The average kindergarten score is 20.

Example words: i–t   m–an   r–o–pe

   1. i–f   _____
   2. s–ee   _____
   3. h–ay   _____
   4. g–o   _____
   5. u–p   _____
   6. h–i   _____
   7. E–d   _____

Figure 10.4   Continued

8. o–dd   _____
9. y–ou   _____
10. a–t   _____
11. c–a–t   _____
12. m–an   _____
13. sh–i–p   _____
14. b–e–t   _____
15. s–oa–p   _____
16. f–un   _____
17. t–a–me   _____
18. s–eem   _____
19. r–i–pe   _____
20. h–um   _____
21. h–o–t   _____
22. h–as   _____
23. m–e–n   _____
24. h–it   _____
25. c–o–mb   _____
26. s–p–oo–n   _____
27. r–a–ke–s   _____
28. f–l–oa–t   _____
29. s–t–o–p   _____
30. b–r–ea–k   _____

Number Correct   _____

Name _____   **Date** _____

3. Sound Segmentation Ability

Use the three example words to demonstrate how spoken words can be broken apart into their individual sounds (phonemes). This is the opposite of exercise 2. Say each of the words and then invite the student to give the individual phonemes. Place a checkmark in the blank beside each item the student answers correctly. The average kindergarten score is 12.

Example words: pat (p–a–t)   he (h–e)   rope (r–o–pe)

1. my (m–y)   _____
2. hay (h–ay)   _____
3. bet (b–e–t)   _____
4. boat (b–oa–t)   _____
5. fix (f–i–x)   _____
6. mud (m–u–d)   _____
7. sap (s–a–p)   _____
8. peel (p–ee–l)   _____
9. rim (r–i–m)   _____
10. stake (s–t–a–ke)   _____
11. bent (b–e–n–t)   _____
12. shy (sh–y)   _____
13. drop (d–r–o–p)   _____

14. flew (f–l–ew) _____

15. lamb (l–a–mb) _____

16. weep (w–ee–p) _____

17. skit (s–k–i–t) _____

18. row (r–ow) _____

19. this (th–i–s) _____

20. frame (f–r–a–me) _____

21. left (l–e–f–t) _____

22. pie (p–ie) _____

Number Correct _____

The three tests in Figure 10.4 are adapted from the Yopp-Singer Phoneme Segmentation Test. The author, Hallie Kay Yopp, California State University–Fullerton, grants permission for this test to be reproduced. http://teams.lacoe.edu/reading/assessments/yopp.html

recognize and apply spelling patterns by having them read words in lists. Other assessments test students' phonics ability as students are reading words in meaningful passages.

DIBELS Nonsense Word Fluency Subtest

The DIBELS Nonsense Word Fluency (NWF) subtest uses lists of nonsense words such as *vig*, *pav*, and *et* to focus directly on a student's ability to blend letter sounds. This test is designed to be given to students from the last half of kindergarten to the middle of second grade. DIBELS provides over 20 alternate forms of the NWF so it can be used both for screening and progress monitoring. Benchmark scores are provided, K–2, so that teachers will be able to group students appropriately for instruction and provide needed support.

The test giver administers the DIBELS NWF subtest by giving the student a page of phonetically regular nonsense words, tells the student that these are make-believe words, models reading a nonsense word, reads a nonsense word together with the student, then invites the student to read the list of nonsense words. The teacher records the number of letter sounds and nonsense words the student pronounces correctly in 1 minute. Teachers can post their students' DIBELS NWF scores on the DIBELS website and immediately receive electronic reports of each student's progress along with a rank ordering of the whole class.

CORE Phonics Survey

The CORE Phonics Survey (CORE, 2007) is a very popular phonics assessment that can be used both for screening and diagnosis. The CORE Phonics Survey first assesses student knowledge of alphabet letter names and sounds, then assesses student ability to use phonics using sequential lists of regular words and pseudo-words (nonsense words) that contain major spelling patterns. For example, after assessing alphabet knowledge, the CORE Phonics Survey assesses students' ability to recognize and apply consonant spelling patterns including the consonant–vowel–consonant pattern (*sip*, *kem*), consonant digraphs (*when*, *shom*), and consonant blends (*trap*, *stig*). Then the CORE Phonics Survey assesses student ability with vowel spelling patterns including final silent *e* (*tape*, *loe*), vowel teams (*paid*, *joad*), *r*-controlled vowels (*bark*, *gorf*), and variant vowels (*few*, *zoy*). The final two CORE Phonics Survey subtests assess student ability to read lists of multisyllable words containing spelling patterns, and a dictation/spelling subtest that assesses student ability to write initial and final consonants and spell entire words from lists of words dictated by the teacher. There is also a Spanish-language version of the CORE Phonics Survey.

Many teachers use the CORE Phonics Survey for diagnosis and instructional planning. For example, students who score low on a screening assessment will be given the CORE Phonics Survey as a diagnostic assessment. The CORE Phonics Survey allows a teacher to pinpoint exactly which spelling patterns a student knows and doesn't know. With this information, teachers can form small student groups for instruction by combining students that need to be taught the same spelling patterns.

Spelling Inventory

Another way to gain insight into students' phonics ability is by examining their ability to spell. The Primary Spelling Inventory and the Elementary Spelling Inventory are fully explained in *Words Their Way* (Bear, Invernizzi, Templeton, & Johnston, 2008). Like the CORE Phonics Survey, these spelling inventories assesses students' ability to apply phonics knowledge and spelling patterns through sequential stages. Decades of research looking at error patterns in students' spellings have established five stages of spelling development. These stages are commonly known as Emergent, Letter-Name Alphabetic, Within-Word Pattern, Syllables and Affixes, and Derivational Relations (Bear et al., 2008). In the Emergent stage of spelling, students begin by using scribbles and letterlike forms and progress to the use of prominent consonants to represent words. In the Letter-Name Alphabetic stage, students use the names of the letters as a clue to their sounds as they listen carefully to words and try to break them down into their constituent sounds. In the Within-Word Pattern stage, students learn the patterns or chunks of letters that comprise various sounds. In the Syllables and Affixes stage, students are learning about how syllables are combined and the changes that happen in words when prefixes and suffixes are added to words. Finally, in the Derivational Relations stage, students are learning about how words share common Greek and Latin roots and how they affect much of English spelling.

To administer these spelling inventories, the teacher dictates a list of 25 to 26 words containing spelling patterns and invites the student to spell them. The teacher then uses the accompanying Feature Guide to record the sounds and spelling patterns the student spelled correctly and place the student at the appropriate stage of spelling development.

Through ongoing assessment, the teacher can determine whether a student is ready to move on to a new stage of word study. The Primary or Elementary Spelling Inventory can be given three or four times a year to document student growth and determine if students need to be placed in different instructional groups or if the instructional focus needs to change.

PALS Phonics Tests

The Phonological Awareness Literacy Screening (PALS) program provides phonics assessments using graded words lists and passages. To administer the PALS Word Recognition in Isolation subtest the teacher invites the student to read a list of words and marks on the scoring sheet whether the student read each word correctly or incorrectly. A score of 15 or more words correct suggests that the student can read that list of words at his or her instructional level.

The PALS Passage Reading test can also be used to obtain a measure of a student's ability with phonics. Using a series of graded passages, the teacher invites the student to read a passage aloud, marks and totals the student's oral reading errors on the scoring sheet, and uses the total number of errors to determine whether the students can read that passage at the independent, instructional, or frustration level. The scoring sheet also includes a 3-point fluency rating scale that assesses the student's oral reading accuracy, expression, and reading rate.

As with DIBELS, teachers can send their PALS data via computer to PALS headquarters and instantly receive back a variety of useful data summaries. For example, teachers can receive PALS class reports that list which students scored high on the subtests and those students who scored low and will need supplemental instruction. PALS class reports also group students by reading level and knowledge of spelling/phonics concepts. PALS also produces Student Summary Reports that show each student's performance on PALS subtests compared to grade-level benchmarks. Student History Reports provide individual students graphs that plot each student's growth over time on each PALS subtest. PALS also provides Back-to-School reports for each class based on data gathered the previous spring and Year-End Reports that provide an outcome measure of each student's reading achievement.

Informal Reading Inventories

An informal reading inventory (IRI) is an individually administered commercially published reading test composed of two parts: (1) word lists or screening sentences at each grade level for estimating a student's sight word recognition level; and (2) reading passages at each grade level for estimating a student's oral reading accuracy, reading comprehension, and listening comprehension levels. Many classroom teachers use an IRI as a diagnostic assessment with those students identified by a screening assessment as likely to need extra instructional support in reading. Data from an IRI can be used to estimate a student's reading level, identify a student's reading strengths and weaknesses, match students with appropriate reading materials, and group students for instruction.

Informal reading inventories are designed to help a teacher classify a student's reading levels into one or more of the following three reading levels: independent, instructional, and frustration (see Table 10.2).

Administering and Scoring the IRI Word Lists

Begin IRI testing by asking the student to read a word list that is 1 year below grade level and marking and totaling the student's errors on a scoring sheet. The scoring sheet contains guidelines that will place the student at independent, instructional, or frustration level for that graded word list. If the student scores at the independent or instructional level on a word list, then move on to the next higher grade-level list. Continue moving up through the grade-level lists until the student reaches the

Table 10.2   Independent, Instructional, and Frustration Reading Levels

Reading Levels	Description	Performance Ranges
Independent	A student can read text at this level successfully and independently.	95%–100% oral reading accuracy
	The text is too easy for instruction.	Approximately 90% reading comprehension
Instructional	A student can read text at this level successfully, with teacher support.	90%–94% oral reading accuracy
	The text is just right for instruction.	Approximately 75% reading comprehension
Frustration	A student cannot read text at this level.	Below 90% oral reading accuracy
	The text is too hard for instruction.	Below 50% reading comprehension

frustration level. The highest grade level at which a student scores at the instructional level is the level at which the teacher should provide reading texts for instruction. A sample IRI word list appears in Figure 10.5.

Administering and Scoring the IRI Reading Passages

Once the student's instructional level is determined from the word lists, give the student a reading passage that is one level below. When giving a student an IRI passage to read, remind the student to pay attention to the content of the passage. As the student reads the passages aloud, mark the student's oral reading errors on the scoring sheet. Although scoring systems vary somewhat from one published IRI to another, IRIs usually have teachers mark the student's substitutions, omissions, insertions, teacher assists, repetitions, and self-corrections (see Figure 10.6 for a list of widely used informal reading inventories). After the student has finished reading the passage aloud, compare the total number of student miscues to the scoring guide. If the student is reading at the independent or instructional level, repeat the process with the next grade-level passage until the student scores at frustration level. The highest level at which the student scores at the instructional level on the passages is considered his or her instructional level, the level at which reading instruction should be provided.

Running Records

Teachers commonly use running records (Clay, 2000, 2002) to determine a student's reading level by calculating the percentage of words the student reads correctly. Teachers can also use running records to identify a student's reading strengths and

Figure 10.5 Sample Marked IRI Page

	mis-pronun.	sub-stitute	inser-tions	tchr. assist	omis-sions	Error Totals	Self-Correct.	(M) Meaning	(S) Syntax	(V) Visual
The Pig and the Snake										
One day Mr. Pig was walking to his^			1					1	1	
town. He saw a big hole in the										
rope snakes (SC) road. A big snake was in the		1							1	‖
hole. "Help me," said the snake,										
"and I will be your friend." "No, no," (SC)							1			1
said Mr. Pig. "If I help you get										
of bit (SC) out you will bite me. You are			1				1		1	1
a snake!" The snake cried and										
cried. So Mr. Pig pulled the										
snake out of the hole.										
Then the snake said, "Now I am										
bit (SC) going to bite you, Mr. Pig."							1			1
"How can you bite me after										
I helped you out of the hole?"										
said Mr. Pig. The snake said.//										
"You knew I was a snake										
when you pulled me out!"										
TOTALS		1	2				3	1	3	5

ERROR TYPES — ERROR ANALYSIS

Summary of Reading Behaviors (Strengths and Needs)

Note. From *Reading Inventory for the Classroom*, 4th ed., by E. S. Flynt and R. B. Cooter, p. 68, copyright 2001 by Merrill/Prentice Hall. Upper Saddle River, NJ:Merrill/ Prentice Hall. Reprinted by permission.

Figure 10.6   Popular Informal Reading Inventories

Analytical Reading Inventory, 8th ed. Upper Saddle River, NJ: Merrill/Prentice Hall, 2006.
Basic Reading Inventory, 9th ed. (BRI-8). Dubuque, IA: Kendall/Hunt, 2005.
Critical Reading Inventory: Assessing Students' Reading and Thinking, 2nd ed. Upper Saddle River, NJ: Merrill/Prentice Hall, 2007.
Flynt–Cooter Reading Inventory for the Classroom, 5th ed. Upper Saddle River, NJ: Merrill/Prentice Hall, 2007.
Qualitative Reading Inventory IV. New York: Longman, 2005.

weaknesses by analyzing patterns in the words the student misread. Running records are popular because they are quick to administer and they can be used on the spot with any text a student is reading.

Using Running Records to Determine Student Reading Level

To take a running record, the teacher listens to a student read an unfamiliar book aloud while recording the student's errors on a running record scoring sheet. After the student has read, the teacher calculates an accuracy rate (words correctly read divided by total words) and a self-correction ratio (self-corrected errors divided by self-corrections plus errors).

Accuracy

$$\frac{\text{Number of words correct} \times 100}{\text{Total words}}$$

$$\frac{90 \times 100}{100} = 90\%$$

Self-Correction Ratio

$$\frac{\text{Self-corrections}}{\text{Errors} + \text{self-corrections}}$$

$$\frac{15 + 5}{5} = \text{Ratio } 1{:}4$$

The accuracy rate indicates whether the text was at the student's independent reading level (95%–100%), instructional level (90%–94%), or frustration level (below 90%).

The self-correction ratio is revealing because if a student corrects one out of every two or three errors (a ratio of 1:2 or 1:3), this suggests he or she is self-monitoring—that is, she is monitoring her own reading to ensure that it makes sense. If the self-correction ratio is only one self-correction for every 5 errors, this shows that she isn't paying much attention to whether or not what she reads sounds right or makes sense. Figure 10.7 lists guidelines for taking a running record, and Figure 10.8 shows a sample running record.

Using Running Records to Analyze Student Reading Strategies

A student's oral reading errors can be further analyzed to determine to what extent he or she was relying on meaning clues (context), language structure clues (syntax), or visual clues (phonics). For example, if the student says "bike" but the text says "bicycle," the error is consistent with the meaning of the text. Similarly, if student reads "little" when the text says "small," meaning is preserved. In this case, the student needs to be coached to remember to use visual clues as well as meaning clues—to cross-check using at least two sources of information.

Figure 10.7   Guidelines for Taking a Running Record

- The sample text should contain at least 100 words (except in lowest levels of texts).
- The text should be unfamiliar or one that the child has read only once before.
- Use check marks for each correct word and record each attempt in full.
- Use the results of a running record to guide text selection for students' individual and group reading lessons.
- Do not use running records to label the child (Colin is a level G reader).
- Words correct divided by total words equals reading accuracy.
- 95% accuracy and above is an easy text at the child's independent reading level.
- 90%–94% accuracy is a "just right" text at the child's instructional reading level.
- 89% accuracy or less is a hard text at the child's frustration reading level.
- Self-corrections do not count as errors.
- If a line or sentence is skipped, each word counts as an error.
- Repeated errors are counted each time; for example, if the child says "get" instead of "grow" repeatedly (Clay, 2002).
- Errors with proper names are counted only the first time (Clay, 2002).
- If the child gets confused in the text, it is okay to say "Try that again," and point to the place where the child should begin reading again. This counts as one error. Code this TTA for "try that again."
- If the child asks you for the word, it is okay to say the word. This counts as one error. Code this as A for ask and T for told.
- Nonquantifiable behaviors should be noted (e.g., read word-by-word, stopped to comment on ideas in the text, checked picture, often appealed for help with eyes, read in monotone, etc.).
- One teacher reading another teacher's running record should be able to see exactly what the child did and said.
- Finish the running record with a short statement about where you think the child is as a reader (e.g., "Tina read with confidence and seems ready to move on to more difficult texts" or "Ahmad uses initial sounds when decoding unknown words").

Teacher–Student Reading Conferences

Teachers can learn a great deal about students' reading skills and strategies through teacher-student reading conferences. A teacher-student reading conference usually takes place during independent reading time and typically lasts from 3 to 7 minutes, depending on the needs of the student.

Many teachers use teacher-student reading conferences to assess three aspects of a student's reading: attitude toward reading, phonics and fluency, and comprehension. A typical conference follows this format:

1. The teacher invites the student to come to the teacher's desk and bring along the book he or she is reading. The teacher notes the book's title and grade level (if applicable) along with the date of the conference.

2. The teacher asks the student attitude and interest questions such as, "Why did you choose this book?" "Have you read other books like this?" "What are some of your favorite books that you've read recently?" "How do you feel about reading in general?" As this discussion occurs, the teacher takes notes for later use in recommending other books of interest or genre to the student.

Figure 10.8 Sample Running Record

Running Record Sheet

Child's Name: Emmorie Hughes   Grade: 1   Date: October 17

Teacher: Sylvia Read   Text Level: P

Reading Accuracy %: 87   Self-Correction Rate: 1:3

Reading Level: _____ Independent (95-100%)   _____ Instructional (90-94%)   _X_ Frustration (below 90%)

page #	Title: I Can't Said the Ant						E	SC	E M S V	SC M S V
1	√	√	talking ^sc √ taking	√			1			v
	√	√	√	a such	loud a	crash clatter	3		ms ms ms	
	√	raced rushed	√	√	√		1		msv	
	So ^sc To	√	√	√	√	√	1			msv
	Then There	√	√	√			1		ms	
	√	√	√	pot pouring	√		1		s	
	- ^sc was	√	crashed ^sc cracked	√				2		msv sv
	√	- a	√	√			1		ms	

<u>Analysis of Errors and Self-Corrections</u>: Emmorie makes very good use of context and sentence structure. Analysis of her oral reading errors suggests that she has good command of consonants and initial consonant blends. She seems to recognize word beginnings accurately, but then substitute other letter-sounds in the middle and endings of words. I would suggest helping Emmorie achieve better balance in her oral reading by paying more attention to print cues rather than context as she does now. This text is currently above her instructional level, so I would suggest trying her out on a level M text to see if she reads more successfully.

3. The teacher asks the student to read aloud a paragraph or page from the book. During this time the teacher takes notes on words the student struggles with and also on the student's overall oral reading fluency. The teacher may look for patterns of oral reading errors such as spelling patterns that occur in multiple missed words, high-frequency words that will need to be taught, or the manner in which the student approaches an unfamiliar word.

4. The teacher asks the student to retell the book's content to get a measure of his or her reading comprehension. This part of the conference is described in a subsequent section of this chapter.

Many teachers record notes from their teacher–student conferences on Teacher–Student Conference Record pages (Figure 10.9). Each page can hold notes from three separate conferences with each student. Multiple pages for each student are kept in alphabetical order in a three-ring binder. Teachers frequently review these notes to look for evidence of reading progress and reading instruction areas that need attention. These notes are also helpful during parent–teacher conferences as a source of data in explaining a student's reading ability to the parents.

ASSESSING FLUENCY

Fluency is generally defined as reading accurately, quickly, and with good expression. Just because some students may be able to recognize and blend spelling patterns accurately does not guarantee they will be able to read fluently. Much of fluency assessment these days focuses on accuracy and rate. Teachers also need to monitor how expressively their students read.

DIBELS Oral Reading Fluency Subtest

Perhaps the most well-known DIBELS subtest is the Oral Reading Fluency (ORF) subtest (see Figure 10.10). To administer the ORF, the teacher gives a student a grade-level passage to read aloud, sets a timer, and counts the number of words the student reads in 1 minute. The teacher also notes the student's oral reading errors on a teacher scoring sheet. The teacher subtracts the number of errors the student made from the number of total words the student read in 1 minute to come up with the number of words the student read correctly per minute (WCPM). This single WCPM score is a measure of both rate and accuracy, but not expression. As with all DIBELS subtests, the ORF is administered frequently throughout the year and increases in student performance are graphed so that the rate of improvement can be monitored for instructional planning.

DIBELS provides benchmark scores for the ORF so that teachers may determine which of their students are at or above grade level (benchmark), slightly below grade level (strategic), or well below grade level (intensive). Table 10.3 shows DIBELS WCPM benchmark scores for the ORF subtest.

Oral Reading Fluency Scale

In addition to assessing the rate and accuracy components of oral reading fluency with measures such as the DIBELS ORF, it is also important that teachers be able to assess the expressiveness of their students' oral reading. The Oral Reading Fluency Scale (Pinnell et al., 1995) is a four-point rating scale that measures expressiveness based on

Figure 10.9   Teacher–Student Reading Conference Record

Student Name _____

Teacher–Student Reading Conference Record

(attitude * fluency * comprehension)

Date _____   Title _____

Comments _____

_____

_____

_____

_____

_____

Words misread _____

Date _____   Title _____

Comments _____

_____

_____

_____

_____

_____

Words misread _____

Date _____   Title _____

Comments _____

_____

_____

_____

_____

Words misread _____

phrasing, expressive interpretation, and rate. The Oral Reading Fluency Scale (Figure 10.11) is designed to be used with narrative text because narration and dialogue work well to elicit expressive oral reading. To administer the Oral Reading Fluency Scale, the teacher gives a passage to the student and instructs him or her to read it aloud as if reading it to someone who has not heard it before. The test developers recommend using a passage that the student has previously read silently. As the student reads, the teacher compares the student's oral rendition to the Oral Reading Fluency Scale descriptors and assigns a score of 1 to 4. A close examination of a student's score can provide the teacher with information about which aspects of oral reading fluency students can do well and which aspects need additional instruction. The Oral Reading Fluency Scale can be found at http://nces.ed.gov/pubs95/web/95762.asp

Figure 10.10   Sample DIBELS Student Report

Name: G, JERAME
ID: 15288
Class: Adams 3rd #1
Grade: Third
Year: 2001-2002
School: Adams
District: Test District

Dynamic Indicators of Basic Early Literacy Skills
Student Report

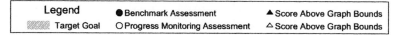

PHONEMIC AWARENESS

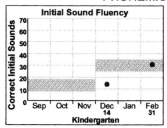

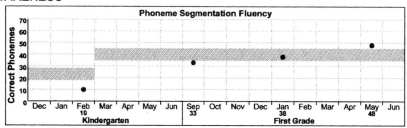

ALPHABETIC PRINCIPLE

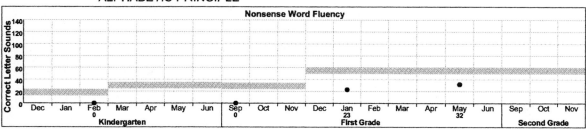

VOCABULARY

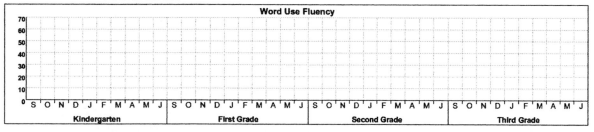

FLUENCY AND COMPREHENSION

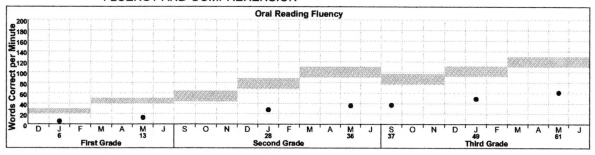

Note. © 2000–2004 DIBELS Data System, http://dibels.uoregon.edu. Reprinted with permission.

04/09/2004, 9

Table 10.3   DIBELS Oral Reading Fluency Benchmark Scores (6th Ed.)

	Beginning of Year	Middle of Year	End of Year
First Grade			
Low risk		>20	<40
Some risk		8–20	20–40
At risk		<8	<20
Second Grade			
Low risk	>44	>68	>90
Some risk	26–44	52–68	70–90
At risk	<26	<52	<70
Third Grade			
Low risk	>77	>92	>110
Some risk	53–77	67–92	80–110
At risk	<53	<67	<80
Fourth Grade			
Low risk	>93	>105	>118
Some risk	71–93	83–105	96–118
At risk	<71	<83	<96
Fifth Grade			
Low risk	>104	>115	>124
Some risk	81–104	94–115	103–124
At risk	<81	<94	<103
Sixth Grade			
Low risk	>109	>120	>125
Some risk	83–109	99–120	104–125
At risk	<83	<99	<104

Compiled from data retrieved from http://dibels.uoregon.edu/benchmarkgoals.pdf

Assessing Vocabulary and Oral Language

Assessing lower-level reading skills such as alphabet knowledge, phonemic awareness, phonics, and fluency is relatively easy. It is not hard to accurately count the number of letter names a student knows or how many words per minute a student can
read correctly. Assessing higher-level reading skills such as vocabulary and comprehension is much more difficult because it is harder to measure growth in a student's
knowledge of word meanings or ability to use comprehension strategies. This section
describes assessment of vocabulary and oral language together because the two con-
structs overlap to such a large degree. Two common oral language assessments are

Figure 10.11 Oral Reading Fluency Scale

4. Reads primarily in larger, meaningful phrase groups. Although some regressions, repetitions, and deviations from the text may be present, these do not appear to detract from the overall structure of the story. Preservation of the author's syntax is consistent. Some or most of the story is read with expressive interpretation. Reads at an appropriate rate.

3. Reads primarily in three- and four-word phrase groups. Some smaller groupings may be present. However, the majority of phrasing seems appropriate and preserves the syntax of the author. Little or no expressive interpretation is present. Reader attempts to read expressively and some of the story is read with expression. Generally reads at an appropriate rate.

2. Reads primarily in two-word phrase groups with some three- and four-word groupings. Some word-by-word reading may be present. Word groupings may seem awkward and unrelated to the larger context of the sentence or passage. A small portion of the text is read with expressive interpretation. Reads significant sections of the text excessively slowly or fast.

1. Reads primarily word-by-word. Occasional two- or three-word phrases may occur—but these are infrequent and/or they do not preserve meaningful syntax. Lacks expressive interpretation. Reads text excessively slowly. A score of 1 should also be given to a student who reads with excessive speed, ignoring punctuation and other phrase boundaries, and reads with little or no expression.

Source: Adapted from *Listening to Children Read Aloud: Oral Fluency*, by G. S. Pinnell, J. J. Pikulski, K. K. Wixson, J. R. Campbell, P. B. Gough, & A. S. Beatty, 1995, Washington, DC: U.S. Department of Education, National Center for Education Statistics. Available at http://nces.ed.gov/pubs95/web/95762.asp.

the Student Oral Language Observation Matrix (SOLOM; Reutzel & Cooter, 2008) and the Critchlow Verbal Language Scale (CORE, 2007).

The Student Oral Language Observation Matrix

The Student Oral Language Observation Matrix (SOLOM) is a general assessment of student oral language development designed for use with English language learners (Figure 10.12). The SOLOM measures student language development with 5-point scales in five language areas: comprehension, fluency, vocabulary, pronunciation, and grammar. For example, a student whose very limited vocabulary makes conversation nearly impossible would earn a score of 1 on the vocabulary scale. A student who frequently uses incorrect words would earn a vocabulary score of 3, and a student who is fully capable of using English vocabulary and idioms would earn a vocabulary score of 5.

Critchlow Verbal Language Scale

The Critchlow Verbal Language Scale (CORE, 2007) is also an oral language assessment that focuses on vocabulary knowledge. The scale is a list of vocabulary words that have very clear opposite words (*large–small*; *hot–cold*). The teacher pronounces each word from the list and records whether or not the student is able to generate an opposite word. The Critchlow Verbal Language Scale includes scoring guidelines that help identify a student's approximate vocabulary grade level. There is also a Spanish-language version of the Critchlow Verbal Language Scale.

Figure 10.12 Student Oral Language Observation Matrix

Name _____   Date _____

	1	2	3	4	5
Comprehension	Cannot understand simple conversation	Only understands conversational language spoken slowly and includes repetitions	Can understand most conversations if the speech is slow	Understands almost everything at normal speed, but may require some repetitions	Understands class conversations and discussions without difficulty
Fluency	Speech is halting and fragmentary; makes it extremely difficult to initiate a conversation	Usually silent or hesitant due to language limitations	Often the speech is interrupted while the student searches for the right word or expression	Generally fluent in class discussions, but may lapse sometimes into word searches	Fluent and effortless conversations
Vocabulary	Very little vocabulary makes conversation nearly impossible	Limited vocabulary and often misuses words	Frequently uses incorrect words, and speech is limited by insufficient vocabulary	Sometimes uses inappropriate terms or must rephrase due to limited vocabulary	Fully capable of using vocabulary and idioms
Pronunciation	Difficult to understand due to severe pronunciation problems	Pronunciation problems make it necessary for student to repeat himself or herself often	Pronunciation problems cause listeners to have to listen closely; some misunderstandings	Always intelligible, but may have heavy accent or inappropriate intonation problems	Normal pronunciation and intonation
Grammar	Acute problems with grammar and syntax making speech nearly unintelligible	Grammar and syntax problems often force student to repeat himself or herself and stick to simple/familiar patterns	Frequent errors with grammar and syntax that sometimes alters meanings	Sometimes makes grammar or syntax errors	Appropriate grammar and syntax usage

Stages of Development

Stage 1: Score of 5–11 = Not proficient in English

Stage 2: Score of 12–18 = Limited English Proficiency (Emergent)

Stage 3: Score of 19–24 = Limited English Proficient (Developing)

Stage 4: Score of 25 = Fully English Proficient

Source: Reutzel, D. Ray; Cooter, Robert B., *Strategies for reading assessment and instruction: Helping every child succeed,* 3rd Edition, © 2007, p. 119. Adapted by permission of Pearson Education, Inc., Upper Saddle River, NJ.

Although there are a number of ways to assess students' levels of comprehension, such as recording how well they can fill in a graphic organizer after reading or have them write a brief summary of a reading passage, most reading comprehension assessment will take one of two forms: asking students to respond to comprehension questions or asking students to retell what they have read. For informal instruction-based assessment, teachers can generate comprehension questions on their own. For more formal assessment purposes, teachers can use published reading passages and questions such as an informal reading inventory. When listening to students retell a passage, teachers may be content to get an overall sense of a student's comprehension of a passage or they may choose to probe a student's retelling with follow-up questions looking for the student's grasp of specific information.

Assessing Reading Comprehension Through Questioning

Many teachers like to assess students' reading comprehension informally during instruction. There are several ways for teachers to generate questions from students' instructional reading materials. Teachers may make notes about the completeness and quality of students' responses. At other times, teachers may want to assess comprehension more formally with a preexisting assessment that might be used to establish the grade level of a student's reading ability or to look more diagnostically at aspects of a student's comprehension including student knowledge of critical vocabulary, ability to make inferences, or ability to apply comprehension strategies.

Teacher-Generated Questions

One simple way for teachers to generate comprehensions is to use elements of text structure. With narrative text teachers generate questions about a story's setting, major characters, the central problem of the story if there is one, important events, the story's conclusion, and the story's theme. For example, in the story *Little Red Riding Hood*, a teacher might ask questions such as:

Setting	Where does this story take place?
	Is it long ago, in our time, or in the future?
Characters	Who are the main characters?
	What can you tell me about _____?
Problem	What is _____ trying to do?
	What problem is _____ facing?
Events	How did this story begin?
	What happened next? and after that?
	What other important things happened in the story ?
	How did the story end?
Theme	What is a lesson we can learn from this story?

If the reading passage is an informational text, teacher-generated questions should focus on main ideas and details. For example, consider the following information passage and the accompanying questions:

> *There are many kinds of motorcycles. Some are made for riding on dirt trails. These motorcycles, often called dirtbikes, have knobby tires to*

avoid slipping on loose dirt and large shock absorbers for riding over rocks and bumps. Some motorcycles, called touring motorcycles, are made for driving long distances on interstate highways. These motorcycles have very large motors for driving at high speeds for long periods of time, windshields to protect the riders from the wind and bugs, and saddlebags to hold the riders' clothing and personal supplies for long trips. Other motorcycles, called cruisers, are made for shorter rides around town or on local highways. Cruisers also have large motors and are often very loud.

Main idea   What is the main idea of this passage?

What are some different kinds of motorcycles?

Details   What does this passage tell us about dirtbikes?

Why do dirtbikes have knobby tires?

Published Questions

Some comprehension assessments consist of reading passages with related comprehension questions for students to answer. For example, most commercially published informal reading inventories include six to eight comprehension questions after each reading passage. Teachers ask the comprehension questions and keep track of the number of questions the student answers correctly. Teachers can also keep track of the number of literal-level and inferential-level questions the student answers correctly to get a sense of how well the student is able to comprehend information that is explicit in the text and how well he or she can make inferences and "read between the lines." Informal reading inventories include a scoring guide for each passage to help determine if the student's reading comprehension level is independent, instructional, or frustration level for that passage. Other examples of published comprehension questions are the comprehension questions contained in basal reading program unit tests, the PALS Comprehension subtest that measures students' comprehension through multiple-choice questions provided after the Reading in Context passages, and the comprehension subtests of nationally standardized tests such as the Gates-MacGinitie Reading Test and the Iowa Test of Basic Skills.

Assessing Reading Comprehension with Retellings

An alternative to using questions for comprehension assessment is to invite students to retell the content of reading passages. Begin by having the student retell with a general prompt such as "Tell me what this is about." When the student finishes the initial retelling, ask "What else can you remember?" When it seems that the student has exhausted his or her memory, begin asking specific probing questions to cover information the student did not include in the retelling. If the passage is narrative, probing questions can be based on story grammar elements. For example, a question to probe the student's knowledge of a major event would be "How did Little Red Riding Hood and Grandma escape from the Big Bad Wolf?" Teachers should also include inferential-level probing questions of narrative texts such as "Why do you think the Big Bad Wolf didn't eat Little Red Riding Hood when he first met her in the woods?" If the text is informational, probing questions should focus on main ideas and details the student omitted from the retelling. For example, "What did this passage tell us about touring motorcycles?"

When scoring a retelling, teachers can make notes about the information that a student includes in the initial retelling and also the additional information the student recalls based on the probing questions. A general rule of thumb is that when a student can retell approximately 90% of the important information from a passage that indicates that the student comprehends that passage at the independent level (easy reading). Approximately 75% recall suggests that the student comprehends the passage at the instructional level (just right for instruction). Less than 50% recall suggests that the passage is at the student's frustration level (too hard).

ASSESSING WRITING

There are three levels of writing assessment that occur in schools. Large-scale, formal assessment happens at a district or state level and involves students in third grade or above. The second level is classroom assessment that looks at the progress of an individual student over time using writing samples that represent both the best possible work a student can do and pieces that represent a student's daily work. The third level is personal assessment or self-assessment for which students keep portfolios and reflect on their own work (Spandel, 2007).

With young writers in kindergarten through third grade, there are rubrics that can be used to look at children's writing trait by trait. Rubrics for young children focus on what students can do, not what they can't do. They are intended for classroom use only, not for large-scale assessment. Rubrics can also facilitate students' self-assessment.

Six traits is the most commonly used set of rubrics. The six traits are ideas, organization, voice, word choice, sentence fluency, and conventions (Spandel, 2007). When students learn about these traits and think about them as they are writing, they become better able to see and describe what good writing is. Note that conventions is only *one* trait; in the past, correctness of spelling and punctuation have been overemphasized. Not only does an overemphasis on conventions vastly oversimplify the nature of good writing, it also sends a message to students that correctness is all that counts. Students who struggle with conventions, but who have wonderful ideas, interesting word choice, or fabulous voice, begin to think of themselves as poor writers and often learn to dislike and avoid writing. When teachers focus on all of the traits and help children to see what they do well as well as ways they could improve their writing, then assessment becomes a way to teach rather than just a way to label students' work with a grade or score.

ASSESSING STUDENTS' READING ATTITUDES AND INTERESTS

When students enjoy reading, they tend to read a lot. When students read a lot, they tend to become better readers. The National Assessment of Educational Progress (NAEP, 2005), has documented year after year that those students who read most read best. Along with assessing students' ability to decode words and comprehend meaningful texts, it is important that teachers also assess students' reading attitudes and interests. As teachers come to know how students feel about reading and what kind of reading materials students enjoy, they will be better able to adjust instruction and provide reading materials and activities that increase students' appreciation of reading and broaden their reading experiences. Teachers can assess students' reading attitudes and interests several ways, including observing student reading behaviors and using attitude and interest inventories.

Observing Students' Reading Behaviors

Perhaps the most basic way to assess students' reading attitudes and interests is to observe their behaviors with books and reading classroom reading activities. Teachers can use the following indicators to develop a reading attitudes checklist for each student that can be completed and included in the student's assessment folder or portfolio.

- Demonstrates eagerness to read.
- Views reading as a source of pleasure and relaxation.
- Views reading as a source of information.
- Shares favorite reading materials with others.
- Actively participates in reading lessons.
- Reads independently for age-appropriate lengths of time.
- Chooses appropriate-level independent reading material.
- Chooses to read a wide variety of genres.
- Chooses to read informational books.
- Persists during challenging reading tasks.

Figure 10.13   Reading Attitude Interview

Name _____   Date _____

Attitude

Tell me how you feel about reading at school.

Tell me how you feel about reading at home (times, materials).

Tell me about yourself as a reader. How good are you at reading?

Do you ever talk about books with your friends?

What kind of books do you like to read? Do you have any favorite genres, authors, or topics?

What are some books you have read lately?

How do you choose books to read?

What are some things you have learned from reading?

Fluency

How well can you read words?

How do you feel about reading out loud in class?

What do you do when you come to a tricky word?

Comprehension

What do you do to help yourself understand what you read (before, during, and after reading)?

How are stories different from informational books?

Do you ever connect what you read to yourself, other books, or other things?

How can you tell if a book is factual or fiction?

What do you do when something that you read doesn't make sense to you?

Summary Comments

Is there anything else you want to tell me about your reading?

Using Attitude and Interest Inventories

Along with observing students' reading behaviors, teachers can use more formal instruments to assess students' reading attitudes and interests. The Reading Attitude Interview is a collection of interview questions that teachers commonly ask students during teacher–student reading conferences. In addition to finding out about students' attitudes and interests, the Reading Attitude Interview (Figure 10.13) also probes students' awareness of their own use of reading strategies. The assessment data generated from this interview instrument will help teachers know which aspects of word identification, fluency, and comprehension students need more help with.

A very popular assessment instrument for measuring students' attitudes toward reading is the Elementary Reading Attitude Survey (ERAS; McKenna & Kear, 1990) based on the comic strip character Garfield. The ERAS consists of 20 questions that measure students' attitudes toward both recreational reading (i.e., How do you feel about reading for fun at home?) and academic reading (i.e., How do you feel about reading your school books?). Above each question are four Garfield images ranging from very happy to very unhappy. The teacher reads each question aloud to the students as they follow along on their printed copies. The students then mark the Garfield image that most closely reflects their attitude toward that question. The teacher scores the student responses creating individual and class scores for recreational reading, academic reading, and total reading. The ERAS was piloted nationally with 18,000 students to establish its reliability and validity.

Teachers can modify the ERAS to also measure students' attitudes toward content and instruction in other subject areas. Do this by photocopying one page of the ERAS questions and images, to cover the questions with correct tape, and then compose and type in new questions. For example, before teaching a science unit on the water cycle, a teacher created a modified ERAS using the Garfield images and questions such as:

1. *How much do you like learning about science in school?*
2. *How much do you like reading books about science?*
3. *How much do you like doing science projects in school?*
4. *How much do you like learning about oceans, lakes, and rivers?*
5. *How excited are you about evaporation?*

FOR ENGLISH LANGUAGE LEARNERS

Learning About ELL Students

The term *ELL* suggests that English language learners are a homogeneous group, when in fact they come with vastly varying degrees of educational backgrounds and familiarity with English and other languages. An understanding of ELL students' literacy and language backgrounds is necessary for teachers to make informed decisions about instructional placements, materials, and activities. Lenski, Ehlers-Zavala, Daniel, & Sun-Irminger (2006) suggest the following questions as a guide to gathering important background information and creating profiles of ELL students. Data can be gathered through observing students and interviewing them, their parents, and others who know them well.

- What languages does the student know and use?
- What types of alphabets does the student know?
- What is the student's cultural background?
- What does the student enjoy doing out of school?
- What has the student said or what stories has the student told?
- What has happened to the student recently that has been important or of great interest?
- What kinds of stories does the student enjoy?
- What activities is the student involved in?
- What is the student's family situation?
- Has the student left anyone behind in his or her home country?
- Who are the student's best friends?
- What personal belongings does the student bring to class or wear? (p. 27)

She used her modified ERAS as a pre/post assessment to measure changes in her students' attitudes toward science learning after participating in her literature-based science unit.

 ## CONCLUDING THOUGHTS

All classroom teachers should be fully committed to the goal of helping every student read at or above grade level by the end of each school year. Because many students begin the school year already reading below grade level or don't make adequate progress to meet that goal, classroom teachers must be equipped to determine the source of students' reading problems. Some students will have difficulty recognizing common spelling patterns and will experience decoding problems. Other students may do fine with decoding, but lack the background knowledge and vocabulary to comprehend the meaning of the words they decode. Teachers must be able to screen students to determine which ones are at risk of developing reading problems and to diagnose the source of those problems. Ongoing progress monitoring tells teachers which students are benefiting from classroom reading instruction and are making adequate progress, and which students need additional instructional interventions.

Teachers need not undertake this responsibility alone. Grade-level teaching teams can collaboratively review student assessment data and plan instruction to meet students' needs. School-level resource personnel can also be valuable resources for assisting with assessment and suggesting instructional strategies and interventions. As educators work and plan together with vision and persistence, real differences will be realized in student reading achievement.

The assessments described in this chapter are just a sampling of what is available to teachers for screening students for reading problems, diagnosing reading strengths and needs, monitoring progress, and measuring outcomes. The Southwest Educational Development Laboratory (SEDL) has a website that lists many reading norm-referenced and criterion-referenced assessments in both English and Spanish. It is a wonderful resource for teachers and others who are looking for reading assessments. The SEDL website may be found at http://www.sedl.org/reading/rad/list.html.

 ## SUGGESTED ACTIVITIES TO EXTEND YOUR LEARNING

1. In an in-class group discussion, brainstorm with your classmates accounts of children you know who may be facing environmental, physiological, emotional, language, and instructional factors that may interfere with their learning. For example, a child you know from a dysfunctional family who gets very little academic support at home, or a child struggling to learn English. What steps could be taken to help such children overcome these factors?

2. Interview a teacher or a school district curriculum leader. Find out what standardized tests are given, for what purposes, and how they were chosen. Also find out what informal classroom assessments are given and how the data may be used to plan instruction. How well do the formal and informal assessments described provide a comprehensive look at students' education needs and progress?

3. Go onto several assessment websites. Explore and see what assessments are available for reading screening, diagnosis, progress monitoring, and outcome measuring. What assessment materials may be downloaded? Suggested websites are:

Oregon Analysis of Assessment Instruments
    http://idea.uoregon.edu/assessment/index.html

DIBELS
    http://dibels.uoregon.edu/

PALS
    http://pals.virginia.edu/

SEDL
    http://www.sedl.org/reading/rad/list.html

Texas Primary Reading Inventory
    http://www.tpri.org/

Florida Center for Reading Research: Assessment Programs
    http://www.fcrr.org/assessmentReadingFirstDiagnosticMeasures.htm

REFERENCES

American Educational Research Association (2000). AERA Position statement on high-stakes testing in pre-k–12 education. Washington, DC: American Educational Research Association.

Bear, D. R., Invernizzi, M., Templeton, S., & Johnston, F. (2008). *Words their way: Word study for phonics, vocabulary, and spelling instruction* (5th ed.). Upper Saddle River, NJ: Merrill/Prentice Hall.

Clay, M. (2002). *An observation survey of early literacy achievement*. Portsmouth, NH: Heinemann.

Clay, M. M. (2000). *Running records for classroom teachers*. Portsmouth, NH: Heinemann.

Consortium on Reading Excellence (2007). *Assessing reading: Multiple measures, K–8* (2nd ed.). Novato, CA: Arena Press.

Cooter, R. B., Flynt, E. S., & Cooter K. (2006). *The Cooter/Flynt/Cooter Comprehensive Reading Inventory: Measuring reading development in regular and special education classrooms*. Upper Saddle River, NJ: Merrill/Prentice Hall.

Denton, C. A., Ciancio, D. J., & Fletcher, J. M. (2006). Validity, reliability, and utility of the observation survey of early literacy achievement. *Reading Research Quarterly*, *41*(1), 8–34.

Fawson, P. C., Ludlow, B. C., Reutzel, D. R., Sudweeks, R., & Smith, J. A. (2006). Running records: Achieving reliable results. *Journal of Educational Research*, *100*(2), 113–126.

Fuchs, D., & Fuchs, L. S. (2006). Introduction to response to intervention: What, why, and how valid is it? *Reading Research Quarterly, 41*(1), 93–99.

Good, R. H., & Kaminski, R. A. (2002). *Dynamic indicators of basic early literacy skills* (6th ed.). Eugene, OR: Institute for the Development of Educational Achievement.

Good, R. H., Simmons, D. C., & Kame'enui, E. J. (2001). The importance and decision-making utility of a continuum of fluency-based indicators of foundational reading skills for third-grade high-stakes outcomes. *Scientific Studies of Reading*, *5*(3), 257–288.

Griffith, P. L., & Olson, M. W. (1992). Phonemic awareness helps beginning readers break the code. *The Reading Teacher, 45*(7), 516–523.

Helman, L. A. (2005). Using literacy assessment results to improve teaching for English-language learners. *The Reading Teacher, 58*(7), 668–677.

Invernizzi, M. A., Landrum, T. J., Howell, J. L., & Warley, H. P. (2005). Toward the peaceful coexistence of test developers, policymakers, and teachers in an era of accountability. *The Reading Teacher, 58*(7), 610–618.

Kaminski, R. A., & Good, R. H. (1996). Toward a technology for assessing basic early literacy skills. *School Psychology Review, 25*, 215–227.

Lenski, S., Ehlers-Zavala, F., Daniel, M. C., & Sun-Irminger, X. (2006). Assessing English-language learners in mainstream classrooms. *The Reading Teacher, 60*(1), 24–34.

McKenna, M. C., & Kear, D. J. (1990). Measuring attitude toward reading: A new tool for teachers. *The Reading Teacher, 43*(9), 626–639.

National Assessment of Educational Progress (2005). *Reading report card.* Washington, DC: U.S. Department of Education. Retrieved from http://nces.ed.gov/nationsreportcard/

National Reading Panel. (2000). *Teaching children to read: An evidence-based assessment of the scientific research literature on reading and its implications for reading instruction. Report of the subgroups.* National Institute of Child Health and Human Development. Retrieved from http://www.nichd.nih.gov/publications/nrp/smallbook.cfm

Pinnell, G. S., Pikulski, J. J., Wixson, K. K., Campbell, J. R., Gough, P. B., & Beatty, A. S. (1995). *Oral reading fluency scale.* U.S. Department of Education, National Center for Education Statistics. Retrieved from http://nces.ed.gov/pubs95/web/95762.asp

Reilly, M. (2007). Choice of action: Using data to make instructional decisions in kindergarten. *The Reading Teacher, 60*(8), 770–776.

Reutzel, D. R., & Cooter, R. B. (2007). *Strategies for reading assessment and instruction: Helping every child to succeed* (2nd ed.). Upper Saddle River, NJ: Merrill/Prentice Hall.

Spandel, V. (2007). *Creating young writers: Using the six traits to enrich writing process in primary classrooms* (2nd ed.). Boston: Pearson.

Reading Interventions for Struggling Readers

11

by John A. Smith

Portrait of An ESL Struggling Reader: Lupe Learns to Read

Lupe's family is from Mexico, though she was born in the United States. Her father speaks no English and her mother speaks a limited amount of English. Lupe is a limited English speaker as well. Spanish is the primary language in her home.

When Lupe started second grade, she was reading books at a C level in the guided reading (Fountas & Pinnell, 1996) framework. Her teacher, Mrs. Checketts, was concerned, but ready to provide her with all the instruction and extra help that she could get her hands on. Lupe had gone to the resource teacher at the beginning of the year, but only as an at-risk student, not as a documented special education student. When the resource teacher's caseload grew too high, she and Mrs. Checketts met together and developed a series of in-class, teacher-led interventions designed to meet Lupe's needs. The resource teacher coordinated the America Reads tutors and made sure that they met with Lupe almost daily.

Mrs. Checketts met with Lupe daily for small-group instruction in which they read and reread little books that were at Lupe's instructional reading level. She was also given time to read those same books independently while Mrs. Checketts met with other groups. Once a week, she read with a partner out of a basal reading series, one that provided lots of practice with familiar stories like Frog and Toad by Arnold Lobel.

Lupe also participated in writing workshop each day. At the beginning of the year, she liked to use her alphabet card to write simple sentences such as "I like apple." By the end of year she was writing simple stories such as "The girl went to the pet store and bought a bird. The bird is red and yellow and green. She bought food for the bird and a cage. She likes the bird a lot. Her mom does not. She says the bird is messy and loud."

The principal of the school also organized an after-school reading program for at-risk students. Classroom teachers were paid to work with students in small guided reading groups 3 days a week after school. After the tutoring hour was over, the students went to the Boys and Girls Club until they were picked up.

By the end of the year, Lupe was reading books at the K and L levels. She really liked to read Junie B. Jones and Magic Tree House books. She continued to return to old favorites like Are You My Mother? and the Clifford books. Her ability and enjoyment of reading were evident when she chose to read or play Sight Word

Bingo for free time. Her fluency was improving rapidly and she could retell what she had read with some detail. Mrs. Checketts felt good about sending her on to third grade with reading skills on a par with many other students in her grade.

——————— 🐸 🐸 🐸 ———————

Contrary to claims by some commercial publishers, there are no infallible reading programs that will bring every struggling reader to grade level and beyond (Pressley, 2002). The best bet for teachers to ensure that all students learn to read well is to (1) determine the causes of student reading problems through careful observation and assessment, (2) provide intensive instructional interventions that focus on essential components of reading that struggling students need, (3) continually monitor the effects of the interventions, and (4) make ongoing instructional adjustments as needed (Reutzel & Cooter, 2007).

Educators nationwide increasingly rely on the three-tier model described in Chapter 2 to provide differentiated reading instruction that will meet the needs of all learners, particularly those who struggle learning to read. Tier One is the foundational classroom reading program that all students receive. Tier Two is the additional in-class reading instruction provided to students who are somewhat below grade level. Tier Three is intensive additional instruction provided to students who read significantly below grade level. Tier Three instruction is often part of a resource program provided by special education or ELL teachers.

When students are identified as not making sufficient reading progress with the Tier One classroom reading program, teachers should intervene by increasing instructional intensity (Torgesen, 2004) through providing more minutes of focused, small-group Tier Two reading instruction in the regular classroom. If Tier Two reading instruction doesn't produce the needed gains in reading achievement, then the classroom teacher should consult with school resource personnel to develop a Tier Three intervention such as placement in a Title 1 or special education resource program. This chapter provides additional information about steps that can be taken to support students who struggle learning to read. Topics include:

🐸 The need for reading instruction interventions

🐸 Strong classroom-based instruction

🐸 In-class interventions

🐸 Resource program interventions

🐸 Using assessment data to plan instruction

🐸 Enlisting parent support

🐸 School-level interventions

 ## THE NEED FOR READING INSTRUCTION INTERVENTIONS

Good news! According to the Nation's Report Card (National Assessment of Educational Progress [NAEP], 2007) overall reading achievement among fourth-grade students in the United States is at its highest level ever. Overall reading scores have been creeping steadily up since NAEP began in 1971. In 2007, fourth-grade students scored an average 221 points on NAEP out of a possible 500, up from 217 in 1992 and 208 in 1971 (see Figure 11.1).

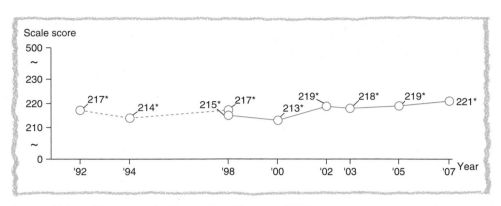

Figure 11.1 Average Fourth-Grade Reading Achievement Scores on the 2007 National Assessment of Educational Progress

Source: National Assessment of Educational Progress, 2007.

However, the increase in overall fourth-grade reading scores masks a huge problem in American education: the achievement gap (see Table 11.1). Although White and Asian/Pacific Islander students scored an average of 231 and 232 points, respectively, out of 500 possible points on the NAEP test, Black, Hispanic, and American Indian students scored an average of 203, 205, and 203 points, respectively—a nearly 30-point gap. Much of the achievement gap is associated with poverty. Students who were eligible for free and reduced lunch scored an average of 205 points on the NAEP test, whereas students who were not eligible for free and reduced lunch scored an average of 232. The achievement gap is also associated with English language proficiency. Students whose primary language was other than English (who were able to be tested) scored an average of 188 points on the NAEP test, whereas their English-speaking classmates scored an average of 224. Learning disabilities also affect reading achievement.

Table 11.1 2007 NAEP Fourth-Grade Reading Achievement by Subgroups

Racial/Ethnic Group	2007 Reading Achievement Score
Asian/Pacific Islander	232
White	231
Hispanic	205
American Indian	203
Black	203
Language Group	
Proficient English speakers	224
English Language learners	188
Income Group	
Noneligible for free/reduced lunch	232
Eligible for free/reduced lunch	205
Disability Group	
Nondisabled	224
Disabled	191

Source: National Assessment of Educational Progress, 2007.

Students who were classified as disabled scored an average of 191 points on the NAEP, whereas students who were not disabled scored an average of 224.

The message is clear: Not all students in the United States are learning to read at acceptable levels. And if educators continue providing the same instruction as they have before, disadvantaged students will continue to lag behind.

Fortunately, research suggests that the percentage of students who struggle to learn to read can be reduced from current estimates of 20% to 40% to levels around 5% with effective instruction (Invernizzi, 2001; Torgesen, 2004). High-quality classroom reading and writing instruction, supplemented by intensive well-designed in-class and resource program interventions for those students who need it, holds great promise for supporting struggling readers and closing the achievement gap.

FOR STRUGGLING READERS

Struggling Readers Need Well-Informed Teachers

People in professional disciplines such as law and medicine keep up on research and practice by reading professional journals and attending conferences. So too should teachers keep up on the most effective instructional practices. There are many ways to do this. Most school districts offer professional development workshops for teachers. Universities offer graduate courses and programs. State departments of education offer endorsement programs. Professional education associations such as the International Reading Association (see the IRA website at http://reading. org) publish reading journals and sponsor national-, state-, and local-level conferences and workshops. All teachers should develop and maintain a professional attitude of keeping up in the field. Look for and take advantage of professional development opportunities as they come around. Make sure your school has a professional library for teachers and subscriptions to high-quality journals such as IRA's *The Reading Teacher*. Get involved in local-, state-, and national-level professional associations by serving on committees and governing boards. Search for information online at state department of education websites, the U.S. Department of Education, and professional associations. There is much knowledge available about teaching reading effectively. Take advantage of it for your own professional benefit and the benefit of your students.

THE CLASSROOM TEACHER IS RESPONSIBLE

A central, overarching principle regarding interventions for struggling readers is that classroom teachers are responsible for the reading achievement of *all* their students. Some teachers, when they send their struggling students to a resource teacher such as special education, assume that the resource teacher takes over the responsibility for those students' learning and achievement. This incorrect assumption may lead classroom teachers to feel less urgency about assessing students to pinpoint their instructional levels and reading strengths and needs and to provide the amount and type of instruction struggling readers need. Resource teachers also need to understand that they serve to support the classroom teachers' instructional program. As classroom and resource teachers recognize their respective responsibilities and roles in supporting struggling readers they will be able to work together more effectively to ensure that struggling readers receive the cohesive and coordinated instruction that is needed. They will share student reading assessment data and plan together which concepts need to be taught and reviewed, in what sequence, at what pace, and with which instructional materials.

 ## STRONG CLASSROOM-BASED READING INSTRUCTION

Interventions for struggling readers must be built on the foundation of a strong comprehensive classroom reading program. Classroom teachers, when considering how to help bring struggling readers to grade level, should first review the Tier One instruction they are providing in their classrooms. Is the classroom environment literacy-rich, including a strong, well-organized classroom library and large amounts of instructional charts and posters displayed on classroom walls? Is there a strong classroom focus on oral language development so that students will know the meanings of the words they are learning to decode? Is there an effective word identification program that follows a logical, cumulative sequence and that features explicit teacher explanation and modeling along with opportunities for students to practice applying skills? Does the classroom reading program teach students to activate their background knowledge, recognize and use text structure, and select and apply comprehension strategies to engaging informational and literary texts? Is there a vibrant writing program that features whole-class and individual instruction in writing genres and techniques, ample amounts of time for students to write at length about topics of personal choice and importance, and opportunities for students to share and publish their writing? Only when all of these critical instructional pieces are in place will intervention be effective.

In many schools, once a strong classroom reading program is in place the next step for helping struggling readers is for teachers to provide Tier Two interventions—additional in-class instruction that is intensive and focused. Finally, for struggling readers who don't respond to a strong Tier One classroom reading program supplemented by Tier Two in-class intervention, there are Tier Three resource program interventions including Title 1, Reading Recovery, special education, and programs for English language learners.

 ## IN-CLASS INTERVENTIONS

Contrary to some perceptions, there is not a separate, unique set of reading skills or reading instruction interventions reserved for struggling readers. Joseph. Torgesen (2004), director of the Florida Center for Reading Research and a leading authority on preventing and remediating reading difficulties, writes:

> Perhaps the most important conclusion to draw from recent intervention research is that intervention instruction should

FOR STRUGGLING READERS

Creating Reading Materials for a Nonreader

Similar to the language-experience approach (explained more fully in Chapter 3), you can write a piece of text about the child. Begin with an introductory paragraph that includes the child's name and other important information about him or her.

Travis is 8 years old. He lives in Jonesboro. His mom is a nurse. His brother's name is Joey.

Travis and the tutor can practice reading this material until he knows it fairly well and then you can write a second page with his input.

Travis likes to catch bugs. He likes ladybugs a lot. He also likes to catch praying mantises. They are sometimes brown and sometimes green. He keeps them in his bug box. He got his bug box for his birthday from his grandpa.

Travis and his tutor then practice this reading material over the course of several days until he can read it fairly fluently and accurately. You can keep creating pages of the book for the child to use with the tutor. You can write about things he enjoys, school rules, playground routines, lunchtime activities, and so on.

Each sentence in the story should be written on a sentence, then cut apart and reassembled by the child. The child should eventually be able to reassemble the whole paragraph or page using the cut-apart sentences. The child should also write a sentence every day. It could be a sentence from the story or a new one. He or she should try to write it without looking at the text but with help from the tutor to listen for sounds and write them down. Also, each day a word should be added to a portable word wall or dictionary card, which can be used in the future to help the child with writing sentences.

After the child has experienced success with this teacher-created text, the tutor can move on to using easy books that appeal to the child. Instead of writing every sentence on sentence strips, missed words are written on index cards. On subsequent days, the missed words are practiced. When the child can correctly read the word on the index card on 3 separate days (indicated with a check mark or smiley), then the card can be retired.

None of this volunteer work with struggling readers is meant to replace expert instruction from the classroom teacher. This is supplementary help that is meant to extend the work initiated by the teacher.

Source: Adapted from *Classrooms That Work: They Can All Read and Write*, 3rd ed., by Patricia M. Cunningham and Richard L. Allington, 2002, New York: Addison-Wesley Longman.

focus on the same major dimensions of knowledge and skill that are taught in the regular classroom but must be more *explicit* and *intensive* than classroom instruction to prevent or remediate reading difficulties. (p. 363)

In other words, all reading instruction should center on the same basic set of reading skills: alphabet knowledge, phonemic awareness, phonics, fluency, vocabulary, comprehension, and writing. The exact blend and intensity of skills instruction will vary according to students' levels of reading achievement and need, but the focus remains on the same skill set.

Rather than recommending specific programs to address struggling student reading problems, Torgesen recommends that instruction for struggling readers needs to be more *explicit* and more *intensive*. Explicit instruction, as described in Chapter 5, requires that teachers (1) clearly explain and model reading concepts and skills; (2) provide students with guided practice opportunities where teachers lead students in practicing the skill on follow-up examples; (3) provide students with independent practice opportunities to apply reading skills on their own, with teacher supervision and feedback; and (4) assess students' abilities to apply the skills and plan follow-up instruction. Explicit instruction also makes use of precise instructional teacher-language, finger-pointing, and routines so that students know when it's their turn to listen to the teacher, when it's their turn to participate, and how they should respond.

Intensity of instruction refers to how much time is allocated for intervention instruction and the size of the instructional groups. The farther below grade level that students are, the more instructional minutes they should receive each day and each week. Students who need intensive intervention should be taught in either a one-on-one setting or else in small instructional groups of two to four students at most.

MORE INSTRUCTIONAL TIME

In many classrooms students, regardless of their reading ability, receive the same amount of reading instruction. The National Reading Panel (NRP, 2000) has made it clear that students who struggle to learn to read need more instructional time than those who learn to read easily. Teachers may provide extra instructional time through longer instructional groups or extra instructional groups for struggling readers. For example, top reading groups may only meet two or three times per week with the teacher for instruction, whereas struggling reader groups need to meet with the teacher every day. Top reading groups may discuss what they've read and plan their reading for the next day or two; struggling readers may receive daily intensive reading skills instruction. Additional instructional time may also be provided through individual tutoring and through before- and after-school instructional programs that are discussed in subsequent sections of this chapter.

FOCUSED SMALL-GROUP INSTRUCTIONAL INTERVENTIONS

One way to increase instructional intensity is to provide reading instruction to students in small, differentiated instruction groups. When reading assessment identifies groups of students with similar reading problems, it makes sense that teachers meet with those students in small groups to address their particular needs together.

Adjusting the size of small groups is a further way to increase intensity. Whereas an instructional group size of five to seven may be appropriate for students reading at grade level, smaller groups of two to four are most appropriate for struggling readers.

Instructional groups also need to be flexible—that is, a particular student's group membership will change over time according to his or her progress and development. A student wouldn't remain in a phonemic awareness group all year, but rather may move into groups focusing on phonics, fluency, and comprehension as specific skills are mastered.

Research focusing on small-group interventions for struggling readers (Kosanovich, Ladinsky, Nelsen, & Torgesen, 2007) suggests a number of ways to vary small-group Tier Two reading instruction to meet struggling readers' specific needs:

- Vary the size of the groups (three to five for struggling readers; five to seven for others).
- Vary the number of days each week that groups meet with the teacher for instruction (daily, two to three, or four to five times per week).
- Vary the number of minutes of small-group instruction (10, 20, or 30 minutes).
- Vary the instructional focus (skills focus or guided reading focus).
- Vary the content and instructional level of small-group lessons.

Many common small-group reading lessons that are effective for on-level students are also effective for struggling readers, but will need to be taught more explicitly and with more opportunities to practice and apply the skills being taught. Such lessons can focus on a wide variety of essential reading skills, from foundational reading skills such as alphabet knowledge and phonemic awareness to more advanced reading skills such as phonics and fluency.

Environmental Print

Some struggling kindergarten students still may not understand the concept of word. In small-group lessons, the teacher and students could examine various kinds of environmental print (fast-food bags, cereal boxes, toy packaging, etc.) and use them to create student-made books. For example, first-grade teacher Martha Whitaker had a photo album of street signs, store signs, billboards, and candy wrappers that her students enjoyed looking through and pointing out letters that they were learning. Other teachers invite students to bring environmental print to class to be displayed on an environmental print wall.

The Language-Experience Approach

Another powerful strategy to use in small groups is the language-experience approach (LEA; Nelson & Linek, 1999; see also Chapter 3). Using small blank books, students can draw pictures or glue in magazine pictures and then dictate text that goes with the illustration. The teacher writes the text in conventional print and the book becomes personalized reading material for the student's reading lessons. This strategy is excellent for teaching children that print carries meaning and with repeated practice reading the text aloud, the student learns one-to-one matching of print and voice, the role of punctuation in reading, sound–letter relationships, and the pleasure of creating and reading one's own language. This strategy works particularly well with English language learners. It is important to preserve the student's syntax and grammar when taking dictation so that the student is not confused when trying to read the text.

Elkonin Boxes

When a group of students lack sufficient phonemic awareness, it is helpful to work with an Elkonin box. This is simply a row of boxes used to help students segment the sounds in words. For example, the word *run* has three sounds: /r/ /u/ /n/. Using a series of boxes, the student pronounces each sound individually and at the same time pushes a small marker, such as a penny or a unifix cube, into each box to represent each sound. This physical act of pushing a marker helps students internalize that each sound in a spoken word can be represented by a written letter (see Figure 11.2).

Figure 11.2 An Elkonin Box

When working with a small group, each student can have a blank row of boxes that has been laminated for durability and a set of markers. The teacher tells the students a word, helps them say the word slowly, stretching out the sounds, as each child pushes a marker into a box for each sound he or she hears.

Letter Manipulatives

Small-group instruction is an ideal time to have struggling readers work with magnetic letters or other letter manipulatives to make words. Using metal cookie sheets, students can make words and manipulate the letters to transform the words according to the teacher's directions. For example, when working with a small group that needs to better understand how to use onsets and rimes to decode words, teachers can direct the students to make the word *light* on the cookie sheet and then tell them to "change the *l* to an *n* to make the word *night*." Teachers can keep changing the initial letter or letters until many *ight* words have been spelled and read. Adams (1990) lists the 37 most common rimes (see the following list) and points out that as students learn to recognize these rimes and to substitute initial letter sounds they will be able to unlock about 500 primary-level words.

37 Most Common Rimes

ack	ain	ake	ale	all	ame	an	ank	ap	ash	at	ate
aw	ay	eat	ell	est	ice	ick	ide	ight	ill	in	ine
ing	ink	ip	ir	ock	oke	op	or	ore	uck	ug	ump
unk											

Decodable Texts

Even accomplished pianists continue to practice musical scales so that the fingering patterns remain automatic. Piano scales are not Chopin, but practicing piano scales enables pianists to play Chopin. Beginning readers, particularly those who are struggling, can benefit from similar practice opportunities provided by reading decodable texts that contain a high percentage of decodable words (*Dan will sit in the van*).

Decodable texts provide opportunities for intensive practice at blending letter sounds and spelling patterns for students who need additional review to attain automaticity. Focused repeated opportunities to practice and apply reading skills help the "lightbulb" come on for many struggling students. Decodable texts should not be used lock-step with an entire class or used any longer than necessary, but should be considered as another tool in an instructional toolbox that will help meet the needs of beginning readers. There are several simple steps many teachers use when reading decodable texts with struggling readers.

Focus the Reader

When reading one-on-one with a struggling reader, teachers can point to the words as the student reads them. This helps the student stay focused and also keeps the pace from dragging. When the student misses a word and continues to read on without self-correcting, the teacher taps lightly several times on the page below the missed word. One of two things happen: Often the student returns to the word, studies it, and then reads it correctly and continues on. However, sometimes the student returns to the word, studies it, and is still unable to read it. When a student is unable to decode a missed word, there are several options for helping the student decode the word.

Prompt the Student

The first option is to prompt the student into the blending process. Do this by slowly modeling the blending process, stretching the sounds of the word. Pronounce the first couple of sounds of the word slowly, then hang back and allow the student to take over the blending process and finish the word.

Blend Word Parts

Another option is to help the student put together the "word parts" by blending the onsets and rimes. Onsets are the word beginnings, usually the consonant or consonants that come before the vowel. Rimes are the vowel and the consonants that come after it. Pig-Latin is built on the principle of onsets and rimes (at-c*ay*, ink-bl*ay*). Table 11.2 shows several words divided into their onsets or rimes.

To help students blend word parts using onsets and rimes, teachers can cover the onset with an index finger and focus on decoding the rime first. Then when the student has figured out the rime, the teacher can uncover the onset and help the student blend the onset with the rime he or she has just studied. For example, to help a student decode the word *stick*, cover the *st* and help the student decode *ick*. Ask, "What does

Table 11.2   Onsets and Rimes

Word	Onset	Rime
cat	c	at
blink	bl	ink
chop	ch	op

this part of the word (*ick*) sound like?" If the student cannot pronounce /ick/ then say, "What sound does *i* make?" Provide the student with the /i/ sound if necessary. Then ask, what will *i* say with *ck* added on?" When the student can pronounce /ick/, uncover the *st* and ask, "What does *ick* say with *st* added on the front?" If the student needs extra support the teacher might add only the *t* to produce *tick*, then the *st* to produce *stick*. For longer words (for example, *stretcher*), focus on each spelling pattern individually (*str–et–ch–er*). Have the student figure out each of the spelling patterns and then blend them left-to-right to pronounce the word. When the student has successfully blended the word, it is often helpful to invite him or her to reread the entire sentence to get one more practice opportunity to blend the word in the context of an entire sentence.

Learning this "building" process is very important for students who struggle with word identification. After going through this process repeatedly with students, they begin applying it themselves, a big step toward independent word identification.

Blend Individual Sounds

The third option when a student cannot decode a word is to use the word to reteach the blending procedure. Say to the student, "Let's say this word the slow way together sound-by-sound: /s/ /t/ /i/ /ck/. Point to the letters as you pronounce their sounds. Now, let's say it together the fast way. Now you say it fast" (student says the word *stick*). With longer words, go through this blending process with parts of the word and then combine. After the student has correctly read the missed word, have him or her reread the entire sentence.

Distinguish Irregular Words

Irregularly spelled words such as *love*, *said*, and *is* do not follow the common spelling patterns and cannot be sounded out. Experienced reading teachers quickly distinguish between regular and irregularly spelled words. When words follow the spelling patterns (regular), teachers should help students decode the words using the procedures already described. However, when a word contains an irregular spelling, teachers should simply tell students that the word does not follow the pattern or rules, and provide its pronunciation. For example, teachers might say something like this:

> *This is the word* is. *It doesn't follow the rules. It looks like it should say* /i/ /s/. *But the* s *makes a* /z/ *sound in this word, so you say* is. *Can you read the word* is *in the sentence?*

Many teachers like to put irregularly spelled words on an "outlaw words" word wall and review the words with the class daily. Students generally learn to recognize irregularly spelled words simply through the sheer repetition when they are given ample opportunity to encounter such words repeatedly in decodable texts *and* in the context of meaningful texts.

Repeated Reading

Repeated reading (Chomsky, 1978; Samuels, 1979) allows students to become familiar with printed words and spelling patterns through repeated exposures to the same text. Similar to good music instruction, repeated reading has students read a passage over and over until they can read it fluently, then move on to another passage.

Samuels (1979) suggests that teachers begin by selecting an interesting passage of about 150 words at the student's instructional level. Next, read the passage aloud to the student and discuss content and vocabulary as needed. Have the student read the passage aloud and use a stopwatch to measure how many seconds it takes the student to read the passage. Tell the student how long the reading took and discuss any errors. If the reading takes longer than 1 minute, add the additional seconds to 60 (1 minute and 12 seconds is recorded as 72 seconds). Have the student practice reading the passage alone silently two or three times, then again out loud with the stopwatch. Show the student his or her time after each reading of the passage. Repeat this process several times until the student's performance has peaked. Performance usually peaks after three or four readings of the same passage.

Repeated readings can be very motivational as students monitor their performance and want to improve. Teachers may want to construct a chart to record and graph each student's repeated readings times (see Figure 11.3). The following formula lets you calculate each student's reading rate in words per minute.

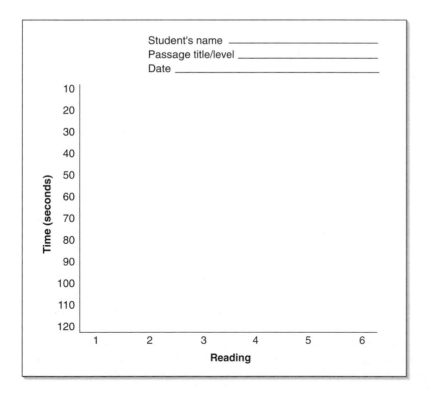

Figure 11.3
Repeated Readings
Line Graph

*(60 × total number of words in the passage) divided by the elapsed
time (in seconds) equals words per minute*

You can also get a score that combines both rate and accuracy by subtracting the number of words misread and multiplying 60 times the number of correct words. This is similar to the DIBELS Oral Reading Fluency subtest (CWPM, correct words per minute). CWPM has been shown to be a very good indicator of general reading ability.

ONE-ON-ONE INSTRUCTIONAL SUPPORT

Students who are struggling with reading need more instructional time and attention than they can get from the classroom teacher alone. One-on-one tutoring provided by certified resource teachers, paraprofessionals, and adult classroom volunteers, and even older, more advanced students can be very effective in providing struggling students with opportunities to practice reading skills the teacher has previously taught in small-group lessons (Pressley et al., 2001).

Effective one-on-one tutoring generally includes attention to three major aspects of reading (Invernizzi, 2001). Some tutoring sessions may focus on ensuring that students are learning and mastering letter–sound correspondences, phonemic awareness concepts, and phonics skills. Other one-on-one sessions may focus on providing struggling students' with oral reading fluency practice as an adult listens to the student reading aloud and provides support and instructional feedback. Whether the texts for fluency practice are natural-language stories, controlled-vocabulary decodable books, or leveled reading books, they must be at the student's instructional reading level. Tutoring sessions provide a wonderful opportunity for students to improve their ability to comprehend text. In one-on-one settings, tutors can pinpoint information students understand, identify gaps in students learning, and help students construct meaning from text in a very personal and supportive manner. Invernizzi (2001) writes, "probably the best way to intellectually engage a child is through casual conversation between the tutor and the student as they read a story together" (p. 463). Structured tutoring programs generally include attention to all three reading instruction emphases in daily 30-minute lessons.

 ## RESOURCE PROGRAM INTERVENTIONS

Teachers should consult with school resource personnel to consider placing struggling students in a Tier Three resource reading program when in-class instructional interventions do not provide the needed levels of improved reading achievement. There are several kinds of resource programs, each designed to meet the needs of a specific group of struggling readers. Because classroom teachers bear the primary responsibility for reading instruction and student achievement, student placement in resource reading programs should be considered only when in-class interventions have been thoroughly tried and found insufficient. Tier Three resource programs such as Title 1, Reading Recovery, special education, and English language learning programs are designed for struggling readers who may lack adequate background and preparation for learning, who may have a reading disability, or who are learning English.

TITLE 1

As described earlier, Title 1 (formerly called Chapter 1) is a federally funded program that provides additional reading teachers to schools in low-income communities. Students who qualify for placement in Title 1 reading programs are those students who are reading below grade level, but who are not thought to have a reading disability. Teachers often refer to Title 1 students as slower learners who simply need extra support. Traditionally, Title 1 reading teachers have provided 30 minutes of daily reading instruction in "pull-out" programs where students left their home-room and received Title 1 instruction in small groups in a resource room "down the hall." Although the extra small-group Title 1 reading instruction was intended to supplement classroom reading instruction, it often had unintended consequences such as (1) students' missing important instruction in other subjects during the time they were pulled out, (2) Title 1 reading instruction being unrelated to classroom instruction so that struggling readers were being asked to learn two reading programs rather than one, and (3) the stigma attached to leaving the classroom for extra help. More recently, Title 1 reading teachers have been encouraged to provide in-class additional instruction that is coordinated with the classroom reading program.

READING RECOVERY

Reading Recovery (Clay, 1993) is a one-on-one pull-out program for students in the bottom 20% of first-grade classes. Reading Recovery teachers provide 30 minutes of daily instruction that includes five components. First, the Reading Recovery teacher and the student reread a familiar leveled book together. This is generally a book that was used the day before for instruction and practiced at home with family that evening. Second, the Reading Recovery teacher takes a running record of the student reading the familiar book and places the running record in a three-ring binder to document that student's reading growth and needs. The third component of the Reading Recovery lesson is a short phonics lesson, often using magnetic letters to explore and form word families to reinforce spelling patterns. The fourth component is a brief dictation activity where the teacher helps the student compose, then write a brief meaningful sentence. The teacher also writes the sentence on a cardstock sentence strip that is read by the student, then cut into individual words for further practice at home. The final component of the Reading Recovery lesson is for the teacher to introduce a new leveled reader to the student. The teacher helps the student read through the book, then sends it home for further reading with the family, and to be used as the familiar book for the next day's lesson.

SPECIAL EDUCATION

Special education (SPED) is a federally funded program that provides teachers to serve students who have been identified through extensive testing as having a reading or learning disability. Title 1 students are generally considered to be lower-ability students who are performing at their capacity, whereas special education students are considered to be normally bright students whose low classroom performance is due to some sort of disability. Once a student has been identified and placed in special education, the SPED teacher uses data from thorough diagnostic assessment to pinpoint the student's reading problems and then develop an individualized education plan (IEP) that becomes a legal contract between the school and the student's family. Special education reading instruction typically focuses on providing very specific and sequenced direct instruction.

ENGLISH LANGUAGE LEARNER PROGRAMS

Many millions of students in U.S. schools come from homes where English is not the primary language. These students often struggle to learn reading simply because they are not yet proficient in English, the language of most classroom instruction and reading texts. Research on English language learners (August & Shanahan, 2006) has identified several important themes that guide effective reading and writing instruction for ELL students. First, literacy instruction that focuses on phonemic awareness, phonics, fluency, vocabulary, and comprehension has "clear benefits" for ELL students. In other words, the basic processes of learning to read apply to all learners regardless of language background. Second, although the basics of learning to read are key to all learners, oral proficiency in English is also critical for ELL students to learn to read and write in English. Unfortunately, research also suggests that instruction in oral English is often overlooked. Research also points out that most forms of literacy assessment are inadequate for identifying ELL students' instructional strengths and needs, making placement decisions for ELL students, and planning instruction that meets ELL students' needs.

Many U.S. schools now have certified or endorsed ELL teachers who serve ELL students, often in pull-out resource programs. ELL programs generally focus on developing students' oral English proficiency while at the same time providing instruction in basic reading and writing skills. As with all Tier Three resource programs, it is imperative that classroom and ELL teachers collaborate in reviewing student achievement and diagnostic data to plan instruction that is coordinated between classroom and ELL programs and that focuses on students' instructional needs.

EFFECTIVE ESL INSTRUCTION

Effective ESL instruction uses grade-level curriculum in the content areas as the basis for teaching both language and key curriculum objectives. ESL students deserve and need to be exposed to grade-appropriate content-area objectives. So content-based ESL instruction integrates content from multiple subject areas into thematic units.

Sheltered instruction (Echevarria, Vogt, & Short, 2004) is a research-based model for teaching English language learners through content-area learning. Students are taught the specialized patterns of language use that are unique to academic subjects while also learning functional language skills. Through sheltered instruction lessons, ESL students learn to read and understand expository prose, write persuasively, argue different points of view, take notes from lectures or text, make hypotheses and predictions, and analyze and synthesize information.

The sheltered instruction lesson should have:

- Clearly defined content objectives that are supported by the delivery of the lesson
- Clearly defined language objectives that are supported by the delivery of the lesson

- Age-appropriate content concepts
- Supplementary materials to make the lesson clear and meaningful
- Meaningful activities that integrate lesson concepts
- Students engaged 90%–100% of the time
- Appropriate pacing

During sheltered instruction lessons, teachers must:

- Make explicit links to students' background knowledge
- Emphasize key vocabulary
- Modulate rate of speech and syntax
- Explain academic tasks clearly
- Use a variety of techniques to make content concepts clear
- Provide opportunities for students to use strategies
- Use scaffolding techniques
- Use a variety of question types, particularly those that involve higher-order thinking
- Provide lots of opportunities for interaction between and among the teacher and students
- Use pairs, triads, and small groups to support the language and content objectives
- Provide sufficient wait time for student response
- Provide, when able, opportunities for students to clarify key concepts in their first language (L1)
- Provide hands-on materials or manipulatives
- Use activities that integrate reading, writing, speaking, and listening
- Review key vocabulary
- Review key content concepts
- Provide feedback to students
- Conduct assessments of learning throughout the lesson

TESOL STANDARDS

The professional organization Teachers of English to Speakers of Other Languages has an excellent and extensive website containing the ESL Standards for Pre-K–12 students: http://www.tesol.edu. It also publishes professional journals and books to support teachers of English language learners.

USING ASSESSMENT DATA TO PLAN INSTRUCTION

Not all students who struggle with reading have the same reading needs. As described in Chapter 1, reading might be thought of as having two major com-ponents: word identification and comprehension. Accordingly, Torgesen (2004) describes two general categories of struggling readers. Many struggling readers have adequate background knowledge and oral language skills, but lack the word identification skills to process print effectively. For these readers, instruction should focus on letter–sound correspondences, phonemic awareness, phonics, and fluency instruction. And as these lower-level skills improve, reading comprehension should simultaneously improve because word identification no longer constrains these students' reading ability.

Other struggling students, unfortunately, have problems with both word identification and oral language. Even when such students make progress with word identification, they still struggle with comprehension because they don't know the meanings of many of the words they've learned to identify. These readers need focused instruction in letter–sound correspondences, phonemic awareness, phonics, and fluency, along with oral language vocabulary and comprehension strategies.

Note that both types of struggling readers have problems with word identification and that both types of struggling readers will need instruction in lower-level print processing skills. Reading teachers must be able to gather and interpret assessment data effectively to determine the most appropriate combination of reading skills that each struggling reader needs to get on track to reach grade-level reading ability.

A very effective way for teachers to use reading assessment data to plan instruction is meeting together in data-study meetings. Once a month grade-level teacher teams in many schools meet to review assessment data and plan instruction. In some schools data-study meetings take place during regularly scheduled teacher preparation time during the school day. At other schools the principal arranges for a team of substitute teachers to take over classes at a grade level while teachers meet to review data. If there is a school reading coach on staff, that person also attends the grade-level data-study meetings to share observations from the data, make suggestions, and offer to help teachers implement instructional plans. The most common use of assessment data in planning instruction is for grouping students for instruction. There are two types of data used to do this: progress-monitoring and diagnostic data.

Progress-Monitoring Data

In many data-study meetings teachers bring color-coded printouts of progress-monitoring data that show which students read at grade level, which students read somewhat below grade level, and which students read significantly below grade level. For example, teachers may bring printouts of DIBELS assessments (Good & Kaminski, 2002; Good, Simmons, & Kame'enui, 2001) that rank-order students from highest to lowest within each classroom. The names of students at or above grade level are highlighted in green. The names of students somewhat below grade level are highlighted in yellow, and students significantly below grade level are highlighted in red. Depending on how many students fall into each category in each classroom, teachers discuss students in each group individually by name and then form groups of students at the same level for small-group instruction. Teachers teach these groups for a month, monitor how well students progress, then regroup students as appropriate during the following month's data-study meeting. A highlight of data-study meetings is when teachers discuss struggling readers by name and brainstorm and share instructional strategies and materials designed to help accelerate struggling students' progress.

DIAGNOSTIC DATA

Whereas progress-monitoring data focus on student's reading levels, diagnostic data focus on individual students' specific reading strengths and needs. Many teachers do diagnostic testing on students below grade level and group students for instruction, not by achievement level, but instead by need in specific reading skill areas. Using the assessment concept of drilling down described in Chapter 10, teachers track backward from fluent oral reading to phonics, to phonemic awareness, to letter–sound knowledge until they isolate the root cause of a student's reading problems. For example, teachers in some data-study meetings use diagnostic assessment data from the CORE Phonics Survey (Consortium on Reading Excellence [CORE], 2007) or the Qualitative Spelling Inventory (Bear, Invernizzi, Templeton, & Johnston, 2008) to identify which reading skills or spelling patterns are troublesome to their struggling students and then group students together who need instruction on these specific patterns. One group of student may need instruction in short vowel sounds including CVC words and short vowel words with consonant blends and digraphs. Another group may be struggling with long vowel patterns and will receive instruction in final silent *e* and vowel team patterns. Teachers in some data-study meetings group students with a combination of progress-monitoring and diagnostic data—using the progress-monitoring data as a first pass toward grouping students for instruction, then using the diagnostic data to fine-tune the actual groupings.

PEARSON
myeducationlab

Assessment, Remediation, and Diagnosis

Go to MyEducationLab, "Assessment, Remediation, and Diagnosis," and read the article "Linking Formative Assessment to Scaffolding."

As you read this article, notice how teachers can use formative assessment data to plan instruction to better meet students' learning needs.

- How can you incorporate assessment/instruction principles to enhance your students' reading achievement?
- How can assessing students' prior knowledge improve instructional effectiveness?
- How can students be taught to self-assess in order to improve their own learning?

ENLISTING PARENT SUPPORT

An important instructional goal shared by many teachers is that each struggling reader receives 10 to 15 minutes of individual reading time with a teacher or another adult each school day. Parent (or grandparent) volunteers can play an important role in helping teachers reach that goal. During back-to-school night at many schools, teachers give parents a form asking if they might be willing to volunteer in the classroom each week or month. Parents who indicate that they would be able to volunteer an hour each week or month are contacted and scheduled so that, when possible, teachers can have an hour of parent volunteer time several days each week.

Because struggling readers are often poor decoders (Pressley, 2002), parent volunteers are often asked to read with struggling students to build fluency and automatic word recognition. Reading texts might include (1) decodable books, (2) familiar guided reading books, and (3) children's literature books the children chose. Teachers can meet with parent volunteers to show them how to provide opportunities for students to practice reading the spelling patterns being studied in class. For example, parent volunteers can listen and help as students who need to work with decodable texts read books from the *Reading for All Learners Program* (Hofmeister, 1996), which has helpful prompts for volunteers and teachers at the bottom of each page.

Teachers can also provide parent volunteers with guided reading books for one-on-one reading with struggling readers. These books are at each student's instructional level so that, through repeated readings of them, the students gain the confidence and facility they need to feel like and actually become successful readers. Parent volunteers can also be given pointers on how to read and discuss books that the children choose to help build background knowledge and vocabulary and to provide positive experiences of reading together for pleasure. Students generally feel it is a privilege to read one-on-one with parent volunteers.

SCHOOL-LEVEL INTERVENTIONS

Schools that provide effective reading instruction are characterized by strong instructional leadership that brings classroom teachers, resource personnel, and family and community resources together to review school-level reading instruction needs, brainstorm available resources, and together develop school-level programs that complement and supplement classroom and resource reading instruction.

One school envisioned and implemented an early morning volunteer tutoring program for struggling readers. Classroom teachers recommended struggling students to participate in the program that involved community volunteers who arrived at school 1 hour before the beginning of the school day to tutor students in the school library using lessons materials provided by the students' classroom teachers. Because the school was on the late bus schedule, this time was convenient for everyone. Between 20 to 30 community volunteers arrived each morning and tutored 1 to 3 students each.

Another school noticed that many students congregated on the school playground before school during the 30 to 40 minutes between being dropped off by their parents and the beginning of the school day. The school's media coordinator, realizing that the media center was vacant during this time, proposed an early morning teacher read-aloud time when faculty members took turns, usually not more than once per month, inviting those students into the media center each morning to listen to teacher read-alouds rather than waste time on the playground. Students learned that it was a special privilege to be in the media center before school and that any rowdiness would see them quickly back out on the playground.

Still another elementary principal coordinated the morning schedules of the Title 1, special education, speech and language, ELL resource teachers, and paraprofessional teacher's aides so that this group of adults could arrive en masse as an instructional support team in classrooms serving struggling readers. This allowed for a daily full hour of very focused small-group reading and writing instruction for students who needed it the most.

The point to be made is that each school has unique instructional needs and available resources. With the right vision and commitment, enterprising educators can develop school-level programs that provide the additional focused reading instruction needed to help all students succeed.

PEARSON
myeducationlab

Special Needs

Go to MyEducationLab, "Special Needs," and read the article "Every Child Will Read."

As you read this article, notice how school-level interventions, in addition to classroom-level interventions, are necessary to ensure success for students with special needs. School-level interventions include careful scheduling, assessment programs, and community involvement.

- What are two school-level interventions that can help every child learn to read successfully?
- How can school administrators facilitate teacher collaboration for the benefit of their students?
- How can community members support school efforts to support struggling readers?

CONCLUDING THOUGHTS

The most effective classroom intervention for struggling readers is a knowledgeable, committed teacher. These teachers develop comprehensive and effective classroom reading and writing programs that address all of the essential elements of reading from oral language and print conventions to high-level fluency and comprehension strategies. Such comprehensive classroom programs are effective and adequate for many students. However, knowing that no single program will meet the instructional needs of all students, effective teachers use assessment data to identify which students are functioning below, or well below, grade level and provide them with additional in-class differentiated small-group instruction to meet specific reading needs. And because some students face significant challenges in learning to read, effective teachers consult with school-level resource personnel to design interventions for students who struggle most.

Teachers who are committed to seeing that all of their students become successful readers increase and focus instruction as needed to meet all students' needs. Effective teachers always keep their focus on students.

SUGGESTED ACTIVITIES TO EXTEND YOUR LEARNING

1. Identify a struggling reader in your family or neighborhood. Offer to tutor him or her twice per week, for about 40 minutes, for 8 to 10 weeks. Focus on (1) assessment, (2) meaningful reading, (3) word study, and (4) spelling in each lesson. Use some of the assessment techniques described in Chapter 10 to identify specific areas of need. Use some of the instructional techniques described in this chapter to strengthen the student's reading in those specific areas. Keep a tutoring journal of the assessment and instructional techniques you tried, which ones were most effective, and the student's progress.
2. Interview a classroom teacher and, if possible, a special education teacher and a Title 1 teacher about the struggling readers they teach, the assessment and instructional methods they use, and their observations about how best to help struggling readers.

REFERENCES

Adams, M. J. (1990). *Beginning to read: Thinking and learning about print.* Cambridge, MA: MIT Press.

August, D., & Shanahan, T. (2006). *Developing literacy in second-language learners: Report of the National Literacy Panel on Language-Minority Children and Youth.* Mahwah, NJ: Erlbaum.

Bear, D. R., Invernizzi, M., Templeton, S., & Johnston, F. (2008). *Words their way: Word study for phonics, vocabulary, and spelling instruction* (4th ed.). Upper Saddle River, NJ: Merrill/ Prentice Hall.

Chomsky, C. (1978). When you still can't read in third grade: After decoding, what? In S. J. Samuels (Ed.), *What research has to say about reading instruction* (pp. 13–30). Newark, DE: International Reading Association.

Clay, M. M. (1993). *Reading recovery: A guidebook for teachers in training.* Portsmouth, NH: Heinemann.

Consortium on Reading Excellence. (2007). *Assessing reading: Multiple measures, K–8,* (2nd ed.). Novato, CA: Arena Press.

Cunningham, P. M., & Allington, R. L. (2002). *Classrooms that work: They can all read and write* (3rd ed.). New York: Addison-Wesley Longman.

Echevarria, J., Vogt, M., & Short, D. J. (2004). *Making content comprehensible for English learners: The SIOP model* (2nd ed.). Boston: Pearson.

Fountas, I., & Pinnell, G. (1996). *Guided reading: Good first teaching for all children.* Portsmouth, NH: Heinemann.

Good, R. H., & Kaminski, R. A. (2002). *Dynamic indicators of basic early literacy skills* (6th ed.). Eugene, OR: Institute for the Development of Educational Achievement.

Good, R. H., Simmons, D. C., & Kame'enui, E. J. (2001). The importance and decision-making utility of a continuum of fluency-based indicators of foundational reading skills for third-grade high-stakes outcomes. *Scientific Studies of Reading, 5*(3), 257–288.

Hofmeister, A. M. (1996). *Reading for all learners.* Logan, UT: Academic Success for All Learners.

Invernizzi, M. A. (2001). The complex world of one-on-one tutoring. In S. Neuman & D. Dickinson (Eds.), *Handbook of early literacy research.* New York: Guilford Press.

Kosanovich, M., Ladinsky, K., Nelsen, L., & Torgesen, J. K. (2007). *Differentiated reading instruction: Small group alternative lesson structures for all students.* Tallahassee: Florida Center for Reading Research. Retrieved from http://www.fcrr.org/assessment/pdf/smallGroupAlternativeLessonStructures.pdf

National Assessment of Educational Progress. (2007). *Reading report card.* U.S. Department of Education. Retrieved from http://nationsreportcard.gov/reading_2007

National Reading Panel. (2000). *Teaching children to read: An evidence-based assessment of the scientific research literature on reading and its implications for reading instruction. Report of the subgroups.* National Institute of Child Health and Human Development. Retrieved from http://www.nichd.nih.gov/publications/nrp/smallbook.cfm

Nelson, O. G., & Linek, W. M. (1999). *Practical classroom applications of language experience: Looking back, looking forward.* Boston: Allyn & Bacon.

Pressley, M. (2002). *Reading instruction that works: The case for balanced teaching* (2nd ed.). New York: Guilford Press.

Pressley, M., Wharton-McDonald, R., Allington, R., Block, C. C., Morrow, L., Tracey, D., et al. (2001). A study of effective first-grade literacy instruction. *Scientific Studies of Reading, 5*(1), 35–58.

Reutzel, D. R., & Cooter, R. B. (2007). *Strategies for reading assessment and instruction: Helping every child to succeed,* (3rd ed.). Upper Saddle River, NJ: Merrill/Prentice Hall.

Samuels, S. J. (1979). The method of repeated readings. *The Reading Teacher, 32,* 403–408.

Torgesen, J. K. (2004). Lessons learned from research on intervention for students who have difficulty learning to read. In P. McCardle & V. Chhabra (Eds.), *The voice of evidence in reading research.* Baltimore: Brookes.

Putting It All Together

by Sylvia Read

12

A DAY IN MR. GREEN'S FIRST-GRADE CLASSROOM: IMPLEMENTING A FIVE-PART LITERACY INSTRUCTION FRAMEWORK

A 3-hour literacy block allows teachers to plan for and teach students in every area of the reading and language arts curriculum. Provided in this chapter are the morning schedule and activities that are typical of classrooms in which high-quality instruction is occurring.

At Mr. Green's school, classes begin at 9:15 a.m. and dismiss at 3:30 p.m. Thirty-five percent of the school's students are eligible to receive free or reduced lunch. He does not have a paid classroom aide, but is fortunate to have several dedicated parent volunteers who help in his classroom, especially during the 3-hour literacy block, which is divided up like this:

8:00–9:00 a.m.:	Before school
9:00–9:15 a.m.:	Students arrive
9:15–9:25 a.m.:	Class business
9:25–10:00 a.m.:	Teacher read-aloud and singing
10:00–10:30 a.m.:	Whole-class word study
10:30–11:30 a.m.:	Differentiated small-group instruction, independent reading and centers time
11:30–11:45 a.m.:	Recess time
11:45 a.m.–12:30 p.m.:	Writing workshop
Afternoon	

Mr. Green's curricular emphases, decisions, and actions are based on a set of personal beliefs about literacy teaching and learning. They are:

- To be fully effective, literacy instruction must include the following instructional components: teacher read-aloud, independent reading, word study, guided reading, and writing.
- A flexible literacy instruction framework provides both needed consistency and coverage.
- Literacy instruction requires a 2$1/2$- to 3-hour instructional block of time.
- Struggling readers need more instruction and more instructional time. All students need reading instruction matched to their needs.

- Assessment is an integral and necessary component of instruction.
- Children need boundaries to feel physically and emotionally safe.
- Children need consistency in daily school routines (ideally, at home too).
- Children learn to behave appropriately through modeling, experience, and positive feedback.
- Children need to be able to make choices in order to feel invested in their learning and behavior; however, too many choices are overwhelming.
- The teacher's job is to balance choice and structure, to provide modeling and feedback, and to let children know that they are *seen*, both literally and metaphorically.
- Finally, all of his first-grade students should leave his class at the end of the year reading at or above grade level.

8:00–9:00 A.M.:   BEFORE SCHOOL

Even though school doesn't officially start for another 75 minutes, some of Mr. Green's students begin trickling in, eager to tell him of their latest family events and to see what they will be doing that day. Most of these early arrivers visit for a few moments and then head outside to the playground to begin burning off a fraction of their limitless energy.

A few of them are Mr. Green's struggling readers. He has identified about 6 of his 23 students as needing extra support in reading, and has made it a priority that each of these students gets one-on-one reading time every day with him, a parent volunteer, or a university practicum student. He takes advantage of this before-school teaching opportunity with a warm invitation of, "Hey, let's read together for a few minutes." He pulls an extra chair next to his desk and the two of them sit side-by-side as he listens to one of the students read aloud from a self-selected sustained silent reading (SSR) book, a preprimer, or a page of decodable phonics practice sentences. As the student reads, he helps with word identification when appropriate, discusses the content of the text, and makes brief notes in a three-ring binder that contains anecdotal records for each of his students.

When he is not reading with a student during this morning time, he is reviewing plans for the day, making instructional materials, or heading to the copy machine to run off another hundred pages of the half-and-half paper his students use each day during writing workshop. He really enjoys this early morning time that allows him to pay special attention to some of his students and get a running start on the day.

9:00–9:15 A.M.:   STUDENTS ARRIVE

The first bell rings, the classroom door flies open, and most of Mr. Green's 23 students begin hanging coats and backpacks on the hooks on the back wall. Some students bring him zipper freezer bags containing the take-home books they have been reading with their parents. Later during the day these bags will be checked in, refilled with new take-home books, and returned to the students. During this 15 minutes, students may converse quietly with friends, browse in the classroom library, play "center" games such as Concentration, read alone or with a partner at a self-selected classroom location, or work on a project at their desks. A few students continue to trickle in right up the official beginning of the school day.

9:15–9:25 A.M.:   CLASS BUSINESS

The final bell rings, students head for their seats, and the school day officially begins. Most of the time, the students' desks are arranged in a horseshoe configuration with the open end of the horseshoe toward the board at the front of the room. A large tan rug lies on the floor in the middle of the horseshoe. Mr. Green regularly alternates between activities at the desks and on the rug, which helps students who need to move and get their wiggles out. In the back of the classroom are two round tables that serve as a listening center, a place for small-group instruction, and other miscellaneous activities.

Mr. Green collects the last of the zipper freezer bags, takes roll and lunch count, and then spends a few minutes welcoming everyone, doing a brief monologue about something silly that happened to him or his family, and providing a preview of the day's highlights. Often, he provides this "morning message" in written form on the board. The students enjoy reading along and trying to predict upcoming words as he writes. Today's morning message, "This afternoon, we'll start a new art project and go to the library," also provides an opportunity to examine a meaningful written text for familiar spelling patterns and word parts. Brady comes to the board and underlines the *th* digraph in *this* and *the*. Sally and Trent each underline an *r*-controlled vowel in *afternoon* and *start*. Jill also underlines the *st* consonant blend in *start*. Tim, a future linebacker, proudly announces that the word *pro* is part of the word *project*. Mr. Green also examines the sentence and points out that there are two more *r*-controlled vowels waiting to be found.

The daily Pledge of Allegiance provides a wonderful opportunity to strengthen students' familiarity with print conventions. Mr. Green consults his class list and announces that today's "pledge pointer" is Abbey. Abbey importantly strides to the front right corner of the room where the American flag hangs above the words to the pledge printed on a piece of chart paper. When she is ready to begin, Mr. Green says, "Stand for the pledge." The class stands and reads the pledge aloud, following along as Abbey uses a yardstick to point to the words. For most of his class this daily opportunity to see left-to-right, top-to-bottom and to match the individual printed words to the, by now, memorized text is very effective in strengthening literacy foundation concepts.

The time for class business ends each morning with the instruction, "Make sure you have two or more silent reading books, and nothing else, on top of your desk and then come to the rug. Remember, I want you to choose books that *have words you know*." This reminds students to choose books at their independent or instructional level so that silent reading becomes an effective time to build automaticity through reading and rereading words with familiar spelling patterns and word parts in context. Some students hurry to the classroom library to get books, others search their backpacks, and many pull books from inside their desks. As the students seat themselves on the rug, Mr. Green scans the desks to make sure that each student will have several independent reading books ready to read when the time comes.

Because it's early in the year, some of the students are reading "Sam books" (short decodable text readers they are familiar with) whereas other students read *Frog and Toad* or other *I Can Read* books. A few read from preprimers, while some read class-made books from language experience lessons. As the months go by, the students read more challenging texts including some easy and some hard chapter books.

The next 40 minutes is devoted to three activities: a brief sharing time, an interactive teacher read-aloud, and singing. Mr. Green's sharing time is typical. His 23 students each have one designated day each week for sharing, although he frequently allows some students to share on other days on an "emergency" basis. Having sharing time on the rug, with the students seated close together, provides a nice, more intimate atmosphere for sharing. Each student takes a minute to tell about a family event, or show and describe an interesting object. Mr. Green asks each student a question or two, providing added opportunities for the students to use and develop their oral language skills, and encourages their classmates to do the same.

As sharing time concludes he reads aloud a picture book. This morning's teacher read-aloud is *Cookies* from Arnold Lobel's Newbery Honor book *Frog and Toad Together*.

Mr. Green first introduces the theme of the story by telling the students of a Saturday afternoon last week when he was watching a football game on TV when he should have been mowing the lawn. He describes how he knew he shouldn't watch the ballgame that afternoon when the lawn needed to be mowed and how he needed *willpower* to put down the chips, get up off the couch, and start the lawnmower. After elaborating on the term *willpower*, he asks his students if any of them could tell about a time when they needed willpower to do something they knew they should do. After several accounts of cleaning rooms, changing diapers, and other mostly household chores, he asks the students to listen carefully to the story to see how Frog and Toad needed willpower to do something they needed to do.

Mr. Green reads *Cookies* aloud, stopping briefly to ask a question or when he senses that some clarification would be helpful. As the story concludes and he closes the book, he asks, "Well, what did you think?" His students respond with comments such as "I liked the part when Frog let the birds eat all the cookies" and "I liked the part when Toad said he was gonna go home and bake a cake." After all of the major story parts have been mentioned, he raises the discussion to a more personal and thoughtful level by asking, "How did you feel when Frog let the birds eat all the cookies? Is there a lesson in this story?" After the discussion, he tells the students, "Later today some of you will read *Cookies* during our small-group work."

A favorite part of each school day is when Mr. Green's 12-string guitar comes out of its case for a usually raucous, always spirited sing-along. Mr. Green and his students sing lots of children's songs, grown-up songs that are appropriate for children, and songs that they write together as a class. Most days they begin with a song Mr. Green chooses, usually a new song that they are learning or reviewing. Then the day's "song chooser" student selects an additional song from the growing "Songs We Know" list posted on the wall.

Today Mr. Green chooses to do a class songwriting activity based on the song "She'll Be Coming 'Round the Mountain." Mr. Green begins by singing the song to his class, adding lots of emphasis and expression to make the song lively. After the students have heard him sing the song, Mr. Green displays the lyrics prewritten on a piece of chart paper. He writes all of the song lyrics on chart paper and tapes a coathanger to the back of each chart at the top. The coathangers make the charts easy to hang up and display, and also easy to store on a chart rack.

With the song lyrics chart in view, Mr. Green reads the words to the students, pointing to the words as he says them, and discusses them. Now that the words have been both musically and visually introduced, Mr. Green leads the class in singing the song several more times until they sing it confidently.

On this particular song lyrics chart, Mr. Green replaces the words "coming 'round the mountain" with a blank space each time they appear in the lyrics:

She'll be _____ when she comes

Mr. Green and his students brainstorm a list of things "she" could be doing "when she comes." With some modeling, prompting, and syllable adjusting from Mr. Green, the list grows to include a variety of activities such as: "riding on her skateboard when she comes," "eating lots of donuts when she comes," "reading Boxcar Children when she comes," and "dancing in the ballet when she comes." As new lines are composed, Mr. Green fills in the words on the blank spaces on the chart paper. The final, and students' favorite, line of the new song is, "She'll be playing in the Superbowl when she comes."

Mr. Green and his students sing the song again, but now with their own new lyrics. A discussion of syllables helps the students understand why some words work well in the song and some don't. After the class enthusiastically sings their rewritten version of "She'll Be Coming 'Round the Mountain," one or two students take turns as song choosers and the singing continues.

The emotional and literacy benefits of singing time are tremendous. First of all, singing creates a sense of community better than almost any other classroom activity. The songs are generally upbeat, often silly, and help get each school day started on a very positive note. Mr. Green's students' eyes sparkle as they sing and bounce to the catchy rhythms.

Mr. Green also gets a lot of instructional mileage from singing. Each day, one of his students gets to be the "song pointer." Like the pledge pointer, the song pointer points to the words on the song lyric chart with a yardstick as the students sing. By springtime, Mr. Green's students can do this accurately and confidently. He also leads the students in examining the printed lyrics for familiar spelling patterns and word parts. The song lyric charts soon become colorfully decorated with circles and underlines as students take markers in hand and highlight the contraction in *She'll*, the *ing* in *coming* and the other verbs, and annotate the fact that *skateboard*, *boxcar*, and *superbowl* are compound words. The powerful motivating influence of music makes daily singing time into a highly effective component of Mr. Green's literacy instruction.

10:00–10:30 A.M.: WHOLE-CLASS WORD STUDY

After teacher read-aloud and singing, Mr. Green begins a whole-class word study lesson. Several weeks ago, he began introducing his students to the vowel teams spelling pattern (*ai*, *ay*, *ea*, *ee*, *oa*, and *ow*). Last week he introduced the A Teams (*ai* and *ay*). Today he plans to introduce the E Teams (*ea* and *ee*). He begins by displaying a chart of long *a* and long *e* vowel team word families (see Figure 12.1). After a quick review of the A Teams, he introduces the *ea* and *ee* spelling patterns.

Teacher Explanation

Mr. Green begins the lesson with explicit teacher explanation and modeling of the concept. He explains to the students that the *ea* and *ee* spelling patterns both have two vowels and both make the long *e* sound. Mr. Green draws his students'

Figure 12.1 Vowel
Team Spelling
Patterns

A Teams		E Teams	
<u>ai</u>	<u>ay</u>	<u>ea</u>	<u>ee</u>
paid	day	leaf	feed
rain	say	team	jeep
wait	play	heat	sweep
trail	stay	cream	screen
paint	away	treat	freeze
chain	today	teach	cheese

attention to the *ea* words on the chart and makes sure that his students are watching carefully as he underlines and explains the *ea* patterns in each word. He then asks, "Whose turn is it to read first?" to remind the students that they are to listen as he models reading the column of *ea* words, showing how the initial consonants and consonant blends combined with *ea* and a final consonant (or consonants) to create the words.

Interactive Guided Practice

Mr. Green and his students read the column of *ea* words together several times aloud together as a class. He teasingly points out that "fifth-grade students are so smart they can start at the bottom of a list and read the words going up to the top." The students protest that they can too, and take great delight in proving it. Mr. Green invites several students to come to the chart, take marker in hand, and underline the *ea* pattern in several words as he had modeled previously.

As the class begins to read the words confidently, they move to "show-off" reading. Mr. Green asks several students to choose three friends, stand, and read the words aloud to the class.

Independent Practice

Mr. Green concludes the lesson by giving each student a blank index card and inviting them to search for and write *ea* words on the index cards during their independent reading and reading at home. Tomorrow, when they will bring the cards with the *ea* words that they've found, Mr. Green will have the students create a class *ea* "word hunt" chart with their words. Mr. Green expects that some of the *ea* words they'll find will not fit the pattern (*bread, spread, breath*). Such exceptions provide a good opportunity to further clarify and reinforce the concept as the students discriminate whether or not the vowels in each word make a long *e* sound. The final component of the day's decoding lesson (finding the spelling patterns in connected text) will take place during the next classroom activity, shared reading.

Differentiated Small-Group Instruction

Because Mr. Green has assessed his students' reading, he knows that one size does not fit all when it comes to reading instruction. His struggling readers need to read below-level texts that are at their instructional level. His students reading at grade level need to read grade-level texts. Last, some students are reading above grade level and they need to read texts that challenge them, allowing them to keep growing as readers.

To manage the differing needs of his students, Mr. Green spent the first few weeks of the school year teaching the students to do center work. His centers are simple, yet the students are engaged in worthwhile reading and writing tasks that help them consolidate their skills. While students rotate among the centers, Mr. Green can meet with his small groups.

There are four groups. Time doesn't permit meeting with every group every day, but Mr. Green meets with his struggling readers every day. Two groups include students who are reading at or near grade level. He meets these groups every other day. The fourth group includes the students who are reading above grade level. They are reading a children's novel and Mr. Green meets with them twice a week.

With one of the two groups of students reading at or near grade level, he projects an overhead transparency of the first page of *Cookies* directly onto the board. He selects a student to serve as the pointer. The student grabs a pencil, sits in the chair next to the overhead projector, and points to the first word on the transparency. Again Mr. Green asks the students, "Whose turn is it to read first?" He reads the first page aloud to them, with the student pointing to the words as he reads. Then he invites the students to read the page aloud with him, leading the class in several choral readings of the page.

The next part of this reading lesson, finding and underlining spelling patterns in the shared reading sentences, is very important. It is this whole-to-parts step that explicitly links the daily decoding lessons to the students' reading of connected text. He begins this portion of the shared reading lesson by asking the familiar question, "Who can find some of our spelling patterns on the first page of *Cookies*?" The students are very familiar with a number of spelling patterns they have learned and immediately hands go up as students scrutinize the sentences. Responding in their standard procedure, Liz says, "Sentence one, the word *Toad* has a vowel team with *oa*." Using a marking pen, Mr. Green underlines the *oa* in *Toad*, then asks, "Who else can find a spelling pattern?" Becca similarly points out, "In sentence two, the word *ate* is a tickle word. Again Mr. Green underlines the identified spelling pattern. Bryce adds, "In sentence one, the word *some* is a tickle word." I use this opportunity to teach why the word *some* looks like but is not a tickle word, making a short *u* sound rather than long *o* it would make if it followed the pattern. They add *some* to their list of "outlaws," words that don't follow the rules. In the next few minutes they discover together that *baked*, *even*, *taste*, and *made* are tickle words; *Frog*, *smell*, and *cried* contain blends; and that *these*, *they*, and *that* contain digraphs. They also add *one* and *said* to their list of outlaws. The board is thoroughly marked up, and the students can plainly see that most of what they read is simply combinations of familiar spelling patterns.

They conclude the pattern-finding portion of the shared reading lesson with one more choral reading of the page, returning from the parts to the whole. Tomorrow,

PEARSON
myeducationlab

Organizing for Instruction

Go to MyEducationLab, "Organizing for Instruction," and watch the video *Guided Reading*.

As you view the video, notice the flow of the lesson from beginning to end. What small-group lesson components described in this textbook were represented in the video? Which components were missing?

• What were the prereading activities the teacher used to prepare the student for reading the selection?
• How did the students read the book? What are the advantages of this method?
• What did the teacher do to build students' oral reading fluency?

Mr. Green will have these groups reread this page and add one or two more pages. Next week, when this group of students can all read *Cookies* reasonably well, Mr. Green will turn it into a readers' theater by underlining Frog's dialogue in red on the overhead transparency, and Toad's dialogue in blue. The nondialogue "narrator" parts won't be underlined. Students will have a chance to read each part (Frog, Toad, or Narrator), practice, and then perform the story as a readers' theater. Mr. Green's objective is to build his students' oral reading fluency while having fun with children's literature.

Independent Reading and Centers Time

As Mr. Green calls his first reading group to meet him at the back table, some of his other students go back to their desks where their independent reading books are waiting. The students select from among the books on their desks and begin reading silently to themselves. So that independent reading time is not wasted, Mr. Green enforces two rules: no talking, and no leaving your seat. During independent reading time Mr. Green quietly conducts reading conferences with his students. Though the students do not talk to each other, the murmurs of their "silent" reading fill the room with a pleasant hum.

In the fall, Mr. Green's first graders independently read for 10 minutes each day. Over the weeks and months, he gradually lengthens the time until, by early March, they read silently each day for 20 minutes. Each day during independent reading, he scans his class list and designates three or four students as "special readers" who get the privilege of choosing a special place in the classroom to read. Popular independent reading places include the rug, the old overstuffed couch in the corner, and the authors' chair. He also scans the students' book selections occasionally to make sure that they aren't showing off, pretending to read *Harry Potter* or some other book above their independent or instructional reading level.

Teacher–Student Reading Conferences

In-between reading groups, Mr. Green fits in a few teacher–student reading conferences. The reading conferences quickly cover three aspects of his students' reading: reading attitude and interests, oral reading fluency, and comprehension. He begins by asking students what book they have chosen and why, and jotting down the date of the conference, title of the book, and its level. They discuss the students' reading interests such as favorite genre and how they learn about and select books. Then he asks the student to read a paragraph aloud as he make notes in a three-ring assessment binder about words or spelling patterns the student struggled with, reading rate, and expression. Finally he asks the student to tell him what the book is about, occasionally probing the student's knowledge of setting, characters, events (or main ideas and details for expository texts) and asking for opinions about the book. To complete the reading conference, he often recommends other books of potential interest, or teaches a brief spontaneous mini-lesson on an appropriate strategy, or assigns the students to reread a passage to practice fluency or to deepen understanding. These notes are very helpful in identifying students with similar needs, tracking students' progress, and determining instructional topics.

Parent Volunteers

Most mornings during independent reading time, a parent volunteer arrives in the classroom. During back-to-school night in September, Mr. Green had distributed a sign-up sheet for volunteers, asking who might be able to volunteer weekly, monthly, or on call as needed. Five parents indicated they could volunteer 1 hour each week, so Mr. Green set up a schedule for each of them to come in on a different day of the week.

In early October, Mr. Green identified six students who needed extra instructional support. He decided that the best use of the parent volunteers was to supervise the extra reading practice for his six struggling readers in the area of basic decoding skills (Perfetti, 1985). He met with the parent volunteers and showed them a simple procedure for reading together one-on-one with these struggling readers.

1. Take the student to the sofa in the corner of the classroom and preview the text Mr. Green has selected (sometimes an *I Can Read* book; sometimes a decodable text, or both) for the student.
2. Point to the words in a sweeping motion while the student reads aloud.
3. When the student misreads a word, tap on it to refocus the student on the word.
4. If the student still cannot identify the word, the parent can either (a) prompt the student by pronouncing the beginning of the word and allowing the student to finish it, (b) help the student blend the letter sounds left-to-right, or (c) "break and make" the word by covering the onset, decoding the rime, and then putting the two parts of the word back together.
5. Finally, the parent volunteer makes notes about the one-on-one reading session, recording the title and page numbers of text read together, and also any words or spelling patterns that the student struggled with.

The goal is for each struggling reader to get 15 minutes of one-on-one reading time with either Mr. Green or a parent volunteer each day. Mr. Green has a reading schedule and a list of appropriate reading texts, and the system works very smoothly. Each parent volunteer arrives in the classroom, goes to Mr. Green's desk to see which student is next on the schedule to be read with and which reading text to use, and takes the student to the couch and reads with them. Then the parent volunteer calls the next student over. Mr. Green also asks the parent volunteers to read with the middle and top students on occasion as well because all students enjoy reading to the volunteers. Mr. Green is absolutely convinced that these parent volunteers make a huge contribution to the reading success of his struggling readers.

11:30–11:45 A.M.:   RECESS TIME

11:45 A.M.–12:30 P.M.:   WRITING WORKSHOP

Mini-Lesson

After 15 minutes of running around outside, Mr. Green's students return to the classroom and find sitting places back on the rug in the center of the classroom, ready to begin writing workshop with a daily 10–15-minute mini-lesson (Atwell, 1998; Avery, 2002). Today's mini-lesson focuses on dialogue. Mr. Green stands in front of the classroom, next to an overhead projector getting ready to write on a transparency version of the students' writing paper that is being projected onto the board. For the past 4 or 5 days, the mini-lessons have been demonstrations of including dialogue in stories. Today, Mr. Green plans to add several sentences to their ongoing class story. The students watch and read along as Mr. Green writes:

Cassie asked, "Where is my pencil?" "It's on the floor," said Juan.

Mr. Green and his students read the sentences again together and then discuss how the quotation marks help readers know who's speaking and what's being said. Then he continues on with the class story, adding the following sentence:

Joanne said, "Hey, that's my pencil, not Cassie's."

They read the sentence together and note again, briefly, how the quotation marks help readers know what the people in a story are saying. As the day's mini-lesson concludes, the students return to their seats with the reminder, "Remember to put talking and quotation marks in your stories. I want to know what the people in your stories are saying to each other."

After the mini-lesson, Mr. Green takes a quick status of the class, recording what each student will be working on that day. If a student is starting a new piece of writing, he listens to their ideas, which gives him the chance to give the students a little feedback. If a student says, "My dog," he'll ask, "What about your dog?" If a student says, "How I feel," he might say, "How do you feel?" He rarely has students say that they can't think of anything to write about. If they do, he offers them suggestions based on what other students are writing about. Often that helps. Sometimes a brief conversation about family sparks an idea. Sometimes nothing helps and he suggests that the student browse the classroom library for a few minutes, knowing that all writers are readers and that books inevitably spark ideas. Most children find choice motivating; some children need more specific directions, in which case it can be helpful to give a limited range of choices.

Silent Writing

When everyone is seated at their desks, they begin 10 minutes of silent writing. The purpose of silent writing is to give the students uninterrupted time immediately after the mini-lesson so that they may apply the information from the mini-lesson to their writing while it is still fresh on their minds. Everybody writes, including Mr. Green. Nobody talks and walks around the classroom during silent writing.

The students write on paper he calls half-and-half paper. It is lined on the bottom half and has room for drawing on the top half. This paper allows them to write or to organize their ideas through drawing when needed. At the beginning of the school year the students drew extensively, with very little writing. Mr. Green would go from desk to desk, saying, "Tell me about your picture," and then adding a caption below the students' drawings. Soon the students wanted to write their own captions and Mr. Green would help them get started. Over the weeks and months, they drew less and wrote more. By the end of the year, many students will totally discontinue the drawing and use the top half of the paper for their revisions. Mr. Green keeps a large supply of this half-and-half writing paper in a small basket at the back of the classroom, and his students know to always keep four to five extra sheets of this paper in their writing folders.

Free Writing Time and Conferences

The 20 to 30 minutes after silent writing are spent in what Mr. Green calls "free writing time." During this time, the students may choose to remain at their seats and continue with their writing, write with a partner, illustrate a book they have written, or have a writing conference with Mr. Green.

Consistently throughout the year, about half of Mr. Green's students each day choose to remain at their seats, continuing their writing. He spends this time moving from seat to seat, dragging a first-grade chair, conferencing with these students. His conferences always begins with an invitation, "Would you please read it to me?" he asks. He sits beside the student's desk and follows along as the student reads aloud. Much of the writing at this point is invented spelling which he encourages with a continual reminder to, "Just write the sounds that you hear." When a student has written an invented word *that he cannot read*, he writes the correct spelling in very small letters above the word(s) on the student's paper. Words with invented spellings that Mr. Green can read are left alone. The only reason he writes the correct spelling for the few words he can't read is to help him remember what is written when it comes time for typing and printing the story for publication. He does not tell his students that they must correct their spelling at this point, and the notations do not seem to bother or inhibit any of the students' expressiveness.

During a writing conference, Mr. Green and the student discuss the content of the story first. Then Mr. Green often asks what the student plans to add next, or he asks for more details. For example, Doug is writing about a sleepover at his grandma's house. Mr. Green tells him that he's very curious about Grandma and would like to know more about what Grandma looks like, and what she does and says. Occasionally he will also provide a spontaneous individual mini-lesson on some aspect of conventions (usually putting space between words, use of periods or capital letters, and or spelling). This free writing time is often the most challenging part of his day because he'll often have three to five students waving to him, indicating that they are ready for a conference. He generally replies with another standard, yet cheerful, response, "Keep writing. I'll be there as quickly as I can."

Authors' Chair

When Mr. Green notes, during a conference, that a student has four to five pages of new writing, he suggests that the student go to the board and sign up for the authors' chair. Usually, three or four students each day read their writing from the authors' chair, which is the final activity during writing workshop and provides a daily 10- to 15-minute opportunity for the students to give and receive feedback about each other's writing. The students who have signed up take turns sitting in the large brown overstuffed thrift store chair and reading their pages of new writing to their classmates who are seated back on the rug.

When a child shares his or her writing, the other children have a very important job: They must listen carefully and respond thoughtfully. This, too, must be modeled and taught. Mr. Green models what listening looks like and sounds like and also what it doesn't look like. The audience responds to the writing in several ways. They tell the author what they heard in the writing, what they liked, and what parts may have confused them. Sometimes the author wants ideas on where to go next with the writing, and in that case the audience can make suggestions and offer ideas. Mr. Green also models ways to respond to others' writing positively, how to ask genuine questions, how to politely explain what parts were confusing and possibly make gentle suggestions for change. Whether or not the author takes the suggestions and uses them to revise is entirely up to the author, but Mr. Green records the suggestions on sticky notes so the author can incorporate the suggestions into their writing the following day. He also offers specific praise when students have incorporated the skill or strategy of the day's mini-lesson. Authors' chair is not just a time for celebrating student writing, but also a time to reinforce the day's lesson.

Publishing

When Mr. Green explained to his students that he would soon begin making books out of their writing, the class decided that you can't make a book out of one page, or two pages, or even five or six pages. Mr. Green suggested that at least eight or nine half-and-half pages of writing would be enough to make a book. He taught the students how to number their draft pages and staple them together so they wouldn't waste time each day shuffling and reordering pages.

When one of his students has written enough for a book, the student brings it to Mr. Green to be published. They review the story together in a brief editing conference. Mr. Green helps the student add periods and capital letters and fix a few spellings. Then a parent volunteer, a college practicum student, or Mr. Green types the student's story on a computer (correcting the remaining spelling and punctuation errors like a real editor), electronically pastes the sentences into a Word book template, then prints the book pages for the student to illustrate. When the illustrations are completed, the student's biographical "author information page" is added at the end, the cover and back pages are added, and the book is bound using the comb-binding machine in the teachers' workroom. The finished book is then presented to its proud author to be celebrated in class and taken home to be cherished and praised by family members. Mr. Green places photocopies of the books in a section of the classroom library for students to read during independent reading time. The original handwritten half-and-half-page manuscripts are saved in each student's portfolio folder to be reviewed and shared at parent conference time.

Mr. Green's daily writing workshop lasts nearly 1 hour. Because his students are so highly motivated by having their writing published, they love writing, and the writing workshop time goes by quickly. In fact, the students are very disappointed if they have to miss writing workshop due to a school assembly or some other interruption. After writing workshop, Mr. Green and his students are ready for lunch.

AFTERNOON

Altogether, Mr. Green and his students spend about 3 hours each morning engaged in reading and writing activities. After lunch, he reads aloud a chapter from a novel each day while his students listen intently on the rug. Math comes next for about 40 minutes, followed by activities from either a science or social studies unit. These activities often involve informational children's book read-alouds and content-area writing. The school day concludes with students going to either physical education or music.

The procedures and routines become so familiar to Mr. Green's students that they can tell a substitute teacher or a parent how the classroom operates after having been in his class for only a few weeks. Students in Mr. Green's class feel safe, a key ingredient for student learning. They are engaged in meaningful reading and writing activities throughout their school day. The density and richness of the instruction in Mr. Green's classroom ensures that students will grow as readers and writers.

CONCLUDING THOUGHTS

Perhaps the largest challenge teachers face is how to provide instruction that is appropriate to a classroom of students who are reading and writing at a wide variety of ability levels. Although some of the instruction described in this chapter is done through whole-class teaching (Cunningham, Hall, & Defee, 1998), Mr. Green accommodates differences in students' abilities. For example, teacher read-alouds provide vocabulary and background knowledge learning, and positive emotional associations with books for students at all levels. During independent reading all students benefit from the practice and reinforcement of reading self-selected texts at their instructional or independent levels. Mr. Green also provides differentiated small-group instruction based on an assessment of their needs.

Writing workshop is wonderful for accommodating students of differing reading and writing ability levels. Students at all levels can write at a comfortable personal pace and receive support and guidance through individual conferences that are specific to their writing needs. Additionally, all students are highly motivated by writing on self-selected topics and seeing their finished works in print.

Another instructional benefit of using a comprehensive balanced literacy instruction framework is the synergy that occurs among the various instructional components. For example, teacher read-alouds provide students with vocabulary and background knowledge that help them make sense of their reading during shared and guided reading lessons. Word study lessons familiarize students with spelling patterns that they use during independent reading and also during writing workshop. Conversely, writing workshop gives students opportunities to explore letter–sound relationships and spelling patterns they encounter in their reading.

For approximately 3 hours each morning "students were involved, almost nonstop, with words: hearing, reading and studying words; sharing and playing with words; singing and dramatizing words; and writing and illustrating words" (Smith, 1998, p. 21). Allington (1980) argues that one of the best predictors of improvement in reading ability is the number of words that students process during reading lessons. In other words, authentic literacy activities such as independent reading, partner reading, shared reading, guided reading, and writing facilitate reading achievement whereas filling in blanks on worksheets is of little or no instructional value (Anderson, Hiebert, Scott, & Wilkinson, 1985). Although scheduling large blocks of time for literacy instruction in primary grades may be a challenge, it is an investment that teachers simply must make.

REFERENCES

Allington, R. L. (1980). Poor readers don't get to read much in reading groups. *Language Arts, 57*(8), 872–881.

Anderson, R. C., Hiebert, E. F., Scott, J. A., & Wilkinson, I. A. G. (1985). *Becoming a nation of readers: The report of the Commission on Reading.* Washington, DC: National Institute of Education.

Atwell, N. (1998). *In the middle: New understandings about writing, reading, and learning.* Portsmouth, NH: Heinemann.

Avery, C. (2002). *And with a light touch: Learning about reading, writing, and teaching with first graders.* Portsmouth: NH: Heinemann.

Cunningham, P. M., Hall, D. P., & Defee, M. (1998). Nonability-grouped multilevel instruction: Eight years later. *The Reading Teacher, 51*(8), 652–664.

Perfetti, C. A. (1985). *Reading ability.* New York: Oxford University Press.

Smith, J. A. (1998). Mr. Smith goes to first grade. *Educational Leadership, 55*(6), 19–22.

Spelling Patterns We Use

CVC	can, bed, sit, hog, rub
Blends	<u>sn</u>ip, fa<u>st</u>, <u>br</u>and
Digraphs	mu<u>ch</u>, <u>sh</u>ed, <u>th</u>is, wi<u>th</u>, <u>wh</u>en
Final Silent *E*	same, drive, rope, tube
Vowel Teams	m<u>ai</u>d, pl<u>ay</u>; gr<u>ee</u>n, t<u>ea</u>m; c<u>oa</u>ch, b<u>ow</u>l
***R*-Controlled Vowels**	c<u>ar</u>d, f<u>or</u>, h<u>er</u>, b<u>ir</u>d, t<u>ur</u>n
Diphthongs	b<u>oy</u>, p<u>oi</u>nt; l<u>ou</u>d, c<u>ow</u>; ch<u>ew</u>; str<u>aw</u>
Open Syllables	<u>be</u>, <u>hi</u>, <u>ba</u>by, <u>re</u>play, <u>ro</u>bot
Consonant-*LE*	ap<u>ple</u>, pud<u>dle</u>, un<u>cle</u>, wres<u>tle</u>
Chunks	b<u>all</u>, <u>nigh</u>t, g<u>oo</u>d, z<u>oo</u>m, s<u>ing</u>, l<u>ong</u>, <u>ank</u>, <u>tion</u>

Spelling Patterns and Chunks List

 ## SHORT VOWEL CVC WORDS

a: cab, jab, lab, tab, add, bad, dad, fad, had, lad, mad, pad, rad, sad, bag, rag, tag, wag, am, dam, ham, jam, Pam, ram, Sam, an, ban, can, Dan, fan, Jan, man, pan, ran, tan, van, cap, gap, lap, map, nap, rap, sap, tap, zap, gas, pass, bat, at, bat, cat, fat, hat, mat, pat, rat, sat, ax, Max, tax, wax, Jazz

e: Ed, bed, fed, led, red, Ted, wed, beg, bell, fell, sell, tell, well, yell, hem, Ben, den, hen, men, pen, ten, yes, bet, get, jet, let, met, net, pet, set, vet, wet, yet

i: bib, fib, rib, bid, did, hid, kid, lid, rid, if, big, dig, fig, gig, jig, wig, Bill, dill, fill, gill, hill, ill, Jill, kill, mill, pill, quill, till, will, dim, him, Jim, rim, Tim, in, bin, fin, pin, sin, tin, win, dip, hip, lip, nip, quip, rip, sip, tip, zip, hiss, kiss, miss, it, bit, fit, hit, kit, knit, lit, mitt, pit, quit, sit, wit, fix, mix, six, fizz, Liz

o: Bob, cob, job, rob, rod, cog, dog, fog, hog, jog, log, doll, Tom, on, bop, cop, hop, mop, pop, top, dot, got, hot, lot, not, pot, rot, ox, box, fox, pox

u: cub, rub, tub, bud, dud, mud, bug, dug, hug, rug, tug, gum, hum, yum, bun, fun, gun, run, sun, cup, pup, us, bus, fuss, but, cut, hut, nut, rut, buzz, fuzz

 ## SHORT VOWEL WORDS WITH CONSONANT BLENDS

a: blab, crab, drab, grab, slab, back, pack, black, snack, act, fact, clad, glad, Brad, raft, flag, brag, drag, snag, camp, clam, clamp, damp, lamp, slam, ramp, scram, stamp, swam, tram, clan, bran, plan, span, and, band, brand, grand, land, hand, sand, stand, ant, pant, plant, clap, flap, scrap, slap, snap, strap, trap, wrap, ask, class, grass, cast, fast, last, past, flat, that, brat, scat, spat, swat e: Fred, sled, sped, left, held, elf, self, smell, spell, belt, felt, melt, help, stem, fence, end, bend, blend, lend, mend, send, spend, tend, trend, bent, cent, dent, sent, spent, tent, vent, went, step, crept, kept, slept, swept, wept, desk, dress, best, crest, nest, pest, rest, test, vest, west, zest, next, text

i: crib, kick, sick, stick, skid, slid, squid, sniff, gift, lift, twig, milk, silk, drill, frill, grill, skill, spill, still, film, slim, swim, trim, grim, slim, swim, trim, limp, grin, skin, spin, prince, wind, hint, lint, mint, tint, glint, print, splint, sprint, squint, blip, clip, drip, flip, grip, skip, slip, snip, trip, lisp, crisp, bliss, fist, list, mist, wrist, twist, flit, grit, skit, slit, spit, split, twit

o: blob, slob, snob, block, clock, lock, rock, sock, soft, clog, frog, slog, smog, pond, crop, drop, flop, plop, slop, stop, cost, lost, slot, spot

u: scrub, stub, spud, stuff, plug, slug, drug, snug, bump, jump, pump, spun, stun, dunk, junk, skunk, bunt, hunt, punt, plus, bust, dust, just, must, rust, trust

SHORT VOWEL WORDS WITH CONSONANT DIGRAPHS

ch: bench, bunch, catch, chap, chat, check, chest, chick, chill, chin, chip, chop, chunk, crutch, ditch, fetch, flinch, hatch, hitch, itch, latch, lunch, match, much, munch, patch, pitch, punch, rich, switch, such, trench, which, witch

sh: bash, brush, bush, cash, crash, fresh, hush, mash, mush, rash, rush, shed, shelf, dish, fish, shin, ship, gosh, Josh, shock, shop, shot, shred, shut, splash, swish, trash, wish

th: bath, Beth, math, moth, path, than, that, them, then, thin, thrill, thud, with

wh: what, when, whim, whip, whop

LONG VOWEL SILENT E WORDS

a: face, lace, race, fade, made, wade, safe, cage, page, bake, cake, fake, Jake, lake, make, quake, rake, sake, take, wake, bale, dale, gale, male, pale, sale, tale, came, fame, game, lame, name, same, tame, cane, Jane, mane, pane, ape, cape, tape, base, case, ate, date, gate, hate, Kate, late, mate, rate, cave, Dave, gave, pave, save, wave, daze, faze, gaze, haze, maze

e: Pete, Gene, Steve, these, scene

i: dice, ice, mice, nice, rice, vice, hide, ride, side, tide, wide, knife, life, wife, bike, dike, hike, like, file, pile, dime, lime, time, dine, fine, line, mine, nine, pine, vine, wine, pipe, ripe, wipe, fire, hire, tire, wire, wise, bite, kite, quite, site, dive, five, hive, live, size

o: lobe, robe, code, rode, Coke, joke, poke, woke, yoke, hole, mole, pole, role, sole, dome, home, bone, cone, tone, zone, dope, hope, rope, hose, nose, rose, note, vote

u: Sue, cube, tube, dude, rude, huge, Duke, mule, rule, dune, June, tune, cute, mute, fuse

LONG VOWEL SILENT E WORDS WITH BLENDS AND DIGRAPHS

a: brace, place, space, trace, blade, grade, shade, trade, stage, flake, brake, shake, snake, stake, stale, whale, shame, chase, crave, grave, shave, slave, blaze, craze, glaze, graze

i: bribe, scribe, tribe, price, slice, spice, thrice, twice, bride, glide, pride, slide, stride, strife, spike, strike, smile, while, chime, crime, grime, prime, slime, shine, spine, swine, twine, whine, gripe, snipe, stripe, swipe, sprite, white, write, drive, strive, thrive, prize

o: globe, probe, broke, choke, smoke, poke, spoke, stroke, stole, whole, slope, chose, those, drove, stove, froze

u: Sue, blue, clue, glue, true, Bruce, prune, chute, flute

VOWEL TEAM WORDS (VOWEL DIGRAPHS)

ai: aid, maid, paid, raid, fail, hail, jail, mail, nail, pail, rail, sail, tail, aim, gain, lain, main, pain, rain, vain, bait, wait

ay: bay, day, hay, jay, lay, may, pay, ray, say, way

ea: pea, sea, tea, peace, easy, read, bead, lead, leaf, beak, leak, peak, weak, deal, heal, meal, real, seal, veal, beam, seam, team, bean, dean, lean, mean, heap, leap, eat, beat, heat, meat, neat, seat, tease, peace, leave, weave

ee: bee, fee, knee, see, free, tree, three, deed, feed, need, reed, seed, weed, greed, beef, peek, seek, week, feel, heel, kneel, peel, seem, queen, seen, teen, beep, deep, jeep, keep, peep, seep, weep, beet, feet, meet

oa: load, road, toad, loaf, soak, coal, foal, goal, foam, roam, loan, moan, soap, boat, coat, goat, moat, oat

ow: mow, low, row, sow, tow, bow

VOWEL TEAM WORDS WITH BLENDS AND DIGRAPHS

ai:	snail, trail, claim, plain, slain, brain, chain, drain, grain, train, Spain, sprain, stain, strain, faint, paint, saint
ay:	clay, play, slay, gray, pray, tray, stay, spray, stray, sway
ea:	flea, each, peach, beach, bleach, reach, preach, screech, speech, teach, plead, bleak, creak, freak, sneak, speak, squeak, streak, tweak, squeal, steal, cream, dream, gleam, scream, steam, stream, clean, cheap, beast, east, feast, least, yeast, cleat, please, cheat, pleat, treat, wheat, greasy, weave, leave
ee:	free, three, tree, bleed, breed, freed, greed, speed, tweed, cheek, creek, Greek, sleek, steel, wheel, green, screen, creep, sheep, sleep, steep, sweep, cheese, fleet, greet, sheet, sleet, sweet, tweet, street, breeze, freeze, sneeze, squeeze, sleeve, sneeze, wheeze
oa:	broach, coach, poach, roach, cloak, croak, groan, boast, coast, roast, toast, float, gloat, throat
ow:	blow, crow, flow, grow, show, snow, bowl, own, grown

R-CONTROLLED VOWEL WORDS

ar:	bar, car, far, jar, tar, star, card, hard, yard, large, dark, bark, Mark, park, spark, shark, arm, charm, farm, barn, yarn, harp, art, cart, chart, part, smart, start
or:	or, for, nor, porch, storm, born, corn, horn, morn, sort, sport; ore, bore, core, chore, horse, more, pore, score, shore, snore, sore, store, tore, wore; door, moor, poor, floor
er:	her, clerk, jerk, germ, term, fern, stern, verse, Bert, nerve, serve, swerve
ir:	fir, sir, bird, girl, firm, dirt, flirt, shirt, skirt, birth, third, first, thirst, squirt
ur:	fur, church, urge, surf, turkey, curl, burn, turn, curse, nurse, purse, hurt, curve

VOWEL DIPHTHONG WORDS

oy:	boy, joy, toy
oi:	choice, voice, boil, coil, foil, oil, soil, spoil, toil, coin, join, joint, point, noise, poison, moist
ou:	couch, ouch, loud, proud, bounce, bound, ground, mound, pound, round, sound, count, house, mouse, out, pout, shout, trout, mouth

ow:	bow, cow, how, now, pow, wow, crowd, flower, power, shower, tower, owl, down, town, plow, brow, chow, crowd, growl, clown, brown, crown, drown, frown
aw:	claw, flaw, draw, jaw, law, paw, raw, saw, straw, thaw, hawk, crawl, scrawl, shawl, dawn, fawn, lawn, yawn
ew:	dew, few, knew, mew, new, blew, brew, chew, crew, drew, flew, grew, threw, screw, stew, view

OPEN-SYLLABLE WORDS

baby	become	bicycle	donate	human
nature	behind	silent	local	bugle
favorite	believe	direction	moment	humor
bacon	beside	final	notice	lunar
David	between	library	polite	music
labor	beyond	microscope	program	nuisance
major	department	private	protect	pupil
paper	destroy	direct	professional	puma
favor	female	final	robot	rumor
famous	pretend	giant	focus	super
later	prevent	hibernate	Homer	tumor
nation	remember	library	locust	tutor
radio	remove	microscope	motor	scuba
savor	respect	primary	nobody	tuba
stable	responsible	rifle	notice	
staple	return	Friday	police	
stadium	rewriting		donut	
	secret			

CONSONANT-LE WORDS

adorable	ankle	apple	bubble	circle
comfortable	crackle	giggle	handlebar	incredible
horrible	impossible	invisible	mumble	people
puddle	puzzle	rattle	remarkable	terrible
tremble	turtle	vegetable	hustle	wiggle

MISCELLANEOUS CHUNKS

These chunks are irregular spellings.

ack:	back, black, crack, flack, hack, Jack, lack, Mack, pack, rack, sack, shack, slack, snack, stack, tack, track, whack, yack
all:*	all, ball, call, fall, hall, mall, tall, wall
ank:	bank, blank, clank, crank, drank, flank, Frank, plank, prank, sank, shrank, spank, tank, thank, yank
ash:	bash, cash, clash, crash, dash, flash, gash, hash, lash, mash, rash, slash, smash, stash, trash, wash
ell:	bell, cell, dell, dwell, fell, sell, shell, smell, spell, swell, tell, well, yell
est:	best, jest, nest, pest, rest, test, vest, west
ick:	brick, chick, click, Dick, flick, lick, pick, Rick, sick, slick, stick, thick, tick, trick, wick
ight:*	bright, fight, flight, fright, knight, light, might, night, right, sight, slight, tight
ing:*	bring, cling, ding, fling, king, ping, ring, sing, sling, spring, sting, string, swing, thing, wing, wring, zing
ink:*	blink, brink, chink, clink, drink, kink, link, mink, pink, rink, shrink, sink, slink, stink, think, wink
ock:	block, cock, clock, dock, flock, lock, mock, rock, smock, shock, sock
old:*	bold, cold, fold, gold, hold, mold, old, scold, sold, told
oo (as in *zoo*):*	boo, moo, too, zoo, food, mood, goof, proof, roof, moon, noon, soon, spoon, boom, doom, broom, room, zoom, coop, loop, hoop, snoop, stoop, cool, fool, pool, drool, spool, school, loose, moose, choose, boot, root, booth, tooth, smooth, snooze
oo (as in *good*):*	good, hood, wood, stood, hoof, woof, book, cook, hook, look, took, brook, crook, shook, cookie, rookie, foot, soot
ould:*	could, should, would
tion:*	action, fraction, motion, nation, potion, station
uck:	buck, chuck, cluck, duck, luck, muck, pluck, snuck, stuck, truck, tuck, yuck
ump:	bump, clump, dump, grump, jump, lump, pump, plump, slump, stump, thump
unk:	bunk, chunk, clunk, drunk, flunk, hunk, junk, punk, plunk, slunk, sunk, spunk, stunk, trunk
y as long e	baby, berry, daddy, muddy, puppy, penny, marry, cherry, bunny, candy, hurry, study
y as long i	by, cry, dry, fly, fry, guy, my, pry, sly, spry, sty, try, wry, apply, rely, reply, satisfy

SILENT LETTERS

wr (silent w)	write, wrap, wrong, wreck, wrench, wrist
kn (silent k)	knee, kneel, knit, knack, knock, knob, knuckle, know, known, knowledge, knight
mb (silent b)	dumb, numb, crumb, thumb, lamb, bomb, climb, comb, plum, plumber, tomb
gn (silent g)	sign, gnome, gnu

HARD AND SOFT SOUNDS

The letter *C* generally makes its "soft" sound when followed by the letters *E*, *I*, and *Y*.

The letter *G* generally makes its "soft" sound when followed by the letters *E* and *Y*.

The letter *G* followed by the letter *I* can make either its hard or soft sound.

Hard *C*	Soft *C*	Hard *G*	Soft *G*
cat	city	game	germ
cake	circle	gas	gentle
come	cement	go	gym
cold	cent	gum	gypsy
cup	cycle	girl	giant
cut	cyclone	give	ginger

CONTRACTIONS

I am	I'm
you are	you're
we are	we're
they are	they're
he is	he's
she is	she's
he has	he's
she has	she's
I have	I've
you have	you've
we have	we've
they have	they've

will not	won't
cannot	can't
have not	haven't
did not	didn't
do not	don't

Final Silent E
Flashcards

made	hide
robe	cube
Jane	pine
note	tube

same	mane
cape	cane
ride	bite
rode	dude

Vowel Team Flashcards

rod	road
got	goat
pan	pain
net	neat

mad	maid
bat	bait
red	read
men	mean

Spelling Pattern Bingo

		FREE		

cab	den	bit	Bob	mud
hat	red	fin	mop	rug
van	ten		got	fun
zap	jet	rip	hot	gum
mad	fed	wig	jog	nut

chat	bake	price	rain	cream
fright	bring	flash	how	toy
jaw	shed		whale	choke
heat	slight	swing	mash	down
boil	claw	lawn	treat	point

Spelling Test Page

Name _____   Name _____   Name _____

1. _____   1. _____   1. _____

2. _____   2. _____   2. _____

3. _____   3. _____   3. _____

4. _____   4. _____   4. _____

5. _____   5. _____   5. _____

6. _____   6. _____   6. _____

7. _____   7. _____   7. _____

8. _____   8. _____   8. _____

Glossary

Accretion the process of adding information to one's existing schema.

Alphabetic principle the understanding that the sounds in spoken words are represented by alphabet letters in printed words.

At-risk students students who, for any number of reasons, are struggling to learn to read and are at risk of reading failure.

Automaticity the point where readers can identify printed words effortlessly, quickly, and accurately so that attention can be allocated to comprehension.

Balanced reading instruction an instructional philosophy popular in the late 1990s that focused on combining phonics and comprehension instruction.

Basal reading programs basic reading programs used by many schools. Basal reading programs, sometimes called core reading programs, include a teacher's manual, student reading books, and accompanying instructional materials.

Benchmark a standard or performance level that students should be able to achieve. For example, third-grade students should be able to read a third-grade or level P book.

Big books enlarged-format picture books that enable teachers to highlight print concepts for small and large groups of students.

Blending sounds the process of blending the speech sounds represented by printed letters to pronounce words (*c-a-t*: *cat*).

Choral reading a pair, small group, or whole class of students reading a text aloud in unison, often together with a teacher, generally as a form of instructional support.

Chunk teachers often refer to common word endings or rimes such as *all, ock, ight,* and *ing* as chunks.

Comprehension strategies procedures that students intentionally apply to improve reading comprehension, such as predicting, clarifying, questioning, and summarizing.

Comprehensive reading instruction framework an expanded version of balanced reading instruction that focuses on teaching and combining *all* major aspects of reading and writing.

Consonant blend two consonant letters side by side wherein you hear both consonant sounds: *sp*ot, *tr*ip, *blend.*

Consonant digraph the *ch, sh, th,* and *wh* consonant pairs wherein you do not hear either consonant sound, but rather a different sound.

Constructivism a theory of learning that proposes that students construct their own understanding of the world by interacting with it and reflecting on their experiences.

Context the meaningful aspect of text that students combine with phonics and sentence structure to identify words.

Core curriculum a current term for a basal reading program that provides instructional materials and strategies for teaching all essential elements of reading and writing.

Criterion-referenced tests standardized tests that compare students to a criterion or benchmark level of performance. This test reports what percentage of students from a class or school has mastered specific instructional concepts. The emphasis is on informing instruction.

Critical comprehension the highest level of comprehension where, like a film or literary critic, students go beyond understanding a text to evaluating the quality of a text.

Cross-checking　the process of confirming word identification accuracy by making sure that printed words look right (phonics), sound right (sentence structure), and make sense (context).

Cueing systems　sources of information, including letter–sound relationships (phonics), meaning (context), and sentence structure (syntax), that readers use to identify printed words.

Decodable texts　texts with a very high percentage of decodable words (*Dan can fan Nan in the tan van*) that provide focused opportunities for students to practice reading spelling patterns.

Decoding　using letter–sound, contextual, and syntactic information to identify printed words.

Diagnosing　the process of looking very closely at various aspects of a student's reading, such as phonemic awareness, sight word recognition level, oral reading accuracy, and reading comprehension to identify specific reading strengths and needs.

Diphthong　the *oy, oi, ou, ow, ew,* and *aw* vowel pairs wherein you do not hear either vowel sound, but rather a different vowel sound, sometimes called a vowel variant.

Direct instruction　teaching reading skills to students very explicitly, clearly, and sequentially, as opposed to letting students infer or guess.

Divergent responses　when we expect students to have differing responses to questions or problems, we expect divergent responses. The opposite is convergent responses, for which there is one right answer.

Evaluative questions　questions that ask students to evaluate the effectiveness of a piece of writing. "Did the author convince you that Sally was a trustworthy person?" "How did the author convince you?" "Was this a good story?"

Explicit and systematic　instruction that features clear, direct teacher explanation and modeling of a cumulative sequence of instructional concepts.

Expository text　informational text, often about science and social studies topics, as opposed to narrative text (stories).

Expressivist tradition　in writing instruction, this tradition emphasizes having students find their personal voices and develop their identities through writing.

Final silent *e*　the common spelling pattern wherein the silent *e* on the end of a word often

makes the preceding vowel "say" its long vowel sound, as in *same, tide, bone,* and *tune.*

Fluency　reading with sufficient speed, accuracy, and expression so that readers can devote most of their attention to comprehension of the text.

Frustration level　the reading difficulty level at which a student is unable to identify more than 90% of printed words in a text or understand more than 50% of a text's meaning and thus is likely to become frustrated.

Gradual release of responsibility　a teaching model wherein a teacher (1) models a reading skill to students, (2) performs the skill with students together, and (3) invites students to perform the skill for the teacher. A synonymous term is "reading to, with, and by students."

Graphic organizer　a visual organizer such as a map, web, chart, or diagram that shows relationships.

Graphophonic cues　a technical term for letter (graph)–sound (phonic) information that readers use to identify printed words.

Guided reading　a reading group instruction strategy by which the teacher introduces an instructional-level text and then listens to and teaches group members individually as they each read at their own pace.

Independent reading　students reading texts at their instructional or independent level, often as the teacher instructs other students in small groups.

Independent reading level　when a student can read a text with 95% accuracy or better, the text is at the student's independent reading level.

Individually administered test　any test administered to students one-on-one, as opposed to group-administered tests.

Inferencing　the process of drawing conclusions as we read, given the evidence in the text and what we know about the world. For example, if the text says that the main character sees smoke in the distance, we may infer that there is a fire.

Inferential comprehension　the level of comprehension where readers must draw on their background knowledge to fill in gaps and make sense of text (reading between the lines). Also called implicit comprehension.

Inferential questions　questions that require the reader to draw conclusions based on evidence in the text and background knowledge. "Why was Sally's jacket torn and dirty?" Maybe Sally's jacket was torn and dirty because the text says that she had been playing in an abandoned building, and usually abandoned buildings are dirty places.

Inflected when a word has an ending attached to it, such as it*s*, wash*es*, and brush*ed*.

Informal reading inventory (IRI) a reading test that uses a series of graded word lists and passages to identify a student's reading level and reading strengths and needs.

Instructional reading level when a student can read a text with 90% to 94% accuracy, the text is at the student's instructional reading level.

Instructional support instructional techniques such as providing students with vocabulary and background knowledge, prereading texts aloud to or in unison with students, and helping students to identify printed words. Teachers should vary the amount of instructional support they provide based on students' needs.

Interactive read-aloud a very effective way to teach comprehension when the teacher engages the students by previewing the book, asking for predictions and connections to prior knowledge, stopping at purposeful moments to emphasize specific ideas in the text, asking guiding questions, and using oral or written responses to bring closure to the selection.

Interactive writing similar to language-experience approach, except the teacher shares the pen with the students. The teacher invites students to come to the chart paper and write words or parts of words that the teacher has chosen.

Interventions additional reading instruction programs provided to students who do not make adequate progress with the classroom core reading program.

Invented spelling beginning writers spelling words the way they sound (*wen* for *when; wuns* for *once*), rather than conventionally. Invented spelling is a transitional stage on the road to conventional spelling.

Language-experience approach (LEA) a reading instruction strategy for beginning readers through which students express their ideas about a topic to their teacher, who writes the students' words on chart paper and then teaches the students to read their own words.

Learning disability a learning problem that hinders a student from learning to read at an expected level.

Leveled books short picture books that increase in gradual levels of difficulty according to characteristics such as word and sentence length, familiarity of words and concepts, print and illustration placement, and font size.

Listening comprehension the ability to comprehend text that is read aloud, rather than provided in print form. Listening comprehension is often seen as a measure of a student's background knowledge and vocabulary.

Literacy learning the learning of both reading and writing.

Literal comprehension the basic level of comprehension where readers recognize information that is clearly provided in the text (it's there in black and white). Also called explicit comprehension.

Literal questions questions that can be answered simply by reading and finding the answer right there in the text. "What color was Sally wearing in the story?" The text reads "Sally's red jacket was torn and dirty."

Literature circle a teaching model wherein a small group of students read a text on their own and then get together to discuss their responses, connections, questions, and favorite parts.

Low-SES students low-socioeconomic students or students from low-income families.

Manipulating sounds students changing speech sounds to create words (*pan-pat-sat-mat-man-fan*).

Manipulatives physical letters such as letter flashcards and plastic magnetic letters that students can handle and manipulate during instructional activities.

Mapping a common teaching strategy for building students' background knowledge by writing a topic (such as *mammals*) in the middle of a board and then writing students' brainstormed examples (*bears, cows, dogs, mice, horses*) around the topic word.

Masking activity a word identification teaching strategy: a teacher covers parts of words using index cards with cutout slots to help students decode words part by part.

Mastery teaching a direct instruction teaching approach in which students must completely master a concept, such as CVC words, before they may move on to learn a subsequent concept, such as consonant blends.

Meaning-change miscues reading errors that change the meaning of a sentence or passage. For example, "Bob slept in his *horse*," instead of the intended word *house.*

Meaning-preserving miscues reading errors that do not change the meaning of a sentence or passage. For example, "Bob slept in his *home*," instead of the intended word *house.*

Meaningful texts texts that are written to convey meaning, as opposed to decodable texts that are written to provide decoding practice.

Metacognition the higher-order thinking that we do when we actively monitor and control our thought processes while learning. In short, we think about our thinking.

Mini-lesson a 5- to 10-minute reading or writing lesson that highlights a single instructional concept.

Miscues a more current term for oral reading errors, including students' substituting, inserting, and omitting words while reading.

Nonsense words made-up printed words such as *shap* and *bime* that are often used in reading tests to assess a student's ability to decode.

Norm-referenced tests standardized tests used to compare groups of students to other groups of students, for example, comparing schools to other schools within a district or districts to other districts within a state. The emphasis is on comparing groups.

Onset the consonant(s) at the beginning of a syllable or one-syllable word (*c*an, *st*op, *ch*ip, *str*eet).

Oral language teachers often use this term to refer to a student's vocabulary size and ability to express oneself with words. Oral language is one of the foundations of printed language.

Outcome measuring assessment that shows how well students are doing at the end of a school year.

Phoneme a speech sound. The word *sat* has three phonemes: /s/ /a/ /t/. The word *chop* has four letters, but only three phonemes: /ch/ /o/ /p/.

Phonemic awareness students' understanding that spoken words are composed of individual speech sounds (/p/ /a/ /n/), that can be segmented, blended, and manipulated to form other spoken words. Phonemic awareness is the conceptual

foundation for readers blending the sounds of printed letters to read printed words.

Phonics a method of teaching beginning readers to read and pronounce words by learning the sounds of letters, letter groups and syllables.

Predictable text beginning reading texts with very explicit repetitious sentence patterns that support students' use of sentence structure and context to identify printed words. Examples of predictable texts include "Brown bear, brown bear what do you see? I see a red bird looking at me" and "Would you, could you in a box, would you could you with a fox."

Preprimer reading books reading instruction books at the beginning first-grade level.

Primer reading books reading instruction books at the middle of first-grade level.

Print conventions characteristics of print, including left-to-right, top-to-bottom, and punctuation.

Progress monitoring assessments that are given frequently throughout a school year to show how quickly students are progressing in reading.

Pull-out programs Title 1, special education, speech and language, and other intervention or resource programs that are provided by a resource teacher in a resource room outside the student's own classroom. Pull-out programs are sometimes criticized for being disconnected from students' classroom reading instruction.

R-**controlled vowels** a spelling pattern in which the letter *r* follows a vowel and changes its pronunciation, as in *car, her, sir, for,* and *fur.*

Reading Recovery a popular reading intervention program designed for struggling first-grade students to help them to catch up to grade level. Reading Recovery features daily one-on-one tutoring in word study, meaningful reading, writing, and running record assessments.

Reciprocal teaching a lesson format for teaching four comprehension strategies; the teacher models *predicting* passage content, *clarifying* unfamiliar words, *questioning* content, and *summarizing* a passage, followed by students applying the same four strategies.

Reliability the *consistency* characteristic of tests. You can be sure that data from reliable tests are accurate and consistent.

Repeated reading   an instructional strategy for building students' oral reading fluency by having them read and reread a passage multiple times, often to a stopwatch, and charting the amount of improvement each time.

Repetition   when a student reading aloud stops and rereads one or more words. Some informal reading inventories count repetitions as errors. Others do not.

Resource teachers   Title 1, special education, speech and language, and other teachers who provide special services to struggling students.

Retelling   a student's oral summarizing of a passage. Often used as a measure of reading comprehension.

Rime   the vowel and consonant(s) that form the ending part of a syllable or one-syllable word (c*an*, t*ime*, b*oat*, c*ar*). Good readers learn to mix and match printed onsets and rimes to identify words.

Round-robin reading   the traditional reading group practice of having students taking turns reading aloud one at a time in order.

Running record   a quick reading assessment: a teacher listens to a student read a passage aloud, notes the number of words missed, and calculates an oral reading accuracy percentage to place students in instructional-level texts. Teachers can also use running records to analyze patterns in students' oral reading errors to determine reading strengths and needs.

Say something   a structure for increasing the amount of discussion that occurs during a read-aloud. Students choose a partner first; then, when the teacher stops the reading, the partners face each other and "say something" about the text.

Scaffolded writing   a child decides what sentence she wants to write and then the teacher draws lines to represent each word in the sentence. The child writes each word to the best of her ability on the lines provided.

Schema theory   this theory purports that all humans have rules or scripts for organizing their understanding of the world. New information is understood best when children can connect it to their existing schema for an idea.

Scope and sequence   a *list* of reading skills to be taught in a reading program and the *sequence* in which they are to be taught.

Screening   an assessment usually given early in the school year to identify students who are likely to have problems learning to read so that instructional interventions may be provided.

Segmenting sounds   the ability or process of hearing a spoken word and breaking it into its individual sounds (*cat*: c–a–t). Segmenting is the opposite of blending.

Self-correction   when a reader misreads a word, recognizes the error, and goes back and corrects the error without teacher direction. Generally viewed as a positive indication that students are monitoring the meaningfulness of their reading.

Self-correction ratio   the number of self-corrections a student makes compared to the total number of oral reading errors.

Shared reading   a reading instruction strategy for early readers in which a teacher introduces a text to students, often through a picture walk; reads the text aloud to the students; reads the text aloud in unison with the students; has the students read the text aloud to the teacher; and then provides follow-up reading skills instruction.

Sight vocabulary   often refers to two kinds of words: (1) very common words (*a, the, and*) that readers quickly memorize from seeing them so often and (2) irregularly spelled words (*of, does, one*) that must be memorized because they can't be sounded out.

Spelling patterns   common printed letter combinations such as consonant blends and final silent *e* that students learn to recognize and use to identify printed words.

SSR   sustained silent reading. A popular term for students reading silently on their own, often while the teacher provides instruction to other students in small groups.

Story grammar   elements such as setting, characters, events, and theme that are common to almost all stories.

Structural analysis   using word parts such as prefixes, suffixes, contractions, and compound words to identify words.

Subtext strategy   a way to teach inferencing with students that involves them imagining what characters might be saying in the illustrations of books and creating speech or thought bubbles containing their words.

Syntax   the structure of sentences (subject–predicate, adjective–noun, etc.) that readers combine with letter sounds (phonics) and meaning (context) to identify words.

Teacher modeling   teachers modeling to students how to apply a reading skill or strategy.

Validity   the *appropriateness* characteristic of tests. The DIBELS Initial Sound Fluency subtest is valid for measuring aspects of phonemic awareness, but it is not a valid test for measuring reading comprehension. Teachers should only use tests to measure aspects of reading that they were designed to measure.

Vowel team   a spelling pattern, sometimes referred to as a vowel digraph, in which two vowels appear side-by-side and the first vowels "says" its long sound and the second vowel is silent, as in p*ai*d, s*ay*, st*ea*m, f*ee*d, b*oa*t, and m*ow*. Vowel teams are not to be confused with vowel diphthongs in which two vowels make a different sound, as in p*oi*nt and ch*ew*.

Webbing   see *mapping*.

Word bank   a collection of word cards that a student has learned, often stored in a zipping plastic bag or recipe box. Word banks are used for reviewing words students have learned and also during writing as a spelling reference.

Word families   words that share a common spelling pattern, such as the *an* family: *an, ban, can, Dan, fan, man, pan, ran, tan,* and *van*. Word families provide instructional examples for teaching spelling patterns.

Word identification   another instructional term for using letter–sound, contextual, and syntactic information to identify printed words. Word identification is more comprehensive than phonics, which focuses only on using letter sounds to help pronounce words.

Word structure   see *structural analysis*.

Word study group   a small group of students pulled together for extra instructional sessions in a word study concept.

Zone of proximal development   term coined by Vygotsky for the difference between what a child can do with help and what he or she can do without guidance.

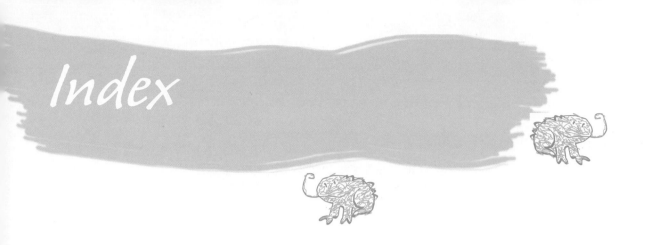

Index

Page numbers followed by *f* indicate figure; those followed by *t* indicate table.